Capital Ideas

Capital Ideas

THE IMF AND THE RISE OF FINANCIAL LIBERALIZATION

Jeffrey M. Chwieroth

PRINCETON UNIVERSITY PRESS

PRINCETON AND OXFORD

Copyright © 2010 by Princeton University Press

Published by Princeton University Press, 41 William Street,
Princeton, New Jersey 08540
In the United Kingdom: Princeton University Press, 6 Oxford Street,
Woodstock, Oxfordshire OX20 1TW

All Rights Reserved

Library of Congress Cataloging-in-Publication Data

Chwieroth, Jeffrey M., 1975– Capital ideas : the IMF and
the rise of financial liberalization / Jeffrey M. Chwieroth.
    p.   cm.
  Includes bibliographical references and index.
  ISBN 978-0-691-14231-9 (cl.: alk. paper)—ISBN 978-0-691-14232-6 (pb.: alk. paper)
1. International Monetary Fund. 2. Financial services industry—Deregulation.
3. Finance—Government policy. 4. Credit control. 5. Financial crises. I. Title.
  HG3881.5.I58C49 2010
  332.1—dc22   2009028486

British Library Cataloging-in-Publication Data is available

This book has been composed in Galliard

Printed on acid-free paper. ∞

press.princeton.edu

Printed in the United States of America

10 9 8 7 6 5 4 3 2

FOR KATIE

per sempre.

Contents

Figures and Tables

Preface

I BEGAN AND FINISHED this book when the world economy was in financial crisis. When I started graduate school in autumn 1997, the financial turmoil that would sweep across Asia and then move on to Russia and Latin America had just begun. In winter 1998 I was fortunate to have the opportunity to participate in Benjamin J. Cohen's course Theoretical Issues in International Political Economy, a seminar devoted to international money and finance taught by one of the leading authorities on the subject.

The course sparked my intellectual interest in understanding why governments would expose themselves to the vagaries of international capital flows by reducing controls on the movement of capital in and out of countries—a process known as capital account liberalization. As events unfolded in Asia and beyond, and many countries turned to the International Monetary Fund for assistance, I became interested in the role the Fund played in all of this. Critics of the Fund charged it with having precipitated the crisis by indiscriminately encouraging governments to liberalize their capital controls prematurely. In line with the typical characterization of the Fund as promoting "one size fits all" policy templates, the conventional wisdom for some time became that the Fund had uniformly pushed capital account liberalization on emerging markets and developing countries.

But once I started to look more closely at the Fund's policy prescriptions, it became clear that there was much more diversity of thought within the Fund than suggested by the conventional wisdom. Some staff members had been enthusiastic about forcing the pace of liberalization and ruling out the use of capital controls, while others argued for a more gradual approach and were sympathetic to the use of controls in some circumstances. I became curious about the origin of these diverse beliefs and how they developed and evolved. It was then that I became interested in *constructivism*.

At the time, constructivism was just beginning to have a significant impact on the field of international relations. In the 1998 50th anniversary edition of *International Organization*, Robert Keohane, Peter Katzenstein, and Stephen Krasner famously identified the debate between rationalism and constructivism as the primary point of contestation in international political economy. In 1998 there was still very little work on what we now might call "constructivist political economy," yet I did find some inspiration from two important books that I was assigned to read in Cohen's course.

One was Cohen's *The Geography of Money*. Those of us who know Jerry well know that he is an economist by training, and thus he might be forgiven for not taking the role of ideas seriously. But Jerry, of course, has never been one to be confined by narrow disciplinary or ontological boundaries. In fact, when one reads *Geography* closely, one finds many constructivist sentiments expressed. Another important source of inspiration was Kathleen's McNamara's *The Currency of Ideas: Monetary Politics in the European Union*. Kate—who was kind enough to offer comments on this project when it was still at an early stage—was one of the first to examine systematically the role that ideas play in international money and finance. Jerry's and Kate's books, both published in 1998, helped me to develop my own arguments about the role of ideas.

As my interest developed into my Ph.D. dissertation and later this book, I found that existing approaches to international organizations, particularly state-centric and principal-agent theories, were inadequate to explain how the Fund's view of capital account liberalization developed and changed. These existing approaches could not explain how or why IMF staff members advocated liberalization without directives or encouragement from leading member states. Principal-agent theory could explain why the staff might have autonomy, but it could not adequately explain what preferences the staff would pursue given this autonomy. I therefore became increasingly interested in the inner workings of international organizations. I was drawn to arguments made by sociologists and constructivists about the roles of professionalization, administrative recruitment, learning, and adaptation.

However, I also found that many of these arguments emphasized structure at the expense of agency. Staff members of international organizations were typically depicted as creatures of habit who, once socialized into a particular structure, could not recognize, resist, or reshape these habits. I found this portrait to be unsatisfying and have thus sought in this book to develop a more strategic and agent-centered constructivist approach. It enables us to bring into sharper focus important battles over norm interpretation and application.

When I submitted a first draft of the manuscript to Princeton University Press in May 2008, the world economy was once again in crisis. At the time things appeared bad, but little did we know how bad it would get. Soon after I was offered a contract, the financial system went into meltdown, and developed country governments broke with long-standing taboos and policy norms by partially nationalizing their financial institutions. The subprime crisis soon thrust the IMF back into the lending business and stirred calls to transform it into a global supervisor of financial regulations. Economic hard times have generated many signs that the norms of financial governance are changing, but as of this writing it is still too soon to reach definitive conclusions. Nonetheless, it is clear that given recent member state commitments to treble its resources and strengthen its mandate, the IMF will likely play a central role in defining future norms of financial governance. It is therefore incumbent upon scholars to better understand how it approaches this task. This is the core theoretical motivation for this book.

Because this book is a significantly revised version of my Ph.D. dissertation at the University of California, Santa Barbara, much of my intellectual debt goes to my professors in Santa Barbara. My greatest intellectual debt is to Jerry Cohen, who has taught me a great deal about international money and finance and the world economy. Our conversations have always been enjoyable, and I could not have imagined writing this book without his insight and friendship. Jerry recognized early on the potential for constructivist political economy and was always ready to offer some assistance on how to strengthen my arguments. Over the years Jerry has taught me not only what it means to be scholarly, but also how to be a scholar. He is my intellectual hero and role model.

I would also like to thank the other members of my Ph.D. dissertation committee—Garrett E. Glasgow and Peter E. Digeser, who were always helpful, offering comments, suggestions, encouragement, and friendship. In addition to my dissertation committee, I would also like to thank other professors from UCSB: John T. Woolley, Cynthia S. Kaplan, Aaron Belkin, Lorraine M. McDonnell, and M. Stephen Weatherford.

I also owe a great debt to Rawi Abdelal. Rawi, who was writing his own book on capital controls at the same time, is an exemplary scholar. While some researchers writing on the same subject matter might be inclined to compete, Rawi set the standard for what it means to be cooperative. He shared with me advice on where to look for information as well as which individuals to interview and how to gain access to them. I hope one day I can reciprocate the great favors he has done for me.

I am also grateful to all of those who read various parts of the book along the way and provided me with much needed comment and encouragement: Kirsten Ainley, Dave Andrews, Pablo Beramendi, Jacqueline Best, Mark Blyth, Stuart Brown, Barry Buzan, Ben Clift, Scott Cooper, Lucia Coppolaro, Mark Duckenfield, Axel Dreher, Randy Germain, Emiliano Grossman, Lloyd Gruber, Emilie Hafner-Burton, Michael Hall, Rodney Bruce Hall, Bob Hancké, Eric Helleiner, Randy Henning, Kim Hutchings, Nicolas Jabko, Daphne Josselin, Joe Jupille, Robert Kissack, Mathias Koenig-Archibugi, David Lake, Ralf J. Leiteritz, Charles Lipson, Walter Mattli, Kate McNamara, Bessma Momani, Kristoff Nimark, Susan Park, Craig Parsons, Lou Pauly, Johannes Pollak, Dave Richardson, Razeen Sally, Len Seabrooke, Uli Sedelmeier, Ken Shadlen, Duncan Snidal,

Mike Tierney, Alfred Tovias, Maarten Vink, Jim Vreeland, Robert Wade, Andrew Walter, Kate Weaver, Wesley Widmaier, and Cornelia Woll.

I was also fortunate to be invited to present earlier versions of different aspects of this book at the University of Chicago, Sciences Po, Duke University, and the College of William and Mary. I benefited greatly from comments from the participants at these seminars, as well as those at various annual meetings of the American Political Science Association, the International Studies Association, and the International Political Economy Society, where parts of this study were also presented. I also greatly appreciate the financial resources provided to me by the London School of Economics and Syracuse University. I would also like to thank Richard Baggaley and Chuck Myers of Princeton University Press for their help and patience during the review process, as well as the anonymous reviewers for their useful suggestions. Richard Isomaki also deserves thanks for his assistance with copyediting the manuscript.

The staff and Executive Board directors of the IMF also deserve special thanks. Contrary to popular depictions, I found the organization and those who work within it to be transparent, forthcoming, and candid about how things work and evolve within the Fund. I am grateful for the time I spent there as a visiting scholar in 2005. For graciously hosting and advising me I thank Simon Johnson. I am also grateful to the scores of current and former staff, directors, and government policymakers who spoke with me on the record, as well as others who shared their views with me in private. This book, and the conclusions I reach within it, would not have been as sound without their assistance. For invaluable assistance exploring the IMF Archives, I thank Premela Isaac and Jean Marcouyeux.

Words cannot express the love and gratitude I have toward my parents, Frank and Linda Chwieroth. Their support for their sons has been unconditional throughout all the years of our lives. The fact that after raising me, they watched without resentment as I moved across the country and around the globe far away from them speaks volumes about the strength of their love for and commitment to their children. I one day hope to be able to emulate this love and commitment. My brother Brian has also been a source of inspiration and support. Although he followed my father by getting a Ph.D. in physics, he has never let me suffer too much from "physics envy." My grandfathers—Leon Morse and Frank Chwieroth—also deserve mention for blazing the trail as the first ones in my family to attend university. At an early age I learned from them that an education could lead to incredible opportunities, such as helping to inaugurate the atomic age or designing sophisticated antennae to grace the tops of the world's tallest buildings. Thanks also should go to my dog Flavio, who was always there to remind me that playing Frisbee in the park is often just as important as reading another IMF report. Brett Caloia also deserves thanks for being a source of strength in my life for the last twelve years. I consider him to be a part of my family and am grateful for all the times he provided me with a place to go when I needed a break.

Finally, I want to thank my wife, Katharine Canada, to whom this book and my life are dedicated. Katie has been by my side since graduate school and has supported me every step of the way. She has endured more discussions about the IMF and capital account liberalization than any classically trained musician should ever have to. Along the way, she ensured I always had her love and famous chocolate chip cookies to keep me going, even when times were difficult. Jerry Cohen once equated passionate love with international monetary cooperation, in that both are difficult to sustain. This may be true. But having the chance to be with Katie reminds me everyday why it is so important to keep trying.

Jeffrey M. Chwieroth
London, April 2009

Abbreviations

ABS	asset-backed securities
AIG	American International Group
APD	Asia and Pacific Department
AER	*American Economic Review*
AFR	African Department
BCBS	Basel Committee on Banking Supervision
BIBF	Bangkok International Banking Facility
BIS	Bank for International Settlements
BRICs	Brazil, Russia, India, China
C-20	Committee of Twenty
CAS	Central Asia Department
CB	Central Banking Department
CCL	Contingent Credit Line
CDO	Collateralized Debt Obligation
CDS	Credit Default Swap
CEA	Council of Economic Advisers
CRA	Credit Rating Agency
EC	European Community
ECB	European Central Bank
EEC	European Economic Community
EMU	Economic and Monetary Union
EP	Economist Program
ER	Exchange Restrictions Department
ERM	Exchange Rate Mechanism
ETR	Exchange and Trade Restrictions Department
EU	European Union
EURO	European Department
EURO1	European I Department
EURO2	European II Department
FASB	Financial Accounting Standards Board
FRBNY	Federal Reserve Bank of New York
FSA	Financial Services Authority
FSAP	Financial Sector Assessment Program
FSB	Financial Stability Board
FSF	Financial Stability Forum
G-7	Group of Seven
G-10	Group of Ten

G-20	Group of Twenty
G-24	Group of Twenty-Four
GAB	General Arrangements to Borrow
GFSR	*Global Financial Stability Report*
GSE	government-sponsored enterprise
HKCE	heterodox, Keynesian, Continental European (economics department)
IASB	International Accounting Standards Body
ICM	International Capital Markets Department
ICMR	*International Capital Markets Report*
IEO	Independent Evaluation Office
IET	interest equalization tax
IIF	Institute of International Finance
IMF	International Monetary Fund
IO	International Organization
IOSCO	International Organization of Securities Commissions
ISDA	International Swaps and Derivatives Association
ISI	import-substitution industrialization
LTCM	Long-Term Capital Management
MAE	Monetary and Exchange Affairs Department
MBS	mortgage-backed securities
MCM	Monetary and Capital Markets Department
MED	Middle Eastern Department
NGO	nongovernmental organization
OECD	Organization for Economic Cooperation and Development
OTC	over-the-counter (derivatives)
PA	principal-agent
PDR	Policy Development and Review Department
RES	Research Department
ROSC	Report on Observance of Standards and Codes
SDR	Special Drawing Rights
SDRM	Sovereign Debt Restructuring Mechanism
SEAP	Southeast Asia and Pacific Department
SEC	Securities and Exchange Commission
SIV	structured investment vehicle
TARP	Troubled Assets Relief Program
UN	United Nations
WEO	*World Economic Outlook*
WHD	Western Hemisphere Department
WTO	World Trade Organization

Capital Ideas

CHAPTER ONE

Introduction

FEW ISSUES have attracted as much controversy as the removal of controls on international capital flows—a process known as capital account liberalization. The International Monetary Fund has been at the center of this controversy. The formal rules of the IMF provide member states with the right to use capital controls, and these rules have not changed significantly since the organization was founded in 1945. But informally, among many staff within the Fund in the 1980s and 1990s, capital controls, once part of economic orthodoxy, became identified as an economic heresy. Although liberalization was not encouraged indiscriminately, the belief that the free movement of capital was desirable—what I call the norm of capital freedom—became the new orthodoxy.

Critics of the Fund have subsequently charged it with encouraging governments to liberalize their controls prematurely, thereby precipitating the wave of financial instability that swept much of East Asia in 1997–1998 before moving on to Russia and Latin America.[1] Critics also used this wave of financial instability to renew charges that the Fund was promoting "one size fits all" policies that ignored the different circumstances of its member states. Without a careful examination of the evidence, many critics of the Fund have jumped to the conclusion that the IMF staff uniformly advocated capital account liberalization. In examining a critical case of how international organizations (IOs) work and evolve, this book shows that many of these criticisms are unfounded.[2]

While the staff shared a belief that capital freedom was desirable in the abstract long run, they conducted a vigorous internal debate about how to proceed toward this goal. To put it differently, though the staff adopted the norm of capital freedom in the 1980s and 1990s, they disagreed about how this norm should be interpreted and applied. As I discuss more fully below, this finding not only has important empirical implications for critics of the IMF, it also has important theoretical implications for scholars seek-

---

[1] Joseph Stiglitz, *Globalization and Its Discontents* (New York: W. W. Norton, 2002), p. 15; Padma Desai, *Financial Crisis, Contagion, and Containment* (Princeton, N.J.: Princeton University Press, 2003), p. 217.

[2] See also IEO, *The IMF's Approach to Capital Account Liberalization* (Washington, D.C.: IMF, 2005), which also documents variation in the IMF's advice but, in contrast to this book, does not seek to explain it.

ing to understand the behavior of IOs. Existing scholarly accounts of IOs, as well as critics of the IMF, devote insufficient attention to the possibility that a norm, once adopted, can be subject to a struggle over its interpretation and application. This book seeks to strengthen our understanding of IOs in general and the IMF in particular by bringing these important battles over norm interpretation and application into sharper focus.

Within the halls of the IMF these debates over norm interpretation and application took the form of a struggle between "gradualists" and supporters of a "big bang." Gradualists emphasized sequencing (i.e., ensuring that certain supporting policies and institutions are in place before additional liberalizing measures are undertaken), while big-bang proponents argued for a rapid move to liberalization. In addition, though both groups generally agreed that controls on capital outflows were inappropriate, gradualists viewed temporary controls on inflows as legitimate in some circumstances, whereas big-bang proponents saw even selective restraints on capital mobility as outside the boundaries of legitimate policy. As a result, though the staff collectively shared a belief in the long-run desirability of liberalization, they often offered conflicting analyses and recommendations on how to proceed toward it.

In the mid-1990s, big-bang proponents gained the upper hand within the Fund, and their informal advocacy of liberalization converged with an initiative to amend the IMF Articles of Agreement to give the Fund the formal mandate to promote liberalization as well as fuller jurisdiction over the capital account policies of its members. In granting the Fund fuller jurisdiction over the capital account, the initiative would have prohibited governments from imposing virtually all types of controls without Fund approval and would have committed governments to liberalizing existing controls. The amendment also would have enabled the IMF, for the first time in its history, to include capital account liberalization as a condition for accessing its financial resources.

In the event, the initiative failed. Proponents of the big-bang approach and the amendment saw their efforts undermined by the financial crises in Asia and beyond. Although the financial crisis that struck Mexico in 1994–1995 had moderated support for the big-bang approach, it was the Asian crisis, which many attributed to "disorderly liberalization" undertaken without regard to sequence, that played a decisive role in discrediting this interpretation and application of the norm of capital freedom. Since the Asian crisis the IMF has been much more cautious in encouraging liberalization, emphasizing sequencing and bestowing greater legitimacy to selective restraints on capital mobility.

Nonetheless, in the decade between the Asian and subprime crises, a period of norm continuity within the Fund, the tacit presumption was that the main risks to financial stability lay with poor fundamentals and institutions within emerging markets, thus placing the onus largely on these countries. Among emerging markets this norm interpretation and application generated much resentment. Emerging markets were encouraged to adjust their policies and implement structural reforms in line with universalist standards and codes that were largely Anglo-American in content, even though emerging markets had little, if any, input into the design of these standards and codes. Within the Fund scant attention was given to "supply-side" regulatory measures aimed at financial market participants based in the financial centers of developed countries; a prescription consistent with an alternative interpretation, often advocated by emerging markets and developing countries, that stresses factors intrinsic to the operation of international capital markets as contributing to financial instability and sees supply-side regulatory measures as intergal to capital account management.

But there are signs that the subprime crisis that erupted in developed countries in summer 2007 is stirring changes within the Fund. Following the partial nationalization of many of their leading financial institutions, developed countries have launched a number of initiatives to reregulate international financial markets. During the subprime crisis the Fund has also come out strongly in favor of regulatory measures aimed at financial market participants in developed countries. However, even though capital inflows played an important part in fueling housing bubbles in the United States and other countries, there has yet to be any significant efforts to overturn the norm of capital freedom.

This book thus explores the inner workings of the IMF to understand the evolution of the staff's approach to capital controls and why it changed so dramatically. In doing so, it offers an important investigation of how IOs operate and change over time. Much of the focus is on intraorganizational processes that gave rise to debates among the Fund's staff over the legitimacy of controls and their liberalization and on how these internal debates shaped the organization's behavior. While not discounting the importance of formal rules and the significant influence of member states, this book shows that the IMF staff exercised significant autonomy in developing their approach. Normative and behavioral changes in IOs, this book demonstrates, are driven not just by new rules or the influence of member states but also by the evolving personnel configurations, beliefs, debates, and strategic agency of their staffs.

MOTIVATION

The IMF's approach to capital account liberalization is not simply a matter of historical interest. Capital account liberalization continues to be an important concern of the IMF, scholars, and the official and private financial communities. The issue remains, as Barry Eichengreen suggests, "an oldy but a goody."[3] Indeed, a recent IMF strategy paper identifies "understanding capital account liberalization" as one of nine vital "responses" to the contemporary "challenge of globalization." Attesting to the ongoing importance of the issue to the Fund, the strategy paper observes: "There is no solid body of analysis on how best to proceed. This is a challenge to which the Fund must rise."[4] In rising to this challenge, the IMF staff continue to strengthen and tailor their advice on liberalization and the use of controls.

Capital account liberalization also remains an important concern of some governments. The European Union (EU) and the United States view liberalization as one of their top policy priorities; with Brussels pushing for it in the context of accession negotiations, and Washington insisting upon it in recent trade agreements with Chile, Singapore, and South Korea, as well as in its ongoing "strategic dialogue" with China. But the EU and U.S. positions have, on occasion, diverged from the IMF's approach, thus revealing important aspects of the political economy of the organization. For instance, in the context of Bulgaria's and Romania's accession negotiations, the IMF recommended the maintenance of selective controls, while EU officials opposed them. Similarly, the United States and the IMF have clashed over the need for China to liberalize its capital account. While the United States, in seeking to intensify pressure on the Chinese currency to appreciate, argues that China should liberalize more rapidly, some IMF staff members claim that China should slow down its liberalization until it strengthens its financial system and achieves greater exchange rate flexibility.[5]

The subprime crisis has also brought renewed attention to the regulation of international capital flows. The recycling of savings and trade surpluses from Asia and oil-exporting countries stirred "capital flow bonanzas"[6] into the United States and other developed countries that generated abundant liquidity and, when channeled through poorly regulated finan-

[3] Barry Eichengreen, "Capital Account Liberalization and the Fund," High Level Seminar on Capital Account Liberalization and the IMF, Swiss Ministry of Finance, Bern, Switzerland, 12 December 2005.

[4] IMF, *The Managing Director's Report on the Fund's Medium-Term Strategy* (Washington, D.C.: IMF, 2005), p. 8.

[5] Eswar Prasad, Thomas Rumbaugh, and Qing Wang, "Putting the Cart before the Horse? Capital Account Liberalization and Exchange Rate Flexibility in China," IMF Working Paper 05/01 (Washington, D.C.: IMF, 2005).

[6] Carmen M. Reinhart and Vincent R. Reinhart, "Capital Flow Bonanzas: An Encompassing View of the Past and Present," NBER Working Paper 14321 (Cambridge, Mass.: NBER, 2008).

cial systems, housing bubbles of historic proportions. These bonanzas are not unique to the subprime crisis; in fact, both the 1980s debt crisis and the Asian financial crisis were preceded by massive capital inflows and the recycling of trade surpluses that created asset price bubbles that eventually burst.[7] Because the risk-taking behavior of financial market participants cannot be regulated perfectly, a few prominent academic economists have advocated taxes on capital inflows, along with a coordinated agenda to tackle global macroeconomic imbalances, as a way of reducing the size of these bonanzas.[8] Others point to controls on outflows as a means to manage "sudden stop" disruptions in capital flows, such as those faced by many emerging markets when the contagion from the subprime crisis spread from developed economies.[9] Indeed, as a number of emerging markets have turned to restrictions on outflows to manage pressures from the subprime crisis, some prominent observers have suggested we are perhaps witnessing "the return of capital controls."[10]

The subprime crisis has also opened up space for greater consideration of regulatory measures aimed at financial market participants in developed countries. One prominent issue for capital account management has been the procyclicality of regulatory policies and industry practices, which amplify the "boom and bust" cycle in financial markets by contributing to the expansion of lending during economic upturns and the collapse of lending during downturns. The Group of Seven (G-7) leading developed countries, though initially slow to come around to the idea, now solidly supports introducing greater countercyclical tendencies through the development of new principles and regulations. The Group of 20 (G-20) leading developed and emerging economies—which has recently replaced the G-7 as the principal forum for leaders to discuss key issues in the global economy—also has directed regulators and standard setters to develop recommendations to mitigate procyclicality. The procyclicality of regulatory policies and industry practices will likely remain a priority for policymakers for the near future.

Current efforts to reform the IMF are also linked to its approach to capital account liberalization. Much of the resentment felt by emerging

---

[7] Carmen M. Reinhart and Kenneth Rogoff, "Is the 2007 U.S. Financial Crisis So Different? An International Historical Comparison," *American Economic Review* 98, no. 2 (2008), pp. 339–344.

[8] Dani Rodrik and Arvind Subramanian, "We Must Curb International Flows of Capital," *Financial Times*, 25 February 2008.

[9] Guillermo Calvo, "The New Bretton Woods Agreement," in *What G20 Leaders Must Do to Stabilise Our Economy and Fix the Financial System*, ed. Barry Eichengreen and Richard Baldwin (London: Vox.Org Publication, 2008), pp. 53–55.

[10] Willem Buiter, "The Return of Capital Controls" 20 February 2009, available at http://www.voxeu.org/index.php?q=node/3104.

market countries toward the Fund stems from critical perceptions of its handling of the Asian financial crisis. Officials from emerging markets blame the Fund not only for pushing countries to liberalize prematurely but also for its general failure in the 1990s to warn of crises that were on the horizon. The Fund's response to the Asian crisis, which placed the burden of adjustment on emerging markets by mandating austerity, deep structural reforms, and the implementation of standards and codes, generated additional criticism and resentment.[11]

This resentment, and the sustained period of global expansion and macroeconomic imbalances from 2002 to 2007, led emerging markets, the Fund's traditional client base, to "self-insure" by paying off early their outstanding IMF loans, and accumulating massive stockpiles of reserves and developing bilateral and regional liquidity arrangements so as to avoid having to borrow from the Fund in the future. Self-insurance, along with the pursuit of export-led growth strategies, helped create the global imbalances that played a role in generating the underlying conditions for today's crisis. Without adequate reforms to restore the faith of emerging markets in the Fund, the risk is that these countries will continue to opt for self-insurance rather than collective insurance, with the result being that the cycle of inflow bonanzas could repeat itself.

Because the IMF's income model depends heavily on interest charges from outstanding loans, the Fund's legitimacy problems created a budgetary crisis for the organization. In response, it has been forced to adjust its own policies, downsizing staff and developing a new income model. The Fund has also begun a comprehensive overhaul of the way it lends money, which has included the introduction of new, more flexible lending instruments. The Fund's member states have also pursued modest governance reforms by agreeing to a slight increase in the relative voting power of emerging markets and developing countries. At the time of writing, these initiatives were pending approval by various national parliaments, with the subprime crisis prompting the G-20 to accelerate the timetable and scope of governance reform.

The Fund's approach to capital account liberalization is not only an important "cause" of current reform efforts, but an important "effect" of such efforts. One of the core lessons of the Asian crisis was that the Fund must develop a broad agenda in monitoring the economies of its member states (what it calls "surveillance") and subjecting its borrowers to conditionality, that is, setting requirements to obtain loans. Yet this lesson cuts

---

[11] Morris Goldstein, "IMF Structural Conditionality: How Much Is Too Much?" Institute for International Economics Working Paper No. 01–04 (Washington, D.C.: Institute for International Economics, 2001); Martin Feldstein, "Refocusing the IMF," *Foreign Affairs*, 77, no. 2 (1998), pp. 20–32.

against efforts to "streamline" conditionality and against member states' interests in avoiding intrusiveness on the part of the IMF.

If surveillance and conditionality pertaining to choices about social institutions is to be perceived as legitimate and politically acceptable, the organization itself must be seen as legitimate and accountable to those member states where this advice and conditional lending is extended. Thus, as Eichengreen concludes, "The debate over capital account liberalization leads, as all roads seem to do these days, to the need to reform governance and representation in the Fund."[12] If the interests and experiences of emerging markets are genuinely incorporated into the IMF (and other key international forums), then reform of the organization, which aims to strengthen its legitimacy and accountability, could foster among emerging markets a sense that surveillance and conditionality (as well as standards and codes) are legitimate and politically acceptable, which, in turn, could encourage greater compliance. Genuine participation from emerging markets could also translate into changes to how the IMF approaches capital account liberalization by giving greater weight to measures, such as supply-side regulation, that align with the interests and experiences of those countries. Without this participation, emerging markets may turn their back on the IMF and the universalist standards and codes it promotes through the pursuit of self-insurance as well as the development of alternative regionally defined norms of financial governance, a process that Eric Helleiner calls "regulatory decentralization."[13]

The historical and contemporary relevance of these issues suggests that understanding the process of normative change within the Fund deserves close attention. Moreover, understanding how the Fund works and evolves has become increasingly important. As recently as October 2008 the IMF seemed to be slipping towards terminal irrelevance. For several years, the demand for its loans had been in sharp decline, as emerging markets were awash with private capital flows and many of them pursued self-insurance strategies. Even after summer 2007, as the world sank into financial crisis, there was little demand for its resources. But the intensification and spread of the crisis in autumn 2008 has changed all of this.

The IMF is now no longer at the margins of financial governance. It has been thrust back into lending business and faced with calls for it to play a more central role as a global supervisor of financial regulators. The G-20 has also agreed to treble the IMF's financial resources and to strengthen its mandate to develop recommendations and engage in surveillance. In addition, the staff is also currently engaged in a number of high-profile

[12] Eichengreen, "Capital Account Liberalization and the Fund."

[13] Eric Helleiner, "Reregulation and Fragmentation in International Financial Governance," *Global Governance*, 16, no. 1 (2009), pp. 15–20.

exercises, such as those concerning global macroeconomic imbalances and sovereign wealth funds. These exercises place the staff at the center of efforts to define "exchange rate manipulation" and to identify "best practices" for government-owned investment funds.[14] All of this suggests that the Fund is positioned to play a central role in defining future norms of financial governance, and thus it is incumbent upon scholars to strengthen our understanding of how it approaches this task.

The evolution of the Fund's approach to capital account liberalization also has important theoretical implications for how scholars understand IO behavior and change. Not surprisingly, the Fund's approach to capital account liberalization has attracted much attention from academics and policymakers. In line with a state-centric approach to IOs, the conventional wisdom for some time, exemplified by Jagdish Bhagwati's[15] and Robert Wade's[16] writings on the "Wall Street–Treasury Complex," was that the Fund's approach resulted from its management acceding to pressure from U.S. officials, who in turn were shaped by demands from the private financial community. But this view has been shown to be problematic.

Rawi Abdelal's interpretation of the construction of the formal rules of international finance challenges some elements of this view.[17] Abdelal's legalistic narrative shows that the U.S. Treasury was at best indifferent to the initiative to amend the Articles in the mid-1990s, and that Wall Street was opposed. The strongest support came from IMF managing director Michel Camdessus and West European governments.

But this revisionist interpretation is *incomplete*, as it fails to explore the decisive influence of the staff and their internal debates on changes to organizational behavior. In focusing largely on the construction of *formal* IMF rules rather than *informal* behavior by the staff, the revisionist interpretation does not dig deeply into the inner workings of the organization to explain how it actually behaves and evolves. If formal IMF rules and the staff's informal approach were always in alignment, then we would not need to go further than the revisionist interpretation. But they were not always aligned.

---

[14] Rodrigo Rato, "Statement on the Executive Board Decision to Approve New Framework for Surveillance," IMF Press Release No. 07/137, 21 June 2007; IMF, *Sovereign Wealth Funds—A Work Agenda* (Washington, D.C.: IMF, 2008).

[15] Jagdish Bhagwati, "The Capital Myth: The Difference between Trade in Widgets and Dollars," *Foreign Affairs* 77, no. 3 (1998), pp. 7–12.

[16] Robert Wade, "The Coming Fight over Capital Flows," *Foreign Policy,* Winter 1998–1999, pp. 41–54. See also Wade and Frank Veneroso, "The Asian Crisis: The High Debt Model versus the Wall Street-Treasury-IMF Complex," *New Left Review,* March–April 1998, pp. 3–22.

[17] Rawi Abdelal, *Capital Rules: The Construction of Global Finance* (Cambridge: Harvard University Press, 2007).

On the contrary, there was a great deal of what principal-agent (PA) theorists call "slippage" between formal IMF rules and the staff's actions, with many staff members in the 1980s and 1990s encouraging liberalization even though formal rules to this day give member states the right to use controls. In fact, the initiative to amend the Articles in the late 1990s was in large part an exercise in empowering the staff with more tools to encourage a policy that many of them had already been promoting informally for nearly a decade. Formal rules, of course, matter, but a fuller understanding of how IOs work and evolve requires a focus on the staff, their beliefs, and their internal debates that shape the organization from within. Indeed, the story of the Fund's approach to capital account liberalization is more about these factors than it is about member states' construction of formal rules.

The behavior of IOs has generated a great deal of recent interest in the scholarly literature. Three general approaches have emerged. One is state-centric, viewing IOs as creatures and instruments of their member states. While offering useful insights, this approach ignores IOs' considerable autonomy, which is partly a result of deliberate actions by member states and partly due to the internal characteristics of IOs.

Drawing on PA theory, a second approach, while generally focusing on IOs' external environment, treats them as autonomous creatures. This approach explores factors that lead member states to delegate authority in the first place, and the efficacy of control mechanisms that states use to rein in IOs that behave undesirably. But this approach, while expecting autonomous behavior by IOs, offers little insight into what the staff will actually do with its autonomy. This approach also tends to place disproportionate emphasis on the role of external factors, and thus tends to overpredict the extent to which organizational behavior is externally driven.

A third approach turns its attention to the internal environment of IOs, offering sociological and constructivist arguments that emphasize the role of organizational culture in shaping staff preferences and the propensity for change. But this approach often fails to investigate the sources of these preferences and thus ends up treating organizational culture as an inert social environment that is impervious to demands for change. An overly structuralist and static depiction of staff behavior is thus offered, one that marginalizes the possibility and efficacy of strategic agency among the staff. Sociological and constructivist approaches therefore tend to underpredict the potential for organizational change and obscure the role the staff plays in facilitating it.

In addition to these theoretical shortcomings, each of these approaches tends to give inadequate attention to the diversity of beliefs that exist within IOs. Overlooked, then, is the possibility that a norm, once adopted, can be subject to a struggle over its interpretation and application. By contrast, these struggles over interpretation and application feature prominently in this book.

THE ARGUMENT

Building on sociological and constructivist approaches, this book focuses largely on the staff, their beliefs, and the internal debates that shape the work and evolution of IOs. The evolution of the staff's beliefs is critical for understanding IO behavior as these beliefs specify legitimate goals and means for the organization to pursue. These beliefs imbue the social world with meaning, shaping the manner in which external demands and events are interpreted and the responses that the staff will entertain and, potentially, implement. Thus, if we want to understand how IOs work and evolve, then we must attend not only to member states' interests but also to beliefs that prevail within IOs and the internal processes and debates shaping these beliefs.

This book is not the first to investigate beliefs that prevail within IOs, but this field of inquiry is hardly crowded. Although there has been an important revival of scholarly interest in IOs, there has been remarkably little empirical research that seeks to uncover how they actually work. As Michael Barnett and Martha Finnemore observe, "Scholars are only now beginning to treat seriously the internal workings of these organizations and ask hard questions about how to approach them analytically."[18] This book seeks to contribute to this important area of inquiry by posing a number of hard questions about IOs in general and the IMF in particular. More specifically, this book asks: How does normative change occur within IOs in general and the IMF in particular? What actors are responsible for normative change?

In its sixty-year history the IMF has developed considerable autonomy and influence, transforming itself from a relatively minor and marginalized organization to a powerful global actor at the center of financial governance. In doing so, the Fund has evolved into an organization that has its own distinct goals and interests. The staff in particular has developed a significant amount of autonomy. It is the staff members who conduct the bulk of the IMF's tasks; they formulate policy proposals for consideration by member states, exercise surveillance, carry out loan negotiations and design the programs, and collect and systematize detailed information. But how the staff approaches its tasks remains understudied. By investigat-

---

[18] Michael Barnett and Martha Finnemore, *Rules for the World: International Organizations in Global Politics* (Ithaca, N.Y.: Cornell University Press, 2004), p. x.

ing the internal workings of the Fund that shape the evolution of the staff's beliefs, this book seeks to rectify this shortcoming.

I argue that five intraorganizational processes—professionalization, administrative recruitment, adaptation, learning, and entrepreneurship—largely shaped the evolution of beliefs and influenced the adoption, interpretation, and application of the norm of capital freedom. The beliefs of the staff of any organization are linked to the beliefs that prevail within the profession(s) from which it recruits.[19] Although some studies allude to the importance of professionalization in shaping organizational behavior, few scholars have systematically and rigorously studied how professionalization actually functions. This book does otherwise, devoting special attention to how the Fund's relationship with the profession of economics shapes its behavior.

Professions are major agents in the construction of understandings, meanings, and standards of behavior. John Maynard Keynes was an early proponent of the view that the economics profession exercised what political scientists Michael Barnett and Raymond Duvall call "productive power" or what sociologists Donald MacKenzie, Fabian Muniesa, and Lucia Siu call "performativity."[20] Keynes once famously quipped:

> The ideas of economists . . . are more powerful than is commonly understood. Indeed, the world is ruled by little else. Practical men, who believe themselves to be quite exempt from any intellectual influence, are usually the slaves of some defunct economist. Madmen in authority, who hear voices in the air, are distilling their frenzy from some academic scribbler of a few years back. I am sure that the power of vested interests is vastly exaggerated compared with the gradual encroachment of ideas . . . [S]oon or late, it is ideas, not vested interests, which are dangerous for good or evil.[21]

However, much scholarship in international political economy neglects this power of professions. On the other hand, sociologists, as well as scholars of epistemic communities, have long recognized that professions wield

[19] Paul J. DiMaggio and Walter J. Powell, "The Iron Cage Revisited: Institutional Isomorphism and Collective Rationality in Organizational Fields," *American Sociological Review* 48, no. 1 (1983), pp. 147–160; Peter A. Hall, ed., *The Political Power of Economic Ideas* (Princeton, N.J.: Princeton University Press, 1989).

[20] Michael Barnett and Raymond Duvall, "Power in Global Governance," in *Power in Global Governance*, ed. Michael Barnett and Raymond Duvall (Cambridge: Cambridge University Press, 2005), pp. 1–32; Donald MacKenzie, Fabian Muniesa, and Lucia Siu, *Do Economists Make Markets? On the Performativity of Economics* (Princeton, N.J.: Princeton University Press, 2007).

[21] John Maynard Keynes, *The General Theory of Employment, Interest, and Money* (London: Macmillan, 1936), pp. 383–384.

this type of power based on their unique claims to socially recognized expertise.[22] I therefore draw on the insights of these scholars to investigate how professions can socially (re)construct understandings, meanings, and standards of behavior.

Since, as I argue later in the book, it is difficult to make a case for capital account liberalization on a pure efficiency or evidentiary basis, one must examine how it became constructed as desirable. Though economists (and other professionals) tend to present their views as based solely on technical knowledge, evidence, and internal truth tests, this information is in fact value laden and the product of human interpretation. Economists create, teach, and disseminate not only technical models of how economies work but also normative conceptualizations of how economies should be organized. These technical models and normative conceptualizations provide a lens through which economists develop shared diagnoses about the problems economies face and the appropriate solutions to them. Economists serve, as Peter Haas suggests, as the "cognitive baggage handlers" of these lenses.[23]

Professional training, in which individuals are exposed and socialized, both implicitly and explicitly, to particular beliefs is often the source of this "cognitive baggage." By the 1970s, most academic economists had come to define capital account liberalization as desirable. A "wide consensus had emerged among economists," Jean Tirole observes: "capital account liberalization—allowing capital to move freely in and out of countries without restrictions—was unambiguously good."[24] Exposure of cohorts of graduate students to this belief fostered an informal transnational network of economists who supported the norm of capital freedom.

This informal network then sought to insert its beliefs within the decision-making processes of the Fund, and the Fund—which recruits almost exclusively from the economics profession—saw its behavior affected accordingly. In the mid-1980s, recruitment and promotion patterns brought to senior positions a new cadre of staff members who, as a result of their professional training, were inclined to view liberalization as desirable. This new cadre replaced retiring members of staff, many of whom had joined the IMF in the 1940s and 1950s and, because of the experience

[22] See, for instance, MacKenzie, Muniesa, and Siu, *Do Economists Make Markets?*; Peter M. Haas, "Introduction: Epistemic Communities and International Policy Coordination," *International Organization* 46, no. 1 (1992), pp. 1–35; Emanuel Adler and Haas, "Conclusion: Epistemic Communities, World Order, and the Creation of a Reflective Research Program," *International Organization* 46, no. 1 (1992), pp. 368–390.

[23] Haas, "Introduction," p. 27.

[24] Jean Tirole, *Financial Crises, Liquidity, and the International Monetary System* (Princeton, N.J.: Princeton University Press, 2002), p. ix.

of the 1930s and their professional training, shared different beliefs about the desirability of liberalization. As a result, the normative outlook of the Fund changed.

But professionalization and administrative recruitment are not the whole story. Real-world events also matter, and organizational staff members can develop and refine their beliefs through experience. Yet experiences do not come with "instruction sheets," as Mark Blyth suggests.[25] Prevailing beliefs can give rise to particular understandings of experiences, thus channeling the lessons that emerge and making existing interpretations "sticky" and resistant to change. Individuals tend to take seriously information that confirms their interpretations and to discount evidence that disconfirms them.

Consequently, the staff often interpreted events—such as the Asian financial crisis—to warrant ad hoc changes in beliefs about how to proceed to a particular goal (i.e., beliefs about legitimate means, such as a greater emphasis on sequencing) without any corresponding change in support for a particular goal (i.e. beliefs about legitimate ends, such as capital freedom). I find this process of *adaptation* to have occurred often in the Fund's history. Real-world experiences, however, usually failed to induce a shift in underlying goals, or what might be called *learning*. A change from the norm of capital control to capital freedom (or vice versa) proved cognitively difficult without personnel changes that brought alternative interpretations to bear on experiences.

Though the staff in the 1980s and 1990s collectively shared the view that capital freedom was desirable in the abstract long run, a vigorous internal debate continued over how this norm should be interpreted and applied. A "battle of ideas" ensued between gradualists and big-bang supporters. This internal debate was very much a reflection of a similar intellectual battle occurring within the economics profession. While professionalization and administrative recruitment can help foster norm adoption, they can also facilitate the formation of subcultures within an organization, as new recruits bring contrasting interpretations and applications of a norm that reflect unsettled debates within the profession from which they were recruited. Although academic economists generally agreed that capital freedom was a desirable long-run goal, they disagreed over how to proceed toward it. Academic economists debated the emphasis to be placed on sequencing and whether allowances should be made for selective capital controls. These intradisciplinary debates helped create subcultures within the Fund, with some staff inclined to favor gradualism

[25] Mark Blyth, *Great Transformations: Economic Ideas and Institutional Change in the Twentieth Century* (Cambridge: Cambridge University Press, 2002), p. 7.

while others supported a "big bang" approach. These subcultures in turn provided an ideational basis for internal bureaucratic struggles. Thus, while the staff collectively shared the belief that capital account liberalization was desirable in the long run, members disagreed over the means to proceed toward this goal and whether to make allowances for temporary and selective deviations from it.

In contrast to existing approaches to IOs, I pay close attention to these important debates over norm interpretation and application and in doing so seek to reveal the crucial role of staff *strategic agency*, that is, the use of detailed means-ends calculations to maximize particular goals. These goals are not solely material in nature; rather they also reflect a commitment to particular beliefs and action that is directed at changing the preferences of others so that they better reflect these beliefs. Martha Finnemore and Kathryn Sikkink describe this process as one of "strategic social construction" in which "actors are making detailed means-ends calculations to maximize their utilities, but the utilities they want to maximize involve changing the other players' utility function in ways that reflect [their] normative commitments."[26]

This agent-centered approach contrasts with the structure-centered approach that characterizes much sociological and constructivist work. This work depicts agents as overly socialized creatures locked in to particular interests because of socialization dynamics associated with particular social structures. Agents are often presented as unable to engage in action beyond the "logic of appropriateness."

While not denying the importance of structure, this book develops a more strategic and agent-centered approach and a more dynamic conception of normative change. This approach, what Nicolas Jabko calls "strategic constructivism," enables a sharper focus on the persuasive and expressive practices that agents use to give meaning to particular events and to frame and construct what is appropriate and possible.[27] Many of the actors in this book are thus best understood to be what Finnemore and Sikkink call "norm entrepreneurs." These actors, though partially socialized by their social environment, retain a capacity to (re)construct it strategically through persuasion, social pressure, material incentives, and positions of leadership. This book finds that the discursive influence of these entrepreneurs depends on their ability to cast a set of events as representing a "crisis" for opposing views and to frame new initiatives so that they resonate with prevailing organizational beliefs, principles, and practices.

---

[26] Martha Finnemore and Kathryn Sikkink, "International Norm Dynamics and Political Change," *International Organization* 52, no. 4 (1998), pp. 887–918 at p. 910.

[27] Nicolas Jabko, *Playing the Market: A Political Strategy for United Europe, 1985–2005* (Ithaca, N.Y.: Cornell University Press, 2006), p. 8.

Professionalization, administrative recruitment, adaptation, learning, and norm entrepreneurship are thus critical for understanding how IOs in general work and evolve and how the Fund in particular adopted, applied, and interpreted the norm of capital freedom. But straightforward bureaucratic politics also matters. Indeed, in the 1990s, some staff—as well as management and the IMF board directors—were motivated by a desire to expand the Fund's mandate in order to reassert its authority in an era when highly liquid capital markets threatened the institution with increasing irrelevance. The belief that liberalization was desirable mattered for these actors because it served as a crucial means for them to articulate their interests and to build coalitions with other like-minded actors. Beliefs therefore not only shape the interests of actors but also the coalitions that form among them.

Yet the professional norms of an organization's staff can also trump bureaucratic motives for budget maximization and task expansion. Where new initiatives are not consistent with the skill set and expertise of an organization's staff, the organization can prove reluctant to expand. Indeed, in the context of the subprime crisis, the IMF, with its core expertise in macroeconomics, has opposed transforming itself into a global supervisor of financial regulators precisely for this reason.

In crafting these arguments this book seeks to add greater methodological and empirical rigor to sociological and constructivist approaches. Emanuel Adler suggests that greater attention to methodology and empirical testing is the "major missing link" for these approaches.[28] One particularly egregious flaw is that these approaches typically assume that professional training socializes individuals to adopt particular beliefs without investigating and demonstrating this claim empirically. As a result, these studies tend to be impressionistic at best, rarely supported by detailed evidence that traces the effect of professionalization.

I seek to inject greater methodological and empirical rigor by employing a mixed-method research design to better demonstrate and trace the effects of beliefs about capital controls. A survey of nearly 300 economists is employed to explore the socialization dynamics associated with professional training. I also create a new dataset that codes the professional training characteristics of over 400 IMF staff to trace the effect of professionalization and administrative recruitment on organizational behavior. I utilize process-tracing that employs original archival data and extensive interviewing and contact with IMF and government officials as well as members of the private financial community to offer a detailed analysis of

---

[28] Adler, "Constructivism and International Relations," in *Handbook of International Relations*, ed. Walter Carlesnaes, Thomas Risse, and Beth Simmons (London: Sage, 2003), pp. 95–119 at p. 109.

the Fund's adoption, interpretation, and application of the norm of capital freedom. I also supplement these sources by drawing on the rich secondary literature on the Fund and contemporary news accounts.

OUTLINE OF THE BOOK

The goal of this book is to explore the processes that drive normative change and behavior in the IMF. Without denying the importance of member states' influence, this book turns its attention to the decisive role played by the staff and the intraorganizational processes that shaped how the organization adopted, interpreted, and applied the norm of capital freedom. The following chapters elaborate on these themes and arguments.

Chapter 2 begins by critically reviewing existing approaches to IOs. Building on sociological and constructivist approaches, it elaborates on the importance of examining the internal workings of IOs to better understand how they behave and evolve. It then develops more fully the role of professionalization, administrative recruitment, learning, adaptation, and strategic agency in stirring normative change "from within."

Chapter 3 consists of two parts. The first part traces the evolution of the economic profession's beliefs about capital controls from the late nineteenth to the late twentieth century. These beliefs are important because they served as a critical determinant of how the IMF staff viewed capital freedom. I identify eight schools of thought: neoclassical, Keynesianism, "neoliberalism,"[29] neoclassical synthesis, post-Keynesianism, monetarism, new classical, and new Keynesianism. Although these schools of thought offer starkly different views on a number of issues, one critical issue that divides some of them and unites others is the respective assumptions they make about the efficiency with which market actors use information. These different understandings of market behavior engender contrasting associated standards of behavior.

Keynesians, post-Keynesians, and some new Keynesians are broadly united by the view that factors intrinsic to the operation of international capital markets limit the extent to which market actors use information efficiently; the result often being myopia, herding, and rationing, which manifests itself in capital inflow "bonanzas" followed by abrupt and "sudden stops" and reversals. Because these factors are intrinsic to the operation of international capital markets and are difficult, if not impossible, to

---

[29] Throughout the book, I use scare quotes to differentiate this school of thought, which emerged in the 1930s, from the broader neoliberal continuum that comprised many schools of thought.

eliminate, capital controls are legitimated as an essential policy instrument. But these schools of thought prevailed within the economics profession only for a short period of time, if at all. The heyday of Keynesianism was roughly from the mid-1930s to early 1960s; new Keynesianism emerged in the late 1970s and strengthened in the 1990s; while post-Keynesianism has been generally confined to the margins of the profession.

By contrast, what broadly unites neoclassicals, "neoliberals," neoclassical synthesists, monetarists, new classicals, and most new Keynesians within what I call the *neoliberal* continuum of thought is the view that market actors use information more or less efficiently. Because international capital flows are seen as generally reflecting economic and policy trends (at least in the long run), this continuum of thought prioritizes policy adjustment and structural reform, not capital controls, as the appropriate course of action to minimize financial instability. The neoliberal continuum of thought, which prevailed from the early 1960s through the 1990s, thus unites behind the view that capital freedom is a desirable long-run goal. But whereas neoliberals disagree with Keynesians, post-Keynesians, and some new Keynesians over the desirability of capital freedom itself, they disagree with one another over how the norm should be interpreted and applied. Although they agree that capital freedom is a desirable long-run goal, neoclassical synthesists and most new Keynesians disagree with neoclassicals, monetarists, and new classicals on two important issues: they place greater emphasis on sequencing, and they are more sympathetic toward temporary and selective capital controls. These differences within the neoliberal continuum of thought played an important role in fostering the development of subcultures within the Fund.

The second part of chapter 3 investigates, rather than assumes, the importance of professional training as a mechanism of socialization. Original survey data is employed to establish a link between these schools of thought, professionalization, and subsequent beliefs held by actors. The evidence is highly suggestive that there is a strong link between professional training in particular academic departments where capital freedom was viewed as desirable and subsequent beliefs that legitimate it. The survey evidence also reveals importance differences within the economics profession over how to proceed toward capital freedom.

Chapter 4 explores events from the early postwar years until the early 1960s. Collectively shared Keynesian beliefs produced widespread support in the 1940s and 1950s for the view that unfettered capital mobility— particularly for short-term flows—was undesirable and that controls were essential. Capital control was the norm. This norm had two bases of support. First, the IMF membership generally supported the legitimacy of controls. The United States, though it chose not to employ controls and viewed them more skeptically than most of the IMF membership, tended to accommodate their use. Other Fund members lent greater support, with a number of other leading members, particularly in Western Europe, fearing the disruptive effects of speculative capital flows.

Second, IMF recruitment patterns ensured that the staff would support capital controls. In the 1930s and 1940s, Keynesian-minded academic economists played an important role in helping to construct the norm of capital control. Through their participation in the Bretton Woods delegations and the professionalization of their graduate students, these economists helped define the range of policy options that could be entertained by the Fund staff. When the staff members came to draw on their training to diagnose economic problems and to form policy judgments, the Keynesian content of this training helped ensure that the legitimacy of controls would be upheld, even when it contradicted the preferences of powerful principals, such as the United States and West Germany. Many staff members recruited in the 1940s and 1950s would serve in senior positions until the 1980s. Reflecting the enduring influence of professionalization, these staff remained largely supportive of controls throughout this period, even when U.S. officials began to take a more critical view of controls in the 1960s and 1970s.

Still, there were developments during this early period that foreshadowed the eventual unraveling of the norm of capital control. During a brief interval, 1945 to 1947, U.S. officials promoted a return to neoclassical orthodoxy. In the context of the 1947 economic crisis in Britain and Western Europe, U.S. officials undermined what remained of expectations that governments could turn to exchange and cooperative controls when unilateral capital controls proved ineffective. In a second critical development, governments began to turn to means other than capital controls, such as official financing, to manage disruptive capital flows. Finally, in the early 1960s, the creation of the Code of Liberalization of Capital Movements among members of the Organization of Economic Cooperation and Development (OECD) and steps to liberalize some controls among members of the European Community (EC) revealed the gradual emergence of new preferences that were more supportive of greater capital freedom.

Chapter 5 explores the decade of the 1960s. As Jacqueline Best argues, the 1960s were a period when Keynesianism was "hollowed out" and replaced by the neoclassical synthesis.[30] U.S. officials, reflecting the rise of advocates of the neoclassical synthesis to prominent policymaking positions, offered support to several changes to formal IMF rules that enhanced capital freedom. U.S. officials also began to insist that controls be

[30] Jacqueline Best, *The Limits of Transparency: Ambiguity and the History of International Finance* (Ithaca, N.J.: Cornell University Press, 2005).

used as only *temporary* policy measures and sought to redefine speculative flows—the chief villain of the international monetary system for Keynesians—as a "normal" feature of the international financial system.

Despite these changes to the IMF's formal rules and its external environment, the staff retained a Keynesian understanding of market behavior. Countries' experiences with greater capital freedom did, however, lead staff members to adapt some their beliefs. Staff reports began to show appreciation for the benefits that greater capital freedom could provide and to place greater emphasis on policy adjustment, as opposed to controls, as an appropriate means to deal with disruptive capital flows. But here and elsewhere there is evidence that prevailing beliefs channeled how the staff responded to experience. The Fund's personnel configuration of Keynesian-minded economists made the organization largely unreceptive to the possibility that liberalizing all capital flows was desirable, even though some leading principals—particularly the United States and West Germany—were advocating such a view. As a result, the staff members adapted their existing beliefs to the perceived limits of Keynesianism but failed to learn new ones that identified complete capital freedom as a desirable goal. The receptivity of the staff to adapting beliefs was in turn facilitated by the overlap of these adaptations with the Fund's emerging approach to balance-of-payments adjustment.

Chapter 6 turns its attention to the international monetary reform negotiations of the 1970s. Acting as a "norm leader," U.S. officials insisted on changes to formal IMF rules so that they seemingly directed the staff to encourage liberalization, at least in circumstances where controls impeded balance-of-payments adjustment. Although the Fund's external environment became even less permissive of the norm of capital control, the staff and organizational behavior did not demonstrate much substantial normative change. Remarkably, U.S. norm leadership, changes to formal IMF rules, and the collapse of the Bretton Woods system of exchange rates failed to induce significant change in the legitimacy lent to controls by the informal staff approach.

Chapters 7 and 8 explore the decades of the 1980s and 1990s. Without a legal mandate or active encouragement from member states or management, some staff members began to encourage, though not indiscriminately, capital account liberalization. Professionalization, administrative recruitment, learning, and norm entrepreneurship were critical in stirring normative change.

A realignment of IMF personnel occurred in the 1980s, which saw new staff, whose training inclined them to view capital freedom as desirable in the long run, replace long-serving staff who had joined in the 1940s and 1950s. This realignment helped to shift the normative outlook of the organization. This realignment also made the staff more receptive to viewing countries' experiences as demonstrating the desirability of liberalization.

But the new IMF personnel configuration in the 1980s, like the one in earlier periods, channeled how the staff responded to experiences. The split between the gradualists and big-bang supporters was shaped not only by ongoing debates within the economics profession over sequencing and temporary controls, but also by the subsequent application of different interpretations to the same experiences. For instance, supporters of each approach drew different lessons from Chile's experience in the 1990s with market-based controls on capital inflows. Whereas big-bang supporters interpreted the controls as an imperfect substitute for adjusting policies and recommended their removal, gradualists saw them as temporarily safeguarding the weak and poorly regulated financial system from capital flow volatility and therefore supported their use. In the battle of ideas that ensued, norm entrepreneurship proved critical.

The general enthusiasm for capital freedom underpinned the initiative to amend the Articles in the late 1990s. But divisions opened among the membership over the desirability of the amendment. When the Asian crisis erupted, and questions arose about the Fund's response to it, support for the amendment and capital freedom dampened greatly. The initiative subsequently failed.

In line with neoliberal understandings, the staff initially identified poor policies and institutions as responsible for the crisis, while downplaying the impact of self-fulfilling market expectations and herding behavior. This interpretation legitimated policy adjustment and structural reform, not controls on outflows, as the appropriate response. Thus, when Malaysia imposed controls on outflows in 1998 to deal with contagion from the crisis, it was subjected to severe criticism.

But the crisis and the Malaysian outcome, which some perceived to be successful, did prompt some staff members and academic economists to reconsider and challenge prevailing beliefs. A small, but influential, set of staff members and academic economists achieved some success in advancing an alternative Keynesian-inspired interpretation of the crisis. Advocacy within the Fund for this alternative interpretation has subsequently led the staff to pay greater attention to factors intrinsic to the operation of international capital markets that can give rise to financial instability. Some staff and academic economists, harkening back to Keynes, have even raised the possibility of *permanent* restraints on short-term capital inflows. Greater controversy surrounds controls on outflows, but Malaysia's rapid recovery from the crisis has led the staff to become more accommodative of their use in crisis situations.

The financial instability in Asia and beyond was thus widely perceived within the Fund to be a "crisis" for the big-bang approach. However, although the Asian crisis undermined staff support for the big-bang approach (but, interestingly, not among some member states), it failed to discredit belief in the long-run desirability of capital freedom. A belief in the long-run desirability of capital freedom channeled the staff response, leading staff to attribute the means used to proceed toward this goal ("disorderly liberalization"), rather than the goal itself, as responsible for financial instability. This adaptation has led to an almost complete unraveling of support within the Fund for the big-bang approach, but not for capital account liberalization per se.

Chapter 9 explores the decade of norm continuity between the Asian and subprime crises. Although greater legitimacy was attached to temporary and selective controls, the onus, as evidenced by the development and promotion of standards and codes, remained on what emerging markets should do to minimize financial instability, with little consideration being given to regulatory measures aimed at financial market participants in developed countries. This approach, which has generated much resentment from emerging markets, is shown to have been due to the preferences of leading principals as well as intraorganizational factors.

The reluctance of the Fund to entertain regulatory measures in developed countries is linked, like many things seem to be, to its legitimacy problems. By eschewing supply-side regulation, the Fund reinforced the perception of many emerging markets and developing countries that it is not responsive to their interests and experiences. To prevent these countries from turning their back on the Fund, some have advocated, and the IMF has slowly started to implement, reforms to formal governance of the organization to give these countries greater "voice." But while potentially useful, such reforms overlook the intraorganizational processes at the heart of this book that are shown often to exert a decisive influence on organizational behavior. With its emphasis on intraorganizational processes, this book suggests that the pursuit of formal governance reforms alone will likely be insufficient to improve the legitimacy of the IMF. Chapter 9 therefore concludes by offering some reform proposals aimed at these intraorganizational processes that seek to encourage greater intellectual diversity within the Fund. Such diversity, along with greater consideration of measures, such as supply-side regulation, could help improve the organization's legitimacy by ensuring the Fund's policy prescriptions better reflect the diverse interests and experience of its membership.

Finally, the epilogue traces changes through spring 2009 that have occurred to the Fund's approach during the subprime crisis. We are potentially entering a period of profound normative change, with many developed countries having broken with long-standing taboos and policy norms and showing a growing interest in reregulation. But at the time of this writing there have yet to be significant efforts to reverse the norm of capital freedom. The Fund, however, has become a more vocal proponent of regulatory measures aimed at financial market participants in developed countries. Although it is still too soon to reach definitive conclusions, new and heterogeneous preferences of the Fund's principals as well as adaptation and norm entrepreneurship are likely candidates underpinning this policy shift.

Significantly, the subprime crisis has resulted in symbolic efforts to strengthen the influence of emerging markets, such as the decision to convene the leaders of the G-20, rather than the G-7, to discuss the reform agenda. Membership of key international forums has also been expanded to include some emerging markets. But it is still unclear whether such efforts will prove substantively important. If not, we could witness growing resentment, self-insurance and regulatory decentralization, as emerging markets turn their backs on the key international forums and the norms they promote.

CHAPTER TWO

Normative Change from Within

THIS BOOK delves deeply into inner workings of the IMF, opening up the black box of the organization so that we can better grasp how intraorganizational processes, in addition to the influence of member states and formal rules, shape organizational behavior and change. In the first part of this chapter, I critically review state-centric and PA approaches. While offering useful insights, these approaches cannot shed adequate light on how IOs, endowed with considerable autonomy, approach their various tasks. The narrow focus of these approaches on material incentives and information leads them to overlook how the staff, their beliefs, and their debates can shape how IOs work and evolve.

In the second part of this chapter, I therefore break with these approaches, viewing the staff's collectively shared beliefs, shaped through ongoing processes of interaction, as a critical determinant of IO behavior. But I by no means imply that IO staff share one uniform position. On the contrary, a key objective of this book is to bring to light not only internal processes that shape the adoption of norms but also the internal debates, oft neglected in the existing literature, that shape how norms are interpreted and applied. Although I build on sociological and constructivist approaches, I do not adopt them uncritically. I instead seek to augment their overly structuralist and static accounts with a more strategic conception of agency and a more dynamic account of how normative change occurs "from within" IOs.

In exploring the productive power of the economics profession, I emphasize that it can serve as an agent of social construction. The shift within economics in the 1960s and 1970s toward viewing capital account liberalization as desirable played an important part in triggering normative change within the IMF. Common professional training and administrative recruitment patterns, which brought new recruits exposed to this belief into the Fund, helped to foster within it widespread belief in the long-run desirability of capital account liberalization. But professionalization and administrative recruitment also fostered subcultures within the Fund, as staff members, though sharing a belief in the long-run desirability of capital freedom, brought with them different interpretations and applications of the norm that reflected ongoing debates within the economics profession. In addition to professionalization and administrative recruitment, I also elaborate how adaptation, learning, and entrepreneurship shaped the process of endogenous normative change.

PRINCIPAL-AGENT APPROACHES AND THE U.S.-CENTRIC CONVENTIONAL WISDOM

PA theory offers the state of the art for rationalist approaches to IOs.[1] PA models are premised on the assumption that IOs are rational actors that pursue their own set of interests, which can lead to "shirking" and "slippage" when these interests run contrary to those of their member states. IO autonomy and influence is derived in the first instance from the act of delegation itself, which provides management and staff with a set of specific tasks to perform. IOs develop additional autonomy and influence through control over information, the ability to "hide" particular actions, and specialization. Member states' heterogeneous preferences and collective action problems among and within member states are also said to further IO autonomy and influence.

Ultimately, PA theorists expect autonomous IO behavior within "zones of discretion" that are based on a calculation that includes the benefits of delegation and the costs of control mechanisms to rein IOs in. Control mechanisms include administrative and oversight procedures, information disclosure requirements, screening and selection of personnel, and efforts and threats to amend organizational mandates or to withhold financial contributions. Member states also may rely on "fire alarms," that is, third-party oversight mechanisms—such as nongovernmental organizations (NGOs)—that monitor and evaluate IOs' performance. Although PA theorists expect IOs often to adopt, interpret, and apply norms on their own initiative, given their desire to elucidate agency problems and the efficacy of various control mechanisms, much of their empirical focus has tended

---

[1] For an overview of PA approaches to IOs, see Darren G. Hawkins, David A. Lake, Daniel L. Nielson, and Michael J. Tierney, "Delegation under Anarchy: States, International Organizations, and Principal-Agent Theory," in *Delegation and Agency in International Organizations,* ed. Hawkins, Lake, Nielson, and Tierney (Cambridge: Cambridge University Press, 2006), pp. 3–38. For important empirical applications to the IMF, see Lawrence Broz and Michael Brewster-Hawes, "U.S. Domestic Politics and International Monetary Fund Policy," in Hawkins et al., *Delegation and Agency,* pp. 77–106; Erica R. Gould, "Money Talks: Supplementary Financiers and International Monetary Fund Conditionality," *International Organization* 57, no. 3 (2003), pp. 551–586; Gould, "Delegating IMF Conditionality: Understanding Variations in Control and Conformity," in Hawkins et al., *Delegation and Agency,* pp. 255–280; Lisa L. Martin, "Distribution, Information, and Delegation to International Organizations: The Case of IMF Conditionality," in Hawkins et al., *Delegation and Agency,* pp. 140–164.

to be on instances in which organizational behavior and normative change is engineered by initiatives "from above."

The state-centric conventional wisdom also offers a view of normative change from above. This view essentially sees a delegation chain flowing from the private financial community to U.S. officials to IMF management to the staff. Highlighting the influence of the "Wall Street–Treasury Complex," Bhagwati claims the U.S. Treasury and Wall Street financial interests left the Fund "relentlessly propelled toward embracing the goal of capital account convertibility."[2] "The U.S. Treasury," according to Wade, "has been leading a campaign to get the main international economic and financial institutions to promote capital liberalization," primarily because "the United States has a powerful interest in maintaining and expanding the free worldwide movement of capital." This interest would be furthered by "the revision of the IMF's constitution (its articles of agreement) to require countries to commit themselves to capital account liberalization as a condition of membership." Wall Street, for its part, is "in favor of open capital accounts worldwide," and thus supported the initiative to amend the Articles.[3]

PA and state-centric approaches usefully identify some of the external processes that can shape normative change at the IMF from above. The IMF currently has 186 member states to which the organization is technically accountable for all its operations. Member states are each represented by a top economic policy official—usually the finance minister or head of the central bank—in the Board of Governors, which meets annually and makes overall strategic decisions. Daily decisions are made by the Executive Board, currently composed of twenty-four executive directors each representing either a single-nation constituency (as is currently the case for the United States, Japan, Germany, France, Great Britain, Saudi Arabia, China, and Russia) or regional multiple-nation constituencies. In between the two boards is the ministerial-level International Monetary and Financial Committee—formerly known as the Interim Committee from 1974 to 1999—which is charged with advising the governors and issuing directions to the board. The committee—which meets twice a year—is composed of twenty-four governors, each of whom has a country counterpart and voting power commensurate with the country's status on the Executive Board.

IMF member states are thus not represented equally. Although the boards operate by consensus rather than formal vote-taking, the voting power of members is taken into account in determining the degree of

---

[2] Bhagwati, "The Capital Myth," p. 12.
[3] Wade, "Coming Fight," pp. 45, 47.

consensus and thus serves as a key informal element in decision-making.[4] Historically, the United States has always been the largest financial contributor to the Fund's resources and has enjoyed the largest proportion of the votes. Currently, the U.S. director controls 16.77 percent of total votes on the board, though in the Fund's early years of operation the U.S. share exceeded a third of total of votes.

Most decisions must command a majority of votes, so the U.S. director must garner support from other countries. U.S. officials therefore often engage in informal and private discussions with other country officials to build support for their initiatives. As a result, when the U.S. director does raise an issue or position within the IMF board, she can do so, according to Treasury Secretary Timothy Geithner, "without triggering counterproductive reactions and a hardening of positions."[5]

Enhancing the power of the U.S. director is her capacity to veto certain decisions—such as increases in financial contributions—that require a special majority of 85 percent. In theory, EU countries could also vote together to exercise a veto; but these countries do not, as yet, coordinate their positions within the Fund. Emerging markets and developing countries are in even less of a position to exert a veto; virtually all are grouped and dispersed over a dozen multimember constituencies, many of which are led by a director from Europe. The United States thus remains the only country with an effective veto.

Standing member state financial contributions ("quotas") provide the Fund with significant autonomy from its principals, as it does not have to raise funds or negotiate with governments on a regular basis. However, under the IMF Articles, a general review of the adequacy of existing quotas must be conducted at least every five years. If these reviews result in the approval of a quota increase, then a special majority of members must ratify it. Within the United States, requests for quota increases, which must gain approval from Congress, have provided legislators with opportunities to scrutinize the Fund.[6]

Preference heterogeneity and collective action problems among key actors that make up the Fund's most powerful member have often complicated IMF operations. Congress has proven capable of bringing significant pressure to bear on the Fund, both through its direct relations with the IMF and indirectly through pressure on the U.S. Treasury. In some in-

[4] Leo Van Houtven, *Governance of the IMF: Decision Making, Institutional Oversight, Transparency, and Accountability*, IMF Pamphlet Series No. 53 (Washington, D.C.: IMF, 2002), p. 23.

[5] Timothy Geithner, "Testimony before the House Banking Subcommittee on General Oversight and Investigations," U.S. Treasury Press Release RR-2380, 21 April 1998.

[6] Broz and Brewster-Hawes, "U.S. Domestic Politics."

stances, congressional opposition can strengthen the U.S. position within the Fund, enabling U.S. officials to use the threat of an intransigent Congress in order to leverage their preferences. In other instances, Congress can offer a real constraint on the U.S. position, reducing the scope of the preferences the Treasury can project or support.

The United States (and other leading member states) also wields significant informal influence over the Fund.[7] Historically, the United States' international leadership role has been critical. In the Fund's early years, for instance, it was customary for potential borrowers to approach the U.S. director about the possibility of a loan before dealing with the IMF management and staff. "The practical question in those years in any prospective large use of Fund resources," writes former U.S. director Frank Southard, "was whether the United States would agree."[8]

U.S. officials also derive a private and subtle form of influence through their regular contact with IMF management and staff. In contrast to most emerging markets and developing countries, the United States (and other G-7 countries) can afford to devote significant human and analytical resources to managing IMF relations.[9] U.S. Treasury officials often seek to raise the profile of an issue and a particular approach to it through their informal influence. According to Geithner, "This approach has involved, for example, encouraging IMF staff to undertake research on the economic aspects on an issue . . . [and] work[ing] to engage IMF Management on the issue and encourag[ing] the Managing Director to address the issue in public fora and international meetings."[10]

Much more important is the fact that IMF staff rarely present a recommendation that could generate U.S. disapproval, though this possibility does, as I detail later in the book, occur. For sensitive issues, U.S. views often are sought before recommendations are put to the board. Other leading member states also seem to enjoy a similar degree of influence. For instance, Susan Strange, writing in the early 1970s, suggested that "since about 1965 it has been taken for granted that no proposal before the board will be pressed to a decision if Germany opposes it. The Japanese

[7] Randall Stone, "The Scope of IMF Conditionality," *International Organization* 62, no. 4 (2008), pp. 589–620.

[8] Frank A. Southard, *The Evolution of the International Monetary Fund*, Princeton Essays in International Finance No. 135 (Princeton, N.J.: International Finance Section, Department of Economics, Princeton University, 1979), pp. 19–20.

[9] Ngaire Woods and Domenico Lombardi, "Uneven Patterns of Governance: How Developing Countries Are Represented in the IMF," *Review of International Political Economy* 13, no. 3 (2006), pp. 480–515; IMF, *External Evaluation of IMF Surveillance: Report by a Group of Independent Experts* (Washington, D.C.: IMF, 1999), pp. 13, 34.

[10] Geithner, "Testimony before the House Banking Subcommittee on General Oversight and Investigations."

power to control decisions is probably more recent."[11] Staff recommendations thus often develop through an informal iterative process with leading member state officials.

Finally, appointment decisions give leading member states a degree of influence over the Fund. The IMF Articles provide for the managing director to be appointed by the board. In practice, though G-20 countries pledged in spring 2009 to end the practice, by long-standing convention the position of managing director has gone to the candidate favored by Western European member states. The appointment of a European managing director is "balanced" by the convention that U.S. officials select the first deputy managing director.[12] Although IMF management is not subservient to leading member state interests, their nationality and professional background, usually in their respective country's finance ministry or central bank, make them highly aware of American and European concerns and more likely to think like American and European insiders.

Many of the factors highlighted by the state-centric conventional wisdom and the PA approach feature prominently in this book. But although member states often play an important part in shaping IMF behavior, the extent of their influence within the Fund is often overestimated. This influence tends to be particularly strong only in specific high-profile cases where economic and geopolitical objectives are at stake.[13] But, in most cases, leading member states do not dictate the Fund's behavior. As Ngaire Woods observes, "[The] set of ideas [shared by the Fund staff] is not a direct reflection of the interests of the most powerful members of the organization, even though powerful members get to influence it."[14]

The preferences and power and IMF principals instead constitute what Woods calls the "outer structural constraint" in which the management and staff operate.[15] But this constraint often tells us more about what the staff cannot do than what they actually can and will do. Indeed, although

---

[11] Susan Strange, "IMF: Money Managers," in *The Anatomy of Influence: Decision-Making in International Organizations*, ed. Robert W. Cox and Harold J. Jacobson (New Haven: Yale University Press, 1971), pp. 263–297 at p. 285.

[12] The position of deputy managing director was not established until 1949. In 1992, when two new deputy managing director positions were created, the U.S.-selected deputy managing director became known as the first deputy managing director. The appointment of a European managing director is also "balanced" by the convention that U.S. officials appoint the president of the World Bank.

[13] Randall Stone, *Lending Credibility: The International Monetary Fund and the Post-Communist Transition* (Princeton, N.J.: Princeton University Press, 2002); Stone, "The Political Economy of IMF Lending in Africa," *American Political Science Review* 98, no. 4 (2004), pp. 577–592.

[14] Ngaire Woods, *The Globalizers: The IMF, the World Bank, and Their Borrowers* (Ithaca, N.Y.: Cornell University Press, 2006), p. 56.

[15] Woods, *The Globalizers*, p. 2.

the Fund staff likely could not have encouraged liberalization without U.S. support for the principle of capital freedom, this book finds, remarkably, little evidence to support the state-centric argument that the staff approach was dictated by the influence of member states alone. Power politics and Wall Street financial interests were not irrelevant, but they also were not the sole or even the decisive factor in shaping organizational behavior.

PA theorists help us to understand why normative change might be driven by agents rather than principals. But PA theory is less helpful in accounting for the processes that shape how IO preferences form and change. It is not that PA theorists do not expect IOs to possess autonomy, but rather that they generally fail to explain adequately what preferences IOs will pursue and how these preferences will change given their autonomy. PA theory, as some leading proponents acknowledge, is limited by "its inability to make general claims about what agents do with the autonomy they possess."[16]

Most PA theorists rely on relatively thin assumptions to specify agents' preferences. One common assumption is that staff members will be motivated by career incentives to adopt management's preferences in order to advance within the organization.[17] Career incentives may also lead the staff to adopt management's preferences so that they can spread blame onto the institution as a whole in case of policy failures. But, as I detail in chapters 7 and 8, these incentives cannot adequately explain normative change within the Fund when the staff adopted the norm of capital freedom *prior* to any clear indication that management favored it, and then later management sent mixed signals on how this norm should be interpreted and applied.

Relations with member states raise another set of incentives that some suggest shape staff behavior.[18] Since the IMF has no automatic right of access to confidential statistics or key policymakers, the staff must rely heavily on the cooperation of member states to ensure it can do its job properly. Adverse analysis or controversial policy prescriptions from the staff thus risks a member state closing off access. These incentives, some claim, have fostered a culture of clientism, with the staff reluctant to challenge or criticize rigorously for fear of losing access and thereby damaging their career

[16] David A. Lake and Matthew D. McCubbins, "The Logic of Delegation to International Organizations," in Hawkins et al., *Delegation and Agency*, pp. 341–368 at p. 344. See also p. 343 n. 1 and Gould, "Delegating IMF Conditionality," pp. 282–283, 307–308.

[17] Thomas D. Willett, "Toward a Broader Public-Choice Analysis of the International Monetary Fund," in *Governing the World's Economy*, ed. David Andrews, C. Randall Henning, and Louis W. Pauly (Ithaca, N.Y.: Cornell University Press, 2002), pp. 60–77.

[18] Woods, *The Globalizers*, p. 58.

prospects.[19] Although such concerns likely weighed on the minds of some staff members, these particular incentives cannot explain why many staff members argued so forcefully for liberalization. Such a stance certainly raised the risk of incurring the ire of some member state officials.

Finally, some presume that the IMF, particularly its management, is interested in budget maximization and task expansion.[20] As I show in chapters 7 and 8, budget maximization and task expansion were likely on the minds of some within the Fund, as the proposed amendment to the Articles would have brought greater financial resources and authority to the IMF at a time of highly liquid capital markets. But even for these actors it was the belief that capital freedom was desirable, rather than some material consideration, that enabled bureaucratically motivated individuals within the Fund to articulate their interests and to build internal coalitions. Moreover, it is less obvious that bureaucratic considerations were shared by all actors within the Fund, particularly during the 1980s and early 1990s when the Fund had its hands full with managing the debt crisis and the transition economies in Eastern Europe and the former Soviet Union.

Ultimately, the influence of member states and IMF management is best understood as playing a supporting rather than leading role in the evolution of the organization's approach. U.S. support for the principle of capital freedom and the transition of Western Europe and Japan to capital account openness in the 1980s and 1990s loosened the outer structural constraint in which the staff operated. This new preference configuration made it easier for the staff to stake out an approach that would previously have been difficult to sustain, but this new approach did not stem directly from these preferences. It was not until the mid-1990s that the staff received active encouragement from leading member states as well as IMF management, thus reinforcing from above the process of normative change that had already occurred largely from within. We therefore need to investigate and theorize the processes of preference formation and change more fully. An examination of the inner workings of the Fund is thus necessary.

STAFF AUTONOMY AND INFLUENCE

The staff enjoy a great deal of autonomy and influence over IMF operations. It is the staff's agenda-setting capacity, which developed and solidified in the 1950s and early 1960s, that is perhaps the most important

[19] IMF, *External Evaluation of IMF Surveillance*, p. 36.

[20] Ronald Vaubel, "A Public Choice Approach to International Organization," *Public Choice* 51, no. 1 (1986), pp. 39–57.

feature that gives the staff such autonomy and influence.[21] The board considers only those recommendations that the staff have prepared and presented to it. To be sure, the staff members are well aware of the preferences of board directors, and some leading member states are, in selected cases, capable of advancing their interests through informal contacts with staff early in the country consultation, loan negotiation, or policy preparation process. But most recommendations are the product of the staff.

Because directors do not generally see staff mission briefs in advance of country consultations or loan negotiations, they cannot easily influence the content of staff analysis and prescriptions before they take place. Therefore, in most instances, directors can do little more than direct the staff to encourage, or not, a particular policy in the future, but they can do little to change the content of country consultations or loan programs under consideration. As a result, even though directors are formally empowered to veto a particular loan program, in practice they have rarely done so, generally confining their interventions to minor changes to staff proposals. The board's limited "ownership" over the positions the staff take in country consultations and loan negotiations has historically been and continues to be an issue of concern for many directors.[22]

The agenda-setting capacity of the staff is the result of the IMF's bureaucratic division of labor, the staff's privileged access to information, and their expertise. Board directors, even the U.S. director and her staff, do not have the expertise, time, or resources to construct loan programs, carry out country consultations, or collect and systematize the necessary data. As Miles Kahler notes, "The United States supported these expansions of staff autonomy [in the 1950s and early 1960s]. In part it had no choice; meticulous design of country programs required a degree of expertise and information that executive directors and their staffs could not provide."[23] This constraint is even more binding for many emerging markets and developing countries, which, as I have suggested, can afford only a limited number of officials devoted to IMF relations.

Further deference from the board stems from the fact that loan program negotiations and country consultations are conducted by the staff via on-site missions to member states. If the board were to direct the staff mem-

[21] Barnett and Finnemore, *Rules for the World*, p. 50; Martin, "Distribution, Information, and Delegation."

[22] Southard, *Evolution of International Monetary Fund*, p. 7; Martin, "Distribution, Information, and Delegation," p. 154; IMF, *External Evaluation of IMF Surveillance*, pp. 13, 34.

[23] Miles Kahler, "The United States and the International Monetary Fund: Declining Influence or Declining Interest?" in *The United States and Multilateral Institutions: Patterns of Changing Instrumentality and Influence*, ed. Margaret Karns and Karen Mingst (Boston: Unwin Hyman, 1990), pp. 91–114 at p. 96.

bers to modify their recommendations, then negotiations with a potential borrower would have to be reopened—an undesirable outcome for an organization designed to provide rapid financing in times of crisis. On-site missions also enable the staff to gather extensive data and perform sophisticated econometric analysis, which they in turn employ to support their recommendations. The staff members are sometimes the best and only available source of data on a country, and they often acquire information on the condition that they do not disclose it to other member states.[24] By contrast, most directors are political appointees with a relatively higher rate of turnover than the staff and therefore with comparatively less knowledge or experience with which to challenge the diagnoses and prescriptions of the staff.

This book features several types of autonomous behavior on the part of the staff. Although scholars conventionally see autonomous staff behavior as present only when the staff overcome opposition from powerful members or act contrary to member states' interests, it also manifests itself in more subtle ways.[25] For instance, staff advocacy of liberalization in the 1980s and early 1990s can be viewed as a case where the Fund pursued an approach toward an issue for which its leading member state had relatively weak preferences. Because at the time U.S. officials were not particularly strong proponents of capital freedom, the Fund staff had wide latitude for autonomous action. The staff subsequently used this wide latitude to develop an approach that did not stem directly from member states' demands. Although this approach may have helped some member states, such as the United States, realize their interest in capital freedom, they did not impose it on the staff. In this sense, the staff demonstrated autonomous behavior by deciding how, among the several possible ways states' interests could be advanced, these interests were best served, and also by developing an approach to an issue that at the time many powerful members deemed a low priority.

But scholars subscribing to the conventional view of IO autonomy will also find plenty of evidence in this book to suggest the IMF did act autonomously. For instance, the Fund staff did, on occasion, fail to act on and carry out member states' demands. As discussed later, in the context of the international monetary reform negotiations of the 1970s, U.S. officials insisted upon changes to formal IMF rules that seemingly directed the staff to advocate liberalization, especially in circumstances where controls were used to prevent exchange rate adjustment. But the staff generally failed to do so.

---

[24] Martin, "Distribution, Information, and Delegation," pp. 161–163.
[25] Barnett and Finnemore, *Rules for the World*, pp. 27–28.

The staff also demonstrated conventional autonomous behavior by developing an approach that ran against the preferences of many of its member states. For instance, some staff members went against the preferences of some EC/EU governments by advocating liberalization as early as the mid-1980s, even though these governments did not come to agree on the desirability of capital freedom until the early 1990s. More recently, as suggested earlier, the staff have, on occasion, opposed EU and U.S. efforts to force the pace of liberalization in particular countries. Finally, it is worth noting that the staff, via their advocacy of capital freedom, demonstrated a form of autonomous behavior through their efforts to transform the broader international normative environment and member states' perceptions of their interest in capital freedom.

ORGANIZATIONAL CULTURE

Sociological and constructivist approaches provide some useful insights for understanding why and how the staff members, given some autonomy, approach their tasks in a particular way. These approaches, while recognizing that IOs operate within an outer structural constraint, see IOs as possessing considerable autonomy because of the legitimacy they derive as expressions of various forms of authority.[26] This authority can enable IOs to imbue social objects with meaning and create norms in ways that are often unintended and even undesired by their member states. As a result, IOs will often display "pathological" behavior, evidencing performance problems or failure to achieve their mandated goals.

To understand what IO staff members do with their autonomy and how their preferences develop and evolve, scholars working within these approaches have turned their attention to internal bureaucratic processes and organizational culture. Organizational culture can be broadly defined as the set of collectively shared beliefs that shape how the staff interpret and understand their environment, select and processes information, and arrive at particular decisions. Simply put, organizational culture is the collectively shared beliefs about "how things are done" within a particular

---

[26] On sociological approaches, see Chris Argyris and Donald A. Schön, *Organizational Learning* (Reading, Mass.: Addison-Wesley, 1978); Edgar Schein, *Organizational Culture and Leadership* (San Francisco: Jossey-Bass, 1992). On constructivist approaches, see Barnett and Finnemore, *Rules for the World*. For important empirical applications of both approaches to the IMF, see Sarah Babb, "The IMF in Sociological Perspective: A Tale of Organizational Slippage," *Studies in Comparative International Development* 38, no. 2 (2003), pp. 3–27; Barnett and Finnemore, *Rules for the World*; Bessma Momani, "Limits on Streamlining Fund Conditionality: The International Monetary Fund's Organizational Culture," *Journal of International Relations and Development* 8, no. 2 (2005), pp. 142–163.

bureaucracy, encompassing ideologies, norms, language, and routines that orient action and govern expectations and behavior. These collectively shared beliefs bound individual rationality, defining how staff members interpret, negotiate, and approach their tasks as well as conditioning how they interpret initiatives for change. Staff members within a particular organizational environment recognize and internalize not only formal routines, rules, and procedures but also informal collectively shared beliefs about how to approach tasks.

As an organization matures over time a particular culture becomes deeply embedded and inert. New staff members come to adopt this culture through a process of socialization. Organizational ideologies, norms, language, and routines become "taken-for-granted" assumptions about "how things are done." Since collectively shared beliefs are no longer openly debated, the staff members are depicted as overly socialized creatures of habit, with their behavior fully determined by the logic of appropriateness. Thus, it is said, that organizational behavior can be easily predicted given knowledge of a particular organization's culture. In addition, one can also predict that resistance will emerge to initiatives for change that threaten established ways of doing things. Staff members will tend to interpret signals from their external environment selectively, adapting their actions to existing collectively shared beliefs rather than learning new ones.

The Fund's Organizational Culture

It would be an overstatement to suggest that the Fund staff hold one distinct set of collectively shared beliefs. Indeed, one of this book's core claims is that scholars must pay greater attention to internal debates to better understand IOs' behavior. Nonetheless, it is possible to specify general assumptions about how things are done within the Fund that are more or less shared by all staff. Four elements may be identified: hierarchical, technocratic, bureaucratic, and homogeneity.

There is a clear hierarchy within IMF departments that corresponds with seniority and experience. Indeed, a recent IEO survey of 621 IMF staff members finds that 87.9 percent of respondents saw the Fund's organizational culture as "hierarchical."[27] The need for the Fund staff to formulate proposals and craft loan programs in a timely and urgent fashion has contributed to its hierarchical organization. As Joseph Stiglitz reminds us, "The institution has a hierarchical structure, not uncommon among organizations that are designed to deal with crises; one cannot have intel-

---

[27] Karin Lissakers, Ishrat Husain, and Ngaire Woods, *Report of the External Evaluation of the Independent Evaluation Office* (Washington, D.C.: IMF, 2006), p. 49.

lectual debates on the best way to fight a fire in the midst of a fire."[28] Along similar lines, Camdessus reportedly once indicated that "the intellectual discipline will be maintained while I am here—we deal with crises and we cannot have our troops rethinking strategy on the field of battle."[29]

But hierarchy, whatever its merits in ensuring a timely and rapid response, also complicates matters. Bessma Momani, for instance, reports that staff members recognize that they will be promoted according to the quality of their technical skills and years of service rather than for working effectively with country officials.[30] This engenders biases in the staff toward improving technical skills and crafting economically sound arguments, rather than toward cultivating relations with country officials and paying due attention to political feasibility.

Hierarchy also creates a form of "silo mentality" within departments that tends to inhibit coordination and communication across departments. A 1991 internal IMF review finds that staff members tended to develop "a sense of allegiance to an individual department, which rewarded loyal service and was protective of its staff."[31] Poorly performing staff members are rarely reprimanded and, at worst, are transferred to less influential departments. Although interdepartmental coordination and communication has reportedly improved in recent years, there have still been clear instances where it has broken down.

A 1999 external review of IMF surveillance finds knowledge transfer across departments to be deficient. The review uncovered a particularly poor relationship between the Research Department (RES), which then, via the Capital Markets Group, was responsible for monitoring and analyzing international capital market developments, and the Asia and Pacific Department (APD).[32] Disagreements between the two departments precipitated a breakdown in coordination and communication. As a result, the concerns of some RES staff about South Korea's poorly regulated and weak financial sector were not properly reflected in APD's consultations with government officials or in their presentations to the board. An opportunity to warn of problems associated with financial sector fragility and capital account openness was therefore missed.

---

[28] Joseph Stiglitz, "Failure of the Fund: Rethinking the IMF Response," *Harvard International Review* 23, no. 2 (2001), pp. 14–18 at p. 16.

[29] Ian Clark, "Should the IMF Become More Adaptive?" IMF Working Paper WP/96/17 (Washington, D.C.: IMF, 1996), p. 25 n. 1.

[30] Bessma Momani, "IMF Staff: Missing Link in Fund Reform Proposals," *Review of International Organizations* 2, no. 1 (2007), pp. 39–57.

[31] As cited in Momani, "IMF Staff," p. 45.

[32] IMF, *External Evaluation of IMF Surveillance*, pp. 13, 32–33, 66, 72, 102, 108–111, 119.

Along similar lines, a 2006 IEO review of multilateral surveillance finds that staff in what was then called the International Capital Markets Department (now the Monetary and Capital Markets Department—MCM) employ little input from other departments—especially the area departments responsible for relations with country officials—in crafting the *Global Financial Stability Report* (*GFSR*), a leading output of the organization. The area department staff members, for their part, tend to offer negative evaluations of the *GFSR* and fail to incorporate much information or insight from multilateral surveillance conducted by RES or MCM in their bilateral surveillance. Yet the area departments' relationship with RES appears to be asymmetric: while area department staff members do not always seem to be attentive to RES staff input, they do seem to exert a critical influence on any judgment made about individual countries in their respective regions that is found in RES multilateral surveillance outputs, particularly the *World Economic Outlook* (*WEO*).[33]

Because the staff rely strongly on macroeconomic models and econometric evidence to formulate recommendations, the organizational culture of the Fund tends to be "technocratic." In the recent IEO survey of IMF staff, nearly 75 percent of respondents saw the Fund's organizational culture as "technical" and "economistic."[34] Historically, the Fund's tasks have primarily been the preserve of economists, and this continues to be the case.[35] In 2005, nearly two-thirds of the Fund's professional staff and almost three-quarters of its new professional recruits were economists.[36]

The strong technocratic element in the Fund's culture gives economic theory a privileged role in shaping behavior. The content of the Fund's specialized knowledge in economics is therefore a critical determinant of staff behavior. "Expertise, after all," write Barnett and Finnemore, "is what determines what staff put on the agenda and what they do with the slack created."[37] The IMF Articles, which are wholly economic in character, ensure that the staff rely on economic analysis and technical, as opposed to political, considerations as much as possible. In approaching their

---

[33] IEO, *Evaluation Summary: Multilateral Surveillance* (Washington, D.C.: IMF, 2006), pp. 2–3, 11, 13, 21, 27–30; IMF, *External Evaluation of IMF Surveillance*, p. 13, 44.

[34] Lissakers, Husain, and Woods, *Report of External Evaluation*, p. 49.

[35] Babb, "IMF in Sociological Perspective," p. 19; Margaret Garritsen de Vries, "The International Monetary Fund: Economists in Key Roles," in *Economists in International Agencies: An Exploratory Study*, ed. A. W. Coats (New York: Praeger, 1986), pp. 53–66; Richard Goode and Andrew M. Kamarck, "The International Monetary Fund and the World Bank," in *The Role of the Economist in Government*, ed. Joseph A. Pechman (London: Harvester Wheatsheaf, 1989), pp. 231–254.

[36] IMF, *Annual Report, 2006* (Washington, D.C.: International Monetary Fund, 2006), pp. 116, 118.

[37] Barnett and Finnemore, *Rules for the World*, p. 46.

tasks, staff members necessarily rely on their economic training to develop detailed knowledge and to form judgments about "appropriate" policy.

It therefore matters that the Fund is staffed by economists and not political scientists. Economists are trained to concentrate on formulating policies that will maximize efficiency, with less consideration given to political and institutional constraints that can undermine attempts at policy reform. The Fund's technocratic culture thus prioritizes the formulation of prescriptive policies that are academically convincing, but not necessarily policies that are politically feasible. This priority is reinforced by hierarchical elements in the Fund's culture that favor the promotion of individuals for their technical skills rather than their success in dealing with country officials.

Evaluations of the Fund's operations routinely echo these conclusions. A recent external evaluation of IMF surveillance reports a widespread, albeit not universal, perception among the staff members that they "did not see it as their function to come up with policies that, while less than first best, moved the country in the right direction and were politically and institutionally acceptable."[38] A 2004 internal evaluation also finds that "Fund advice fails to take into account existing political constraints, or is so optimistic about the ability of governments to overcome them that it does not consider second-best policy choices that would be consistent both with the maintenance of macroeconomic stability and country-specific political realities."[39] A 1999 external evaluation similarly observes that the staff members "are apparently not as good at suggesting how first-best [policy] might actually be implemented."[40]

Some observers argue that the Fund should do more to recruit midcareer professionals, individuals who enter the Fund "laterally" from academic institutions, the private and public sectors (typically finance ministries and central banks), and other IOs, as opposed to entry-level professionals brought in through the Economist Program (EP). While midcareer professionals may have greater practical knowledge to offer than recruits fresh from graduate training, they may encounter resistance from staff should they seek to approach their tasks in a manner inconsistent with the Fund's way of doing things. The Fund has a "strong culture" regarding operational procedures and the need to build up experience within the Fund to do them properly. The value of significant external experience is therefore often undervalued.[41]

[38] As cited in Willett, "Broader Public-Choice Analysis," p. 75.

[39] IMF, *Biennial Review of the Implementation of the Fund's Surveillance and of the 1977 Surveillance Decision Modalities of Surveillance* (Washington, D.C.: IMF, 2004), p. 12.

[40] IMF, *External Evaluation of IMF Surveillance*, p. 65.

[41] IMF, *External Evaluation of IMF Surveillance*, p. 32.

The IMF's extensive bureaucratization reinforces hierarchical and technocratic elements in the Fund's culture. Nearly three-quarters of staff surveyed by the IEO identified the Fund's culture as "bureaucratic."[42] Most country reports must pass through the Fund hierarchy. A staff mission begins with a briefing paper that describes a particular country's economic situation and specifies a set of recommendations. This brief then travels through the relevant area department from the country desk officer to the regional division chief to the front office senior staff. Comments are offered at each level within the department. Other departments are also invited to comment, though the area department may choose not to incorporate their suggestions.

The Policy Development and Review Department (PDR), which serves a central monitoring and quality control function, then must approve the brief before it finalized. The brief is then sent to management for final approval. These internal dynamics are said to produce the Fund's "line" on a given country.[43] A similar process must be followed when staff members file their "back to the office" report before submitting it to the board.

The common criticism of this extensive bureaucratization is that it produces uniform policy prescriptions that ignore particular economic and political contexts in member states. Area department staff may recognize that PDR will enforce "the Fund way of doing things," and therefore have less of a reason for raising issues or policy prescriptions outside the range of options that are typically deemed legitimate. Bureaucratization, along with the hierarchical nature of the Fund, can thus stifle internal debate and produce "one size fits all" policy prescriptions.

But such an outcome will likely be the case only for issues where the Fund's "line" has been decided and clearly articulated. However, on issues where the Fund's line has not yet been fully developed, there is likely to be sufficient scope for staff to pursue a broader range of policy prescriptions. Indeed, the failure of the Fund to articulate a particular "line" on capital controls and their liberalization provided staff with wide discretion over how to approach capital account issues in various contexts. Also, as I document in later chapters, PDR often sent mixed signals to the staff on the issue, giving them additional leeway on whether to advocate liberalization or to accommodate, even encourage, the use of controls. How capital account liberalization was approached thus often lay with particular mission chiefs and their staff economists, and not with PDR staff, IMF management, or board directors.

Homogenization of staff work is another important element in the Fund's culture. Over three-fifths of staff members in the IEO survey re-

[42] Lissakers, Husain, and Woods, *Report of External Evaluation*, p. 49.
[43] IMF, *External Evaluation of IMF Surveillance*, pp. 24–25.

ported that they find the Fund's organizational culture to be homogenous and conforming.[44] Hierarchy and bureaucratization certainly contribute to pressures to conform to standard ways of doing things. Former Canadian director Ian Clark suggests that the Fund has the "goal of presenting a 'single corporate line'" in its interactions with member states.[45]

Organizational socialization is also important. Margaret Garritsen de Vries, who served as a staff member from 1946 to 1973 and as official Fund historian for nearly three decades, writes about a process of "assimilation" that occurs at the Fund.[46] According to de Vries, "Differences in economists' culture, training, ideology, and background have generally not affected their easy assimilation into the staff or into the Fund's work." De Vries suggests that assimilation occurs fairly rapidly because most staff members share a common professional background.

Work practices also are important. The Fund subjects new recruits to an intensive orientation followed by a two-year training program for new Ph.D.s in which they are rotated across two departments. Individuals also commonly work as members of a team, on missions abroad and at IMF headquarters. According to de Vries, "Teamwork, especially on missions abroad, makes for ready assimilation, particularly since a joint position has to be obtained."

But this conforming organizational culture can stifle internal debate and limit the receptivity of the staff to new ideas. Staff papers sent to the board are supposed to present a "team view," not the view of any particular individual. Dissenting views are not included. Not surprisingly, staff members report that they often are "preoccupied with getting their analysis agreed and accepted internally rather than listening or learning from outside."[47] Some staff members also point to the internal review process, suggesting that it "hinders innovation and flexibility; departments are inhibited from trying to do things differently."[48] Others claim that the need to standardize all internal communication contributes to excessive homogenization.[49]

This discussion helps us to better understand in a general sense "how things get done" within the IMF. By directing our attention to beliefs about how things get done within organizations, the sociological and constructivist approaches provide us some insight into what staff members do

[44] Lissakers, Husain, and Woods, *Report of External Evaluation*, p. 49.

[45] Clark, "Should the IMF Become More Adaptive?" p. 24.

[46] De Vries, "The International Monetary Fund," pp. 57–58.

[47] IMF, *External Evaluation of IMF Surveillance*, p. 33.

[48] IMF, *External Evaluation of IMF Surveillance*, p. 33. See also Van Houtven, *Governance of the IMF*, p. 18.

[49] Momani, "IMF Staff," p. 50.

with the autonomy they possess. These approaches also enrich our understanding of normative change by helping to account for instances where organizational behavior is shaped by the extent to which a particular initiative resonates with an organization's culture.

But these approaches cannot fully account for normative change within the Fund. Although scholars working within these approaches often put forward the staff's beliefs to explain IO preferences, they have thus far devoted surprisingly little attention to how these beliefs develop and change. Instead, in empirical work we typically encounter the staff operating in a more or less fully developed organizational culture. Scattered allusions tend to be made to various factors that shape the staff's collectively shared beliefs, but little systematic or sustained effort is made to investigate their origin.

Yet we need to understand, for instance, not only that the Fund's culture is "technocratic" but also how the content of this technocracy matters. To be sure, staff members draw on their professional training and expertise to craft recommendations, and this is important to understanding how things get done inside the Fund. But a determinant of how things get done that is far more crucial than staff members' credentials as economists is the content of staff training and expertise and how this content has shifted over time.

A more serious deficiency of sociological and constructivist approaches is their treatment of staff agency. In seeking to demonstrate that culture matters, sociologists and constructivists tend to downplay the possibility and efficacy of staff strategic agency. As a result, sociologists and constructivists generally offer overly structuralist and static accounts of organizational change and behavior. Missing is greater attention to the role the staff play in fostering change from within and the "battles of ideas" that can occur among individuals.[50] The staff members do not simply react to initiatives for change; they are also often proactive actors at the forefront of efforts to promote it. A more agent-centered account is thus needed.

THE PRODUCTIVE POWER OF THE ECONOMICS PROFESSION

The IMF staff have strong links to the economics profession. In addition to the fact that most are economists, the IMF deliberately encourages the staff to maintain and develop close links with the profession.[51] These

---

[50] Even Barnett and Finnemore—in *Rules for the World*, chap. 3—tend to neglect internal staff debates in their discussion of the development and expansion of IMF conditionality. Instead, IMF staff members seem to alter the content of conditionality almost seamlessly without any friction or resistance.

[51] De Vries, "The International Monetary Fund," p. 57.

close links are important because professions are critical agents of social construction, possessing a "productive power" that enables them to construct understandings, fix meanings, and define what is legitimate and even possible.

Many of the beliefs shared by the staff originate from the economics profession. Economists are chiefly concerned with understanding the production, consumption, and distribution of goods and services (i.e., developing causal understandings about how economies operate) and using these understandings to develop policies that maximize welfare (i.e., formulating standards of behavior for "appropriate" policy). These causal understandings and standards of behavior in turn provide some of the building blocks for the norms we observe the IMF constructing and advocating. The economics profession, like all professions, is thus a major agent of social construction.

Professions derive a unique form of power from their legitimacy, which, as Magali Larson observes, is "founded on the achievement of socially recognized expertise."[52] Indeed, as Sarah Babb observes, "What makes professions special is that they make rules about which ideas are to be considered knowledge and who is allowed to call themselves an expert."[53] Like other professions, the productive power of the economics profession is based a claim to authoritative knowledge. John Markoff and Veronica Montecinos, for instance, suggest that this authority derives in large part from "membership in a profession believed to possess the knowledge to dispel anxiety."[54] Similarly, others suggest the influence of the economics profession is due to "social deference to expertise."[55] The credentials that economists possess, such as a Ph.D. in economics, thus serve to constitute them as "authorities." And the Fund, because it is staffed primarily by economists, bases much of its legitimacy on claims to expert-based authority.

Economists tend to present their understandings and associated standards of behavior as based solely on technical knowledge, evidence, and internal truth tests. Yet the information that economists provide is not simply technical knowledge based on evidence and internal truth tests. Rather, as Peter Haas suggests, it is "the product of human interpretations

[52] Magali S. Larson, *The Rise of Professionalism: A Sociological Analysis* (Berkeley and Los Angeles: University of California Press, 1977), p. xvii.

[53] Sarah Babb, *Managing Mexico: Economists from Nationalism to Neoliberalism* (Princeton, N.J.: Princeton University Press, 2001), p. 15.

[54] John Markoff and Veronica Montecinos, "The Ubiquitous Rise of Economists," *Journal of Public Policy* 13, no. 1 (1993), pp. 37–68 at p. 41. See also Babb, *Managing Mexico*; Barnett and Finnemore, *Rules for the World*.

[55] Robert Nelson, "Introduction and Summary," in Pechman, *Role of Economist*, pp. 1–22 at p. 3.

of social and physical phenomena."[56] For instance, when Keynesians in the 1940s examined the financial instability of the interwar years they blamed incompletely informed investors for triggering self-reinforcing capital flows. Yet when Milton Friedman examined the same events a decade later he reinterpreted the self-reinforcing capital flows described by Keynesians as rational market discipline.[57]

Even the most ostensibly positive models of economic behavior are saturated with normative and ethical implications. Jacqueline Best and Wesley Widmaier, for instance, argue that the micro and macro divide in economics is more about the relative emphasis placed on private versus public interests than it is about small- or large-scale processes.[58] The economics profession, like all professions, thus has a normative value-laden aspect as well as a technical element. Just as medical doctors are taught to value human life above other goals, economists are taught normative conceptualizations about how economies should be organized.

Technical knowledge (causal understandings) and normative conceptualizations (standards of behavior) offer lenses through which economists develop shared diagnoses about the problems economies face, the kinds of information relevant to understanding these problems, and the array of possible and appropriate policies to remedy them. As the "baggage handlers" of these beliefs, economists shape how ideas "travel." Economists tend to pick up their "cognitive baggage" from professional training. Professional training exposes and socializes an individual to particular understandings and standards of behavior by promoting, both implicitly and explicitly, a particular set of beliefs. "Professional training," observe Finnemore and Sikkink, "does more than simply transfer technical knowledge, it actively socializes people to value certain things above others."[59]

Economists are generally taught to value efficiency over all over objectives. Efficiency serves as a normative guide for evaluating policy, inducing a bias toward policies that remove monopoly and promote the wider and better dissemination of information, and against policies that distort or fix prices and restrict entry. Economists are therefore instinctively inclined to see most restrictions and controls as "inappropriate" because they can introduce distortions and harm efficiency. As Barry Eichengreen

---

[56] Haas, "Introduction," p. 4.

[57] Milton Friedman, "The Case for Flexible Exchange Rates," in *Essays in Positive Economics*, ed. Milton Friedman (Chicago: University of Chicago Press, 1953), pp. 157–203.

[58] Jacqueline Best and Wesley Widmaier, "Micro- or Macro-Moralities? Economic Discourses and Policy Possibilities," *Review of International Political Economy* 13, no. 4 (2006), pp. 609–631.

[59] Finnemore and Sikkink, "International Norm Dynamics," p. 905. See also Peter Evans and Martha Finnemore, "Organizational Reform and the Expansion of the South's Voice at the Fund," G-24 Discussion Paper No. 15 (New York: UNCTAD, 2001), p. 17.

and Charles Wyplosz explain, "Holders of the union card are taught to prize the efficiency of the market and to regard intervention through taxation and controls as welfare-reducing. They are trained to anticipate the incentive of market participants to evade taxes and circumvent administrative restrictions."[60]

Economists are also taught various assumptions about how economies operate, which in turn inform the technical knowledge and normative conceptualizations they develop. Colin Hay, for instance, shows that public choice assumptions of instrumental rationality can lead to pessimistic views about the desirability of public governance.[61] Assessments of the desirability of capital account liberalization have been similarly shaped by assumptions about market behavior and the efficiency with which market actors employ information. For instance, whereas new classicals assume fully informed market actors making an efficient use of information, Keynesians assume incompletely informed market actors relying on conventions. These assumptions, though sometimes adopted more out of analytical convenience than out of true belief, in turn lead to starkly different assessments of the desirability of capital account liberalization. The former legitimates it, while the latter suggests some restraints are necessary.

To explain how expert authority is translated into policy, scholars of epistemic communities focus on "networks—often transnational—of knowledge based experts with an authoritative claim to policy relevant knowledge within their domain of expertise. Their members share knowledge about the causation of social or physical phenomena in an area for which they have a reputation for competence, and a common set of normative beliefs about what action will benefit human welfare in such a domain."[62] Like-minded experts shape policy via a process of administrative recruitment in which they supplant or replace actors informed with alternative perspectives.[63] Organizational sociologists describe a similar process as "normative isomorphism."[64] For these scholars, policy choices

[60] Barry Eichengreen and Charles Wyplosz, "Taxing International Financial Transactions to Enhance the Operation of the International Monetary System," in *The Tobin Tax: Coping with Financial Volatility*, ed. Mahbub ul Haq, Inge Kaul, and Isabelle Grunberg (Oxford: Oxford University Press, 1996), pp. 15–41 at p. 15.

[61] Colin Hay, "Theory, Stylized Heuristic or Self-Fulfilling Prophecy? The Status of Rational Choice Theory in Public Administration," *Public Administration* 82, no. 1 (2004), pp. 39–62.

[62] Peter M. Haas, "Policy Knowledge: Epistemic Communities," in *International Encyclopedia of the Social and Behavioral Sciences*, vol. 17, ed. Neil J. Smelser and Paul B. Bates (Amsterdam: Elsevier Science, 2001), pp. 11578–11586 at p. 11579. See also Haas, "Introduction," p. 3.

[63] Adler and Haas, "Conclusion," pp. 375–385; Haas, "Introduction," p. 30; Haas, "Policy Knowledge," pp. 11582–11583.

[64] Dimaggio and Powell, "The Iron Cage Revisited."

are driven in part by the development of new theories about "appropriate policy" by like-minded professionals, who then acquire power in relevant bureaucracies.

The concepts of epistemic communities and normative isomorphism are relevant to this book's focus on the source of new norms, the processes through which they enter IOs, and the power that emanates from expertise. However, this book departs from this earlier work in several key ways. First, it is difficult to conclude that all the economists featured in this book based their beliefs purely on knowledge claims. The claim that capital freedom is desirable was not derived from careful empirical verification and rigorous internal truth-tests that produced a knowledge-based consensus. On the contrary, no such knowledge-based consensus existed, and the Fund did not adopt the norm of capital freedom simply because liberalization was the objectively "optimal" policy choice. Rather, for many inside the Fund, opposition to capital controls, observes a 1999 external evaluation of IMF surveillance, "was based more on ideology than on a careful consideration of the evidence and the policy alternatives."[65]

Theoretically, the case for capital freedom is based on an analogy with standard theoretical arguments for free trade in goods and services. In a competitive market with perfect information, capital freedom produces a "first-best" equilibrium in which capital is allocated to its most productive resources and residents of different countries engage in welfare-improving intertemporal consumption smoothing.[66] But there are also equally compelling theoretical arguments that suggest some restraints on capital mobility may also be optimal.

One line of argument points to preexisting domestic distortions that could prevent markets from reaching the "first-best" equilibrium. For instance, explicit or implicit government liability insurance could engender "moral hazard," leading domestic financial intermediaries to reach excessively for risk, prompting capital inflow surges. A case therefore could be made, in principle, for the use of capital controls on standard "second-best" grounds. The judicious introduction of a new distortion in the form of capital controls could, in theory, turn out to improve rather than worsen economic welfare.

Though economists do not debate the logic of this argument, most would suggest the "first-best" measure would be to adjust policies so that the distortion is removed. Many economists also would doubt whether a government, in a world of multiple distortions and imperfect policymaking, could actually introduce controls in such a manner as to raise eco-

---

[65] IMF, *External Evaluation of IMF Surveillance*, p. 39.

[66] For a summary, see Maurice Obstfeld and Alan M. Taylor, *Global Capital Markets: Integration, Crisis, and Growth* (Cambridge: Cambridge University Press, 2004).

nomic welfare. The issue, as economist Michael Dooley observes, is not theoretical but empirical.[67]

A second line of argument can be traced to skepticism about the extent to which financial market participants use information efficiently. Strictly speaking, unfettered capital mobility only produces the "first-best" equilibrium in a world of competitive markets and fully informed financial market participants. But there is a strong skeptical tradition that highlights factors intrinsic to the operation of international capital markets—such as information asymmetries—that limit the extent to which financial market participants use information efficiently.[68] Keynesians, post-Keynesians, and some new Keynesians point to evidence that incompletely informed investors often display, successively, excessive optimism and excessive pessimism. These swings in market sentiment can give rise to multiple equilibria in which self-fulfilling market expectations and herding behavior trigger financial instability even in the presence of sound economic and policy trends. A case could therefore be made for the judicious introduction of controls to limit the herding behavior and volatility intrinsic to international capital markets.

The evidence suggests an even more pessimistic evaluation of the optimality of capital freedom when one examines the relationship between liberalization and growth, which is arguably the most important issue for most emerging markets and developing countries. The findings from dozens of statistical analyses are generally mixed with a number of studies finding no or even a negative relationship between capital account openness and growth in emerging markets and developing countries.[69] As a result, economist Pierre-Richard Agenor concludes: "From a purely analytical point of view, it cannot be established *a priori* whether the benefits of financial openness are likely to outweigh its potential costs."[70] A 2003 IMF study similarly observes that "it is difficult to establish a strong causal relationship [between capital account liberalization and growth] . . . [I]f

---

[67] Michael P. Dooley, "A Survey of Academic Literature on Controls over International Capital Transactions," NBER Working Paper 5352 (Cambridge, Mass.: NBER, 1995).

[68] The seminal piece on information asymmetries remains Joseph Stiglitz and Andrew Weiss, "Credit Rationing in Markets with Imperfect Information," *American Economic Review* 71, no. 3 (1981), pp. 393–410. See also Stiglitz, "Capital Market Liberalization, Economic Growth, and Instability," *World Development* 28, no. 6 (2002), pp. 1075–1086; and Stiglitz, "Capital Market Liberalization, Globalization, and the IMF," *Oxford Review of Economic Policy* 20, no. 1 (2004), pp. 57–71.

[69] For an overview of the statistical evidence, see M. Ayhan Rose, Eswar Prasad, Kenneth Rogoff, and Shang-Jin Wei, "Financial Globalization: A Reappraisal," IMF Working Paper WP/06/189 (Washington, D.C.: IMF, 2006).

[70] Pierre-Richard Agénor, "Benefits and Costs of International Financial Integration: Theory and Facts," *World Economy* 26 (2003), pp. 1089–1118 at pp. 1101–1102.

financial integration has a positive effect on growth, there is as yet no clear and robust empirical proof that the effect is quantitatively significant."[71]

Economists thus never reached a knowledge-based consensus that liberalization constituted an "optimal" policy choice. Indeed, some prominent economists, such as Bhagwati and Eichengreen, were critical of how many of their academic colleagues arrived at the view that capital freedom was desirable with a surprising degree of certitude in advance of and in the absence of definitive evidence.[72] Similarly, Stanley Fischer, writing in the wake of the Asian crisis, claimed, "The difference between the analytic understanding of capital- and current-account liberalization is striking. The economics profession knows a great deal about current-account liberalization, its desirability, and effective ways of liberalizing. It knows far less about capital-account liberalization. It is time to bring order both to thinking and policy on the capital account."[73]

The consensus for liberalization was thus not principally knowledge-based; rather it was primarily norm-based. To be sure, a body of evidence did emerge suggesting that liberalization offered some efficiency benefits and that controls introduced distortions and could harm economic performance. This body of scholarship, however, did *not* definitively conclude that at least some restraints on capital mobility was suboptimal. Nonetheless, among some economists beliefs about causal relationships hardened into a neoliberal ideology in which the desirability of liberalization and the inappropriateness of controls became held as an article of faith and was resistant to change even in light of empirical evidence.

Such beliefs can generate particular interpretations of experiences, channeling the lessons that emerge and bounding individual rationality. Individuals may use cognitive shortcuts that draw attention to information that confirms interpretations and discount information that disconfirms them. A "hypothesis-confirming" bias can creep into cognitive processes, in which actors fail to give due consideration to a full sample of information and base their decisions on only those instances that resonate with prevailing interpretations, limiting the range of lessons that might be drawn.[74]

---

[71] Eswar Prasad, Kenneth Rogoff, Shang-Jin Wei, and M. Ayhan Rose, "Effects of Financial Globalization on Developing Countries: Some Empirical Evidence," IMF Occasional Paper No. 220 (Washington, D.C.: IMF, 2003), p. ix. See also pp. 6–7.

[72] Bhagwati, "The Capital Myth"; Barry Eichengreen, "Capital Account Liberalization: What Do the Cross-Country Studies Tell Us?" *World Bank Economic Review* 15, no. 3 (2001), pp. 341–365.

[73] Stanley Fischer, "Capital Account Liberalization and the Role of the IMF," in *Should the IMF Pursue Capital Account Convertibility?* Princeton Essays in International Finance No. 207 (Princeton, N.J.: Princeton Department of Economics, 1998), p. 8.

[74] Richard Nisbett and Lee Ross, *Human Inference: Strategies and Shortcomings of Social Judgment* (Englewood Cliffs, N.J.: Prentice-Hall, 1980).

As a result, when causal beliefs become hardened into articles of faith, they can severely skew and constrain the ways in which actors process and respond to information, eroding standards of evidence associated with a given profession. Norms associated with professional training and organizational cultures can exert similar artificial yet powerful constraints on the way actors interpret the world. For instance, the Fund's technocratic culture biases the staff toward "first-best" policy prescriptions that are academically convincing rather than "second-best" options that are politically feasible. These artificial constraints are not derived from any objective truth, but rather from an unquestioned belief in the appropriateness of a given view.

Such processes feature several times in this book. For instance, as I detail in chapter 7, the prevailing beliefs of some IMF staff members initially severely narrowed their understanding of the extent to which Chile's market-based controls on inflows in the 1990s could "work." Big-bang proponents framed the controls as an inappropriate attempt to substitute for policy adjustments necessary to arrest the inflow surge. Since these individuals viewed the effectiveness of the controls as likely to prove short-lived and to introduce distortions, they insisted upon liberalization. But this framing initially blinded these staff members to the positive benefits the controls provided. In particular, these staff members at first failed to pay sufficient attention to evidence that suggested the controls had lengthened the maturity of capital inflows and, in doing so, potentially helped safeguard the weak financial sector from capital flow volatility. While the use of controls for such a purpose could be justified on "second-best" grounds, it was unlikely to be sanctioned by those who had taken the "first-best" world as an article of faith.

Many of the economists at the center of this book therefore are best characterized as norm-based experts as opposed to knowledge-based experts. Norm-based experts, like knowledge-based experts, are accorded access to decision-making processes because their credentials, reputation, and professional training constitute them as "an authority" on policy. Though presented as "objective knowledge," however, their beliefs are in fact shaped by interpretations linked to professional training, articles of faith, and norms.

PROCESSES OF NORM ADOPTION, INTERPRETATION, AND APPLICATION

Although the Fund's leading member states eventually gave broad support to the norm of capital freedom, they did not impose this norm and a particular interpretation and application of it on the staff. Rather, the Fund's adoption, interpretation, and application of this norm can be largely traced to the staff, their beliefs, and their internal debates. Five processes were vital in stirring the process of normative change: professionalization, administrative recruitment, adaptation, learning, and entrepreneurship.

Professionalization and Administrative Recruitment

Within organizations the emergence of particular beliefs is often decisively shaped by patterns of professionalization and administrative recruitment. The types of experts recruited to particular positions and the credentials demanded can shape the types of policies that an organization entertains and potentially implements. The emergence of particular beliefs within an organization is therefore often tightly linked to the understandings and standards of behavior that prevail within the profession(s) from which an organization recruits.

Most scholars see administrative recruitment as a means through which an IO maintains a particular set of beliefs. For instance, a number of scholars claim that the Fund's recruitment procedures and commitment to English as a working language has skewed employment overwhelming toward graduates of institutions from and natives of English-speaking countries, particularly the United States and Britain.[75] There is much empirical evidence to support this claim. A 1968 study of senior IMF staff revealed that nearly 60 percent were from English-speaking developed countries.[76] By 2004 the staff's composition had not altered dramatically. Nearly 50 percent of senior staff and 40 percent of middle-ranking and junior staff members were from English-speaking developed countries.[77]

Although the Fund faces a relative lack of "passport diversity" among the staff, a far more critical influence on its beliefs is the relative lack of "intellectual diversity." There is an unquestionably high degree of homogeneity in the professional training characteristics of the staff. A 1996 study finds that some 90 percent of new staff recruits with Ph.D.s received them from the United States or Canada.[78] A more recent study finds greater recruitment of Ph.D.s with European training in 1999, but still no recruits with training outside developed countries.[79]

---

[75] Strange, "IMF: Money Managers," p. 269; Woods, *The Globalizers*, p. 52; Ngaire Woods, "The United States and the International Financial Institutions: Power and Influence within the World Bank and the IMF, " in *US Hegemony and International Organizations*, ed. Rosemary Foot, S. Neil MacFarlane, and Michael Mastanduno (Oxford: Oxford University Press, 2003), pp. 92–114 at pp. 108–109.

[76] Strange, "IMF: Money Managers," p. 269.

[77] IMF, *Diversity Annual Report* (Washington, D.C.: IMF, 2004), p. 19. Another 10 percent or so of staff members at all levels were from "other English-speaking countries."

[78] Clark, "Should the IMF Become More Adaptive?" p. 9.

[79] Evans and Finnemore, "Organizational Reform," p. 12.

Some scholars allege that these empirical findings suggest that a particular type of knowledge is embedded within the Fund (i.e., "English-speaking country knowledge" or "U.S. knowledge") and that these recruitment patterns are yet another instrument through which leading member states, particularly the United States, exert control over the Fund. Others suggest that these findings simply reflect the fact that the best economics departments are to be found in the United States—with other English-speaking country institutions following close behind—and that the IMF simply hires the best. What both perspectives fail to grasp is that while recruits may represent "U.S. knowledge" or the "best knowledge," what is far more important is the specific content of this knowledge. While it matters that Fund economists tend to come from U.S. and other English-speaking country institutions, what matters more is that the beliefs that prevail within these institutions have shifted over time, and that we therefore need to investigate the way that this shift has affected IMF practices. Although the geographic composition of staff nationalities and graduate institutions has demonstrated significant continuity, the beliefs about capital controls prevailing within the economic profession and the IMF have evidenced dramatic change.

Administrative recruitment reinforces or maintains a particular culture only when organizational and professional beliefs overlap. Yet when organizational and professional beliefs become decoupled, recruitment can act as an important mechanism for endogenous organizational change, as individuals wedded to a particular view are replaced or supplanted by new recruits sharing alternative views. This process of personnel realignment can facilitate cultural change, albeit usually in a gradual fashion.

PA theorists suggest member states "screen and select" individuals to create particular personnel configurations. Leading member states—particularly the United States—do wield some influence over staff appointments. In theory, the managing director is responsible—subject to the approval of the board—for the appointment and dismissal of the staff. In practice, some suggest leading member states have the capacity to veto particular appointments.[80] But the extent to which member states influence staff appointments should not be overstated. While member states often expend great effort in "screening and selecting" IO management, with the exception of some high-profile episodes, they typically permit IMF management to have wide discretion over staff appointments.

Writing in the late 1970s, former U.S. director Frank Southard observed that:

---

[80] Woods, "United States and International Financial Institutions," p. 109.

The Executive Board recognized early (after a few unhappy episodes) that it should not seek to debate staff appointments. . . . Just as the Board recognized that it should not seek to challenge the Managing Director's appointments to the staff, he in turn recognized that important ones should be privately reviewed with Executive Directors. For example, a director would not be formally proposed for the African Department without careful consultation with Executive Directors elected by the African countries, and because of linguistic and other aspects of Africa, there have been some intense discussions behind the scenes. But I do not recall any case in which a Managing Director felt obliged to propose the appointment of a particular person solely because of representations by Executive Directors, although that does not mean that such representations are without effect. . . . Of course, Executive Directors have not been uniformly and invariably enthusiastic about the Managing Director's proposals. But they recognize that their suggestions should be made privately and that there is no practical alternative to accepting his formal appointments. I do not know of a single instance during my twenty-five years in the Fund in which the Managing Director withdrew a proposed staff appointment because of objections by the Board, although this had occurred earlier in at least one important case.[81]

Some recent staff appointments have also played out along similar lines, with leading member states finding it difficult to block particular appointments. For instance, in 1999, Camdessus reportedly appointed Thomas Dawson as director of the IMF External Relations Department despite opposition from U.S. Treasury Secretary Summers.[82]

Member states have also sometimes initiated changes to IMF recruitment procedures that seemingly contradict PA expectations. IMF recruitment procedures generally require a Ph.D. in economics from one of the leading—usually Anglo-American—economic departments. The Fund currently engages in two kinds of recruitment: the EP, which takes in newly trained Ph.D.s, and midcareer appointments. In a typical year more recruits are brought in at the midcareer level than in the EP.

PA theorists would expect member states, particularly U.S. officials, not to revise these procedures because they should facilitate the emergence of a particular view that more or less aligns with the "Washington Consensus." By permitting the IMF sufficient autonomy, the Fund recruitment procedures should eventually "steer" it toward the preferences of its most powerful principals.

---

[81] Southard, *Evolution of International Monetary Fund*, pp. 8–9.
[82] Author's interview with Thomas Dawson, Washington, D.C., 17 May 2005.

Yet, contrary to PA expectations, the IMF board has initiated some changes to recruitment procedures in an attempt to foster greater intellectual diversity. These attempts to encourage greater intellectual diversity, as opposed to attempts to encourage greater passport diversity, were largely in response to the IMF Administration Department's concern that there was a need to "bring to the Fund a small number of career staff who might approach policy questions from a new and somewhat different perspective."[83]

These recruitment procedure changes were implemented despite opposition from management and staff who believed they would potentially introduce ideas outside the confines of neoclassical economics, thereby weakening the quality of the staff.[84] One therefore cannot necessarily presume that IMF principals engineer recruitment patterns to ensure the "right" personnel (i.e., those more likely to adhere to the Washington Consensus) are "screened and selected."

Recruitment procedures matter not because they are necessarily a direct reflection of member state interests, but rather because, in demanding particular types of individuals and qualifications, they establish a pathway through which new beliefs can be transmitted to an IO. IOs that recruit almost exclusively among individuals with a particular type of training or degree are highly susceptible to developments within that profession; and these developments are therefore crucial for understanding the evolution of organizational beliefs and practices. This is especially likely to be the case in organizations, like the IMF, where most new recruits are drawn from a limited number of academic institutions. Indeed, Peter Evans and Martha Finnemore suggest that the tendency of the Fund to engage in what they call "intellectual monocropping" has been critical in fostering "shared belief in a paradigm."[85]

Adaptation and Learning

But there is more to understanding normative change within IOs than just professionalization and recruitment patterns. Real-world events also matter, and staff members routinely seek to develop, refine, and update their beliefs as a result of new experiences and information. Here adaptation and learning enter in as critical processes.[86] Adaptation involves a

---

[83] As cited in Bessma Momani, "Recruiting and Diversifying IMF Technocrats," *Global Society* 19, no. 2 (2005), pp. 167–187 at p. 177.

[84] Momani, "Recruiting and Diversifying IMF Technocrats," pp. 177–178.

[85] Evans and Finnemore, "Organizational Reform," pp. 10, 9.

[86] On learning and adaptation, see Argyris and Schön, *Organizational Learning*; Ernest Haas, *When Knowledge Is Power: Three Models of Change in International Organizations* (Berkeley and Los Angeles: University of California Press, 1990); Barbara Levitt and James G. March, "Organizational Learning," *Annual Review of Sociology* 14 (1988), pp. 319–340.

change in beliefs about the desirability or possibility of using a given policy instrument or instrument setting without any corresponding change in beliefs about the desirability of a given policy goal. Adaptation can entail changes in organizational language, structures, symbols, and small modifications of behavior. New agendas and strategies may be added to existing ones, but the organization's "implicit assumptions that govern actual behavior, that tell group members how to perceive, think, and feel about things"—what organizational theorists Chris Argyris and Donald Schön call "theories-in-use"—remain relatively unchanged.[87]

Learning, on the other hand, involves a change in beliefs about the desirability or possibility of a given policy goal. To put it differently, adaptation can be thought of as a change in beliefs about "desirable means," while learning can be thought of as change in beliefs about "desirable ends." Learning involves a comprehensive reappraisal of organizational goals, entailing a reexamination of shared beliefs about "how things are done." Organizational ideologies, norms, language, and routines are fundamentally challenged, thereby disrupting the certainty and stability that culture provides in helping an organization navigate an uncertain and complex world. Because collectively shared beliefs embodied in an organization's culture respond to the basic human desire for certainty and stability, many staff members are likely to resist initiatives for change that others derive from learning.

Both adaptation and learning involve processes in which staff members take deliberate action to embed their inferences from experience into an organization's collectively shared beliefs. Staff members actively search for new information to update their beliefs, and this new information can often lead them to pursue new policy directions. But these experiences do not come with "instruction sheets," and thus interpretation shapes how these experiences are processed and understood. Interpretations in turn depend largely on the prevailing beliefs that give meaning to particular experiences and frame the manner in which they are understood. As Barbara Levitt and James March conclude, understandings from experience are influenced "less by history than by the frames applied to that history."[88]

As suggested, interpretations can channel the types of lessons that emerge, bounding individual rationality, inducing a "hypothesis-confirming" bias, and rendering prevailing beliefs "sticky" and resistant to change. Prevailing organizational beliefs, while fostering greater organizational certainty and stability, can therefore end up inhibiting the pro-

---

[87] Edgar Schein, *Organizational Culture and Leadership, Second Edition* (San Francisco: Jossey-Bass, 1992), p. 22; Chris Argyris and Donald Schön, *Theory in Practice: Increasing Professional Effectiveness* (San Francisco: Jossey-Bass, 1974).

[88] Levitt and March, "Organizational Learning," p. 324.

cesses of adaptation and learning by narrowly defining the kind of information that is considered relevant and filtering this information in such a manner as to match these beliefs—a process that J. W. Lorsch calls "strategic myopia."[89] As Edgar Schein notes, prevailing beliefs will inherently shape interpretations of reality and the potential for behavioral changes because individuals and groups "want to perceive the events around us as congruent with our assumptions, even if that means distorting, denying, projecting, or in other ways falsifying to ourselves what may be going on around us."[90]

Certain organizational routines may also inhibit the potential for adaptation and learning. The absence of well-developed mechanisms to transmit "adaptations" and "lessons" across an organization can lead to difficulties in bringing individual or group experiences to bear on organizational practice. Even where such mechanisms may exist, staff members are unlikely to listen to and heed these "adaptations" and "lessons" unless organizational incentives and habits are in place that encourage such behavior. Organizational cultures that encourage conformity, rather than novel or unorthodox thinking, can also seriously limit the opportunity for adaptation and learning. One way these processes manifest themselves within the Fund is via the aforementioned difficulties with interdepartmental knowledge transfer. Although the Fund claims its practice of rotating staff across country and departmental assignments facilitates knowledge transfer, this exchange has been insufficient at times, with the result being several high-profile breakdowns in communication and coordination across various departments, such as the one in South Korea.

To some extent these breakdowns—particularly those that involve inadequate surveillance coordination—can be explained partly by hierarchical, conforming, and "silo mentality" elements in the Fund's culture and partly by straightforward internal bureaucratic competition over turf, budget, and staffs. But, as I show in chapter 7, in the case of South Korea's financial system an equally critical determinant of knowledge transfer failures was strong prevailing beliefs that tended to downplay information that would contradict these beliefs. As Woods suggests in her study of the IMF and World Bank, prevailing beliefs "can lead to a certain kind of blindness and overrigidity . . . that create[s] somewhat of a straight-jacket around the thinking of each organization."[91] Individuals can become overinvested in a particular interpretation and scenario so that they are unable to consider alternative beliefs or outcomes.

---

[89] J. W. Lorsch, "Strategic Myopia: Culture as an Invisible Barrier to Change," in *Gaining Control of the Corporate Culture*, ed. R. H. Kilmann, Mary J. Saxton, Roy Serpa, and associates (San Francisco: Jossey-Bass, 1985), pp. 84–102.

[90] Schein, *Organizational Culture and Leadership*, p. 22.

[91] Woods, *The Globalizers*, pp. 55, 56.

Consequently, when staff members—acting on prevailing beliefs—encounter a mismatch of outcome to expectation (an error), they tend to change their beliefs about legitimate means in an ad hoc fashion rather than changing their beliefs about legitimate goals. As a result, most belief change tends to be adaptation, rather than learning, and thus takes place at the level of policy instruments and instrument settings, as opposed to policy goals. A great deal of normative change therefore tends to be gradual rather than revolutionary; new agendas or policy instruments may be added to organizational practice but without the deeper shift in staff beliefs about desirable goals. Learning is so cognitively difficult that it often depends on a personnel realignment that enables alternative interpretations to be brought to bear on experiences.

Resistance to changing ideas can also be viewed through a rationalist lens. Such resistance may be due to the content of the ideas. Economic theories are quite sophisticated, and each school of thought tends to have strong arguments in its favor. Empirical research is also rarely so conclusive that it sweeps aside prevailing beliefs immediately, which may simply indicate skepticism toward available information rather than channeled adaptation and learning. Moreover, the failure to change goals as opposed to means on the basis of new data could reflect a form of Bayesian updating rather than belief-driven thinking. If actors have strong priors about goals and weak priors about means to achieve those goals, then failure should lead actors to change means before they change goals.

In a broad sense many of the adaptive and learning processes featured in this book can be seen as conforming to such processes. Yet such processes cannot fully account for how adaptation and learning occur because they tell us little about how new data used to update existing beliefs are gathered and interpreted. Bayesian updating (and related notions of skepticism) describe a process in which actors add new data to prior knowledge and beliefs and revise their knowledge and beliefs accordingly. New information affects an actor's probability assessment about how the world works, but does not guarantee that the actor will converge on the "true" way the world works. An actor can still learn the "wrong" lesson from experience.

Exactly what an actor learns will be influenced partly by how new information is processed and interpreted. A focus on bounded rationality and channeled learning helps bring to light this important process. An actor cannot possibly collect and process all information that might bear on a particular set of beliefs. Because information is costly, actors rely on cognitive and normative shortcuts to gather, process, and interpret this information. Actors therefore may seek out and privilege information that confirms their beliefs and give less attention to information that disconfirms their beliefs, thus inducing the "hypothesis-confirming" bias and "strategic myopia" discussed earlier. None of this, of course, suggests that the staff are not engaged in a process that fits Bayesian updating. But what it does suggest is that we cannot fully understand how actors update their beliefs without due attention to the cognitive and normative processes that shape how they process and interpret information.

Interpreting and Applying Norms

Norm adoption does not necessarily mean the end of debate, however. Norms, once adopted, are often followed by a struggle over how they should be interpreted and applied. Indeed, although the Fund is often depicted as promoting a "one size fits all" policy template, there was in fact considerable debate between gradualists and big-bang proponents.

Theories of normative change and IOs, as well as critics of the Fund, generally neglect the possibility that after a norm is adopted a new battle often emerges over its interpretation and application. Normative change is not limited to adoption; it also entails processes of redefinition and implementation. Existing studies typically focus on the adoption stage, assuming that a norm, once adopted, retains a universal and unproblematic interpretation and application. But, as some suggest, this focus is "curious because constructivists in particular should be open to the possibility that norms are open to 'social reconstruction.'"[92] As one group of constructivists recently warned, "Constructivists should resist temptations to reify ... social facts, as any conventional wisdom can always be reconstructed."[93] Indeed, while for some a particular norm may be adequate, for others the same norm may be either too ambitious or too circumscribed.

This book features many instances of battles over norm interpretation and application, such as those between gradualists and big-bang proponents. Focusing on these debates enables us to inject a greater degree of strategic agency into our accounts of IO behavior and normative change. Normative change often depends on norm entrepreneurs within an organization who promote greater acceptance of a new norm, or a new interpretation and application of an accepted norm. Such actors come in different forms and play varying roles at different stages of the process.

Existing accounts tend to focus on how actors operating "from above" (i.e., leading member states or management) or "from below" (i.e.,

[92] Kees Van Kersbergen and Bertjan Verbeek, "The Politics of International Norms: Subsidiarity and the Imperfect Competence Regime of the European Union," *European Journal of International Relations* 13, no. 2 (2007), pp. 217–238 at p. 221.

[93] Wesley Widmaier, Mark Blyth, and Leonard Seabrooke, "Exogenous Shocks or Endogenous Constructions? The Meanings of Wars and Crises," *International Studies Quarterly* 51, no. 4 (2007), pp. 747–759 at p. 755.

NGOs) affect normative change. Earlier I dealt with member state influence quite extensively and therefore concentrate here on briefly examining the influence of IO management and NGOs.

The management of IOs can often be a critical agent in stirring normative change. Finnemore, for instance, traces the important influence of Robert McNamara in shaping the World Bank's shift to poverty alleviation in the 1970s.[94] Along similar lines, Abdelal explores the critical role played by Jacques Delors, Michel Camdessus, and Henri Chavranski in shaping the formal rules governing the use of capital controls among members of the EC/EU, IMF, and OECD, respectively.[95] With respect to the IMF, Clark finds that "for major new departures . . . the *specific* initiative tends to come from management, formulated so as to be consistent with the (strongly-held and usually publicly-expressed) *general* preferences of the major shareholder(s) and the (sometimes latent) preferences of the majority of developing countries. . . . It would appear that management initiative is a necessary condition for taking a major new decision at the IMF. . . . It is not a sufficient condition, however, since . . . a coalition of major shareholders can block any particular proposal."[96]

The role of management in helping to define an issue or problem as amenable to institutional resolution, mediating in negotiations to ensure leading member states agree on this definition, and arranging the necessary coordination to achieve implementation necessarily places it at the center of most efforts to change formal organizational rules. As any scholar of bureaucratic politics would suggest, the incentives for management to seek change are likely to be particularly strong when there are doubts about an organization's continuing relevance. But while the need for relevance will prompt initiatives for change, it is management's beliefs and desire for greater influence—conditional on the normative environment that member states support—that will shape the form of any proposed change.

The expanding array of NGOs and civil society actors engaged in monitoring and consulting with IOs often serves as an additional force for normative change.[97] Lacking material means to influence IOs *directly*, NGOs nonetheless have perhaps exercised their greatest influence *indirectly* via their extensive monitoring and evaluation efforts. These ef-

[94] Martha Finnemore, *National Interests in International Society* (Ithaca, N.Y.: Cornell University Press, 1996).

[95] Abdelal, *Capital Rules.*

[96] Clark, "Should the IMF Become More Adaptive?" p. 22.

[97] Margaret Keck and Kathryn Sikkink, *Activists beyond Borders: Advocacy Networks in International Politics* (Ithaca, N.Y.: Cornell University Press, 1998); Susan Park, "Norm Diffusion within International Organizations: A Case Study of the World Bank," *Journal of International Relations and Development* 8, no. 2 (2005), pp. 111–141.

forts—what is called the "fire alarm" mechanism within the PA approach—can potentially threaten an IO's resources or legitimacy by bringing about greater public awareness in leading member states of perceived problems with its performance. More recently, some IOs have begun to consult NGOs on their operations, enabling some NGOs to enjoy a more direct influence on behavior.

With respect to the IMF, NGOs became increasingly important actors in late 1980s through their moderately successful efforts to urge governments to address conditions in heavily indebted countries. The attention given in 1994 to the "Fifty Years is Enough" campaign was a clear indication that NGO activism would prove to be an enduring feature of the Fund's external environment.[98] NGOs have proven capable of successfully mobilizing public opinion across developed and developing countries, thus drawing greater attention to perceived problems with the IMF's performance, while at the same time advancing a particular normative agenda. Often coming from the left of the political spectrum, NGO activism tends to target the economic hardship often associated with IMF programs. NGO efforts now culminate in massive protests each year during the annual meetings of the IMF and World Bank.

NGOs also seek to influence IMF behavior by lobbying the national parliaments of leading member states to use their "power of the purse" during IMF quota reviews to push for reforms that would hold the IMF more accountable for its activities, while at the same time giving greater consideration to the NGO community's normative agenda. In the United States, NGO activism has helped result in Congress establishing scores of legislative mandates prescribing how the U.S. director should vote on particular issues as well as numerous studies on IMF practices and reform—the most important one having been the creation of the International Financial Institution Advisory Commission (the "Meltzer Commission"), which Congress mandated during its consideration of the 1998 quota review in the context of the Asian financial crisis.[99]

But accounts that focus on management and NGOs, like those that emphasize the role of member states, obscure the role that the organizational staff play in fostering normative change. There is an inherent presumption in these accounts that normative change depends solely on the ability of management or the NGO community to develop and push for initiatives that can mobilize the power of leading member states.

---

[98] Kevin Danaher, *50 Years Is Enough: The Case against the World Bank and the International Monetary Fund* (Cambridge, Mass.: South End Press, 1994).

[99] See International Financial Institution Advisory Commission, *Report of the International Financial Institution Advisory Commission* (Washington, D.C.: Government Printing Office, 2000).

This presumption is usually coupled with an overly static and structuralist depiction of behavior by the staff, casting them as merely reacting to initiatives for change, as opposed to promoting them proactively. Staff members are thus treated as having little strategic agency of their own, and endogenous normative change is more or less ruled out in favor of exogenous normative change.

While any formal rule change will likely involve influence from above and from below, informal changes often can occur from within through staff strategic agency. Indeed, some recent empirical studies point to the role of internal advocacy in fostering normative change at the World Bank, and we should expect similar internal dynamics and processes to matter for normative change at the IMF.[100] Thus, as Barnett suggests, understanding staff behavior requires a "blending of *homo economicus* and *homo sociologicus.*"[101]

Arguing for a more strategic conception of agency and a more dynamic conception of normative change does not contradict an emphasis on the importance of interpretation. Rather, it provides a fuller understanding of how preferences over means and ends are acted upon. Hence the content of the beliefs that actors share and advance are critical, as they give meaning to material trends, legitimate specific policy responses, articulate particular interests, and help form internal coalitions. By defining what policy choices are legitimate and possible, these collectively shared beliefs bound the rationality of actors and shape their interests. Yet actors are not inescapably bounded by these beliefs. Decision making is often based on instrumental rationality, but this rationality is informed and shaped by the beliefs that give meaning to and prescriptions for particular choices.

Internal entrepreneurs emerge because organizations do not possess a single set of interests or a mind-set. Bureaucratic turf battles have been dealt with extensively in the literature, but less attention has been devoted to understanding the ideational basis for internal bureaucratic battles. Theoretically, the ideational basis for these battles can be linked to many of the same internal mechanisms that facilitate the adoption of norms.

While administrative recruitment can serve as a pathway through which a norm constructed in a given profession is transmitted to an IO, it can also transmit intra- and interdisciplinary debates, such as those

---

[100] Anthony Bebbington, Scott Guggenheim, Elizabeth Olson, and Michael Woolcock, "Exploring Social Capital Debates at the World Bank," *Journal of Development Studies* 40, no. 5 (2004), pp. 33–64; Nuket Kardam, "Development Approaches and the Role of Policy Advocacy: The Case of the World Bank," *World Development* 21, no. 11 (1993), pp. 1773–1786.

[101] Michael Barnett, *Dialogues in Arab Politics: Negotiations and Regional Order* (New York: Columbia University Press, 1998), p. 9.

that existed among economists over sequencing and temporary capital controls. Professionalization and administrative recruitment can thus result in the formation of subcultures. These subcultures develop as individuals from different professions or the same profession but with different training are recruited into an organization. New recruits can bring with them different norms or different views of the same norm that may conflict with those of other staff from different professions or with different training. These subcultures in turn offer fertile ground for internal norm entrepreneurs.

Such entrepreneurs can also emerge because individual staff apply different frames to the same experience, thus resulting in variation in the "adaptations" and "lessons" drawn from it. Upon "adapting" or "learning" from experience, staff members then often make great efforts to influence how others interpret experience—a process that Levitt and March call "paradigm peddling" and "paradigm politics."[102] Beliefs are shaped and transformed through ongoing interaction, deliberation, and contestation over the meaning of events via expressive, communicative, or rhetorical practices. These interactions, and the efforts of internal norm entrepreneurs, are likely to prove significant when new events and beliefs can be discursively represented as undermining or posing a "crisis" for prevailing beliefs.[103]

Success depends on an entrepreneur's ability to show that a given failure of policy resulted from an actor's behaving in accordance with a particular belief; and that behaving in accordance with an alternative belief (i.e., the one preferred by the entrepreneur) generates success in short order.[104] In line with sociological and constructivist observations, internal entrepreneurs also are likely to have greater discursive influence if they can illustrate the compatibility between their new initiative and existing organizational beliefs, principles, and practices. In keeping with bureaucratic models of organizations, internal entrepreneurs also will likely find success when their particular initiative appeals to the institutional interests of other actors, enabling an internal coalition for change to be constructed.

The behavior of the IMF is undeniably a central question in today's world economy. The subprime crisis has thrust the Fund back into the lending business amid calls for it also to play a more central role in the supervision and regulation of the international financial system. These developments, along with current efforts to reform the Fund, suggest that it has become

---

[102] Levitt and March, "Organizational Learning," p. 324.

[103] Widmaier, Blyth, and Seabrooke, "Exogenous Shocks."

[104] Jeffrey W. Legro, *Rethinking the World: Great Power Strategies and International Order* (Ithaca, NY: Cornell University Press, 2005).

even more important to understand the various factors and processes that shape "how things are done" within the organization. I have argued that existing approaches only take us so far and that we need to be more aware of the potential for endogenous organizational change. Exogenous factors and processes are certainly critical, but to understand and explain IO behavior better and more fully, we must bring greater focus to processes and actors that operate "from within" IOs that shape the direction and potential for normative change.

I have also suggested that we must devote greater attention to staff strategic agency and battles over norm interpretation and application. Many observers assume that the IMF is a homogenous organization that promotes a uniform set of policies consistent with a singular interpretation and application of a particular norm. But the evidence this book provides suggests that this is not always the case. From the outside the IMF may appear to be monolithic, but from the inside one gains a better appreciation for the lively and vigorous internal debates that characterize many issues and often can result in a diverse set of staff beliefs and practices. The following chapters elaborate and apply these arguments.

CHAPTER THREE

Capital Ideas and Capital Controls

THE STRONG TECHNOCRATIC CHARACTER of the IMF's organizational culture means that economic theory plays an essential role in shaping the content of the staff's expertise. Cycles, trends, and shifts in economic theory shape the content of this expertise by helping to determine what constitutes an economic problem and how such problems are best solved. When the staff members approach their tasks, they necessarily come to rely on the content of their training to develop specialized knowledge and to form judgments about policy. Cycles, trends, and shifts in the beliefs prevailing in the economic profession about capital controls and their liberalization have therefore tended to produce corresponding cycles, trends, and shifts in the staff's approach.

Thus, cycles, trends, and shifts in the content of staff training are vital for understanding organizational behavior and the processes of endogenous change. The first part of this chapter traces cycles, trends, and shifts in the prevailing beliefs of the economic profession about capital controls and their liberalization. The second part provides evidence to substantiate the link between professional training and subsequent beliefs held by actors, an important empirical step that most studies generally neglect.

NEOCLASSICAL ORTHODOXY

The beliefs that gave rise to the norm of capital freedom in the 1980s and 1990s were not without precedent. The classical gold standard, which lasted roughly from 1870 to 1914, had similar normative underpinnings. During this period neoclassical orthodoxy helped form what Keynes famously called "the rules of the game."[1] Governments understood that they were obliged to maintain currency convertibility and a fixed price for their currency in terms of gold. The use of capital controls violated these (unwritten) rules.

In theory, the gold standard was a self-equilibrating system, with adjustment occurring more or less automatically along the lines of the price-

---

[1] John Maynard Keynes, *The Economic Consequences of Mr. Churchill* (London: Hogarth Press, 1925).

specie-flow mechanism. A commitment to currency convertibility at a fixed price meant that deficit (surplus) countries would face a decrease (increase) in their gold reserves. This decrease (increase) in reserves would in turn have a deflationary (inflationary) impact, eventually increasing (decreasing) competitiveness and decreasing (increasing) consumption, thereby returning the balance of payments to equilibrium.

In reality, operation of the gold standard was more complex than the price-specie-flow mechanism depicted, and substantial gold flows failed to take place. Adjustment instead generally took place according to the "rules of the game" in which central banks facilitated a return to equilibrium via changes in the discount rate. Though they lacked a sophisticated understanding of balance-of-payments adjustment, neoclassical economists gradually recognized that the "rules of the game" introduced a role for international capital flows.[2]

According to neoclassical assumptions, markets are perfectly competitive and market actors are fully informed optimizers who make efficient use of information regarding economic and policy trends (or "fundamentals"). As discussed in chapter 2, these assumptions lead neoclassicals to see free trade in financial assets as having welfare effects precisely analogous to those of free trade in goods and services. For these economists, as Eichengreen observes, "The case for free capital mobility is thus the same as the case for free trade but for the subscripts of the model."[3] Capital freedom is therefore desirable because it will produce a "first-best" equilibrium.

Early neoclassical economists saw interest rate differentials as the essential determinant of capital flows.[4] When a central bank experiencing a payments deficit or gold outflow raised its discount rate, it made the market more attractive to investors and led to capital inflows. Discount rate increases therefore worked to stem payments deficits and gold outflows not only through their deflationary impact but also by attracting capital. Even after the tumultuous interwar period, most academic economists continued to see capital flows that helped ease the current account adjustment process as desirable. An influential 1944 League of Nations publication, often attributed primarily to Ragnar Nurske, and capturing the lessons of

[2] Neoclassical economists did not fully incorporate capital flows into their models of balance-of-payments adjustment until 1919 with the publication of the Cunliffe Committee's report on postwar monetary problems.

[3] Eichengreen, "Capital Account Liberalization: What Do the Cross-Country Studies Tell Us?" p. 341.

[4] See, for instance, Frank William Taussig, *International Trade* (New York: Kelley, 1966 [1927]), chap. 17; P. B. Whale, "The Working of the Prewar Gold Standard," *Economica* 4, no. 13 (1937), pp. 18–32.

the interwar period, favorably identified some capital flows as "equilibrating" because they helped restore balance-of-payments equilibrium.[5]

Some short-term speculative flows were also seen as desirable within the context of neoclassical orthodoxy. If a currency moved below its fixed price, speculators, who expected the central bank to play by the rules of the game and take action to stabilize the external value of the currency, would purchase the currency at the depreciated price and help push it back up to its fixed price, easing the adjustment process.[6] Financial instability was said to result only when poor fundamentals undermined the commitment to external balance.

Although there were some exceptions, capital freedom was generally the norm during the gold standard.[7] The onset of World War I brought the era of the gold standard to a close, as governments suspended convertibility. Following the war there was widespread agreement that wartime controls and restrictions should be abolished. Although an attempt was made in the 1920s to reestablish capital freedom and a modified version of the gold standard, the financial crisis of 1931–1933 and the Great Depression led most governments to restrict capital. Although governments had used capital controls in the past, their comprehensiveness and permanence represented an important break with neoclassical orthodoxy. Though their intensity varied, the use of capital controls was widespread. By the beginning of World War II, neoclassical orthodoxy and the norm of capital freedom had met their demise.

KEYNESIANISM

The events of the interwar period were represented as a "crisis" for neoclassical orthodoxy. Leading economists of the era advanced interpretations of these events that overturned neoclassical orthodoxy and the norm of capital freedom and that gave rise to a new set of Keynesian understand-

---

[5] League of Nations Economic, Financial and Transit Department, *International Currency Experience: Lessons of the Inter-war Period* (Geneva: League of Nations, 1944), pp. 15–16, 72 n. 1.

[6] Fred Block, *The Origins of International Economic Disorder: A Study of United States International Monetary Policy from World War II to the Present* (Berkeley and Los Angeles: University of California Press, 1977), p. 5; Barry Eichengreen, *Globalizing Capital: A History of the International Monetary System* (Princeton, N.J.: Princeton University Press, 1996), pp. 31, 73.

[7] Barry Eichengreen and Marc Flandreau, "The Geography of the Gold Standard," in *Currency Convertibility: The Gold Standard and Beyond*, ed. Jorge Braga de Macedo, Barry Eichengreen, and Jaime Reis (London: Routledge, 1996), pp. 113–143.

ings and standards of behavior that dramatically transformed the legitimacy of capital controls. As I detail in chapter 4, these new beliefs would provide the normative underpinnings for the IMF Articles of Agreement.

In interpreting the interwar period, academics and policymakers drew the lesson that exchange rates were to be stable rather than fluctuate. The League of Nations report suggested that "if there is anything that interwar experience has clearly demonstrated, it is that paper currency exchanges cannot be left free to fluctuate from day to day under the influence of market supply and demand. . . . If currencies are left free to fluctuate, speculation in the widest sense is likely to play havoc with exchange rates."[8] Keynes, White, and the broader academic community generally shared these views and sought to create a system of fixed, but adjustable exchange rates.[9]

Scholars conventionally argue that the emergence of the norm of capital control at Bretton Woods was underpinned by the belief that controls were necessary to maintain exchange rate commitments and to permit the policy autonomy needed to promote full employment and to offer social welfare benefits.[10] By permitting policy autonomy, capital controls, as John Ruggie famously described, would help reconcile the competing desires for trade openness and domestic interventionism through the "embedded liberalism compromise."[11] As Ruggie observed, "Governments would be permitted—indeed, were expected—to maintain capital controls."[12] Controls thus offered a means to reconcile what we now think of as the impossible trinity of capital mobility, exchange rate stability, and monetary policy autonomy. This motivation was clear in Keynes's and White's arguments.

Keynes worried about "short term speculative movements or flights of currency" as well as those responding to interest rate differentials.[13] In

---

[8] League of Nations, *International Currency Experience*, pp. 137–138. See also pp. 119, 211 and Ragnar Nurske, *Conditions of Monetary Equilibrium*, Princeton Essays in International Finance No. 4 (Princeton, N.J.: Department of Economics, 1945), pp. 2.

[9] James Boughton, "Why White, Not Keynes? Inventing the Postwar International Monetary System," IMF Working Paper WP/02/52 (Washington, D.C.: IMF, 2002); Boughton, "American in the Shadows: Harry Dexter White and the Design of the International Monetary Fund," IMF Working Paper WP/06/06 (Washington, D.C.: IMF, 2006).

[10] The literature on the Bretton Woods negotiations is voluminous. The best treatment of this particular belief remains Eric Helleiner, *States and the Reemergence of Global Finance: from Bretton Woods to the 1990s* (Ithaca, NY: Cornell University Press, 1994), pp. 33–38.

[11] John Gerard Ruggie, "International Regimes, Transactions, and Change: Embedded Liberalism in the Postwar Economic Order," *International Organization* 36, no. 2 (1982), pp. 379–416.

[12] John Gerard Ruggie, "Embedded Liberalism and the Postwar Economic Regimes," in *Constructing the World Polity: Essays on International Institutionalization*, ed. John Gerard Ruggie (New York: Routledge, 1998), pp. 62–84 at p. 74.

[13] Keynes, "Proposals for an International Clearing Union" (April 1943), reprinted in J. Keith Horsefield, ed., *The International Monetary Fund, 1945–1965: Twenty Years of International Monetary Cooperation*, vol. 1, *Chronicle*, by J. Keith Horsefield, vol. 2, *Analysis*, by

contrast to neoclassicals, Keynes saw interest rate arbitrage flows as posing a problem for economic management. Unlike the gold standard, in which interest rates were aimed at maintaining external balance, Keynes sought to create a system in which interest rates could be geared toward full employment. Capital flows would therefore have to be controlled. "Advisable domestic policies," Keynes argued, "might often be easier to compass, if the phenomenon known as 'the flight of capital' could be ruled out."[14] Later elaborating his views, Keynes suggested:

> Freedom of capital movements is an essential part of the old laissez-fare system and assumes that it is right and desirable to have an equalization of interest rates in all parts of the world. . . . In my view the whole management of the domestic economy depends upon being free to have the appropriate rate of interest without reference to the rates prevailing elsewhere in the world. Capital control is a corollary to this.[15]

Controls were also seen as necessary to ensure capital flight would not disrupt new domestic financial interventionist measures. Keynes explained to the British House of Lords that controls would ensure that "our right to control the domestic capital market is secured on firmer foundations than ever before."[16]

White was also committed to ensuring governments possessed sufficient policy autonomy. Like Keynes, White noted controls "would give each government much greater measure of control in carrying out its monetary and tax policies" by minimizing "flights of capital, motivated either by prospect of speculative exchange gain, or desire to avoid inflation, or evade taxes." In White's view, such capital flows were "the chief cause of foreign exchange disturbances and were not compatible with a system of stable exchange rates."[17] Nurske and the League economists reached similar conclusions.[18]

Margaret Garritsen de Vries and J. Keith Horsefield, vol. 3, *Documents*, ed. J. Keith Horsefield (Washington, D.C.: IMF, 1969), vol. 3, p. 32.

[14] Keynes, "National Self-Sufficiency," *Yale Review* 22, no. 4 (1933), pp. 755–769 at p. 757. See also p. 762.

[15] Keynes, *The Collected Writings of John Maynard Keynes*, vol. 25, *Activities, 1940–1944: Shaping the Post-war World, The Clearing Union*, ed. Donald Moggridge (Cambridge: Cambridge University Press, 1980), p. 149. See also pp. 212, 275–276.

[16] Keynes, "Speech to the House of Lords," 23 May 1944, in *The Collected Writings of John Maynard Keynes*, vol. 26, *Activities, 1941–1946: Shaping the Post-war World, Bretton Woods and Reparations*, ed. Donald Moggridge (Cambridge: Cambridge University Press, 1980), p. 17.

[17] Harry Dexter White, "Preliminary Draft Proposal for a United Nations Stabilization Fund and a Bank for Reconstruction and Development of the United and Associated Nations" (April 1942), reprinted in Horsefield, *International Monetary Fund, 1945–1965*, vol. 3, pp. 67, 66.

[18] League of Nations, *International Currency Experience*, pp. 116–117, 123.

But support for controls—particularly in the 1940s and 1950s—went beyond the conventional focus on reconciling the impossible trinity; it also reflected a strong skepticism of neoclassical assumptions that represented investors as fully informed optimizers. This skepticism stemmed from Keynes's core insight that factors intrinsic to the operation of international capital markets generate pervasive uncertainty that limits the extent to which investors use information efficiently. As Keynes put it:

> We have, as a rule, only the vaguest idea of any but the most direct consequences of our acts . . . [and] the fact that our knowledge of the future is fluctuating, vague, and uncertain renders wealth a peculiarly unsuitable topic for the methods of classical economy theory. . . . About these matters there is no scientific basis on which to form any calculable probability whatever. We simply do not know. . . . Orthodoxy [or neoclassical] theory assumes that we have a knowledge of the future of a kind quite different from that which we actually possess . . . [and] leads to . . . an underestimation of the concealed factors of utter doubt, precariousness, hope and fear.[19]

Rather than assuming that investors develop their expectations efficiently from fundamentals, Keynes assumed that they are myopic and look to each other for signals. Constrained by uncertainty, incompletely informed investors rely on conventions to help them surmise what other actors might do. These conventions consist of intersubjective understandings that investors share about how economies are supposed to behave; and these conventions coordinate actors' expectations about future fundamentals.[20] As Keynes put it, "Knowing that our judgment is worthless, we endeavor to fall back on the judgment of the rest of the world . . . that is, we endeavor to conform with the behavior of the majority or average . . . to copy the others . . . [to follow] a conventional judgment."[21] Financial asset prices, in this view, do not represent their "true value" based on an efficient use of information, but rather what investors think others believe the asset is worth, each of whom is assigning value from the same point of view. As a result, asset prices, in Keynes's view, could diverge from their "fundamental" value.

Moreover, expectations based on conventions could become self-reinforcing and autonomous from underlying fundamentals, leaving

---

[19] Keynes, "The General Theory of Employment," *Quarterly Journal of Economics* 51, no.2 (1937), pp. 209–223 at pp. 213–214, 221–222.

[20] Keynes, in "General Theory of Employment," p. 214, suggested that investors would assume that "existing relations between economic variables . . . [are] uniquely correct in relation in our existing knowledge of the facts."

[21] Keynes, "General Theory of Employment," p. 214.

governments subject to wide swings in market sentiment that were unrelated to fundamentals.[22] These dynamics in turn could inflict devastating economic consequences that veered far from the path that would result if investors were guided as neoclassicals suggest. For Keynes, since market behavior is shaped by conventions, which in turn are informed by prevailing beliefs, then the task for governing the economy becomes constructing institutions to stabilize these expectations so that they conform to expected parameters. Keynes therefore sought to construct a system that would manage the intersubjective nature of financial markets through substantial state involvement.

The state, Keynes argued, should intervene to take permanent responsibility for basic economic decisions concerning the level of investment and saving through "a somewhat comprehensive socialization of investment."[23] State intervention would reduce the role of uncertainty and help stabilize investors' expectations, thus smoothing out the variability in economic performance that the volatile conventions-driven preferences of investors triggered. In each of the two drafts for his International Clearing Union plan, Keynes therefore wrote, "It is widely held that control of capital movements, both inward and outward, should be a *permanent* feature of the post-war system."[24]

The League economists shared Keynes's understanding of market behavior. Adjusting policies, they observed, could be insufficient when panic took hold. The League report suggested that when "flight psychology" prevailed, "no increase in the discount rate may be sufficient to deter it. Indeed an increase in the discount rate, by shaking confidence further, is apt to produce the opposite effect."[25]

White was also skeptical of the neoclassical case for capital freedom. In his doctoral dissertation, White demonstrated that the effects of unfettered capital mobility on the prewar French economy were not unambiguously positive and concluded that "some measure of intelligent control of the volume and direction of foreign investments is desirable."[26]

[22] Keynes, *General Theory of Employment, Interest, and Money*, pp. 315–317.

[23] Keynes, *General Theory of Employment, Interest, and Money*, p. 378. See also p. 164. Keynes never offered a precise definition of what he meant by the socialization of investment or state control of the investment process, but he does offer scattered hints about the creation of institutions of investment planning, see James R. Crotty, "On Keynes and Capital Flight," *Journal of Economic Literature*, 21, no. 1 (1983), pp. 59–65 at pp. 60–61.

[24] Keynes, "Proposals for an International Currency (or Clearing) Union," 11 February 1942, reprinted in Horsefield, *International Monetary Fund, 1945–1965*, vol. 3, p. 13, emphasis added; Keynes, "Proposals for an International Clearing Union [April 1943]," p. 31, emphasis added.

[25] League of Nations, *International Currency Experience*, pp. 162–163.

[26] Harry Dexter White, *The French International Accounts, 1880–1913* (Cambridge: Harvard University Press, 1933), pp. 311–312.

White also questioned whether the neoclassical case for capital freedom was analogous to the case for free trade, observing that "the assumption that capital serves a country best by flowing to countries which offer the most attractive terms is valid only under circumstances that are not always present."[27]

But Keynesian skepticism of capital freedom did not extend to all types of capital flows. Emphasis was placed on controlling short-term speculative capital flows. These flows, as the League report suggested, often were "disequilibrating instead of equilibrating, or instead of simply coming to a stop."[28] "Equilibrating" flows were to be encouraged, however.[29] "Productive" flows and those that provide "genuine new investment for developing the world's resources"—such long-term flows, loans and credits that facilitate trade, and foreign direct investment—were also to be encouraged.[30] In their various drafts for constructing the IMF, both Keynes and White made clear that the Bretton Woods institutions were to promote equilibrating and productive capital flows.

Many Keynesians also frequently sought to make a distinction between "normal" and "abnormal" capital movements.[31] It was generally accepted that these flows could, for the most part, be distinguished according to two criteria. Interest rates were at the core of one criterion: capital moving "downhill" from low to high interest rate economies was identified as normal, while capital flowing "uphill" in the opposite direction was constituted as abnormal. According to another criterion, abnormal flows could also be distinguished from normal flows in that they tended to be "disequilibrating," that is, moving from economies with current account deficits to economies with current account surpluses. With these criteria in mind, capital flight was defined as abnormal.

More significantly, in contrast to neoclassicals, Keynesians saw speculative short-term flows as abnormal. Speculation was observed to occur for the most part in the uphill direction and to be largely unresponsive to

---

[27] White, "Preliminary Draft Proposal," p. 67.

[28] League of Nations, *International Currency Experience*, p. 16.

[29] See Keynes, "Proposals for an International Currency (or Clearing) Union," p. 13; Keynes, "Proposals for an International Clearing Union," p. 32; and White, "Preliminary Draft Proposal," pp. 49–50 for Keynes's and White's views, respectively.

[30] See Keynes, "Proposals for an International Currency (or Clearing) Union," pp. 11, 13; Keynes, "Proposals for an International Clearing Union," p. 32, and White, "Preliminary Draft Proposal," p. 46, for Keynes' and White's views, respectively. On the views of the League economists, see Louis W. Pauly, *Who Elected the Bankers? Surveillance and Control in the World Economy* (Ithaca, N.Y.: Cornell University Press, 1997), pp. 72–73.

[31] See, for instance, Arthur Bloomfield, *Capital Imports and the American Balance of Payments, 1934–1939: A Study in Abnormal Capital Transfers* (Chicago: University of Chicago Press, 1950), pp. 30–32; Marco Fanno, *Normal and Abnormal International Capital Transfers* (Minneapolis: University of Minnesota Press, 1939), especially chaps. 2–3.

changes in the discount rate.[32] Conventions, which generated euphoria and panic, were seen to motivate such behavior. Many Keynesians were particularly concerned that pervasive uncertainty and conventions could trigger "self-aggravating" flows of short-term capital that "fed upon themselves in a self-inflammatory way," leading to crises in the presence of otherwise sound fundamentals.[33]

Keynesianism emerged in the 1930s and 1940s as the dominant set of beliefs within the economics profession. The events of the interwar period had shaken the confidence of a generation of economists in neoclassical orthodoxy. In his presidential address to the American Economic Association in 1940, Frederick Mills reflected upon the climate of opinion at the time:

> If we face the realities of economic life, and set against these realities our theories, our analytic tools, our ability to devise and direct instruments of control, we must confess to inadequacy. . . . This feeling stands in sharp contrast to our nineteenth-century predecessors. Except for a few troubled spirits, these economists felt at home in a mastered world. Their belief was a reflection of the Victorian confidence that certain ultimate values in life had been grasped and cast into institutional molds that would endure. . . . These hopes have not been realized.[34]

In light of such widespread rejection of neoclassical orthodoxy, Nurske commented, "There is now almost universal agreement that capital movements of the unbalancing kind—speculative transfers and capital flight—had better be subjected to control."[35] Arthur Bloomfield perhaps best summarized the climate of opinion at the time:

> It is now highly respectable doctrine, in academic and banking circles alike, that a substantial measure of *direct* control over private capital movements, especially of the so-called "hot money" varieties, will be desirable for most countries not only in the years immediately ahead but also in the long run as well. Unfettered freedom of individuals to transfer funds across national boundaries, while conspicuously violated in actual practice since 1914, has long been a hollowed dogma of tradi-

[32] League of Nations, *International Currency Experience*, pp. 162–163; Bloomfield, *Capital Imports*, p. viii.

[33] Nurske, *Conditions of Monetary Equilibrium*, pp. 2–3 ("self-aggravating"); Bloomfield, *Capital Imports*, pp. 18, 23 ("fed upon themselves").

[34] Frederick C. Mills, "Economics in a Time of Change," *American Economic Review* 31, no. 1 (1941), pp. 1–14 at pp. 1–2.

[35] Ragnar Nurske, "Domestic and International Equilibrium," in *The New Economics: Keynes' Influence on Theory and Public Policy*, ed. Seymour E. Harris (New York: Alfred A. Knopf, 1947), pp. 264–292 at p. 289.

tional economic thought, and in this respect the present-day enthusiasm among economists for exchange control over capital movements represents a sharp break with past orthodoxy. This doctrinal *volte-face* represents a widespread disillusionment resulting from the destructive behavior of these movements in the interwar years.[36]

"NEOLIBERALISM"

Keynesianism was not without controversy, however. Although the climate of opinion in the 1940s favored controls, a small number of economists opposed their use. In Europe, these economists became known as the "neoliberals." Like neoclassicals, these "neoliberals" stressed the desirability of capital freedom.

Although recognizing that speculative flows had been somewhat excessive in the 1930s, the "neoliberals" rejected the Keynesian argument that investor conventions were to blame. Instead, they, like the neoclassicals, represented speculation as a rational reaction by fully informed investors to an efficient reading of fundamentals. In addition to political uncertainty, "neoliberals" saw unorthodox macroeconomic policies as the chief cause of speculative attacks in a system of fixed exchange rates. These unorthodox policies result, as Gottfried Haberler noted, whenever "national policies cease to regard the maintenance of exchange stability as something which must take precedence over all other considerations."[37]

The "neoliberals" also praised, rather than criticized, the discipline that speculative flows imposed on policymakers. As Wilhelm Ropke argued: "The more quickly and thoroughly an entirely new situation is created through the abolition of exchange control, the less will be the danger that through change of Government the course of economic policy might once more become uncertain. . . . It would be exceedingly difficult for any subsequent Government to destroy what has already been achieved, by a return to a 'leftist' course of economic policy."[38] Finally, many "neoliberals" also claimed that controls were incompatible with the principle of individual liberty. Friedrich Hayek, for instance, noted that controls represented "the decisive advance on the path to totalitarianism and the suppression of individual liberty" as well as "the complete delivery of the individual

---

[36] Arthur Bloomfield, "Postwar Control of International Capital Movements," *American Economic Review* 36, no. 2 (1946), pp. 687–709 at p. 687.

[37] Gottfried Haberler, *The Theory of International Trade: With Its Applications to Commercial Policy*, trans. Alfred William Stonier and Frederic Benham (London: W. Hodge, 1950), p. 431 (see also p. 430); Frank Knight, "Achilles' Heels in Monetary Standards," *American Economic Review* 30, no. 1 (1940), pp. 16–32 at p. 20.

[38] Wilhelm Ropke, *International Order and Economic Integration* (Dordrecht: Reidel, 1959), p. 245.

to the tyranny of the state the final suppression of all means of escape—not merely for the rich, but for everybody."[39]

The American banking community shared some of these concerns and sought to block and, when this failed, to modify Keynes's and White's plans for the IMF.[40] In place of the Keynes and White plans, the bankers supported the "key currency" plan formulated by John Williams, a Harvard economist and vice president of the Federal Reserve Bank of New York (FRBNY). The "key currency" plan envisaged a system of stable exchange rates where sterling and the dollar would be freely convertible and form the "key currencies" around which the system was based.[41]

Although they shared the bankers' opposition to controls, the "neoliberals" did not share their enthusiasm for what amounted to a restoration of the modified gold standard of the 1920s. In place of a system of stable exchanges rates, the "neoliberals" made the case for the unthinkable: floating exchange rates. Presaging many of the arguments that Milton Friedman and others would offer in the 1950s (see below), the "neoliberals" made their own case for floating exchange rates.[42] In contrast to League report, the "neoliberals" did not view floating exchange rates as responsible for capital flow volatility. On the contrary, in addition to poor fundamentals, it was fixed exchange rates that were to blame. Anticipating one of the fundamental causes of the collapse of the Bretton Woods system of exchange rates, the "neoliberals" claimed that such systems have a tendency to rigidify with policymakers resisting parity changes until the last possible moment. This type of system in turn encourages speculative flows, as speculators can make a one-way bet on the currency.[43]

Instead of seeing floating as a cause of speculation, the "neoliberals" saw it as means of curbing it. Exchange rate movements in response to

[39] Friedrich Hayek, *The Road to Serfdom* (Chicago: University of Chicago Press, 1944), p. 92 n. 2. By contrast, Keynes and White viewed controls on the investment decisions of a wealthy minority as essential for the preservation of policy autonomy. See Keynes, *Collected Writings*, vol. 25, pp. 31, 149; and White, "Preliminary Draft Proposal," p. 67.

[40] Helleiner, *Reemergence of Global Finance*, pp. 39–49.

[41] John H. Williams, *Postwar Monetary Plans and Other Essays* (New York: Alfred A. Knopf, 1944).

[42] Here I follow the interpretation of Haberler's writings offered in Michael Bordo and Harold James, "Haberler versus Nurske: The Case for Floating Exchange Rates as an Alternative to Bretton Woods," NBER Working Paper 8545 (Cambridge, Mass.: NBER, 2001). This interpretation suggests that prior to the 1950s, Haberler only sought to make the case that the benefits of floating exchange rates were a theoretical possibility. He did not, however, become a strong advocate for floating exchange rates until the publication of *Currency Convertibility* (Washington, D.C.: American Enterprise Institute, 1954).

[43] Knight, "Achilles' Heels in Monetary Standards," pp. 20, 27. Nurske, in *Conditions of Monetary Equilibrium*, p. 8, also recognized this danger inherent in a fixed but adjustment scheme. However, he was optimistic that controls would ensure that speculative attacks were rare.

capital flows would deter speculators from making a one-way bet on the currency. A system of floating exchange rates would also enable a rapid move to convertibility in the postwar era, as governments could avoid the "unsatisfactory" use of controls while they accumulated sufficient monetary reserves to maintain their exchange rate commitments.[44]

The "neoliberals" also doubted the desirability and feasibility of a system of fixed exchange rates that ultimately, in their view, could not be maintained unless governments either cooperated to harmonize their interest rates or weak currency states adopted the monetary policy of strong currency states. Like Keynesians, the "neoliberals" did not view an equalization of interest rates across the globe as desirable. Indeed, another benefit of floating was that it could permit greater policy autonomy while avoiding the use of controls.[45]

Although the "neoliberals" presented a clear alternative to Keynesianism, they were ultimately unsuccessful in preventing the adoption of a system of adjustable pegs and capital controls at Bretton Woods. A change in prevailing beliefs was simply unobtainable. The academic and policymaking communities, according to Michael Bordo and Harold James, were largely "captive of the contemporary perception of the tumultuous events of [the] time."[46] As Robert Skidelsky, one of Keynes's most celebrated biographers, notes, the use of floating exchange rates was simply "beyond the practical or theoretical imagination of the times."[47] Nonetheless, the arguments of "neoliberals" were significant, in that they laid the groundwork for their future intellectual allies of the 1950s and 1960s in the academic and policymaking communities. As this intellectual movement gained strength, it would present a significant challenge to Keynesianism and ultimately contribute greatly to unraveling the norm of capital control.

MONETARISM, POST-KEYNESIANISM, AND THE NEOCLASSICAL SYNTHESIS

The emergence of monetarism in the 1950s presented a formidable challenger to Keynesianism.[48] In the monetarist understanding of market be-

[44] Knight, "Achilles' Heels in Monetary Standards," p. 27. See also p. 23 and Haberler, *Theory of International Trade*, p. 446.

[45] Haberler, *Theory of International Trade*, p. 449; Knight, "Achilles' Heels in Monetary Standards," pp. 25–26.

[46] Bordo and James, "Haberler versus Nurkse," p. 23.

[47] Robert Skidelsky, *John Maynard Keynes: Fighting for Britain, 1937–1946* (London: Macmillan, 2000), p. 193.

[48] Some of the most important monetarist works include Milton Friedman, "The Role of Monetary Policy," *American Economic Review* 58 (1968), pp. 1–17; Milton Friedman and Anna J. Schwartz, *A Monetary History of the United States* (Princeton, N.J.: Princeton University Press, 1963).

havior, known as *adaptive expectations*, there is a short lag between changes in fundamentals and the market's perception of these changes. Market expectations therefore form efficiently in the long run, but not the short run. Awareness of the role of short lags, however, does not translate into concerns, as expressed by Keynesians, about the consequences of uncertainty and conventions. As Jacqueline Best observes, "The monetarist conception of expectations only considers the effects of a lag in communicating transparent economic information. We are one step away from the neoclassical assumption that markets provide information instantaneously, but we are still far from an appreciation of the intersubjective nature of economic processes."[49]

In the 1950s, monetarists (and others) started to argue for moving to a system of floating exchange rates and free capital mobility. Though confined to the margins of the profession, the case for floating steadily gained ground over the next two decades. Arguments for floating were partly an exercise in reinterpreting and reconstructing the events of the interwar period. For proponents of floating, academic economists of the 1930s and 1940s—particularly those responsible for the League report—had fundamentally misinterpreted the experiences of the interwar period. Echoing the arguments of the "neoliberals," monetarists claimed that fixed exchange rates and poor fundamentals were to blame for financial instability rather than floating and convention-driven behavior.

For proponents of floating, speculative attacks were primarily due to the pursuit of unsound policies that were at odds with exchange rate commitments.[50] Consistent with the assumption of adaptive expectations, investors eventually recognized these policy inconsistencies and exerted speculative pressure on the exchange rate. In making his now famous case for floating, Milton Friedman contended:

> In retrospect, it is clear that the speculators were "right"; that forces were at work making for depreciation in the value of most European currencies relative to the dollar independently of speculative activity; that the speculative movements were anticipating this change and hence, there is at least as much reason to call them "stabilizing" as to call them "destabilizing."[51]

[49] Best, *The Limits of Transparency*, p. 179 n. 14.

[50] Haberler, *Currency Convertibility*, p. 25.

[51] Friedman, "Case for Flexible Exchange Rates," pp. 176–177. See also pp. 175, 176 n. 9; Fritz Machlup, *Remaking the International Monetary System: The Rio Agreement and Beyond* (Baltimore: Johns Hopkins University Press, 1968), p. 108; Gottfried Haberler, "The Case against Capital Controls for Balance of Payments Reasons," in *Capital Movements and Their Control*, ed. Alexander Swodoba (Geneva: Sjidhoff-Leiden, 1976).

Speculative flows were thus a rational reaction, delayed by a short time lag, to an efficient reading of fundamentals.

Advocates of floating also drew on some arguments made earlier by neoclassicals and "neoliberals" to press for abandoning the Bretton Woods system of adjustable pegs and capital controls. Like neoclassicals, advocates of floating claimed capital freedom would produce an efficient allocation of the world's capital and enhance economic welfare. Like the "neoliberals," advocates of floating also claimed that floating would deter speculators and provide for greater monetary policy autonomy. To those who suggested that controls could be just as effective in deterring speculation and permitting policy autonomy, Friedman responded: "It is no answer to this argument to say that capital flows can be restricted by direct controls, since our ultimate objective in using this method [floating exchange rates] is precisely to avoid such restrictions."[52]

Not surprisingly, the 1960s was a decade of considerable debate among economists. Yet the principal debate was not between monetarists and Keynesians, but rather between those who sought to preserve Keynesian insights and those who sought to reinterpret them within the neoclassical framework. The former consisted largely of British economists based at Cambridge University as well as some American institutionalists, such as John Kenneth Galbraith. Retaining Keynes's emphasis on uncertainty and conventions, some members of this group later styled themselves as post-Keynesians.[53] Like Keynes, these economists saw *permanent* controls and guidelines as having a legitimate role in market economies. Others writing very much in the Keynesian tradition, such as Charles Kindleberger and Hyman Minsky, later developed approaches that considered financial crises as a product of previous "manias" linked to speculative "euphoria."[54] The key link to the Keynesian tradition was that boom-and-bust patterns were seen as driven as much by dramatic changes in market sentiment as they were by credit expansion.

American economists who sought to reinterpret Keynes offered a challenge to these beliefs. The American reinterpretation of Keynes in the form of the neoclassical synthesis supplanted Keynesianism in the early 1960s as the dominant set of beliefs within the profession, relegating what would become post-Keynesianism to the margins. In spite of the steady

[52] Friedman, "Case for Flexible Exchange Rates," p. 164. See also p. 158.

[53] On post-Keynesianism, see Paul Davidson, "Post Keynesian Economics: Solving the Crisis in Economy Theory," in *The Crisis in Economy Theory*, ed. Daniel Bell and Irving Kristol (New York: Basic Books, 1981), pp. 151–173.

[54] Charles Kindleberger, *Manias, Panics, and Crashes: A History of Financial Crises* (New York: Basic Books, 1978); Hyman Minsky, "A Theory of Systemic Fragility," in *Financial Crises: Institutions and Markets in a Fragile Environment*, ed. Edward I. Altman and Arnold W. Samerz (New York: John Wiley and Sons, 1977), pp. 138–152.

inroads monetarism was making within the profession, the dominance of the neoclassical synthesis in the early 1960s was so great that Paul Samuelson was able to assert confidently that the neoclassical synthesis "is accepted in its broad outlines by all but a few extreme left-wing and right-wing writers."[55]

Samuelson along with Robert Solow, James Tobin and others sought to adapt Keynes's insights so that they could be placed within the broad confines of neoclassical orthodoxy.[56] Like Keynes, neoclassical synthesists argue government intervention is necessary to ensure that investment and employment reaches the appropriate levels in circumstances when prices fail to adjust so that markets clear (i.e., conditions of excess supply or insufficient demand). But whereas Keynesians and post-Keynesians point to conventions to account for investment volatility, neoclassical synthesists instead focus on short-run market imperfections.

The synthesis was fashioned by abandoning the Keynesian emphasis on uncertainty as a pervasive constraint on the efficient use of information, and replacing it with a focus on market errors that prevent actors from forming their expectations efficiently in the short run. This theoretical departure led to what Best calls the "hollowing out" of Keynesianism. In contrast to Keynesianism, this hollowed-out understanding of market behavior sees markets as efficient in the long run. This understanding thus synthesizes Keynesianism and neoclassical orthodoxy by suggesting that markets could err in the short run described by Keynes, but would behave efficiently in the long run described by neoclassicals.

Neoclassical synthesists often point to price stickiness as a short-run market error that prevents the economy from reaching its long-run equilibrium. In his classic treatment, Rudiger Dornbusch explained that unfettered capital mobility often results in the "overshooting of exchange rates" because of the "differential adjustment speeds in goods and assets markets."[57] Monetary expansion stimulates a reduction in nominal and real interest rates, generating capital outflows that precipitate a short-run exchange rate depreciation that "overshoots" the long-run equilibrium. Goods market prices then slowly rise in response to stronger domestic and foreign demand triggered by lower real interest rates and depreciation of the exchange rate, respectively. These price increases in turn lead to a slow

---

[55] Paul A. Samuelson, *Economics: An Introductory Analysis*, 5th ed. (New York: McGraw-Hill, 1961), p. 242.

[56] See, for example, Paul A. Samuelson and Robert M. Solow, "Analytical Aspects of Anti-inflation Policy," *American Economic Review* 50, no. 2 (1960), pp. 177–194; James Tobin, "Inflation and Unemployment," *American Economic Review* 61 (1972), pp. 1–18.

[57] Rudiger Dornbusch, "Expectations and Exchange-Rate Dynamics," *Journal of Political Economy*, 84, no. 6 (1976), pp. 1161–1176 at p. 1162.

rise in real interest rates that, along with enhanced trade competitiveness, generates capital inflows that push the exchange rate back its long-run equilibrium following the monetary expansion.

Dornbusch's treatment, and subsequent neoclassical synthesist work, implied that while markets could be left unfettered in the long run, in the short run a case could be made for government intervention. But lacking the Keynesian emphasis on factors intrinsic to the operation of markets that are difficult, if not impossible, to eliminate, the neoclassical synthesist understanding of market behavior legitimated only *temporary,* rather than permanent, intervention.

The neoclassical synthesis understanding of market behavior has inspired scores of "second-best" arguments for regulating international capital flows. These second-best arguments claim that an ideal government facing one clear distortion or market error could, in principle, improve welfare by introducing controls.[58] Tobin, for instance, pointed to preexisting distortions in goods and labor markets to make the case for a tax on short-term speculative flows. Since "prices in goods and labor markets move much more sluggishly, in response to excess supply or demand, than the prices of financial assets, including exchanges," Tobin "recommend[ed] . . . throw[ing] some sand in the wheels of our excessively efficient international money markets."[59] Other economists writing in this tradition have also suggested a case could be made for controls when other distortions were present, such as tariffs[60] or inflexible real wages.[61]

But arguments for the Tobin tax, like other second-best arguments, are in several important respects decidedly non-Keynesian. First, the implicit presumption of all second-best argument is that any intervention will be reversed once policies have been adjusted so as to remove the distortion or to correct the market error. Since intervention is justified only so long as the distortion or market error prevents markets from reaching their long-run equilibrium, intervention is necessarily a temporary, rather than a permanent, measure. As Dornbusch concluded, controls designed

---

[58] For a survey, see Dooley, "Survey of Academic Literature."

[59] James Tobin, "A Proposal for International Monetary Reform," *Eastern Economic Journal* 4, nos. 3–4 (1978), pp. 153–159 at p. 154. Tobin initially offered the idea in 1972 in a lecture at Princeton University, published as *The New Economics One Decade Older,* The Eliot Janeway Lectures on Historical Economics in Honor of Joseph Schumpeter (Princeton, N.J.: Princeton University Press, 1974). Tobin used his 1978 presidential address to the Eastern Economic Association to float the idea again. See also Barry Eichengreen, James Tobin, and Charles Wyplosz, "Two Cases for Sand in the Wheels of International Finance," *Economic Journal* 105, no. 428 (1995), pp. 162–172 especially at p. 164.

[60] Richard Brecher and Carlos F. Diaz-Alejandro, "Tariffs, Foreign Capital and Immiserizing Growth," *Journal of International Economics* 7, nos. 3–4 (1977), pp. 317–322.

[61] Richard Brecher, "Second-Best Policy for International Trade and Investment," *Journal of International Economics* 14, nos. 3–4 (1983), pp. 313–320.

to slow down the speed of asset market adjustment should only be used as "strictly transitory policy" to offset shocks.[62] In later updating Tobin's argument, Eichengreen and Wyplosz emphasize the need for policy adjustment, noting that while controls can provide countries with fixed exchange rates "the breathing space needed to prepare orderly re-alignments," any realignment also "requires the adoption of supporting macroeconomic policies."[63] Otherwise, controls will in the long run generate increasing distortions and fail to prevent the collapse of any exchange rate commitment.

Advocates of the Tobin tax (and similar policies) also generally envision restriction being applied to a much narrower range of flows than suggested by Keynes and others. Recall that in addition to short-term speculative flows, some Keynesians also foresaw a need for controlling interest rate arbitrage flows. While Tobin tax advocates often stress expansion of policy autonomy as a principal purpose, in contrast to Keynesians, they are generally more optimistic about the benefits of freeing a broader range of capital flows. Indeed, Tobin went to great lengths to point out that the tax was aimed only at discouraging short-term speculation and sought "to obstruct as little as possible international movements of capital responsive to long-run portfolio preferences and profit opportunities."[64]

This discussion leads to the final, and perhaps most important, respect in which neoclassical synthesist arguments for controls differ from Keynesian standards of behavior. Neoclassical synthesists treat speculation as something that should be *managed* via *market-oriented* measures. This view is therefore quite similar in an important respect to arguments for floating. Neither approach seeks to *eliminate* speculation, as Keynes had, but rather seeks only to keep it within certain limits and transfer some of the costs to investors who engage in it. Taxes and floating exchange rates increase the costs of international financial transactions but leave them otherwise unfettered. Indeed, an important aspect of arguments for taxes is that they seek not to distort the stock of net flows. Speculation is thus seen as a normal, if perhaps occasionally excessive, expression of a market economy. The goal is to manage it so that it does not interfere with other policy goals.

This view is decidedly non-Keynesian. For Keynesians, the Tobin tax is insufficient alone to control the volatility that convention-driven market behavior induces. What is required, as Keynes suggested, is stabilization

[62] Rudiger Dornbusch, "Special Exchange Rates for Capital Account Transactions," *World Bank Economic Review* 1, no. 1 (1986), pp. 3–33 at p. 3.

[63] Eichengreen and Wyplosz, "Taxing International Financial Transactions," p. 22.

[64] Tobin, "Proposal for International Monetary Reform," p. 155. See also Eichengreen, Tobin, and Wyplosz, "Two Cases for Sand," p. 165.

of investors' expectations, which can only be accomplished by socializing investment and implementing permanent, not temporary, controls on some capital movements. In contrast to these prescriptions, the Tobin tax offers only a limited policy response and one that reflects an underlying faith in the market.

From a Keynesian perspective, the Tobin tax and similar proposals fail to confront the far more pervasive problems of uncertainty and convention-driven market behavior. Rather than seeing these problems as something that should be managed via market-oriented measures, Keynesian standards of behavior see them as something that should be eliminated via, if necessary, administrative measures (i.e., quantitative limits or outright prohibitions on certain types of financial activity). But Tobin tax proponents seek to avoid administrative measures because they can impose significant administrative costs, create severe distortions, and provide strong incentives for evasion and subsequent widening and tightening of existing restrictions.[65] Indeed, Tobin later remarked that his tax was "proposed in this spirit" of avoiding administrative measures.[66]

In jettisoning the Keynesian understanding of market behavior in the early 1960s, neoclassical synthesists and most of the economics profession also abandoned associated standards of behavior that legitimated controls as permanent policy measures. Whereas Keynesians had constructed the norm of capital control and carved out an exception for "productive" flows, neoclassical synthesists helped construct the norm of capital freedom and carved out an exception for taxes, but only on a temporary basis and only under select circumstances characterized by distortions and short-run market errors. Monetarists, for their part, also contributed to construction of the norm of capital freedom by advancing a standard of behavior that provided no room for controls within the boundaries of legitimate policy practice. In the early 1960s, there thus emerged a general consensus across much of the economics profession that capital freedom was desirable, at least in the long run.

The dominance of the neoclassical synthesis and the steady inroads that monetarism was making in the 1960s meant that most graduate students in economics were instilled with beliefs significantly different from those that had been taught in the early postwar era. In particular, the Keynesian assumption of convention-driven market behavior appears to have lost importance within the profession for some time. A 1985 survey of 212 economics graduate students from leading academic departments finds that only 4 percent believed that the assumption of market actors

[65] Eichengreen and Wyplosz, "Taxing International Financial Transactions," p. 24.
[66] James Tobin, "Prologue," in Haq, Kaul, and Grunberg, *The Tobin Tax*, pp. ix–xviii at p. xi.

behaving according to conventions was "very important," while 51 percent believed that the neoclassical assumption of rational behavior was "very important."[67]

NEW CLASSICAL ECONOMICS AND NEW KEYNESIANISM

The ascendance of the neoclassical synthesis and monetarism in the 1950s and 1960s was the first clear signal that support for Keynesianism was unraveling. But it was the emergence of new classical economics in the 1970s that confirmed its demise and further contributed to the emergence of the norm of capital freedom. These new classical beliefs, which cast markets as rational and efficient in the use of information, hark back to many of the same principles of neoclassical orthodoxy that Keynes had challenged.

The new classical understanding of market behavior argues that actors efficiently form *rational expectations* regarding the market's direction by employing "all available information."[68] Although not all economists abandoned alternative understandings of market behavior, the development of the theory of rational expectations is said to have unleashed a "counter-revolution" within the economics profession.[69]

In fashioning their understanding of market behavior, new classicals sought to ground the behavior of aggregates, such as international capital markets, based on a causal account of the microeconomic behavior of individual market actors. Their micro-foundational account, derived from the neoclassical assumptions that actors optimize and that markets clear, suggests that Keynesian, post-Keynesian, neoclassical synthesist, and monetarist understandings are inaccurate. In the new classical view, "If economic agents optimize, as most economists agree they do, they cannot be irratio-

---

[67] David Colander and Arjo Klamer, "The Making of an Economist," *Journal of Economic Perspectives* 1, no. 2 (1987), pp. 95–111 at p. 105. Interestingly, a 2001–2003 survey of 231 graduate students from the same leading academic departments finds that behavior according to conventions has increased in importance (with 9 percent indicating it was "very important"), while views about the importance of the rationality assumption have evidenced no change. See Colander, "The Making of an Economist Redux," *Journal of Economic Perspectives* 19, no. 1 (2005), pp. 175–198 at p. 188.

[68] See John Muth, "Rational Expectations and the Theory of Price Movements," *Econometrica* 29, no. 3 (1961), pp. 315–360; Robert E. Lucas, "Expectations and the Neutrality of Money," *Journal of Economic Theory* 4, no. 2 (1972), pp. 103–124; Thomas J. Sargent, David Fand, and Stephen Goldfeld, "Rational Expectations, the Real Rate of Interest, and the Natural Rate of Employment," *Brookings Papers on Economic Activity* 1973, no. 2, pp. 429–480.

[69] Mark H. Willes, "Rational Expectations as a Counterrevolution," in Bell and Kristol, *Crisis in Economic Theory*, pp. 81–96.

nal. Irrationality is unnecessarily expensive—it is more expensive than using the available information efficiently."[70] Rational actors will therefore converge to a correct model and understanding of the economy.

Systematic mistakes by markets such as asset bubbles or excesses, self-fulfilling crises, short-run market errors, and lags are impossible since all actors know the structure of the economy. Theoretical support for this view came from the efficient market hypothesis, which suggests that capital markets are "efficient" in that market actors employ "all available information" in determining asset prices.[71] Prices therefore reflect the "true state" of the economy based on fundamentals, thus enabling actors who trade in financial assets to make Pareto-efficient decisions and legitimating unfettered capital mobility. New classicals also point to fundamentals, rather than factors intrinsic to the operation of international capital markets, to explain predictive failures of neoclassical models, such as the famous "Lucas Paradox," which ponders, "Why doesn't capital flow from rich to poor countries," where the marginal return on capital should be higher.[72]

The emergence of the new classical theory of policy credibility was another important theoretical development. It is, as Best observes, "perhaps the most influential variant of new-classical economics in the realm of international finance."[73] In the new classical view, market actors base their expectations on all available information and interpret this information through the "correct" model of the economy. Part of the information actors employ is the credibility of a government's announced policies. If market actors deem a policy to be credible, it is likely to be effective; but if they don't, market actors will respond with actions, such as capital outflows, that undermine the policy. While new classicals claim capital account liberalization is a signal of credibility and leads to inflows, controls (or any type of intervention) are said only to precipitate capital flight.[74]

The only credible policy is, then, the "correct" one, that is, the policy based on new classical understandings and standards of behavior. New classicals suggest market actors employ this model and are therefore capa-

[70] Willes, "Rational Expectations as a Counterrevolution," p. 89.

[71] Eugene F. Fama, "Efficient Capital Markets: A Review of Theory and Empirical Work," *Journal of Finance* 25, no. 2 (1970), pp. 383–417.

[72] Robert E. Lucas, "Why Doesn't Capital Flow from Rich to Poor Countries?" *American Economic Review* 80, no. 2 (1990), pp. 92–96. See also Laura Alfaro, Sebnem Kalemli-Ozcan, and Vadym Volosovych, "Why Doesn't Capital Flow from Rich to Poor Countries? An Empirical Investigation," NBER Working Paper 11901 (Cambridge, Mass.: NBER, 2005).

[73] Best, *The Limits of Transparency*, p. 124.

[74] See Leonardo Bartolini and Allan Drazen, "Capital Account Liberalization as a Signal," *American Economic Review* 87, no. 1 (1997), pp. 138–154.

ble of recognizing which policies are credible. Market sentiment, the theory goes, therefore exercises a significant influence on policy, selecting out those policies that are inefficient and rewarding "proper" practice.

The rational expectations counterrevolution also informed understandings of currency crises. The earliest formal models of currency crises—so-called first-generation models—emerged in the late 1970s.[75] Because investors are assumed to be efficient in the use of information, in this model, currency crises are triggered by governments pursuing unsound policies—often in the form of budget deficits monetized by the central bank—that are inconsistent with exchange rate commitments. Investors recognize this inconsistency and therefore engage in speculative flight, precipitating devaluation. Speculation is thus a rational response to information gathered from an efficient reading of fundaments. From this vantage, speculators do not "cause" the currency crisis; rather, their response is only a symptom of underlying policy failures. Speculators at worst advance the date that foreign reserves are exhausted by unsustainable policies. This understanding of currency crises thus resembles Friedman's analysis of the interwar currency crises, though it lacks the short time lag embodied in the adaptive expectations understanding of market behavior. It is, however, radically different from the Keynesian perspective, which stresses factors intrinsic to the operation of international capital markets that can give rise to self-fulfilling market expectations that develop autonomously from fundamentals.

Alongside the rational expectations counterrevolution came two new lines of argument that undermined the case for interventionist policies, particularly import-substitution industrialization (ISI) and domestic financial interventionism. In the early postwar period Raul Prebisch and other "structuralist" economists, as well as many pioneers of the field of development economics, advocated industrialization through protection as a means to develop infant industries and overcome export pessimism.[76] But these policies came under attack in the late 1960s and early 1970s, with a number of economists pointing to the benefits of integration in the world economy and the costs and distortions of ISI. Of particular relevance for understandings about capital controls was the new discourse on "rent-seeking."[77] A growing number of economists suggested that ex-

[75] Paul Krugman, "A Model of Balance of Payments Crises," *Journal of Money, Credit, and Banking* 11 (1979), pp. 311–325. "Second- and third-generation" crisis models would develop in the 1990s. I examine these developments in chapters 7 and 8.

[76] Hollis Chenery, "The Structuralist Approach to Development Policy," *American Economic Review* 65 (1975), pp. 310–316; Raul Prebisch, *The Economic Development of Latin America and Its Principal Problems* (New York: United Nations, 1950).

[77] Anne O. Krueger, "The Political Economy of the Rent-Seeking Society," *American Economic Review* 64 (1974), pp. 291–303.

change and capital controls not only introduced distortions but also invited corruption, smuggling, and black markets. Liberalization and market-oriented policies, on the other hand, would depoliticize decisions about foreign exchange, thus discouraging harmful rent-seeking activities and promoting growth.

Domestic financial interventionism also came under attack. Many early postwar economists advocated financial interventionism to enhance growth prospects and correct domestic market failures. Controls were seen as necessary to ensure that capital flows could not disrupt these efforts. But beginning in the 1970s financial interventionism was increasingly redefined as "financial repression," harming growth prospects and introducing distortions. Evidence accumulated that liberalizing domestic finance could enhance growth and efficiency, thus undermining an important rationale for capital controls.

In considering how such reforms should proceed, a number of economists, following the pioneering work of Ronald McKinnon and Edward Shaw, concluded that interventionist measures should be gradually removed, and only in the wake of other policy reforms.[78] In particular, macroeconomic stabilization should precede domestic financial liberalization, which should be followed by exchange rate reform and then trade and current account liberalization. Capital account liberalization should occur at the end of this sequence of reforms, with long-term flows liberalized first and restrictions remaining on short-term flows until the end of the process. Because of the differential adjustment speeds of goods and assets markets, early advocates of this argument cautioned that premature capital account liberalization could undermine other reform efforts. As McKinnon warned, "The absorption of substantial amounts of foreign capital during the [trade] liberalization process . . . may be a serious mistake."[79]

The 1970s was thus a decade when support for Keynesianism, post-Keynesianism, and interventionist policies was increasingly confined to the margins of the profession. Indeed, a series of surveys conducted of economists in the 1970s, 1980s, and 1990s across a wide range of issues reveals a shift in the profession toward greater agreement with monetarist and new classical beliefs.[80] In 1980, the demise of Keynesianism seemed so complete that Robert Lucas, in an article entitled "The Death of Keynesian Economics," confidently asserted:

---

[78] Ronald I. McKinnon, *Money and Capital in Economic Development* (Washington, D.C.: Brookings Institution, 1973); Edward Shaw, *Financial Deepening in Economic Development* (Oxford: Oxford University Press, 1973).

[79] McKinnon, *Money and Capital*, p. 4.

[80] For an overview, see Dan Fuller and Doris Geide-Stevenson, "Consensus among Economists: Revisited," *Journal of Economic Education* 34, no. 3 (2003), pp. 369–387.

One cannot find good, under-forty economists who identify their work as "Keynesian." Indeed, people even take offense if referred to as "Keynesians." At research seminars, people don't take Keynesian theorizing seriously anymore; the audience starts to whisper and giggle to one another.[81]

To be sure, since 1980 there has remained considerable debate among economists. Some economists, drawing on second-best arguments, highlight that controls could be welfare-improving. Still, most economists making such arguments seek only to demonstrate that controls could theoretically improve welfare. Such arguments, as Dooley observes, are generally "not policy recommendation(s) . . . since the actual effectiveness of such a program is an empirical question . . . [and there] is no evidence that controls have enhanced economic welfare in a manner suggested by theory." Capturing the views of most economists, Dooley emphasizes that "it would be better to remove the existing distortion rather than introducing another to mitigate the damage inflicted by the first."[82]

Yet some economists remain skeptical of arguments that remove any scope for the use of controls. In the late 1970s, new Keynesianism emerged to "defend the essence of the neoclassical-Keynesian synthesis from the new classical assault," writes N. Gregory Mankiw.[83] Like neoclassical synthesists, new Keynesian understandings of market behavior are premised on the assumption that market actors employ information efficiently in the long run, but not in the short run, where market errors can justify government intervention. For instance, in Joseph Stiglitz and Andrew Weiss's seminal treatment, information asymmetries—a factor intrinsic to the operation of international capital markets—hinder the efficient allocation of credit even when the market is in equilibrium and where there are no sticky prices or government regulation.[84] In this view, unrestrained capital mobility is not necessarily efficient, and some restraints on capital mobility could prove useful. Stiglitz and other new Keynesians, however,

---

[81] Robert Lucas, "The Death of Keynesian Economics," *Issues and Ideas*, Winter 1980, pp. 18–19.

[82] Dooley, "Survey of Academic Literature," pp. 2, i.

[83] N. Gregory Mankiw, "The Macroeconomist as Scientist and Engineer," unpublished manuscript, Harvard University, 2006. On New Keynesianism, see N. Gregory Mankiw, "The Reincarnation of Keynesian Economics," *European Economic Review* 36, nos. 2–3 (1992), pp. 559–565. New Keynesians share with neoclassical synthesists an acceptance of sticky wages and prices and the possibility that markets do not clear. However, in contrast to neoclassical synthesists, some new Keynesians have explored how rational expectations could be used in models with sticky wages and prices. See, for instance, Stanley Fischer, "Long-Term Contracts, Rational Expectations, and the Optimal Money Supply Rule," *Journal of Political Economy* 85, no. 1 (1977), pp. 191–205.

[84] Stiglitz and Weiss, "Credit Rationing."

generally advocate market-based measures as opposed to more comprehensive restrictions suggested by Keynesians and post-Keynesians.[85] Yet among new Keynesians there are some that do doubt the desirability of capital freedom.

Despite this wide range of views, the differences that have remained among most economists tend to one of degree rather than kind. Replacing the early postwar Keynesian consensus has been a set of *neoliberal* beliefs that range along a continuum from the neoclassical synthesis and new Keynesianism to monetarism to neoclassical economics, "neoliberalism," and new classical economics. Although proponents of each of these schools of thought disagree about the desirability and efficacy of government interventionism and the efficiency with which market actors use information, they generally share the view that the capital freedom is desirable, at least in the long run. Debates have persisted within the profession about the importance of sequencing and the role of temporary controls, but few question the long-run desirability of liberalization. This consensus has stood in sharp contrast to Keynesian and post-Keynesian understandings that view unfettered capital mobility as undesirable and permanent controls as essential.

Table 3.1 summarizes the core understandings and standards of behavior associated with these different schools of thought. The critical issue that divides some of them and unites others is their various assumptions about the efficiency with which market actors use information. Keynesians, post-Keynesians, and some new Keynesians are united by an understanding of market behavior that suggests certain factors intrinsic to the operation of international capital markets can give rise to capital flow volatility and financial stability. Currency crises are understood to develop through self-fulfilling expectations that can emerge autonomously from underlying fundamentals. These understandings engender a standard of behavior that controls should be an essential and *permanent* feature of the international monetary system.

On the other hand, what unites the neoliberal continuum of thought is an understanding of market behavior that suggests market actors use information more or less efficiently, and that capital flows generally reflect underlying fundamentals. Currency crises are seen as developing primarily from economic and policy failures. To be sure, there are important differences among the schools of thought that make up the neoliberal continuum. While neoclassical synthesists, most new Keynesians, and monetarists suggest that expectations form efficiently only in the long run because

---

[85] Some post-Keynesians have been critical of Stiglitz for not going far enough in advocating more comprehensive restrictions on capital mobility. See Claude Gnos and Louis-Philippe Rochon, "Reforming the International and Monetary System: From Keynes to Davidson and Stiglitz," *Journal of Post-Keynesian Economics* 26, no. 4 (2004), pp. 613–629.

TABLE 3.1
Monetary Understandings, Crisis Constructions, and Standards of Policy Behavior

School of thought	Understanding of market behavior	Crisis construction	Standards of policy behavior
Neoclassical orthodoxy	Market expectations are based on an efficient use of information regarding fundamentals.	Crises are caused primarily by poor fundamentals in capital-recipient countries.	**Capital freedom:** Capital mobility should be unfettered. Policymakers should adjust policies and implement structural reforms to respond to payments imbalances, capital flow volatility, and financial instability.
Keynesianism, post-Keynesianism, and some elements of new Keynesianism	Market expectations are based on conventions, which can become self-reinforcing and autonomous from fundamentals.	Crises are caused primarily by factors intrinsic to the operation of international capital markets.	**Capital control:** Capital mobility, especially for short-term speculative and interest rate arbitrage flows, should be permanently restricted, via administrative measures, if necessary. "Productive" and "equilibrating" capital flows should be unfettered. Policymakers should implement or intensify controls to respond to payments imbalances, capital flow volatility, and financial instability.
"Neoliberalism"	Market expectations are based on an efficient use of information regarding fundamentals.	Crises are caused primarily by poor fundamentals in capital-recipient countries. Special attention is given to tendency of fixed exchange rates to rigidify and offer one-way bets to speculators.	**Capital freedom:** Capital mobility should be unfettered. Policymakers should employ floating exchange rates to deter speculators and to respond to payments imbalances, capital flow volatility, and financial instability.

of market errors or lags, neoclassicals, "neoliberals," and new classicals claim that expectations form efficiently more or less instantaneously. Neoclassical synthesists and new Keynesians also sanction the use of *temporary* market-based controls to correct for distortions or market failures, while the other schools of thought within the neoliberal continuum do not. But despite these differences, each of the schools of thought that comprise the neoliberal continuum broadly agree that capital freedom is a desirable *long-run* goal and that adjusting policies, rather than imposing controls, is the optimal response to capital flow volatility and financial stability.

TABLE 3.1 (*continued*)
Monetary Understandings, Crisis Constructions, and Standards of Policy Behavior

School of thought	Understanding of market behavior	Crisis construction	Standards of policy behavior
Monetarism	Market expectations are based on an efficient use of information regarding fundamentals in the long run, but in the short run expectations lag fundamentals (adaptive expectations).	Crises are caused primarily by poor fundamentals in capital-recipient countries. Special attention is given to tendency of fixed exchange rates to rigidify and offer one-way bets to speculators.	**Capital freedom:** Capital mobility should be unfettered. Policymakers should employ floating exchange rates to deter speculators and to respond to payments imbalances, capital flow volatility, and financial instability.
Neoclassical synthesis and most elements of new Keynesianism	Market expectations are based on an efficient use of information regarding fundamentals in the long run, but short-run market errors prevent expectations from forming efficiently in the short run.	Crises are caused primarily by poor fundamentals in capital-recipient countries. Special attention is given to domestic distortions.	**Capital freedom:** Capital mobility should be unfettered in the long run with due attention to sequencing. Policymakers may intermittently use temporary market-based restraints on capital mobility to counter preexisting distortions and market errors. Policymakers should adjust policies to remove distortions or to correct for market errors so that temporary restraints may be removed.
New classical	Market expectations are based on an efficient use of information regarding fundamentals (rational expectations).	Crises are caused primarily by poor fundamentals in capital-recipient countries	**Capital freedom:** Capital mobility should be unfettered. Policymakers should adjust policies and implement structural reforms to respond to payments imbalances, capital flow volatility, and financial instability.

EXPLORING AND ASSESSING PROFESSIONALIZATION

The evolution of these beliefs shaped the views of generations of economists. By creating, teaching, and disseminating technical models of how economies work and normative conceptualizations of how economies should be organized, the economics profession served as a critical agent of social construction and socialization. Although a number of scholars assert this to be the case, few, if any, have rigorously and systematically addressed this claim. This is an unfortunate shortcoming. Without evidence linking professional training to subsequent beliefs held by actors, it becomes difficult to sustain the claim that professionalization matters. I seek to rectify this shortcoming by using original survey data to establish a link between professionalization and subsequent beliefs. While uncovering a link between professional training and subsequent belief is hardly counterintuitive, it is a necessary, though largely neglected, empirical step in building any convincing account that stresses the role of professionalization.

The content of professional training, irrespective of the profession, shapes individual beliefs by promoting, both implicitly and explicitly, a particular set of understandings and standards of behavior. Common professional training thus plays an important part in constructing consensual knowledge. As Paul DiMaggio and Walter Powell observe, "[Those] drawn from the same universities and filtered on a common set of attributes . . . will tend to view problems in a similar fashion, see the same policies, procedures and structures as normatively sanctioned and legitimated, and approach decisions in much the same way."[86] With respect to the economics profession in particular, David Colander, author of several studies entitled "The Making of an Economist," similarly concludes:

> Individuals are not born as economists; they are molded through formal and informal training. This training shapes the way they approach problems, process information and carry out research, which in turn influences the policies they favor and the role they play in society. The economics profession changes as cohorts with older-style training are replaced with cohorts with newer-style training. In many ways, the replicator dynamics of graduate school play a larger role in determining economists' methodology and approach than all the myriad papers written about methodology.[87]

Differences and similarities in professionalization therefore may help account for much of the variance in subsequent beliefs about capital controls and their liberalization, the logic being that individuals develop beliefs associated with the particularities of their professional training in economics and then act as "baggage handlers" of these beliefs.

A caveat is in order before proceeding. I do not claim all individuals are socialized by their professional training experience. Behind the pattern of collectively shared beliefs emerging from professional training there might be some individuals who were socialized into these beliefs and others whose prior beliefs led them to self-select into particular economic departments. Yet even those individuals who did self-select into particular economic departments were likely exposed to new understandings and stan-

---

[86] Dimaggio and Powell, "The Iron Cage Revisited," p. 153.
[87] Colander, "Making of an Economist Redux," p. 175.

dards of behavior that, at the very least, reinforced their prior beliefs or led them to extend their beliefs in a way that had not yet been considered. Over time the belief structure of these individuals likely became increasingly robustly embedded in a particular set of collectively shared beliefs, with such beliefs being constantly reshaped and redefined via interaction with other members of the group who shared them.

Neoliberalism, as I define it, represents a broad spectrum of thought. Despite significant differences among the schools of thought that comprise it, each of them to some to extent draws on neoclassical assumptions and believes in the long-run desirability of capital account liberalization. These are two key attributes that constitute a neoliberal economist, and it these specific attributes that I seek to examine.

I begin by using a two-pronged strategy to identify academic departments that were likely transmitters of the norm of capital freedom. First, I rely on earlier observations and research that describes cultures that tended to prevail in various economic departments.[88] This research typically identifies seven leading American economic departments (Harvard, MIT, Chicago, Yale, Berkeley, Stanford, and Princeton) as likely purveyors of neoclassical assumptions. I then construct a more comprehensive list of relevant departments by examining publication frequency data in the *American Economic Review (AER)* from 1963 to 1980, a period when the managing editor primarily published articles that employed neoclassical assumptions.[89] These publication data help to better discern which departments were likely transmitters of the norm of capital freedom to their students. Since during this period the *AER* was primarily publishing articles that employ neoclassical assumptions and models, departments with higher publication frequency should be stronger transmitters of the norm of capital freedom than those with lower publication frequency.[90]

---

[88] W. Lee Hansen, "The Education and Training of Economics Doctorates," *Journal of Economic Literature* 29, no. 3 (1991), p. 1085; Robert J. Lampman, ed., *Economists at Wisconsin, 1892–1992* (Milwaukee: Board of Regents of the University of Wisconsin System, 1993); William J. Barber, "Postwar Changes in American Graduate Education in Economics," in *The Post-1945 Internationalization of Economics,* ed. A. W. Coats (London: Duke University Press, 1996), pp. 12–32.

[89] George H. Borts, "Report of the Managing Editor," *American Economic Review* 71, no. 2 (1981), pp. 452–464 at p. 459.

[90] There is also the possibility that these leading departments simply publish more frequently than others, and thus what is really being captured here is the quality of the department rather than content of the assumptions it promotes. As a way of assessing this possibility, in other work I used this method to examine the frequency of publication in another top economics journal with a slightly different orientation. If this method were capturing quality, then one would expect to find the same leading departments publishing more frequently. But this was not the case. In fact, I found a much smaller number of departments to publish more frequently in this other top economics journal. See Jeffrey M. Chwieroth, "Shrinking the State: Neoliberal Economists and Social Spending in Latin America," in *Constructing*

TABLE 3.2
Top Fifteen Academic Departments According to Publication Frequency
in *AER*, 1963–1980

Berkeley	New York University
Brown	Northwestern
Carnegie Mellon	Pennsylvania
Chicago	Princeton
Harvard	Stanford
Hebrew University (Israel)	Wisconsin
Johns Hopkins	Yale
MIT	

Table 3.2 presents the top fifteen "neoclassical academic departments" as measured by publication frequency in *AER* from 1963 to 1980. It corresponds well with the list of departments that qualitative research identifies as "neoclassical departments." This result increases our confidence that the departments listed in table 3.2 are indeed likely transmitters of the norm of capital freedom. Individuals trained at "neoclassical economic departments" are thus likely to be neoliberals, as I define them, and their professional training characteristics can shed some light on their beliefs.

A brief comment on the content validity of this approach is in order before proceeding.[91] Content validity is the extent to which a given measure adequately captures the full content of the operational definition given for the concept. This validation procedure asks the researcher to consider whether key elements may be omitted from the indicator or inappropriate elements included in it.

Regarding the former, one omitted element is those individuals who advocate capital freedom but did not receive training at one of the aforementioned academic departments. Although my approach may not adequately capture the full array of individuals who support capital freedom, this approach still outperforms alternative approaches, such as one that identifies neoliberals based on whether they were "American-educated."[92] The reason, as I demonstrate more fully below, is that not all American departments were supporters of the norm of capital freedom. On the contrary, some departments—such as those at University of Massachusetts,

---

the International Economy, ed. Rawi Abdelal, Mark Blyth, and Craig Parsons (Ithaca, NY: Cornell University Press, forthcoming).

[91] For a fuller treatment of the validity of this measure, see Jeffrey M. Chwieroth, "Testing and Measuring the Role of Ideas: The Case of Neoliberalism in the International Monetary Fund," *International Studies Quarterly* 51, no. 1 (2007), pp. 5–30.

[92] See Glen Biglaiser, *Guardians of the Nation? Economics, Generals, and Economic Reform in Latin America* (South Bend, Ind.: University of Notre Dame Press, 2002).

Amherst, Michigan State, Rutgers, and the New School for Social Research—are routinely said to be disseminators of "heterodox economics."[93] As numerous methodologists recognize there is usually a trade-off in measurement between parsimony and completeness.[94] Given the theoretical focus on economists and no clear alternative to the one offered here, it seems reasonable to partially sacrifice completeness for parsimony.

Concerning the issue of including inappropriate elements, some may claim the approach does not adequately capture the diversity evident among those who supported capital freedom. In other words, some may see my approach as making an unnecessarily strong homogeneity assumption; that is, that all economists trained at particular academic departments prefer no capital controls. But, as suggested, the approach explicitly recognizes that among supporters of capital freedom there are significant differences of view about the importance of sequencing and the legitimacy of selective restraints on capital mobility. Yet despite these differences there has been a broad consensus that capital account liberalization is a desirable long-run goal. This consensus contrasts sharply with Keynesian and post-Keynesian standards of behavior that deny the desirability of such a goal, even in the long run.

To gain a better understanding of the extent to which professional training serves a socialization mechanism that informs subsequent individual beliefs about capital account liberalization, a web-based survey of 263 randomly selected economists from the top 150 academic departments in world was conducted from January 2006 to April 2007.[95] Individuals were asked to respond to 20 propositions about international capital markets, capital controls and their liberalization.[96] Respondents could "strongly agree," "mostly agree," "mostly disagree," "strongly disagree," or they could indicate "no clear opinion." Respondents were first asked to offer

[93] Hansen, "Education and Training," p. 1063; Barber, "Postwar Changes," p. 25; citing the 2002 report of the department's external evaluation committee, www.umass.edu/economics describes the faculty as "working within several different traditions in economics: Marxian, post-Keynesian, institutionalist, historical, non-Marxian radical political economy, and feminist economists."

[94] David Collier, Henry E. Brady, and Jason Seawright, "Critiques, Responses, and Trade-Offs: Drawing Together the Debate," in *Rethinking Social Inquiry: Diverse Tools, Shared Standards*, ed. Henry E. Brady and David Collier (Lanham, Md.: Rowman and Littlefield, 2004), pp. 195–226 at pp. 221–226.

[95] Respondents were "cold contacted," with a return rate of 16.5 percent, which is quite good for this type of strategy. Data from econphd.net were employed to rank academic departments; see http://www.econphd.net/rank/rallec.htm (accessed 10 June 2005).

[96] A modest number of respondents refrained from answering all the propositions. In private correspondence with the author most of these respondents revealed that they believed their area of expertise was too far removed from some questions and therefore were unable to give relevant answers.

the views they believe they had immediately following completion of their professional training. Since the nature of the data collection exercise necessarily relies on retrospective evaluations, some caution is warranted in interpreting the results. Yet despite the limitations of surveys in general, and of this type of survey in particular, it does offer some important insights into the economics profession, and the results in large part capture how many economists see (saw) these issues.

To gain a better handle on the extent to which professional training helped create consensus among all economists in the sample, I first condense the extreme answers along the support-rejection dimension into a single category; that is, those "strongly agreeing" and "mostly agreeing" are collapsed into a single category, and the same for those "strongly disagreeing" and "mostly disagreeing." I then employ two criteria to explore how much consensus exists. The first criterion is the relative entropy coefficient, which provides a single nonlinear information-theoretic measure that equals 0 if there is perfect consensus, and equals 1 if there is no consensus at all. The second criterion compares the proportion of respondents that fall in the condensed "agree" and "disagree" categories.

Table 3.3 presents the results. Not surprisingly, the entropy statistic suggests the sharpest divisions among all economists in the sample centered on understandings of the behavior of international capital markets (Propositions 1–4), the use of controls to manage capital inflow and outflow surges (8–9, 11–12, 15), the desirability of liberalizing short-term capital flows (17), and big-bang arguments for liberalization (19–20). These are all matters on which economists from each of the school of thought offer significantly different views.

Yet despite the relatively high level of entropy among the responses, the weight of opinion on most of these issues leans toward supporting neoliberal understandings and standards of behavior. In terms of understandings of international capital markets, a majority of respondents upon completion of their training believed international capital markets allocate savings efficiently, supported the efficient market hypothesis, and agreed capital flows play an "equilibrating" role. Slightly less than a majority of respondents also saw capital flows as responding primarily to economic and policy trends. With respect to standards of behavior for the use of controls, a majority of respondents upon completion of their training saw controls as ineffective in managing inflow and outflow surges, viewed controls as distortionary, and disagreed with the more Keynesian-oriented proposition that controls are essential for managing balance-of-payments crises. A majority of respondents upon completion of their training also thought that controls do not make economic sense because alternative policy options are more effective for achieving the same goals. But there are no clear majorities against controls as an essential tool to manage

TABLE 3.3
Propositions and Responses upon Completion of Professional Training, Full Sample

Proposition	Generally agreeing	Generally disagreeing	No clear opinion	Relative entropy
1. The first fundamental theorem of welfare economics (i.e., competitive markets produce an efficient allocation of the world's resources) generally applies to the international capital market. (253)	57.9% (146)	22.6% (57)	19.8% (50)	0.88
2. The efficient market hypothesis (i.e., prices can be viewed as embodying the true value of assets) applies to the international capital market. (249)	55.0% (137)	20.1% (50)	24.9% (62)	0.91
3. International capital flows play an "equilibrating" role in the international monetary system because they help to restore equilibrium in the balance of payments. (246)	52.4% (129)	20.3% (50)	27.2% (67)	0.93
4. International capital flows respond primarily to economic and policy trends. (243)	49.8% (121)	17.7% (43)	32.5% (79)	0.93
5. The free flow of international capital offers residents of different countries the opportunity to pool risks and engage in intertemporal trade. (242)	85.0% (205)	7.9% (19)	7.5% (18)	0.48
6. The free flow of international capital facilitates portfolio diversification of residents of different countries. (242)	89.3% (216)	4.1% (10)	6.6% (16)	0.37
7. Open capital markets impose a valuable discipline upon governments that might otherwise pursue overexpansionary fiscal or monetary policies or tolerate lax practices by domestic financial intermediaries. (240)	68.3% (164)	11.3% (27)	20.4% (49)	0.76
8. When faced with a surge in capital *inflows* policymakers should not implement capital controls as they tend to be ineffectual or distortionary. (240)	55.0% (132)	17.9% (43)	27.1% (65)	0.90
9. When faced with a surge in capital *outflows* policymakers should not implement capital controls as they tend to be ineffectual or distortionary. (239)	51.0% (122)	17.2% (41)	31.8% (76)	0.91
10. Capital controls are an essential tool for the preservation of national economic autonomy. (239)	15.1% (36)	67.8% (162)	17.1% (41)	0.77

TABLE 3.3 (*continued*)
Propositions and Responses upon Completion of Professional Training, Full Sample

Proposition	Generally agreeing	Generally disagreeing	No clear opinion	Relative entropy
11. Capital controls are an essential tool for managing balance-of-payments crises. (239)	18.8% (45)	54.4% (130)	26.8% (64)	0.91
12. Capital controls are an essential tool for managing short-term capital flows. (237)	25.8% (61)	46.0% (109)	28.3% (67)	0.97
13. Capital controls are an essential tool to ensure domestic savings are used to finance domestic investment. (236)	11.0% (26)	69.5% (164)	19.5% (46)	0.74
14. Capital controls are an essential tool for maintaining an adequate domestic tax base. (235)	6.4% (15)	75.3% (177)	18.3% (43)	0.64
15. Capital controls do not make economic sense as there are always alternative instruments more effective for achieving the same goals. (234)	50.4% (118)	22.2% (52)	27.3% (64)	0.94
16. Government restrictions on long-term international capital flows (e.g., foreign direct investment or long-term bank lending) should be abolished altogether. (237)	68.4% (162)	19.4% (46)	12.2% (29)	0.76
17. Government restrictions on short-term international capital flows should be abolished altogether. (231)	38.5% (89)	32.4% (75)	29.0% (67)	0.99
18. Market-based restrictions on capital flows—such as a tax—are preferable to quantitative restrictions. (232)	75.8% (175)	4.3% (10)	20.2% (47)	0.61
19. The lack of credibility in the reform process of developing countries or emerging markets makes it appropriate to act quickly to liberalize the capital account early in the reform process. (233)	28.8% (67)	34.8% (81)	36.5% (85)	0.99
20. The best route to an efficient financial sector in developing countries or emerging markets is to liberalize the capital account. (228)	39.4% (90)	29.3% (67)	31.1% (71)	0.99

Note: The number of respondents in each category is given in parentheses. The total number of respondents is 263. Proportions may not sum to 100 due to rounding.

short-term flows, in favor of abolishing controls on short-term capital flows, or supportive of the big-bang case for liberalization; in fact, the weight of opinion leans in the opposing direction for some of these issues.

Still, views tend toward greater consensus on other issues. All economists upon completion of their training generally agreed that liberalization enables greater risk pooling and portfolio diversification (Propositions 5–6) and that controls on long-term "productive" flows should be abolished (16). The sample widely rejects Keynesian-oriented arguments that lend support to controls as measures to ensure domestic savings are used for investment, to preserve policy autonomy, and to maintain an adequate tax base (10, 13–14). In contrast to Keynes, most economists reject, rather than accept, the proposition that governments should insulate themselves from market discipline (7). Lastly, to the extent restraints on capital mobility are seen as legitimate, this legitimacy is limited to market-based measures and fails to extend to administrative measures (18).

Similarities and differences in the content of professional training likely facilitated these patterns of consensus and dissension. In particular, those respondents trained at "neoclassical departments" are likely to share differing beliefs from those respondents trained at "heterodox" American departments, "Keynesian departments" (such as Cambridge), and Continental European departments (hereafter HKCE departments).[97] Therefore, I divide the sample along these lines and present, in table 3.4, the propositions and answers for each group.

A clear picture emerges from these data. Whereas those trained at "neoclassical departments" evidence relatively strong support for propositions that legitimate liberalization, those trained at HKCE departments show greater skepticism of these same propositions. These two groups tended to have strikingly different understandings of international capital markets upon completion of their professional training. Upon completion of their professional training neoliberal and HKCE economists had significantly different views about the welfare implications of capital freedom

---

[97] On the differences between "neoclassical departments" and British departments, see Martin Ricketts and Edward Shoesmith, "British Economic Opinion: Positive Science or Normative Judgment?" *American Economic Review* 82, no. 2 (1992), pp. 210–215; Ricketts and Shoesmith, *British Economic Opinion: A Survey of a Thousand Economists* (London: Institute of Economic Affairs, 1990). On the differences between "neoclassical departments" and Continental European departments, see Bruno S. Frey, Werner W. Pommerehne, Friedrich Schneider, and Guy Gilbert, "Consensus and Dissension among Economics: An Empirical Inquiry," *American Economic Review* 74, no. 3 (1984), pp. 986–994; Bruno S. Frey and Reiner Eichenberger, "American and European Economics and Economists," *Journal of Economic Perspectives* 7, no. 4 (1993), pp. 185–193. The sample of HKCE economists is significantly smaller than that of neoliberal economists partly because of the relatively few number (36) of HKCE departments among the top 150 academic departments and partly due to a lower response rate (8.8 percent) from respondents in HKCE departments.

TABLE 3.4
Propositions and Responses upon Completion of Professional Training, Neoclassical versus HKCE Departments

Proposition	Generally agreeing		Generally disagreeing		No clear opinion	
	Neoclassical departments	HKCE departments	Neoclassical departments	HKCE departments	Neoclassical departments	HKCE departments
1. The first fundamental theorem of welfare economics (i.e., competitive markets produce an efficient allocation of the world's resources) generally applies to the international capital market. (225 / 28)	62.2%** (140)	21.4%** (6)	19.6%** (44)	46.4%** (13)	18.2%* (41)	32.1%* (9)
2. The efficient market hypothesis (i.e., prices can be viewed as embodying the true value of assets) applies to the international capital market. (221 / 28)	58.4%** (129)	28.5%** (8)	18.1%** (40)	35.7%** (10)	23.5% (52)	35.7% (10)
3. International capital flows play an "equilibrating" role in the international monetary system because they help to restore equilibrium in the balance of payments. (219 / 27)	53.4% (117)	44.4% (12)	19.2% (42)	29.6% (8)	27.4% (60)	25.9% (7)
4. International capital flows respond primarily to economic and policy trends. (216 / 27)	51.4% (111)	37.0% (10)	16.2%* (35)	29.6%* (8)	32.4% (70)	33.3% (9)
5. The free flow of international capital offers residents of different countries the opportunity to pool risks and engage in intertemporal trade. (215 / 27)	86.1%* (185)	74.1%* (20)	6.5% (14)	14.8% (4)	7.4% (16)	11.1% (3)
6. The free flow of international capital facilitates portfolio diversification of residents of different countries. (215 / 27)	90.7%** (195)	77.8%** (21)	3.3% (7)	11.1% (3)	6.0% (13)	11.1% (3)

TABLE 3.4 (*continued*)
Propositions and Responses upon Completion of Professional Training, Neoclassical versus HKCE Departments

Proposition	Generally agreeing		Generally disagreeing		No clear opinion	
	Neoclassical departments	HKCE departments	Neoclassical departments	HKCE departments	Neoclassical departments	HKCE departments
7. Open capital markets impose a valuable discipline upon governments that might otherwise pursue overexpansionary fiscal or monetary policies or tolerate lax practices by domestic financial intermediaries. (214 / 26)	69.6% (149)	57.7% (15)	10.3% (22)	19.2% (5)	20.1% (43)	23.1% (6)
8. When faced with a surge in capital *inflows* policymakers should not implement capital controls as they tend to be ineffectual or distortionary. (212 / 26)	57.0%* (122)	38.4%* (10)	15.4%** (33)	38.4%** (10)	27.6% (59)	23.1% (6)
9. When faced with a surge in capital *outflows* policymakers should not implement capital controls as they tend to be ineffectual or distortionary. (212 / 26)	53.9%** (115)	26.9%** (7)	14.6%** (31)	38.4%** (10)	31.5% (67)	34.6% (9)
10. Capital controls are an essential tool for the preservation of national economic autonomy. (213 / 26)	14.1% (30)	23.1% (6)	70.0%** (149)	50.0%** (13)	15.9% (34)	26.9% (7)
11. Capital controls are an essential tool for managing balance-of-payments crises. (212 / 27)	16.0%** (34)	40.7%** (11)	56.6%* (120)	37.0%* (10)	27.3% (58)	22.2% (6)
12. Capital controls are an essential tool for managing short-term capital flows. (211 / 26)	23.2%** (49)	46.2%** (12)	47.8%* (101)	30.8%* (8)	28.9% (61)	23.1% (6)
13. Capital controls are an essential tool to ensure domestic savings are used to finance domestic investment. (210 / 26)	10.5% (22)	15.4% (4)	71.9%** (151)	50.0%** (13)	17.6%** (37)	34.6%** (9)

TABLE 3.4 (*continued*)
Propositions and Responses upon Completion of Professional Training, Neoclassical versus HKCE Departments

Proposition	Generally agreeing		Generally disagreeing		No clear opinion	
	Neoclassical departments	HKCE departments	Neoclassical departments	HKCE departments	Neoclassical departments	HKCE departments
14. Capital controls are an essential tool for maintaining an adequate domestic tax base. (209 / 26)	4.8%** (10)	19.2%** (5)	78.5%** (164)	50.0%** (13)	16.7%* (35)	30.8%** (8)
15. Capital controls do not make economic sense as there are always alternative instruments more effective for achieving the same goals. (207 / 27)	50.7% (105)	48.1% (13)	20.8% (43)	33.3% (9)	28.5% (59)	18.5% (5)
16. Government restrictions on long-term international capital flows (e.g., foreign direct investment or long-term bank lending) should be abolished altogether. (208 / 26)	69.7%* (145)	53.9%* (14)	17.3%** (36)	38.5%** (10)	12.9% (27)	7.7% (2)
17. Government restrictions on short-term international capital flows should be abolished altogether. (205 / 26)	41.0%** (84)	19.2%** (5)	30.7% (63)	46.1% (12)	28.3% (58)	34.6% (9)
18. Market-based restrictions on capital flows—such as a tax—are preferable to quantitative restrictions. (205 / 27)	77.0% (158)	62.9% (17)	3.9% (8)	7.4% (2)	19.0% (39)	29.6% (8)
19. The lack of credibility in the reform process of developing countries or emerging markets makes it appropriate to act quickly to liberalize the capital account early in the reform process. (206 / 27)	31.5%** (65)	7.7%** (2)	31.5%** (65)	59.3%** (16)	36.9% (76)	33.3% (9)
20. The best route to an efficient financial sector in developing countries or emerging markets is to liberalize the capital account. (203 / 25)	41.4%* (84)	24.0%* (6)	28.1% (57)	40.0% (10)	30.5% (62)	36.0% (9)

Note: The number of respondents in each category is given in parentheses (neoclassical / HKCE). The total number of respondents is neoclassical 232, HKCE 31. Proportions may not sum to 100 due to rounding.

Difference in Proportions Test: * significant at 10%, ** significant at 5%.

(1), the efficient market hypothesis (2), and whether capital flows respond primarily to economic and policy trends (4). Not surprisingly, there were no significant differences as to the "equilibrating role" of some capital flows (3).

There were, however, significant differences between the two groups with respect to the standards of behavior for capital controls. Significant differences are found regarding whether controls should be used to manage inflow and outflow surges (8 and 9) and whether controls are an essential policy tool (10–14), with neoliberal economists consistently opposing restrictions on capital mobility. Somewhat surprisingly, there were no significant differences between neoliberal and HKCE economists on whether capital controls make economic sense (15). Still, there were significant differences between the two groups regarding the abolition of restrictions on long-term and short-term flows (16 and 17), though a majority of HKCE economists did support liberalization in the case of long-term flows and nearly a third of neoliberals expressed reservations regarding liberalizing short-term flows. Sympathy among neoliberals for restrictions on short-term flows likely reflects unresolved differences among the group about the legitimacy of temporary capital controls. Finally, there appear to be no significant differences between neoliberal and HKCE economists regarding their preferences for market-based rather than administrative measures (18).

Upon completion of their training neoliberal economists express a wide range of views on propositions associated with big-bang arguments with no clear consensus (19–20). This likely reflects unresolved debates among them on the importance of sequencing. HKCE economists, on the other hand, appear much more skeptical of big-bang arguments, with a significantly higher proportion of respondents opposing them. For the remaining propositions (5–7), upon completion of their training neoliberal and HKCE economists tended to have relatively similar beliefs, though the former generally supported propositions associated with the norm of capital freedom much more enthusiastically than the latter.

Overall, these results generally confirm that individuals trained in "neoclassical departments" are likely to share beliefs that severely limit the place of controls within the boundaries of legitimate policy practice and that support liberalization as the "appropriate" policy choice. Moreover, those trained in "neoclassical departments" are found to generally disagree with their HKCE colleagues. Finally, the results underscore the importance of recognizing differences of view even among neoliberals, especially in regard to the importance of sequencing and the role of temporary controls in managing volatile short-term capital flows.

Does professionalization also continue to shape and inform the beliefs of neoliberals today? To provide some answers, I asked neoliberals which factors shaped their current beliefs, whether their beliefs had changed since graduate school, and how they currently view the survey propositions. Less than half of the respondents (43.5 percent) indicated that their beliefs have changed significantly since graduate school. The long-term influence of professional training is also suggested by the respondents' answers about which factors they believe shape their current views. Along with country experiences and current research findings, respondents identified professional training as the strongest primary or secondary influence on their current beliefs. Respondents also downplayed the possibility of self-selection, with only slightly more than one-tenth identifying their socioeconomic or political background as a primary or secondary determinant of their current views. The absence of much evidence for strong self-selection effects dovetails with findings from other surveys of economists, which uncover that a significant proportion of graduate students report that their political beliefs changed as a result of their professional training.[98]

Table 3.5 presents the results from asking neoliberal respondents how they currently view the survey propositions. In examining the responses, it seems neoliberal economists by and large continue to express many of the same beliefs they exhibited upon completion of their training. Beliefs remain stable across sixteen of the propositions and, more significantly, in the direction that legitimates capital freedom as desirable. Indeed, for most neoliberal economists the place of capital controls within the boundaries of legitimate policy practice remains the same as it was upon completion of their training.

But the strengthening in the late 1990s of Keynesian-inspired interpretations of the Asian financial crisis, which represented the turmoil as a market panic more than a rational reaction to poor fundamentals, along with greater awareness of the dangers of rapid liberalization and of the potential for short-term flows to trigger financial instability have likely led some respondents to moderate their support for strict neoliberal understandings and standards of behavior.[99] Partially reversing patterns found for views that respondents reported they had upon completing their training, table 3.5 reports a significant increase in reservations about the efficient markets hypothesis (2) and big-bang political economy arguments

---

[98] Colander, "Making of an Economist Redux"; Colander and Klamer, "The Making of an Economist."

[99] Although the survey was conducted from January 2006 to April 2007, one might expect the subprime crisis could lead to further moderation of support.

TABLE 3.5
Propositions and Responses upon Completion of Professional Training versus Current Views, Neoliberal Economists

Proposition	Generally agreeing		Generally disagreeing		No clear opinion	
	Professional training	Current	Professional training	Current	Professional training	Current
1. The first fundamental theorem of welfare economics (i.e., competitive markets produce an efficient allocation of the world's resources) generally applies to the international capital market.	57.4% (58)	58.4% (59)	17.8% (18)	24.8% (25)	24.8% (25)	16.8% (17)
2. The efficient market hypothesis (i.e., prices can be viewed as embodying the true value of assets) applies to the international capital market.	50.5% (51)	48.5% (49)	17.8%** (18)	31.7%*** (32)	31.6%** (32)	19.8%** (20)
3. International capital flows play an "equilibrating" role in the international monetary system because they help to restore equilibrium in the balance of payments.	50.5% (51)	50.5% (51)	23.7% (24)	30.7% (31)	25.7% (26)	18.8% (19)
4. International capital flows respond primarily to economic and policy trends.	54.5% (55)	54.5% (55)	15.8% (16)	20.7% (21)	29.7% (30)	24.7% (25)
5. The free flow of international capital offers residents of different countries the opportunity to pool risks and engage in intertemporal trade.	88.1% (89)	85.1% (86)	6.9% (7)	9.9% (10)	5.0% (5)	5.0% (5)
6. The free flow of international capital facilitates portfolio diversification of residents of different countries.	91.1% (92)	87.1% (88)	3.0% (3)	3.9% (4)	5.9% (6)	8.9% (9)
7. Open capital markets impose a valuable discipline upon governments that might otherwise pursue overexpansionary fiscal or monetary policies or tolerate lax practices by domestic financial intermediaries.	68.3% (69)	67.3% (68)	10.9% (11)	10.9% (11)	20.8% (21)	21.8% (22)
8. When faced with a surge in capital *inflows* policymakers should not implement capital controls as they tend to be ineffectual or distortionary.	50.5% (51)	42.6% (43)	18.8% (19)	25.7% (26)	30.7% (31)	31.7% (32)
9. When faced with a surge in capital *outflows* policymakers should not implement capital controls as they tend to be ineffectual or distortionary.	46.5% (47)	45.5% (46)	13.9% (14)	19.8% (20)	39.6% (40)	34.7% (35)

TABLE 3.5 (*continued*)
Propositions and Responses upon Completion of Professional Training versus Current Views, Neoliberal Economists

Proposition	Generally agreeing		Generally disagreeing		No clear opinion	
	Professional training	Current	Professional training	Current	Professional training	Current
10. Capital controls are an essential tool for the preservation of national economic autonomy.	13.9% (14)	13.9% (14)	65.3% (66)	64.3% (65)	20.8% (21)	21.8% (22)
11. Capital controls are an essential tool for managing balance of payments crises.	19.8% (20)	19.8% (20)	53.5% (54)	52.4% (53)	26.7% (27)	27.7% (28)
12. Capital controls are an essential tool for managing short-term capital flows.	25.7% (26)	25.8% (26)	41.6% (42)	42.6% (43)	32.7% (33)	31.6% (32)
13. Capital controls are an essential tool to ensure domestic savings are used to finance domestic investment.	13.9% (14)	12.8% (13)	64.4%* (65)	76.2%* (77)	21.8%** (22)	10.9%** (11)
14. Capital controls are an essential tool for maintaining an adequate domestic tax base.	6.9% (7)	5.9% (6)	73.3% (74)	81.2% (82)	19.8% (20)	12.8% (13)
15. Capital controls do not make economic sense as there are always alternative instruments more effective for achieving the same goals.	47.6% (48)	51.5% (52)	17.8%* (18)	27.7%* (28)	34.7%** (35)	20.8%** (21)
16. Government restrictions on long-term international capital flows (e.g., foreign direct investment or long-term bank lending) should be abolished altogether.	66.3% (67)	64.3% (65)	17.8% (18)	20.8% (21)	15.8% (16)	14.9% (15)
17. Government restrictions on short-term international capital flows should be abolished altogether.	32.7% (33)	30.7% (31)	33.7% (34)	40.6% (41)	33.7% (34)	28.7% (29)
18. Market-based restrictions on capital flows—such as a tax—are preferable to quantitative restrictions.	76.2% (77)	77.2% (78)	3.0% (3)	3.0% (3)	20.8% (21)	19.8% (20)
19. The lack of credibility in the reform process of developing countries or emerging markets makes it appropriate to act quickly to liberalize the capital account early in the reform process.	30.7% (31)	31.6% (32)	33.6%* (34)	45.5%* (46)	35.6%** (36)	22.7%** (23)
20. The best route to an efficient financial sector in developing countries or emerging markets is to liberalize the capital account.	38.7% (39)	44.6% (45)	26.7% (27)	27.7% (28)	34.6% (35)	27.7% (28)

Note: The number of respondents in each category is given in parentheses. The total number of respondents is 101. Proportions may not sum to 100 due to rounding.

Difference in Proportions Test: * significant at 10%, ** significant at 5%.

for liberalization (19). Standards of behavior that rule out the use of controls have also moderated somewhat, with a significant increase in the proportion of respondents opposing the view that capital controls do not make economic sense (15). But opposition to the use of controls in some circumstances has also hardened somewhat, with a significant increase in the proportion of respondents expressing reservations about using controls to ensure domestic savings are channeled to domestic investment (13).

Thus, since completing their professional training, respondents have experienced a modest, but not a substantial, shift in their beliefs. Indeed, the shift should not be overstated. Recall that over half of respondents indicated that their beliefs have not changed significantly since completing their training. Moreover, though views on the use of controls have moderated somewhat, most respondents continue to subscribe to beliefs that proscribe their use. Current beliefs also seem to see controls as temporary measures to manage occasionally excessive capital flow surges or to deal with domestic distortions rather than as permanent measures to confront factors intrinsic to the operation of international capital markets that are difficult, if not impossible, to resolve. Indeed, respondents failed to significantly moderate their opposition to capital controls as an essential policy instrument (8–14). Although there has been a modest decrease in opposition to the use of controls on inflows (8), the difference in views is not significant. Finally, it should be pointed out that for all four propositions for which we observe a shift in beliefs, it seems to be driven more by belief clarification than by belief change; that is, by respondents shifting to the "generally disagreeing" category from the "no clear opinion" category rather than from the "generally agreeing" category.

Despite its limitations, the use of current beliefs and retrospective appraisals of past beliefs does provide an informative window into the socialization process associated with professional training. Neoliberal economists evidence views that contrast sharply with HKCE economists. Common professional training is found to be associated with similar beliefs about the behavior of international capital markets, the use of controls, and the desirability of liberalization. The results also further bring to light the differences of view that exist among neoliberal economists over the importance of sequencing and the role of temporary controls.

Most respondents also appear to remain fairly committed to the beliefs they had developed by the time their training was complete. Beliefs on most issues remained "sticky," though not absolutely fixed, over time. Thus, to the extent that professional training leaves a firm ideational and normative imprint on a particular individual, these beliefs appear to be relatively stable over time. Indeed, there is a fairly high level of association between beliefs reportedly held upon completion of training and those currently held. Overall, these results provide highly suggestive evidence that professional training imparts a belief structure that continues to inform and shape the views of most individuals over time.

Some readers may object that the survey evidence mainly demonstrates that the "best" economists (i.e., those from leading universities) became and remain skeptical of capital controls. This sentiment contains an element of truth. Indeed, one of this book's core arguments is that because the Fund tends to recruit largely from a select few top-quality academic departments, and, more importantly, because there was shift in the content of professional norms within these departments, the IMF came to define capital freedom as desirable. But it is not entirely accurate to claim that graduates of top-quality economics departments are the "best."

Recall Joseph Stiglitz's telling criticism that the IMF staff "frequently consists of third-rate students from first-rate universities."[100] Most IMF staff economists do possess strong academic credentials, but it seems misguided to claim that these economists, or even those responding to this survey, necessarily advocate the "best" ideas. Graduates from top-quality economics departments do not have a monopoly on the "best" available theories and techniques for analyzing the world economy. Indeed, there are likely to be many high-quality economists who have received their training from departments other than those of leading universities who can offer alternative perspectives on the "best" policy response. In fact, in economics there is rarely one unambiguous "best" policy response.

The cycles, trends, and shifts in economic theory have demonstrated an interesting evolution since the late nineteenth century. To paraphrase Keynes, what was once defined as orthodoxy has often later become redefined as a heresy. Economists at different time periods attached varying degrees of legitimacy to capital controls, and in doing so helped define the range of policy options that could be entertained by those who professed to deploy the specialized knowledge of the profession. Similarities and differences among the various schools of thought and the training they instilled help to explain a great deal of the variance in subsequent beliefs about the norm of capital freedom and its interpretation and application.

Professionalization helped to instill cycles, trends, and shifts in economic theory to generations of graduate students, exposing them to various technical models and knowledge of how economies do operate, as well as related normative conceptualizations and judgments about how economies *should* operate. The survey evidence strongly suggests that

[100] Joseph Stiglitz, "What I Learned at the World Economic Crisis," *New Republic*, 17–24 April 2000, pp. 56–60.

there is a robust link between the content of an economist's professional training and the subsequent beliefs that economist develops about international capital markets, capital controls, and their liberalization. The fact that these beliefs generally endure over time suggests that professionalization and shifts in the content of this professionalization were of critical importance to the Fund's adoption, interpretation, and application of the norm of capital freedom.

CHAPTER FOUR

Capital Controlled

THE EARLY POSTWAR ERA

THE ARTICLES OF AGREEMENT provide many of the formal rules that guide the Fund's operations. Although other formal IMF rules operated differently in practice from the intent of their drafters, as Eichengreen observes, "Capital controls were the one element that functioned more or less as planned."[1] Most governments in the early postwar era employed a range of restrictions that limited capital mobility, with the widespread acceptance of Keynesian beliefs underpinning this norm. Both formal IMF rules and the informal staff approach defined controls as a legitimate policy practice.

This chapter begins by tracing the institutionalization of the norm of capital control into the IMF Articles. It then turns to analyzing two important bases of support for the maintenance of this norm during the early postwar era. One important base of support was the United States and the broader IMF membership, which generally supported restrictions on capital mobility. There was, however, one brief interval between 1945 and 1947 when U.S. officials promoted a return to neoclassical orthodoxy. Two significant events occurred during this interval: the failed attempt at sterling convertibility and an IMF board decision on the use of the organization's financial resources. The former dealt a fatal blow to the expectation that cooperative controls would be used to contain disequilibrating capital flows, while the latter ensured that the Fund's resources could not be used to support "leaky" controls. After this brief interval, U.S. officials became more accommodative, even encouraging, of the use of controls abroad. Perhaps the high point of this orientation was U.S. support for a 1956 board decision that reaffirmed the right of member states to control capital movements "for any reason."[2] This decision deepened formal institutionalization of the norm of capital control within the Fund. But member states' influence and formal rules are only part of the story.

---

[1] Eichengreen, *Globalizing Capital*, p. 94.
[2] Executive Board Decision 541-(56/39), 25 July 1956, reprinted in Horsefield, *International Monetary Fund, 1945–1965*, vol. 3, p. 246.

Missing is attention to a second important base of support: the IMF staff. The staff's autonomy, though limited in the early postwar years, increased significantly in the 1950s and 1960s. By investigating the informal staff approach, we gain valuable insight into how the staff, after acquiring greater autonomy, approached tasks. This chapter shows that the staff endorsed restricting capital movements in the early postwar era, even when such views contradicted the preferences of powerful principals, such as the United States and West Germany. Recruitment patterns were an important determinant of staff support, bringing in most of the initial staff from Bretton Woods delegations and later expanding the size of the staff in the 1950s with additional recruits from the economics profession at a time when Keynesianism generally prevailed. When these additional recruits came to draw on their Keynesian training to form judgments on policy, this helped buttress formal IMF rules that legitimated the use of controls.

Drafting the Articles of Agreement

In drafting the IMF Articles, the Bretton Woods delegations sought to create a system where capital control would be the norm. However, they were also well aware of the difficulties in controlling short-term flows. Therefore, two provisions were envisioned for the Articles that were intended to make controls more effective.

Even though Keynes and White recognized that there would be difficulties in distinguishing between current and capital account transactions, they nonetheless crafted a provision that would have permitted governments to introduce exchange controls to screen current account transactions for illegal capital flows. Another envisioned provision, put forth by Keynes, would have facilitated cooperation to increase the effectiveness of controls.[3] White went even further, proposing that such cooperation be made mandatory.[4]

In addition to such measures, the academic and policymaking communities also considered whether the IMF should use its resources to finance speculative capital flows. However, such a scheme was generally considered to be unworkable given the large amount of resources that would be

---

[3] Keynes, "Proposals for an International Currency (or Clearing) Union," p. 13; Keynes, "Proposal for an International Clearing Union," p. 31.

[4] White, "Preliminary Draft Proposal," pp. 44, 66; White, "Preliminary Draft Outline of a Proposal for an International Stabilization Fund of the United and Associated Nations," reprinted in Horsefield, *International Monetary Fund, 1945–1965*, vol. 3, p. 96. For White's endorsement of exchange controls, see White, "Preliminary Draft Proposal," p. 63.

needed. As the League report observed: "If, in addition to trade and normal transactions, such a fund had to cover all kinds of capital flight, it might have to be endowed with enormous resources. In fact, no fund of any practicable size might be sufficient to offset mass movements of nervous flight capital."[5] The League report also questioned whether governments—particularly the United States—would be willing to provide the resources necessary to offset capital flight. Although the idea was rejected at the time, it would be only a few years time before its merits were reconsidered.

Ultimately, many of the standards of behavior elaborated by Keynes, White, and their supporters were institutionalized in the IMF Articles. Article VI, Section 3 explicitly grants governments the right to use capital controls: "Members shall exercise such controls as are necessary to regulate international capital movements."[6] To ensure that governments are free to impose controls on their own accord, IMF jurisdiction over the capital account is limited to only a small subset of capital flows that are defined as current account payments and consist of "other current business, including services, and normal short-term banking and credit facilities" associated with trade as well as loan repayments and family remittances.[7] A weak form of cooperation is enshrined in Article VIII, Section 2b, which obliges the courts of member states to render unenforceable any exchange contract that runs contrary to the exchange control regulations of another member state that have been approved by the Fund.[8] With the exception of information that would disclose the affairs of individuals or companies, member states are also required to provide the Fund, on request, information on capital movements and holdings.[9]

However, there are several qualifiers in the Articles that weaken some of these pro-control standards of behavior. Some provisions, for instance, seem to remove the right of governments to institute exchange controls to screen current account transactions. For instance, Article VI, Section 3 also states: "But no member may exercise these controls in a manner which will restrict payments for current transactions or which will unduly delay transfer of funds in settlement of commitments." Article VIII, Section 2a similarly prohibits the implementation of "restrictions on the making of

[5] League of Nations, *International Currency Experience*, p. 188.

[6] Articles of Agreement of the International Monetary Fund (22 July 1944), reprinted in Horsefield, *International Monetary Fund, 1945–1965*, vol. 3, p. 194.

[7] Article XIX, Clause I (1–4) of the Articles of Agreement of the International Monetary Fund, p. 206.

[8] Joseph Gold, *International Capital Movements under the Law of the International Monetary Fund* (Washington, D.C.: IMF, 1977), p. 30.

[9] Article VIII, Section 5a of the Articles of Agreement of the International Monetary Fund, p. 196.

payments and transfers for current international transactions."[10] Although some U.S. officials at the time claimed these provisions removed the right of governments to implement exchange controls, this was not the intention of the drafters of the Articles.[11]

But Keynes and White were less successful in obliging member states to assist in the enforcement of each other's capital controls. Opposition to the mandatory cooperative control provisions emerged not only from the American banking community but also from U.S. officials inside the Federal Reserve and the State Department, among whose staff included prominent academic opponents of Keynes, such as Jacob Viner, as well as individuals from Wall Street, such as Dean Acheson, with whom White was forced to consult regarding his proposals. Faced with this opposition, Keynes and White modified their earlier proposals, suggesting that the Fund be granted the authority to *require* the imposition of controls if a member state requested the use of IMF resources to finance a deficit stemming from speculative capital flows. This provision sought to ensure that IMF resources were to be used solely to finance those deficits arising from current account payments or the movement of productive capital.[12] The provision would also put the onus on governments to employ controls to manage speculative flows rather than enabling them to forgo their use by depleting IMF resources.

Yet opposition prevented even this watered-down cooperative measure from being included in the Articles. Still, some of the spirit of Keynes and White's arguments remained. The Articles permit member states to cooperate in controlling capital movements, but they do not require them to do so.[13] Although the Fund cannot require member states to impose controls, Article VI, Section 1 empowers it to *request* they do so in the case of "large or sustained outflows."[14] A government refusing to cooperate with the request can be declared ineligible to use the Fund's resources. Although this provision stripped the Fund of some of its proposed supranational authority, it nevertheless seemingly created a strong incentive for governments to employ controls when faced with capital outflows.

Thus, despite some important qualifications, the overriding norm underpinning the IMF was one of capital control: governments were given the right to regulate capital movements and the Articles were designed to

---

[10] Articles of Agreement of the International Monetary Fund, p. 195.

[11] Helleiner, *Reemergence of Global Finance*, p. 46.

[12] See Keynes, "Proposals for an International Currency (or Clearing) Union," p. 23; and White, "Preliminary Draft Proposal," pp. 49–50; White, "Preliminary Draft Outline," pp. 89–90 for Keynes's and White's views, respectively.

[13] Article VIII, Section 2b of the Articles of Agreement of the International Monetary Fund, p. 195.

[14] Articles of Agreement of the International Monetary Fund, pp. 193–194.

encourage the use of controls. Keynes's statement to the British House of Lords best illustrates the formal institutionalization of this norm into the IMF Articles: "Not merely as a feature of the transition, but as a permanent arrangement, the plan accords to every member government the explicit right to control all capital movements. *What used to be a heresy is now endorsed as orthodox.*"[15]

U.S. POLICY: ACCOMMODATING AND UNDERMINING THE NORM OF CAPITAL CONTROL

Following the Bretton Woods meetings, White explained that, although other governments were free to employ capital controls, "the United States does not wish to have them."[16] Yet U.S. officials, because of Cold War strategic imperatives as well as broader sponsorship for ISI and financial interventionism, did not promote liberalization abroad in the early postwar era.[17] Instead, prior to the collapse of the Bretton Woods exchange rate system, U.S. officials generally accommodated their widespread use abroad. In some instances, U.S. officials even actively encouraged their use.

But there was one brief interval—between 1945 and 1947—when U.S. officials took a more critical approach. During this interval, Keynesian advocates lost favor in the new Truman administration, and members of the banking community emerged in prominent policymaking positions. The United States subsequently turned to promoting a speedy return to neoclassical orthodoxy. Two events stand out during this interval: the attempt at sterling convertibility and an IMF board decision concerning the use of Fund resources.

In the initial months following the war U.S. officials sought to use a loan to pressure the British government to establish current account convertibility; a policy based on the logic of the "key currency" plan.[18] A $3.75 billion loan was advanced to the British government on the condition that they would move to current account convertibility within a year. The move to convertibility proved a failure, lasting only a period of six weeks.

[15] Keynes, "Speech to the House of Lords," p. 17.

[16] As cited in Armand van Dormael, *Bretton Woods: Birth of a Monetary System* (London: Macmillan, 1978), p. 185.

[17] Helleiner, *Reemergence of Global Finance*, chaps. 3–5; Helleiner, *The Making of National Money: Territorial Currencies in Historical Perspective* (Ithaca, N.Y.: Cornell University Press, 2003), pp. 187–197.

[18] Richard Gardner, *Sterling-Dollar Diplomacy: Anglo-American Collaboration in the Reconstruction of Multilateral Trade* (Oxford: Clarendon Press, 1956).

In terms of the IMF approach, the most significant aspect of the failed move to sterling convertibility was the refusal of U.S. officials to sanction the use of cooperative controls. Following the war, Britain and Western Europe suffered from massive capital flight to the United States despite their system of unilateral controls. Subscribing to Keynesian standards of behavior, British and European officials turned to cooperative control measures as the appropriate response. Although the Fund's mandatory cooperate control powers had been significantly watered down, there remained an expectation, though it would prove to be false, that governments would offer their cooperation upon request. Even the U.S. Treasury's commentary on the IMF hinted as much, indicating that while "it is a matter for each country to decide whether . . . it wishes to establish or retain any administrative supervision over foreign exchange transactions . . . a country may find it helpful to cooperate with other member countries in controlling capital movements."[19] At one point in the later stages of the Bretton Woods negotiations U.S. officials even proposed a draft clause that would have required cooperation, though it did not resurface in later discussions.[20]

But the bankers who dominated U.S. policymaking during this brief interval rejected the option of cooperative controls because of concerns that they would prevent New York from becoming a major international financial center that could rival London.[21] U.S. officials also ruled out the use of exchange controls, the other solution Keynes and White had offered as means to strengthen unilateral controls, since they conflicted with the goals of creating a more liberal trading system and moving to convertibility. Instead, U.S. officials offered neoclassical prescriptions, arguing that governments could stem capital flight via deflationary measures. The U.S. refusal to implement cooperative controls demonstrated that such measures could be easily vetoed by a major power.[22] More significantly, the U.S. refusal completely undermined what remained of the expectation that governments would cooperate to assist in the enforcement of each other's controls.

At the same time the attempt at sterling convertibility was unfolding, U.S. officials moved to shape formal rules governing the use of IMF resources to finance deficits arising from capital outflows. The Articles had left considerable ambiguity about whether governments could use IMF resources for such a purpose. Article VI, Section 1 prevents the Fund from

---

[19] U.S. Government, "Questions and Answers on the International Monetary Fund," reprinted in Horsefield, *International Monetary Fund, 1945–1965*, vol. 3, p. 179.

[20] Helleiner, *Reemergence of Global Finance*, p. 47 n. 91.

[21] Helleiner, *Reemergence of Global Finance*, pp. 56, 59–60.

[22] Sterling asset holders inside and outside the overseas sterling area also refused to enforce cooperative arrangements.

financing capital outflows that are "large or sustained," but Article V, Section 3a states that a member state can draw on IMF resources if it "represents that it is presently needed."[23] Policymakers quickly recognized that this ambiguity could potentially enable a member state to use IMF resources to finance "large or sustained" capital outflows (or to acquire such resources unconditionally, another issue that caused bitter debate among the Fund membership in the early postwar era) so long as it could represent that such resources were presently needed.

This possibility, which, if it did occur, would likely require significant American resources, had triggered significant opposition among some U.S. legislators during the ratification debate over the Bretton Woods Agreement. These congressional opponents subsequently found strong support from U.S. Treasury officials who, as Joseph Gold explains, were concerned that "the resources of the Fund . . . might be squandered in financing capital flight from members that maintained overvalued currencies."[24] Neoclassical advocates within the Treasury insisted upon policy adjustment, rather than financing, as the appropriate response to capital flight.

The issue was a matter that required interpretation, and on this occasion it was U.S. power that would resolve the ambiguity. In approving the Bretton Woods Agreement Act in 1945, Congress instructed the U.S. IMF governor and executive director to secure an interpretation that would bar the use of the Fund's resources for purposes "beyond current monetary stabilization," including operations "to meet a large or sustained outflow of capital."[25] The matter was subsequently referred to the IMF board.

In September 1946, shortly after the collapse of the attempt at sterling convertibility, the board interpretation, at U.S. insistence, ruled that IMF resources could be drawn against only "to give temporary assistance in financing balance-of-payments deficits on current account for monetary stabilization operations."[26] Though this interpretation, as Gold observes, was "unduly restrictive," it was entirely consistent with the aims of U.S. officials to promote a speedy move to neoclassical orthodoxy.[27] By restricting governments from using IMF resources to finance capital outflows and refusing to implement cooperative controls, U.S. officials placed the burden on deficit countries to adjust.

[23] IMF Articles of Agreement, p. 191.

[24] Gold, *International Capital Movements*, pp. 23–24.

[25] Section 13a of the U.S. Bretton Woods Agreement Act, reprinted in Horsefield, *International Monetary Fund, 1945–1965*, vol. 2, p. 385.

[26] IMF Executive Board Decision 71-2, (26 September 1946), reprinted in Horsefield, *International Monetary Fund, 1945–1965*, vol. 3, p. 245.

[27] Gold, *International Capital Movements*, p. 24.

However, most deficit countries during this period were unwilling to adjust. The deepening of the European balance-of-payments crisis and the onset of the Cold War led to the end of the brief neoclassical interval and fostered a change of views among U.S. officials about the desirability of financing capital flight. Financing tied to policy conditions subsequently presented itself as the ideal solution, as it enabled U.S. officials to extract some degree of policy adjustment in exchange for financial resources, thus speaking to concerns about the provision of unconditional financing, while at the same time avoiding the use of cooperative and exchange controls, thus promoting the emergence of New York as a financial center and the move to current account convertibility.[28] Reversing their earlier position, U.S. officials came to accommodate financing as a support mechanism for "leaky" unilateral controls.

This financing took the form of the Marshall Plan. Marshall Plan aid along with a series of currency devaluations in 1949 and establishment of the European Payments Union in 1950 helped pave the way for achievement of current account convertibility in Western Europe in 1958. The move to current account convertibility would subsequently have important implications for the evolution of the IMF's approach.

REAFFIRMING THE LEGITIMACY OF CAPITAL CONTROLS

Prior to the achievement of current account convertibility in Western Europe, some IMF board directors questioned whether the Articles permitted the use of exchange controls and multiple currency practices if such measures were deemed necessary to regulate international capital movements. Article VI, Section 3 and Article VIII, Section 2a contain language that seemingly suggests there are limits to the extent governments can use exchange controls to regulate capital flows. Although the drafters at Bretton Woods had claimed that this was not their intention, the issue resurfaced in the 1950s. New concerns also surfaced that Article VIII, Section 3—which states: "No member shall engage in . . . any discriminatory currency arrangements or multiple currency practices except as authorized under this Agreement or approved by the Fund"[29]—prohibited the use of multiple exchange rates to regulate capital flows. These were matters that demanded interpretation. The outcome would set the formal boundaries of legitimate behavior for Fund members.

---

[28] Block, *Origins of International Economic Disorder*, p. 87; Helleiner, *Reemergence of Global Finance*, pp. 62–67.

[29] IMF Articles of Agreement, p. 195.

The matter was initially referred to the IMF staff for analysis. In its analysis the Legal Department concluded that none of the provisions of the Articles prevented governments from using exchange controls so long as they did not interfere with current account transactions. But the Legal Department did conclude that the Articles prevented the use of multiple exchange rates to regulate capital movements.[30]

The Exchange Restrictions Department (ER) staff generally concurred with this analysis, and also raised additional concerns about "defining in advance which restrictions might be regarded as being for capital purposes or otherwise," which they believed would give rise "to considerable if not insuperable difficulties."[31] Keynes and White had been aware of the difficulty in distinguishing between current and capital account transactions, and their opponents had sought to use this issue to prohibit the use of exchange controls to screen for illegal capital flows.[32] But in contrast to those who preferred to rule out exchange controls *a priori*, the staff took a more flexible approach that reflected their general Keynesian outlook.

Recognizing that there was "no *a priori* way of stating what capital controls applied in conjunction with payments restrictions would or would not qualify under Article VI, Section 3," the ER staff recommended "an empirical approach . . . i.e., that of examining each country's restrictions on a case by case basis."[33] When the issue came to the board for discussion, Irving Friedman, then ER director, went further, commenting that the staff were prepared to treat cases where governments used exchange controls to regulate capital movements "sympathetically," even suggesting that they would sanction the use of exchange controls when their impact on current account transactions was "small."[34] The informal approach outlined by Friedman thus accommodated exchange controls as within the boundaries of legitimate policy practice.

The Indian board director sought to extend further the boundaries proposed by Friedman, arguing that the staff approach needed to be generous enough to accommodate "situations in which effective control of capital transfers might not be possible without some check on current payments." However, the U.S. and West German directors—both representing governments who took a more liberal approach to capital

---

[30] "Legal Aspects of Regulations of International Capital Movements," SM/55/74, 16 November 1955 (IMF Archives).

[31] Article VI, CF/S331/CapitalTransfers1956–1959, 11 August 1955 (IMF Archives).

[32] Helleiner, *Reemergence of Global Finance*, p. 41.

[33] Controls on Capital Transfers, SM/56/15, 7 February 1956 (IMF Archives), p. 9 ("no a priori way . . . "); Article VI, p. 3 ("an empirical approach . . . ").

[34] Executive Board Meeting 56/24, 6 April 1956 (IMF Archives), p. 4.

account regulation—blocked this proposal. U.S. director Frank Southard and West German director Otmar Emminger insisted the "rule of reason" the ER staff suggested would be sufficient to accommodate the concerns of the Indian director.[35]

On the issue of multiple exchange rates, the board followed the lead of Belgian director Andre van Campenhout. As the IMF general counsel during its first seven years in operation, Van Campenhout had been, according to Susan Strange, "broadly sympathetic to . . . a conservative and restrictionist view of the functions of the Fund."[36] Now as the Belgian director, Campenhout represented a government that employed a multiple exchange rate regime to regulate capital movements. Van Campenhout, in his reading of the Articles, rejected the expansive interpretation of the Legal Department, claiming that the Fund "had no jurisdiction with respect to discriminatory currency arrangements designed to regulate international capital flows, except insofar as they had a restrictive effect on current payments."[37]

The board eventually reached a general consensus that governments had the right to control capital movements in any way that would not restrict current payments, while recognizing that some exchange controls were also within the formal boundaries of legitimate policy practice. Yet there were still concerns that multiple exchange rates might "embrace some current transactions and that in these cases at least members must seek prior approval of the Fund."[38] The board therefore decided to keep this aspect of the issue under consideration.[39] The final July 1956 decision ultimately reaffirmed the authority of governments to use capital controls and placed them firmly within the formal boundaries of legitimate policy practice: "Members are free to adopt a policy of regulating capital movements for any reason . . . [and] they may, for that purpose, exercise such controls as are necessary . . . without approval of the Fund."[40]

---

[35] Executive Board Meeting 56/24, pp. 4–5. West Germany would eliminate all its controls on capital outflows in 1957, leaving in place only some controls on inflows to dampen exchange rate and inflationary pressures.

[36] Strange, "IMF: Monetary Managers," p. 288.

[37] Executive Board Meeting 56/24, p. 2. See also J. Keith Horsefield and Gertrud Lovasy, "Evolution of the Fund's Policy on Drawings," in Horsefield, *International Monetary Fund, 1945–1965*, vol. 2, pp. 381–427 at pp. 403–404.

[38] Executive Board Meeting 56/24, p. 3.

[39] Although over the years the board has periodically reviewed the right of member states to use multiple currency practices to regulate international capital movements, this right has never been overturned.

[40] Executive Board Decision 541-(56/39), 25 July 1956, reprinted in Horsefield, *International Monetary Fund, 1945–1965*, vol. 3, p. 246.

SUPPORT FOR CAPITAL CONTROLS FROM WITHIN THE IMF

Support for capital controls also came from within the IMF, with the staff approach clearly in line with Keynesian standards of behavior. Although the configuration of member state preferences favored the norm of capital control, these preferences were not the primary determinant of the staff's approach. Instead, the IMF's initial recruitment patterns were of greater significance. These recruitment patterns established a pathway through which the norm of capital control could be transmitted to the IMF.

Most of the initial IMF staff members were recruited from the Bretton Woods delegations and thus shared and helped develop the norm of capital control.[41] According to one IMF official historian, the national delegations had drafted the IMF Articles "against the background of the disturbing capital movements that had taken place during the 1930s," and so as members of the IMF staff they "thought that controls over capital movements might be necessary and beneficial."[42] Additional recruitment in the 1950s—when Keynesianism still generally prevailed within the economics profession—reinforced the beliefs of the staff members who had been recruited from the national delegations. The strength of Keynesianism within the economics profession ensured that it would form, as IMF official historian James Boughton observes, "the bedrock of thinking at the IMF" for much of the early postwar era.[43] This bedrock would remain remarkably solid for decades, with the personnel configuration of the Fund demonstrating significant continuity over the next thirty years. Many of the staff recruited from the Bretton Woods delegations, as well as those who joined the Fund in the 1950s, would remain members of the staff until they retired in the 1980s.

Like Keynes and White, the Fund's staff in the 1940s and 1950s generally looked favorably upon long-term "productive" capital movements as well as those flows that facilitated balance-of-payments equilibrium. In line with these beliefs, a 1953 staff paper concluded: "The growth of large and steady movements of private long-term capital would facilitate the undertaking of some of the adjustments which several countries must make to achieve better international balance. It would also permit more

[41] De Vries, "The International Monetary Fund," p. 54.

[42] Margaret Garritsen de Vries, "Exchange Restrictions: The Setting," in Horsefield, *International Monetary Fund, 1945–1965*, vol. 2, pp. 217–229 at p. 224.

[43] James Boughton, "The IMF and the Force of History: Ten Events and Ten Ideas That Have Shaped the Institution," IMF Working Paper WP/04/75 (Washington, D.C.: IMF, 2004), p. 13.

comprehensive programs of economic development."[44] Yet, also in line with their Keynesian beliefs, staff reports generally identified short-term flows as "undesirable."[45]

The staff were also generally skeptical of the neoclassical case for capital freedom, with one staff report observing, "The theory of capital movements implicit in the neoclassical theory of international trade is almost wholly inadequate in giving guidance to policy concerning the control of capital movements."[46] Moreover, echoing some of the arguments of Keynes and White, the staff generally saw capital controls as legitimate instruments for stimulating employment, protecting domestic capital markets, and managing balance-of-payments pressures. In situations where governments imposed or intensified controls for such purposes one staff report noted, "No disagreement on this subject is likely to arise between the Fund and member states."[47] Indeed, in instances where governments faced capital inflow or outflow surges, such as Canada in 1950 and Europe in 1949, respectively, the staff tended to recommend some form of controls.[48]

In the 1950s the Fund's staff became increasingly concerned about heightened capital mobility. The gradual liberalization of restrictions on current account transactions in Western Europe greatly expanded opportunities for disguised capital flows, enabling investors to take advantage of current account convertibility to evade capital controls. A number of European governments also gradually dismantled their capital controls and some—such as West Germany, Switzerland, and Belgium—moved toward nearly complete capital freedom, thus further heightening capital mobility. In addition, U.S. and British officials gave their tacit support to the emergence of the Eurocurrency markets, with the result being, as Beth Simmons observes, "a growing pool of largely unregulated capital" that further heightened capital mobility.[49]

---

[44] "The Interest and Activity of the International Monetary Fund as Regards the International Flow of Private Capital," CF/S331/CapitalTransfers1946–1955, 16 November 1953 (IMF Archives), p. 3.

[45] "Capital Controls," CF/S331/CapitalTransfers1946–1955, 1955 (IMF Archives), p. 30.

[46] Memorandum of the Capital Movements Committee, CF/S331/CapitalTransfers 1960–1970, 12 April 1960 (IMF Archives), p. 2

[47] "Identification of Capital Control Measures," CF/S331/CapitalTransfers1956–1959, 18 January 1956 (IMF Archives), p. 6.

[48] Eric Helleiner, "Ambiguous Aspects of Bretton Woods: Canadian Exchange-Rate Policy in the Marshall System, 1950–1962," in *Orderly Change: International Monetary Relations since Bretton Woods*, ed. David M. Andrews (Ithaca, N.Y.: Cornell University Press, 2008), pp. 78–99; Horsefield, *International Monetary Fund, 1945–1965*, vol. 1, p. 210.

[49] Simmons, "The Internationalization of Capital," in *Continuity and Change in Contemporary Capitalism*, ed. Herbert Kitschelt, Peter Lange, Gary Marks, and John D. Stephens (Cambridge: Cambridge University Press, 1999), pp. 36–69 at p. 40.

In the context of these developments, the staff became increasingly worried that governments would be unable to regulate capital movements effectively, and that heightened capital mobility would imperil the exchange rate system.[50] These issues, of course, had been of paramount concern to Keynes, White, and their contemporaries. However, whereas Keynes and White had boldly argued for cooperative control measures to help limit capital mobility, this option was now no longer on the table.

The staff therefore turned to recommending the introduction or intensification of unilateral controls, though all the while remaining aware that such measures could at times be counterproductive. A 1950 staff report, for instance, noted: "Exchange restrictions, which have in many cases been devised to prevent the escape of capital have also on occasions strengthened tendencies toward escape."[51] Still, the staff interpreted heightened capital mobility as something requiring greater regulation to insulate governments, not as something that could impose a valuable discipline and prompt governments to adjust policies.

GRADUALLY REDEFINING THE DESIRABILITY OF CAPITAL FREEDOM

By the end of the 1950s, there had been a subtle shift in the attitudes that many West European governments took toward capital freedom. The 1957 Treaty of Rome—which established the European Economic Community (EEC)—directed members to free capital "to the extent necessary to ensure the proper functioning of the Common Market." Later, in 1959, a Code of Liberalization of Capital Movements was created for the Organization for European Economic Cooperation, with a similar code developed for its successor the OECD in 1961. The Code, like the Treaty of Rome, obliged member states to maintain their existing degree of freedom for capital movements and current account invisibles and to pursue further liberalization in both areas.

But most West European governments remained skeptical of the benefits of liberalizing capital—particularly short-term speculative flows— and thus what little progress that was made tended to be in freeing outward foreign direct investment. By the early 1990s, commitments to liberalize for EU and OECD countries would be expanded to encompass a

[50] "Capital Controls," p. 23; "Paper on Capital Controls and Movements in Thirteen Selected Countries," CF/S331/CapitalTransfers1956–1959, 6 June 1956 (IMF Archives), p. 1; Memorandum to the Capital Movements Committee, CF/S331/CapitalTransfers 1960–1970, 12 April 1960 (IMF Archives).

[51] IMF, *Report on Exchange Restrictions, 1950* (Washington, D.C.: IMF, 1950), p. 28.

broader array of capital flows, including short-term speculative flows.[52] But in the early 1960s most members of these organizations did not countenance efforts to greatly increase capital freedom. Nonetheless, even these modest steps toward liberalization were significant in an era when most governments continued to reject the desirability of capital freedom even in principle.

These modest efforts to encourage greater capital freedom were a clear signal that some governments were gradually moving away from the Keynesian beliefs that had prevailed at Bretton Woods. As Eva Thiel observes, "Although the mood in the early 1960s was not in favor of the immediate and total abolition of controls of all forms of capital flows, there was a consensus that joint work towards reaping the economic benefits of freer capital movements should be pursued."[53] Alexandre Lamfalussy similarly notes: "The [OECD] Code amounted to a declaration of principle by developed countries of the world in favor of a wide measure of freedom for capital movements."[54]

These developments would have an important constitutive effect.[55] By institutionalizing the idea that capital freedom was beneficial and should be encouraged, EEC and OECD members began to gradually redefine the legitimate policy practices for their members. By the mid-1990s, the broadened obligations to liberalize, along with the expanded membership of these organizations, helped create a core constituency for capital freedom that consisted of many of the most powerful principals of the IMF. However, it should be underscored that in the early 1960s there was only a gradual and subtle shift in attitudes.

The IMF staff, for their part, took notice of the developments in the EEC and OECD. Some staff members expressed concerns about the jurisdictional implications of the expanded authority of the EEC and OECD over international capital movements. Presaging arguments in the 1990s that there was a "hole" in the international financial architecture with respect to jurisdiction over capital movements, the Fund staff noted, "At present the question of the liberalization of capital transactions on a worldwide basis lies in a no man's land in that it is not covered by

[52] For a detailed examination of the evolution of OECD and EU formal rules, see Abdelal, *Capital Rules.*

[53] Eva Thiel, "Recent Codes-Based Liberalization in the OECD," in *Capital Liberalization in Transition Countries: Lessons from the Past and for the Future,* ed. Age F. P. Bakker and Bryan Chapple (Cheltenham, UK: Edward Elgar, 2003), pp. 85–104 at p. 85.

[54] Alexandre Lamfalussy, "Changing Attitudes toward International Capital Movements," in *Changing Perceptions of Economic Policy: Essays in Honour of the Seventieth Birthday of Sir Alec Cairncross,* ed. Frances Cairncross (London: Methuen, 1981), pp. 194–231 at p. 197.

[55] Abdelal, *Capital Rules.*

any international organization."[56] Yet by and large the issue of capital account liberalization was a field onto which the Fund staff ventured very little.[57] Indeed, one 1960 internal staff memorandum notes "the continued silence of the Fund on the subject of capital transactions" gives "the present impression that it will not take an active role in the matter of freeing capital movements."[58]

The events examined in this chapter reveal both the utility and the limitations of focusing on external dimensions of normative change within IOs. U.S. accommodation of controls, opposition to cooperative controls, and provision of Marshall Plan aid demonstrate the importance of U.S. power in shaping formal IMF rules and the standards of behavior that the staff can support. For instance, even though some staff members supported cooperative control measures, they would have it found it difficult to argue for such measures once U.S. officials had made their opposition known. This chapter also offered evidence of how the U.S. Congress is capable of bringing significant pressure to bear on the Fund. Lastly, a subtle shift in the attitudes that some leading member states took toward capital freedom directs our attention to preference heterogeneity among IMF principals.

But these factors alone do not tell a complete story; we also must be attentive to the informal staff approach and internal organizational processes. For instance, state power alone did not resolve the ambiguity surrounding the use of exchange controls to regulate capital movements. Rather the board delegated to the staff the task of developing their own "rule of reason." Staff members, in line with their beliefs at the time, staked out a flexible informal approach that signaled a willingness to treat exchange controls sympathetically—a policy position that ran contrary to U.S. and West German preferences.

It is perhaps tempting to read the staff position as a reflection of a compromise struck between member states opposed to exchange controls, such as the United States and West Germany, on one hand, and member states more sympathetic toward them, on the other. Although there is no direct evidence to support this conjecture, such an informal compromise may have been struck. Nonetheless, because compromises struck among governments with heterogeneous preferences tend to be ambigu-

---

[56] Memorandum to the Capital Movements Committee; "Current Progress in Europe in the Freeing of Capital Movements," CF/S331/CapitalTransfers1960–1970, 27 June 1960 (IMF Archives), p. 4.

[57] Author's interview with Jacques Polak, Washington, D.C., 16 May 2005.

[58] Memorandum on Progress in the Further Liberalization of Capital Movements by the OEEC, CF/S331/CapitalTransfers1960–1970, 2 February 1960 (IMF Archives), p. 3.

ous, this line of argument again directs us back to how the IMF staff interpreted and resolved this ambiguity, which draws our attention back to the staff's beliefs.

The emergence of new attitudes supportive of greater capital freedom, and the resulting preference heterogeneity among the IMF membership, similarly directs our attention to the informal staff approach and internal organizational processes. Preference heterogeneity among IMF principals may help us understand some reasons for greater staff autonomy, but it does not tell us much about what the staff can be expected to do with this autonomy. We must therefore turn again to the staff's beliefs, which at the time were largely shaped by recruitment patterns.

These beliefs led the staff to stake out a position that, while consistent with the preferences of those members supportive of capital controls, did not stem directly from them. Moreover, contrary to the preferences of those members in favor of greater capital freedom, such as the United States and West Germany, the staff sought to develop ways to better regulate capital rather than free it, thus generating "silence" from the Fund on the subject of liberalization. These developments go against the expectations of those scholars who focus on external factors alone to explain IO behavior, particularly since the IMF is conventionally depicted as the handmaiden of the United States in the early postwar era. The staff, while enjoying less freedom of action in the early postwar era than in later periods, still managed to exert an independent, though modest, impact on policy.

CHAPTER FIVE

The Limits and Hollowness of Keynesianism in the 1960s

KEYNESIANISM generally prevailed during the first fifteen years of the Bretton Woods system, with capital controls situated firmly within the boundaries of legitimate policy practice. But the 1960s were a decade of significant transition. The academic and policymaking communities discarded Keynesianism to varying degrees, replacing it with new beliefs more closely in line with the neoclassical synthesis and monetarism. Although monetarism would steadily gain ground in the academic and policymaking communities, in this decade the neoclassical synthesis had a far greater impact. Capital controls remained within the boundaries of legitimate policy practice, but the beliefs underpinning their legitimacy were notably different. Speculation became seen more and more as a "normal," rather than an "abnormal," part of the international financial system. Moreover, controls were increasingly defined as being at best a temporary response to the limited difficulties disruptive capital flows posed rather than an essential and permanent solution to more pervasive problems.

The United States and West Germany were important advocates of these beliefs. Their support for two new initiatives from IMF managing director Per Jacobsson led to changes to formal IMF rules that would redefine speculation as "normal" and authorize the Fund to finance disruptive capital flows. Advocates of authorizing the Fund to finance such flows saw it as a way to promote greater capital freedom because it would enable governments to avoid the use of controls without abandoning their policy goals. U.S. officials thus began to back away from their early postwar accommodation of controls and came to support official financing not as a means to buttress "leaky" controls but rather as a means to encourage liberalization. Although these formal rule changes aligned with U.S. interests, they were not imposed on the Fund; instead their origins lie in the entrepreneurial efforts of Jacobsson, who had long been committed to neoclassical orthodoxy.

But the informal staff approach did not align entirely with Jacobsson's views or the formal rule changes. In spite of the emergence of the neoclassical synthesis and monetarism, the staff generally retained a Keynesian understanding of market behavior. Yet in contrast to Keynesian standards of behavior, the staff approach evidenced greater support for adjusting policies in response to disruptive capital flows as well as greater appreciation of the benefits of capital freedom. Adaptation, and the degree to which these adaptations fit with existing organizational principles and processes, played a critical role in fostering these changes to the staff's approach.

MANAGING HEIGHTENED CAPITAL MOBILITY

In the 1960s policymakers faced the challenge of managing heightened capital mobility. Although the challenge had surfaced in the past, many of the beliefs that informed policymaking were now rather different. In the early postwar era, most governments, in line with Keynesian standards of behavior, relied on controls to deal with disruptive capital flows. In the 1960s, many developed countries, such as France, still subscribed to these standards of behavior and used controls to support monetary policy auton-omy, exchange rate commitments, and financial interventionism.[1] Most developing countries also continued to employ controls to support ISI, export-led growth, and financial interventionism.[2] Thus, most of the IMF's membership supported the norm of capital control.

But, as detailed in chapter 4, not all governments remained wedded to this norm. Some governments, most notably the United States and West Germany, had begun to turn a more critical eye toward this norm, viewing greater, though not necessarily complete, capital freedom, as desirable and controls as nonessential. As one official IMF historian remarked: "A view that had been dominant before 1930 began to gain ground, namely, that freedom of capital movements was highly desirable in itself."[3] The debate over what to do about heightened capital mobility thus predictably pitted those who favored a more restrictive system versus those who sought to construct a more liberal one.

This debate took place within the context of growing concerns about the adequacy of international liquidity and the deteriorating U.S. balance-of-payments position. Views on how to deal with these concerns therefore played an important part in informing attitudes toward measures to man-age capital mobility. In response to the challenge of heightened capital mobility, policymakers developed a series of ad hoc measures that were designed to limit or offset the disruptive effects of short-term flows. These measures, reflecting the rise of the neoclassical synthesis in U.S. poli-cymaking circles, as well as more supportive attitudes toward capital free-

[1] Helleiner, *Reemergence of Global Finance*, pp. 91–93.
[2] Margaret Garritsen de Vries, "A Convertible Currency World," in Horsefield, *International Monetary Fund, 1945–1965*, vol. 2, pp. 280–297 at pp. 293–295.
[3] De Vries, "A Convertible Currency World," p. 292.

dom in other countries, represented speculative flows as a normal, if perhaps excessive, feature of a monetary system of convertible currencies and one that should be managed but not eliminated.

In 1959, IMF quotas were increased as a first step to address concerns about international liquidity. However, following speculative pressure in 1960 and 1961 on the dollar and sterling, respectively, policymakers came to the realization that this quota increase would be insufficient to address a situation when both the United States and Britain borrowed from the Fund simultaneously. A series of proposals were subsequently drafted that would enable the Fund to borrow from its member states in order to augment its resources. These proposals led to the creation of the General Arrangements to Borrow (GAB) in 1962 (discussed below).

New forms of cooperation also emerged among the monetary authorities and central banks of developed countries that sought to limit the disruptive impact of short-term flows. The Gold Pool was constructed to foster management of the price of gold, and a network of "swap" arrangements was designed to help provide short-term financial assistance to governments that saw the value of their currency come under pressure. These swap networks committed central banks to holding one another's currencies for longer periods, rather than immediately converting them into gold or dollars, and to providing short-term lending of needed currencies.

The Neoclassical Synthesist Shift in U.S. Policy

Faced with a persistent balance-of-payments deficit, caused in large part by a growing volume of capital outflows, U.S. officials devised a series of mechanisms for influencing the direction of these flows. During the early 1960s prominent advocates of the neoclassical synthesis came to exercise a significant influence on policymaking in the Kennedy and Johnson administrations. Kennedy appointed a number of prominent neoclassical synthesists, such as Walter Heller, Robert Solow, and James Tobin, to his Council of Economic Advisers (CEA). Paul Samuelson had served as an advisor to Senator, candidate, and President-elect Kennedy and continued to serve as an informal consultant to the administration.

The CEA shared its influence on policymaking with Robert Roosa, a senior Treasury official, and McChesney Martin, chair of the Federal Reserve. Together, these officials, though sharing a belief in the desirability and efficacy of government intervention, viewed speculative flows as a natural, though sometimes excessive, part of a market economy and one that needed to be managed, but not eliminated, in order to ensure it did not undermine the pursuit of other objectives.

One clear indication of the influence of these beliefs on U.S. policy was the introduction in 1963 of the interest equalization tax (IET), a tax on capital outflows aimed at the purchase of and income drawn on foreign securities by U.S. investors.[4] In line with neoclassical synthesist standards of behavior, the IET was designed to be a temporary market-oriented intervention that would preserve domestic growth objectives while other policies were adjusted to respond to international pressures.

Roosa noted that U.S. officials opted for market-based measures rather than administrative controls because of fears that the latter would "literally congeal the bloodstream of American capitalism."[5] The IET was to be a "transitional measure," Roosa explained, designed to militate against capital outflows "until the other policies already under way succeed in encouraging more balanced flows of capital."[6]

The IET signaled that U.S. accommodation for Keynesian standards of behavior had diminished. To be sure, U.S. officials were concerned about disruptive capital flows. Yet by the 1960s they were more supportive of greater capital freedom than their predecessors at Bretton Woods.

The neoclassical synthesis also informed U.S. support for a series of measures that would facilitate greater capital freedom. As Roosa claimed, the long-term goal of the U.S. government "was to widen the areas of freedom for the movement of capital in response to the competitive forces of the market place."[7] However, this long-term goal did not induce U.S. officials to oppose the use of controls abroad; they instead turned to developing and supporting measures, such as swap networks, that would lessen the need for controls and thus foster greater capital freedom.

Financing and Redefining Speculative Capital Flows

In terms of formal IMF rules, the most significant development during this period was a reinterpretation of the 1946 board decision governing use of Fund resources to finance capital outflows. Recall that U.S. officials had insisted on the 1946 decision to encourage governments to adjust policies in response to capital flight. IMF resources were to be limited to financing only those deficits arising from current account imbalances.[8]

The leading figure in initiating the reinterpretation of these formal rules was IMF managing director Per Jacobsson. Although U.S. officials had

---

[4] Best, *The Limits of Transparency.*

[5] As cited in Helleiner, *Reemergence of Global Finance*, p. 86.

[6] Robert Roosa, *The Dollar and World Liquidity* (New York: Random House, 1967), p. 141. See also p. 52.

[7] Roosa, *Dollar and World Liquidity*, p. 138.

[8] In fact, on at least six separate occasions the board had taken capital account deficits into consideration when making financing available; see Horsefield and Lovasy, "Evolution of the Fund's Policy on Drawings," pp. 412–414. However, Joseph Gold, former IMF general counsel, contends that all of these lending decisions were in accordance with Article 6–1a; see Horsefield, *International Monetary Fund, 1945–1965*, vol. 1, p. 506.

been "instrumental" in the appointment of Jacobsson as managing director in 1956, and would sanction the reinterpretation, they did not devise this policy initiative, nor did they push it on Jacobsson.[9] The evidence instead suggests that Jacobsson acted independently as an entrepreneur for greater capital freedom. Part of the reason for initiative may have been due to simple bureaucratic motives, and it is easy to see how the new mandate and financial resources provided by the board reinterpretation (as well as the GAB) would strengthen the organization's role.

But a far more significant determinant of Jacobsson's actions was the way his own deep commitment to neoclassical orthodoxy served to articulate these bureaucratic motives.[10] As a member of the League of Nations secretariat in the 1920s, Jacobsson had helped to craft reports that recommended a return to capital freedom after World War I. This professional experience left a lasting impression on Jacobsson's beliefs about economics. As his biographer notes: "For the rest of his life he remained convinced that there was a moral quality in economics, a right and a wrong. . . . Once convinced, he mobilized all his energy and ingenuity to ensure that the 'right' policy was applied."[11] From 1931 to 1956 Jacobsson mobilized all his energy and ingenuity as economic advisor and head of the Monetary and Economic Department of the Bank for International Settlements (BIS) to advocate policies consistent with neoclassical orthodoxy. During this period he worked diligently to lobby U.S. and European officials on the need for orthodox policies and a return to full convertibility.[12]

Although Jacobsson recognized the dangers of speculative short-term flows, he did not subscribe to the belief that speculation constituted an abnormal or undesirable practice. Rather, as IMF managing director he argued that they should be regarded as a "normal element in the convertible system." In examining strategies to deal with such flows, Jacobsson consistently argued for relying on financing rather than controls.[13]

---

[9] On the "instrumental" input of U.S. officials, see Miles Kahler, *Leadership Selection in the Major Multilaterals* (Washington, D.C.: Institute for International Economics, 2001), p. 25. See also David Peretz, "The Process for Selecting and Appointing the Managing Director and First Deputy Managing Director of the IMF," Independent Evaluation Office of the International Monetary Fund Background Paper BP/07/01 (Washington, D.C.: IEO, 2007), p. 3.

[10] On Jacobsson's commitment, see Erin Jacobsson, *A Life for Sound Money: Per Jacobsson* (Oxford: Clarendon Press, 1979), pp. 41, 158, 181, 197, 201, 209–210, 224, 228–229, 400–413.

[11] Jacobsson, *Life for Sound Money*, p. 42.

[12] Helleiner, *Reemergence of Global Finance*, pp. 66–67; Jacobsson, *Life for Sound Money*, pp. 195, 214–215, 246–258.

[13] Per Jacobsson, "Current Economic Problems [12 June 1961]," reprinted in *Selected Speeches of Per Jacobsson* (Washington, D.C.: IMF, 1964), pp. 233, 260, 261; Jacobsson, "Monetary Relations between Europe and the United States [24 May 1962]," reprinted in *Selected Speeches*, pp. 174, 198.

Because financing would weaken the need for controls and facilitate greater capital freedom, Jacobsson proposed that the Fund be permitted to finance capital outflows. Jacobsson rejected the argument made earlier by Nurske and the League economists that IMF resources would be insufficient to offset speculative flows. "Even speculators have not got unlimited funds at their disposal," Jacobsson argued, and "it may be that the very knowledge that these new resources can now be mobilized to defend currencies will have a calming effect on the markets."[14]

It is perhaps tempting to interpret Jacobsson's initiative as a case of "screening and selection" by those IMF principals in favor of greater capital freedom. Given Jacobsson's intellectual history, one could conjecture these principals supported his candidacy because they expected him to later propose initiatives that would facilitate greater capital freedom. However, it is important to recall that, because of the long-standing convention that a European holds the IMF managing directorship, Jacobsson's candidacy also would have had to receive support from governments, such as France, that did not subscribe to his views on capital controls. Before supporting Jacobsson's candidacy these governments presumably would have sought some reassurance that Jacobsson would not seek to impose such views on the IMF membership. Moreover, when Jacobsson was appointed in 1956, U.S. officials were still accommodative, even encouraging, of the use of controls, as evidenced by the board decision that gave member states the right to use controls "for any reason." All of this tends to cast doubt on the conjecture that certain member states would have actively sought a candidate based on his views about capital freedom.

Unfortunately, the details surrounding Jacobsson's appointment are not entirely clear. The IMF board does not discuss or compare candidates in formal sessions; instead, an "informal hit-and-miss" procedure is used whereby private discussion takes place until a single candidate emerges with sufficient support.[15] While it is unclear the extent to which governments in favor of capital freedom actively promoted a particular candidate, what does emerge from firsthand accounts of the process is that U.S. officials supported Jacobsson's candidacy because they viewed him as an effective organizational head.

Still, though it would require U.S. support, Jacobsson's proposal was not devised or initiated by U.S. officials. The initiative, in fact, came from

---

[14] Jacobsson, "The Fund in 1961/1962 [6 April 1962]," reprinted in *Selected Speeches*, p. 261.

[15] Kahler, "United States and International Monetary Fund," p. 26; Southard, *Evolution of International Monetary Fund*, pp. 7–8. More recently, the selection of the IMF managing director has become more transparent, but there is still little formal record on which to assess member states' decisions.

Jacobsson. In February 1961, Jacobsson first unveiled his proposal in what one source describes as an "unexpected statement" to the board on future activities of the Fund.[16] The statement appears to have caught the Fund's principals off guard; indeed, in the initial discussion of the proposal the U.S. director noted that it "came as a complete surprise on the U.S. side."[17]

The board subsequently discussed the proposal in two informal sessions, where directors agreed that the proposal warranted further discussion, with several directors offering their support. However, French director Jean de Largentaye and Canadian director Louis Rasminsky opposed the initiative.[18] Rasminsky presciently warned that using IMF resources in the manner Jacobsson proposed would permit greater capital freedom, which in turn would ultimately threaten the exchange rate system.[19] But it was the French government, supported at times by the Dutch and the Belgians, that offered the staunchest opposition to the proposal, as well as the initiative to develop the GAB, arguing that financing, and the borrowing it would require, would provide a substitute for the necessary policy adjustments that should be undertaken by deficit countries.[20] Since most of the financing and borrowing would likely be used to defend the dollar and sterling, it seemed to de Largentaye that the proposal was "a trick of the Anglo-Saxon nations."[21]

The proposal was subsequently referred to the Legal Department, which distributed its memorandum on the subject in May 1961.[22] In the view of the Legal Department the 1946 decision had been incomplete because it ignored provisions in the Articles that permitted the use of IMF resources to finance certain types of capital flows. From this analysis the Legal Department concluded that IMF resources could be used for three purposes: (1) financing current account deficits; (2) financing capital outflows that were not large or sustained; and (3) financing payments deficits caused by those capital flows specified in Article VI, Section 1b(i), which permitted the use of IMF resources for "capital transactions of reasonable amount required for the expansion of exports or in the ordinary course of trade,

[16] Jacobsson, *Life for Sound Money*, p. 359. See Minutes of the Executive Board Meeting EBM 61/5, 10 February 1961 (IMF Archives), p. 26.

[17] Minutes of the Executive Board Meeting, EBM 61/31, 23 June 1961 (IMF Archives), p. 7.

[18] Rasminsky represented a multimember constituency that also contained Ireland.

[19] Horsefield, *International Monetary Fund, 1945–1965*, vol. 1, p. 504.

[20] Minutes of the Executive Board Meeting, EBM 61/31, 21 June 1961 (IMF Archives); Minutes of the Executive Board Meeting, EBM 61/32, 23 June 1961 (IMF Archives), pp. 6–7; Minutes of the Executive Board Meeting, EBM 61/37, 7 July 1961 (IMF Archives), p. 11.

[21] Jacobsson, *Life for Sound Money*, p. 360.

[22] "Use of Fund Resources for Capital Transfers," SM/61/45, 24 May 1961 (IMF Archives).

banking, or other business."[23] The Legal Department therefore recommended that the 1946 interpretation be amended by adding to it the provision "or to finance capital transfers in accordance with the provisions of the Articles, including Article VI."

Adapting to the Limits of Keynesianism: The New Approach of the IMF Staff

The ER and RES staffs weighed in on the issue in a joint June 1961 paper to the board.[24] This paper is particularly illuminating, as it provides the clearest and fullest exposition of the staff's approach prior to the reform negotiations in the 1970s. In the board paper, the staff approach evidences modest change from the early postwar era. With greater support for capital freedom forthcoming from some of the IMF membership, there was now more space for the staff to consider alternatives to Keynesianism, even though these alternatives were not pushed on them.

During this period the staff began to offer prescriptions that were somewhat at odds with Keynesian standards of behavior. Whereas in the early postwar era the staff had demonstrated a proclivity to recommend controls to manage disruptive capital flows, in the 1961 paper they reveal modest support for alternative mechanisms, such as policy adjustment and financing. Although the paper notes that controls could be "useful" for governments facing capital outflows, it goes on to suggest that governments will also have "to adopt policies appropriate to correct the deficit." In particular, governments would have to assess, in consultation with the Fund, "the most suitable interest rate policies to be pursued in response to cyclical and other factors, in a world where capital moves very easily from market to market."[25]

At Bretton Woods, Keynes and White had sought to create a system where governments would be provided sufficient policy autonomy to pursue various national objectives, and controls were to play an integral role in this system. But by the early 1960s this system was slowly unraveling, and in direct contrast to Keynesian standards of behavior, the IMF staff—harking back to standards of behavior consistent more with neoclassical orthodoxy—were suggesting that some governments might need to subjugate macroeconomic policy autonomy to the goal of maintaining external balance.

---

[23] IMF Articles of Agreement, reprinted in Horsefield, *International Monetary Fund, 1945–1965*, vol. 3, p. 191.

[24] "Capital Movements and the Use of the Fund Resources," SM/61/57, 20 June 1961 (IMF Archives).

[25] "Capital Movements and the Use of the Fund Resources," pp. 7, 6. See also p. 11.

But the staff did not uniformly insist on policy adjustment; in cases where sufficient resources were available, the staff welcomed the use of reserves, IMF financing, or assistance from swap networks to offset disruptive capital flows. These measures, the staff argued, would permit governments to avoid the use of controls and to reap the benefits from greater capital freedom. Like Jacobsson, the staff also rejected earlier arguments raised by the League economists that suggested IMF resources would be insufficient to offset short-term capital flows; the staff instead argued that "the very knowledge that sufficient support for a currency is available may well convince speculators that their fears or expectations will not be realized, thus forestalling the undesired outflow."[26]

Some observers attribute the staff's comparatively greater emphasis on policy adjustment and financing to the emergence of the neoclassical synthesis and monetarism within the economics profession.[27] This argument is not fully persuasive, however. While the staff members were surely aware of these academic developments, they did not adopt new understandings of market behavior associated with these schools of thought. Instead, they retained a Keynesian understanding of market behavior despite abandoning their proclivity for prescribing controls. Although the staff paper notes that the liberalization of controls in Europe has "been of great benefit to the international community," the discussion of such benefits is limited to those that had been highlighted by Keynes and White. Emphasis is placed on how postwar liberalization had fostered the growth of short-term banking facilities and productive flows, which in turn had stirred world trade and development. Equilibrating capital flows are also identified as desirable, particularly from the standpoint of inflation-deficit and recession-surplus states.[28]

More significantly, the Keynesian understanding of market behavior features prominently in the staff's analysis. The staff express concerns about the devastating consequences of convention-driven market behavior, "especially as speculation tends to feed upon itself" and can "force a country into a devaluation when it is not in a state of fundamental disequilibrium." Such capital flows, in the view of the staff, "prove to be self-reinforcing in character" and "may well lead to an unnecessary or exaggerated devaluation of the currency concerned." The staff also continued to share some of the concerns of Keynes and White about interest-rate arbitrage flows. Such flows were seen as likely to limit monetary policy autonomy, undermine the system of adjustable pegs, and disrupt financial interventionist efforts.

---

[26] "Capital Movements and the Use of the Fund Resources," p. 6. See also p. 8.
[27] Best, *The Limits of Transparency*, pp. 95–96.
[28] "Capital Movements and the Use of the Fund Resources," pp. 4–5.

According to Boughton, the staff at the time also did not find monetarism or the case for floating to be "particularly persuasive." The case for floating, observes Boughton, "took a long time to influence thinking in the IMF."[29] In 1950, the decision of Canada to float its currency had been viewed as a possible threat to international financial stability. The staff continued to subscribe to this view in the 1960s, noting that floating was "not an acceptable solution to the problems of the main industrial countries arising from large and troublesome capital movements."[30]

Ultimately, continued attachment to Keynesian understandings of market behavior led the staff to lean toward associated standards of behavior, albeit in a modified form. Although the staff paper notes that IMF resources could be used to support liberalization or to help avoid the use of controls, it goes on to suggest that "countries with prospects of large or sustained deficits due to capital outflows would presumably make use of capital controls if corrective measures could not be expected to ensure an early return to equilibrium."[31] Jacques Polak, then RES director, later further clarified that the informal staff approach would be to favor the use of controls over policy adjustment.[32]

Rather than developing new beliefs from the economics profession, adaptation appears to have been critical in stirring a change in the staff's approach. Country experiences offered valuable information that the staff members employed to refine and update their beliefs. As indicated, the staff viewed the gradual liberalization of controls in the 1950s as beneficial in that it helped to stir trade and development and to ease the adjustment process in some countries. Moreover, the use of unilateral controls was seen as increasingly ineffective: "Experience indicates that it is impossible in practice to forestall all capital movements considered to be undesirable . . . [I]mposition is a difficult administrative task out of the reach of many countries and impossible to apply successfully at short notice in countries that do not have them"[33] Positive experiences with liberalization and negative experiences with controls thus led the staff to adapt to the perceived limitations of Keynesian standards of behavior.

An important factor behind the receptive attitude of the staff to these lessons was the overlap between these perceived limitations and existing IMF principles and processes. For instance, the staff's new comparatively greater emphasis on the need for policy adjustment in response to disrup-

[29] Boughton, "Force of History," pp. 15, 17.

[30] "Capital Movements and the Use of the Fund Resources," p. 7.

[31] "Capital Movements and the Use of the Fund Resources," p. 11.

[32] Minutes of the Executive Board Meeting, EBM 61/37, 7 July 1961 (IMF Archives), p. 21.

[33] Memorandum to the Capital Movements Committee, pp. 4–5.

tive capital flows fit well with the implications of the emerging IMF approach to balance-of-payments adjustment. By the late 1950s, Polak, who then served as RES deputy director, had devised what became known as the "monetary approach to the balance of payments."[34] This approach linked external payments deficits to excessive domestic credit creation and implied that the imbalance could be reduced by either fiscal or monetary means. Although the original Polak model evolved to take into account other means governments could use to reduce their imbalances, the model became the foundation for IMF financial programming and conditionality and had profound implications for how the Fund addressed payments imbalances.

First, it implied that the cause of and the solution to payments imbalances lay with the deficit country.[35] The Polak model understood the cause of an imbalance to be one of excess aggregate demand relative to output, which suggested that the solution was to decrease absorption or increase productivity. Since short-term productivity changes are difficult to attain, the Polak model focused the staff's attention on adjusting economic and policy trends, such as excessive budget deficits and credit creation. The Polak model is not wrong to focus on fundamentals in deficit countries. Yet in directing attention to domestic economic and policy trends, the model obscures external causes of payments imbalances, such as the self-fulfilling expectations of financial market participants, which are a cause of so much concern in the Keynesian understanding of market behavior.

The lesson that controls were increasingly ineffective also resonated with the IMF's approach to balance-of-payments adjustment. In addition to focusing attention on economic and policy trends in deficit countries, the IMF approach also implied that measures that failed to address underlying payments imbalances, such as capital controls, would at best produce only a short-term improvement in the balance-of-payments. Although the staff still viewed controls as useful for facilitating the adjustment process, the use of this particular approach to balance-of-payments adjustment led the staff increasingly to view any restriction as an inappropriate substitute for adjusting policies. Growing evidence that controls were ineffective fit with this general principle.

---

[34] The monetary approach did not reflect the influence of monetarism within the Fund. Rather, Polak took a traditional closed economy Keynesian model but widened it so as to examine the money supply as influenced by the foreign balance. See Jacques J. Polak, "The IMF Monetary Model at Forty," IMF Working Paper WP/97/49 (Washington, D.C.: IMF, 1997).

[35] Barnett and Finnemore, *Rules for the World*, chap. 3; Woods, *The Globalizers*, chap. 2.

Disconfirming evidence for Keynesian standards of behavior thus precipitated ad hoc changes to the informal staff approach. New strategies—such as a policy adjustment and financing—were added on to existing ones, while old strategies—such as the use of controls alone to manage balance-of-payments pressures—gradually fell into disuse. But despite these adaptations, the staff by and large continued to subscribe to a Keynesian understanding of market behavior that constituted unfettered capital mobility as undesirable. Underlying organizational "theories-in-use" thus remained relatively unchanged. New information that revealed the limitations of Keynesianism as well as greater support from some leading IMF principals for capital freedom did not lead the staff to abandon their attachment to the norm of capital control. Although the staff adapted to limits of Keynesianism, the personal configuration of the Fund reflected earlier recruitment patterns, which made it difficult for the staff to bring alternative perspectives to bear on experience. Learning therefore proved cognitively difficult.

There is also possibility that the staff altered their approach as a result of informal encouragement from Jacobsson. Although there is no direct evidence for such encouragement, it is reasonable to suppose that it might have existed. As compared to previous managing directors, Jacobsson tended to be more involved in influencing staff research and crafting policy statements.[36]

The appointment of Jacobsson as managing director also decreased the influence of Edward Bernstein, who had been a delegate to Bretton Woods and served as the Fund's first RES director until 1958. There were reportedly significant disagreements on some occasions between Jacobsson and Bernstein over the place of capital controls in easing the adjustment process. Whereas Jacobsson favored policy adjustment, Bernstein was sympathetic to the use of controls to help establish equilibrium. U.S. director Frank Southard also reportedly disagreed with Bernstein's views on a number of occasions, siding more often with Jacobsson.[37] These disagreements eventually precipitated Bernstein's resignation in January 1958, with Polak subsequently replacing him as RES director in June—a position he would hold until 1979. Still, it is important to note that even if informal encouragement from Jacobsson did play a part in shaping the staff's approach, it nonetheless failed to fully overturn the staff's support for controls and Keynesian understandings of market behavior.

---

[36] Jacobsson, *Life for Sound Money*, pp. 299–300.

[37] Edward Bernstein, "The Early Years of the International Monetary Fund," in *International Financial Policy: Essays in Honor of Jacques J. Polak*, ed. Jacob A. Frenkel and Morris Goldstein (Washington, D.C.: IMF, 1991), pp. 58–66 at p. 62.

Formalizing New Beliefs

In the board discussion that followed the June 1961 paper from the ER and RES staff, a debate took place over which capital flows the IMF would be permitted to finance should the 1946 decision be overturned. The discussion focused on where to draw the line between current and capital account transactions and between a "reasonable" and "unreasonable" amount required for the expansion of exports or the ordinary course of trade, banking, and other business. At its core, the debate was thus about the fixing of meanings and the politics thereof. The "winners" would decide what constituted "legitimate" capital flows in the eyes of formal IMF policy.

Predictably, the debate boiled down to a struggle pitting the United States and West Germany against France. The main points of debate centered on interest-arbitrage and speculative flows. With respect to interest-rate arbitrage flows, Southard, Wilfried Guth—the West German director—and others argued the phrase "ordinary course of trade, banking, and other business" needed to reflect changes in the international banking practice since Bretton Woods. The range of ordinary practice of international banking had become wider and the depth of financial intermediation greater, and thus the meaning of the phrase needed to reflect these realities.[38] The IMF general counsel later spoke in favor of this position as well.[39]

On the issue of speculative flows, Southard pointed to the practical difficulties of excluding a priori such capital movements. Southard noted: "It was difficult to make a clear distinction between some speculative waves and what might be called fairly normal capital movements. Undoubtedly under Article VI, Section 1(a), there would be short-term movements which were not large or sustained and which might be a mixture of speculative and non-speculative capital." Southard therefore sought to ensure "that there was no peculiar hostility against speculative movements."[40]

Guth concurred, but went even further, suggesting "it was only natural," in light of events, that "greater freedom of capital movements . . . had greatly contributed to the expansion of world trade and investment." Perhaps concerned about the legitimacy the staff continued to provide to

[38] Minutes of the Executive Board Meeting, EBM 61/31; Minutes of the Executive Board Meeting, EBM 61/32, pp. 3, 5; Minutes of the Executive Board Meeting, EBM 61/37, p. 9.
[39] Minutes of the Executive Board Meeting, EBM 61/32, p. 6.
[40] Minutes of the Executive Board Meeting, EBM 61/37, p. 2.

controls, Guth argued that the Fund "should stand for the principle of freedom of restrictions in this field."[41] The U.S. and West German arguments thus sought to overturn the position that had been staked out at Bretton Woods. Whereas Keynes and his supporters had cast speculative flows, as well as some interest-rate arbitrage flows, as abnormal and illegitimate, Southard and Guth sought to present them as normal and legitimate.

De Largentaye opposed these claims, focusing his arguments on how interest-rate arbitrage flows were disequilibrating for inflation-surplus and recession-deficit countries and how they undermined monetary policy autonomy in inflation-deficit and recession-surplus countries. For the French government, interest-rate arbitrage flows, regardless of whether they are equilibrating or disequilibrating, "always create a conflict between the needs of internal and external stability" and "deprive countries of their autonomy in the handling of interest rates as an instrument of internal stability." Before sanctioning financing for such flows, de Largentaye wanted the staff to spell out in concrete and detailed terms what their suggestion for "the most suitable interest rate policies" involved, in order that policymakers could realize the degree of "restraint and sacrifice involved."[42]

But the French were largely isolated on the board, and the U.S. and West German position prevailed. Due to lingering legal concerns, the board, in July 1961, crafted a new formal policy that was described as a "clarification." The clarification indicated that the 1946 decision "does not preclude the use of the Fund's resources for capital transfers in accordance with the provisions of the Articles, including Article VI."[43] This clarification had significant implications for the evolution of the Fund's practices. As Susan Strange notes: "By this semantic legerdemain the Gordian knot was cut; an amendment to the Fund's rules that was in fact substantial was disguised as merely procedural."[44]

---

[41] Minutes of the Executive Board Meeting, EBM 61/37, pp. 8–9. The U.S. and West German position on speculative flows also received strong support from the alternate executive director representing the multimember constituency of Burma, Ceylon, Japan, and Thailand.

[42] Minutes of the Executive Board Meeting, EBM 61/37, p. 6.

[43] Executive Board Decision 1238-(61/43), 28 July 1961, reprinted in Horsefield, *International Monetary Fund, 1945–1965*, vol. 3, p. 245. See also Minutes of the Executive Board Meeting, EBM 61/43, 28 July 1961 (IMF Archives).

[44] Susan Strange, "International Monetary Relations," in *International Economic Relations of the Western World, 1959–1971*, vol. 2, ed. Andrew Shonfield (London: Oxford University Press, 1976), p. 99.

With board approval for his initiative, Jacobsson used his position as managing director to establish the precedent that the Fund should interpret its new authority liberally, providing governments with a generous time period to arrest capital outflows and still qualify for financing. Governments were to be permitted access to financing so long as "appropriate measures were being taken so that the disequilibrating capital outflow would be arrested . . . within a maximum period of three to five years."[45] This was in contrast to the views of the ER staff, who had argued that governments experiencing a disequilibrating capital outflow should "make use of capital controls if corrective measures could not be expected to ensure an *early* return to equilibrium."[46]

Approval of the GAB followed soon after the board clarification. The first paragraph of the preamble of the GAB further illustrates not only the emergence of greater support for capital freedom among some of the Fund's membership but also the shift toward the construction of formal policy measures that sought to manage speculative flows rather than eliminate them:

> In order to enable the International Monetary Fund to fulfill more effectively its role in the international monetary system in the new conditions of widespread convertibility, including greater freedom for short-term capital movements, the main industrial countries have agreed that they will, in a spirit of broad and willing cooperation, strengthen the Fund by general arrangements under which they will stand ready to lend their currencies to the Fund up to the specified amounts under Article VII, Section 2 of the Articles of Agreement when supplementary measures are needed to forestall or cope with an impairment of the international monetary system in the aforesaid conditions.[47]

The GAB thus enabled governments to avoid the use of controls by providing a means to "cope" with speculative flows through financing and to "forestall" such movements by demonstrating that adequate resources were available should the temptation to engage in speculation arise. Reflecting the ascendance of the neoclassical synthesis and monetarism, "coping" and "forestalling" were developed as means to manage

---

[45] As cited in Gold, *International Capital Movements*, pp. 25–26.

[46] Capital Movements and the Use of the Fund Resources, p. 11, emphasis added. In the board's discussion of the memorandum, Southard expressed concerns that not too much emphasis should be placed on the word "early"; see Minutes of the Executive Board Meeting, EBM 61/37, p. 3.

[47] Executive Board Decision 1289-(62/1), 5 January 1962, reprinted in *Selected Decisions of the International Monetary Fund and Selected Documents*, Eighth Issue (Washington, D.C.: IMF, 1976), p. 98.

rather than eliminate speculative capital flows. Proposals to curtail such flows through a tightening of controls were virtually absent from policy discussions. Indeed, the GAB preamble suggests that the liberalization of such flows was now increasingly seen as desirable, at least among "the main industrial countries." A subsequent quota increase in 1964–1965 provided additional resources to the Fund with the expressed intention to make such funds available to offset capital movements.[48]

The decade of the 1960s was one of transition in the norms guiding IMF operations. The discarding and "hollowing out" of Keynesianism significantly altered the beliefs that informed policymaking. Although some policymakers continued to view controls as essential, the erosion of support for controls was clearly under way. The unraveling of Keynesianism and the norm of capital control within the Fund was reflected in three developments.

First, the U.S. position changed significantly. The new U.S. position, along with greater support for capital freedom from other leading principals, most notably West Germany, meant the outer structural constraint of member states' preferences had loosened modestly, permitting the staff greater space to consider alternatives to Keynesianism. Changes to formal IMF rules constituted a second important development. The 1961 board clarification and the creation of the GAB represented a shift toward constructing policy measures that sought to manage, rather than eliminate, speculative capital flows. The logic underpinning these new formal rules, which encouraged governments to avoid the use of controls, was thus notably different from that elaborated by Keynes and his supporters.

Here the entrepreneurship of Jacobsson appears to have been critical. Jacobsson acted strategically by developing a specific initiative that was consistent with the strongly held general preferences of some of the Fund's leading principals (United States and West Germany). He acted autonomously not only by defining how, among the many possible ways he could advance these preferences, these preferences were best served but also by going against the strongly held general preferences of other leading principals (in particular, France).

Finally, in an environment in which the Fund's outer structural constraint and formal rules became more permissive, the staff began gradually developing a new approach that recognized the limits of Keynesian standards of behavior as well as the benefits of greater capital freedom. Although the staff members were aware of their changing outer structural

[48] Margaret Garritsen de Vries, *The International Monetary Fund, 1972–1978: Cooperation on Trial*, vols. 1 and 2, *Narrative and Analysis*, vol. 3, *Documents* (Washington, D.C.: IMF, 1985), vol. 1, p. 513.

constraint, these new preferences were generally not pushed on them. In fact, heterogeneous preferences that pitted the United States and West Germany against France gave the staff additional autonomy to stake out their own approach. Adaptation was thus a far more crucial factor than member states' influence in shifting the staff's approach.

These adaptations fit well with the implications of the emerging staff approach to balance-of-payments adjustment. But the staff still did not conclude that unfettered capital mobility was desirable in itself. Prevailing beliefs channeled the adaptations drawn from experience, and the personnel configuration of the IMF made learning cognitively difficult. Capital freedom had yet to become a goal for the staff, but later developments would overturn this state of affairs.

CHAPTER SIX

Formal Change and Informal Continuity

THE REFORM NEGOTIATIONS OF THE 1970S

BY THE 1970s even the "hollowed out" version of Keynesianism that had emerged in the 1960s was on the verge of being overturned. Capital controls still retained legitimacy, albeit a weaker form, as defined by formal IMF rules and the informal staff approach. But international monetary reform negotiations in the 1970s would further weaken the legitimacy of controls within the context of the former, though, interestingly, not the latter.

Heightened capital mobility proved to be increasingly disruptive for the Bretton Woods exchange rate system. European and Japanese officials, and the IMF management and staff, made clear their preference for using controls to preserve the system. In these circles, Keynesianism still retained support, though it was significantly weaker than in the past. In accordance with these beliefs, these actors supported an attempt to develop cooperative control measures. However, the initiative failed and the legitimacy of controls was weakened further.

The United States effectively became a norm leader for capital freedom. Controls, even the temporary variety, were cast as illegitimate, with U.S. officials promoting several initiatives and changes to formal IMF rules that sought to limit the circumstances under which their use could be considered legitimate. Yet despite formal change at the IMF there remained informal continuity.

Although U.S. officials successfully pushed through formal rule changes, their success was not matched in terms of altering the staff's informal approach, which proved resistant to adopting a new normative outlook on capital controls. This "slippage" between formal rules and the informal staff approach was due largely to the failure of these formal rule changes to resonate with the staff's prevailing beliefs that continued to lend legitimacy to controls.

INITIATIVES FOR COOPERATIVE CONTROLS

The closure of the gold window in August 1971 led many governments to float their currencies temporarily. Although controls were no longer employed as widely as they had been in the past, they still retained some legitimacy. As Lawrence Krause observed at the time, "Capital movements have been progressively liberalized by most countries, but actions which tend to restrict capital movements do not elicit cries of outrage."[1] In fact, European and Japanese officials, and the IMF management and staff, would not abandon their support for controls for some time.

Events in the early 1970s suggested that unilateral controls were increasingly ineffective. The unilateral tightening of controls by European and Japanese officials had failed to prevent disruptive capital flows from forcing the move to floating.[2] But rather than forcing policymakers to discard beliefs that legitimated controls, these market forces—when *interpreted* through a Keynesian lens—led European and Japanese officials, and the IMF management and staff, to consider cooperative controls to preserve the Bretton Woods exchange rate system.

Interestingly, governments and the IMF management and staff rejected the use of comprehensive exchange controls, which, along with cooperative controls, had been suggested by Keynes and White. In early 1973, the Technical Group on Disequilibrating Capital Flows of the IMF Committee of Twenty (discussed below) rejected such "brutal" controls because they may "involve a degree of administrative restrictions which could damage trade and beneficial capital flows."[3] Attention therefore shifted to cooperative controls.

The closure of the gold window precipitated the launch of several rounds of negotiations that sought to reform the international monetary system. The French government—in two initiatives taken in 1971—promoted the use of cooperative controls. The first initiative—taken two months prior to the closing of the gold window—produced agreement among the Group of 10 (G-10)[4] central bankers to limit their placements of funds in the Eurocurrency market to help stem its growth, marking the first attempt to curb the expansion of this market.

The second initiative—agreed to in December at meetings held at the Smithsonian Institution—led to U.S. officials agreeing to retain their capital controls in order to support the new adjustable peg exchange rates

[1] Lawrence Krause, "Private International Finance," *International Organization* 25, no. 3 (1971), pp. 523–540 at p. 536.

[2] Helleiner, *Reemergence of Global Finance*, p. 103.

[3] "Report of the Technical Group on Disequilibrating Capital Flows [17 May 1973]," in IMF, *International Monetary Reform: Documents of the Committee of Twenty* (Washington, D.C.: IMF, 1974), pp. 78–92 at p. 85.

[4] The G-10 refers to the group of countries that agreed in 1962 to participate in the GAB by making resources available to the IMF. Initially, the G-10 consisted of Belgium, Canada, France, Italy, Japan, the Netherlands, Sweden, the United Kingdom, the United States, and West Germany. Switzerland, then not a member of the Fund, joined the G-10 in 1964.

agreed to at the meetings. The French government also sought to convince U.S. officials to intensify their controls, but they proved unwilling. The two initiatives for cooperative controls became a focus of the reform discussions that began in 1972.

The Fund's membership agreed that the IMF board should prepare a report that would form the basis for discussions at the August 1972 annual ministerial meeting. But as the board began to discuss reform, it found it could not make much progress. In early 1972 the board therefore asked Polak to draft a "sketch" to provide the basis of discussions. Polak recalls that he and other staff members were "concerned about capital mobility and the problems it could cause for countries."[5]

At the time the staff was generally skeptical of unfettered capital mobility, and saw controls as one of several means that governments could employ to maintain their exchange rate commitments in the reformed international monetary system. As one official IMF historian observes, "Some of the Fund staff ha[d] been convinced for several years that disruptive capital movements were the single most important cause of the collapse of the Bretton Woods system and had been studying ways of controlling such capital movements in the reformed system."[6] That the staff diagnosed disruptive capital flows as the "single most important cause" of the collapse of the Bretton Woods exchange rate system is one indication that Keynesianism still exerted an impact on the staff's beliefs. Indeed, other observers claimed that such flows were a symptom of the underlying weaknesses of the exchange rate system, and held that it was these weaknesses—not capital mobility per se—that had destroyed it.[7]

Although the staff were concerned about disruptive capital flows, they also viewed unilateral controls as problematic since "they can never be quite complete and evasion-proof."[8] Cooperative controls, however, were seen as a potentially more effective measure. But because such measures were opposed by some of the Fund's membership, most notably the United States, the staff recognized they would have to tread carefully in advocating them.[9] Yet despite these member state preferences, a 1971 staff

---

[5] Author's interview with Polak.

[6] De Vries, *International Monetary Fund, 1972–1978*, vol. 1, p. 192. See also p. 125; "Private Short-term Capital Flows and Analogous Movements of Central Bank Funds—Short Outline of Study," CF/S331/CapitalTransfers1971, 9 June 1971 (IMF Archives); "Policy Issues Raised by Short-term International Capital Flows," CF/S331/CapitalTransfers1971, 7 July 1971 (IMF Archives).

[7] Gold, *International Capital Movements*, p. 35.

[8] "Policy Issues Raised by Short-Term International Capital Flows," p. 3.

[9] "Reform of the International Monetary System—a Sketch of Its Scope and Content [7 March 1972]," reprinted in de Vries, *International Monetary Fund, 1972–1978*, vol. 3, pp. 3–15 at p. 11.

report asserted that a key issue for discussion should be "factors bearing on the international payments situation, especially the disturbing short term capital flows in mid-1971 threatening the stability of the international monetary system and possible coordination by national governments of policies to help control such flows."[10]

THE UNITED STATES AS A NORM LEADER

In subsequent board discussions U.S. officials reversed the position they had agreed to at the Smithsonian. U.S. officials began to advocate privately the liberalization of capital controls.[11] The shift in U.S. policy was due in part to the realization that greater capital freedom would help preserve policy autonomy by helping to underwrite fiscal and payments imbalances. But Helleiner adds that the shift in U.S. policy "was largely influenced by advocates of neoliberal thought" who had acquired important positions within the U.S. Treasury.[12] One prominent advocate was Treasury Secretary George Schultz, an MIT-trained economist and former dean of the University of Chicago business school. Prior to his appointment as Treasury Secretary in May 1972, Schultz had been an advocate of greater capital freedom.[13] Other leading neoliberal intellectuals, such as Gottfried Haberler and Milton Friedman, also had close ties to the Nixon and Ford administrations and shaped their policy positions. At the August 1972 annual IMF ministerial meeting, Schultz publicly announced U.S. opposition to capital controls for the first time and indicated that the United States would dismantle its controls by December 1974.[14] The speech was reportedly drafted by Friedman.[15]

The eventual IMF board report on international monetary reform strongly reflected U.S. leadership and the rise of neoliberalism. The report suggests greater capital freedom would encourage "the growth of international trade" and increase "the economic well-being of developed and

---

[10] De Vries, *International Monetary Fund, 1972–1978*, vol. 2, p. 788.

[11] De Vries, *International Monetary Fund, 1972–1978*, vol. 1, p. 137.

[12] Helleiner, *Reemergence of Global Finance*, p. 115.

[13] George P. Schultz and Kenneth W. Dam, *Economic Policy Beyond the Headlines*, 2nd ed. (Chicago: University of Chicago Press, 1998), pp. 119–121.

[14] IMF, *Summary Proceedings—Annual Meeting of the IMF, 1972* (Washington, D.C.: IMF, 1972), pp. 35, 41. See also de Vries, *International Monetary Fund, 1972–1978*, vol. 1, p. 167. The United States actually abolished its controls even earlier, in January 1974.

[15] Kenneth W. Dam, *The Rules of the Game: Reform and Evolution in the International Monetary System* (Chicago: University of Chicago Press, 1982), p. 224; and Paul Volcker and Toyoo Gyohten, *Changing Fortunes: The World's Money and the Threat to Monetary Leadership* (New York: Random House, 1992), pp. 118, 120.

developing countries." Capital freedom is praised as providing an "efficient intermediation in channeling funds to investment projects." The report also casts capital mobility as a valuable discipline on governments, because it "served at times to prompt decisions on new measures . . . in circumstances in which the need for policy changes has been inadequately appreciated or such changes have been unduly delayed."[16] European and Japanese officials however, continued to support a place for capital controls in the reformed system.[17] The final board report therefore recognizes these strongly conflicting preferences.

In 1972, the IMF's membership created the Committee of Twenty (C-20) to draft concrete reform proposals. Although members of the C-20, as Louis Pauly indicates, were drawn "from the major constituencies of the Board of Governors of the IMF, a staff taken from the finance ministers and central banks of the leading monetary powers did the real work; they in turn assigned a group of technical experts to examine the problem of speculative capital flows."[18] The Report of the Technical Group on Disequilibrating Capital Flows was submitted to the C-20 in May 1973. According to Lamfalussy, "The views expressed in the technical group's report . . . may be taken as representing the broad trend of official thinking on capital controls at the end of the Bretton Woods era."[19]

In line with the continued subscription of some governments to Keynesian standards of behavior, the report argues that the collapse of the system of adjustable pegs in March 1973 tended to strengthen the case that capital controls, particularly those employed in cooperation with others, should play a role in the reformed system.[20] IMF managing director Pierre-Paul Schweitzer, who had succeeded Jacobsson upon his death in 1963, also shared these views.[21]

But these views clashed with the U.S. position, and the report reflects these disagreements. Although the report suggests controls could play a role in the reformed system, their place within the boundaries of legitimate policy practice was to be narrowed. The report claims there was no need for permanent controls on capital flows and suggests certain limitations should be placed on their use.

[16] "Reform of the International Monetary System [18 August 1972]," reprinted in de Vries, *International Monetary Fund, 1972–1978,* vol. 3, pp. 19–56 at pp. 47, 48.

[17] De Vries, *International Monetary Fund, 1972–1978,* vol. 1, pp. 18, 132, 136–137.

[18] Pauly, *Who Elected the Bankers?* p. 97.

[19] Lamfalussy, "Changing Attitudes," p. 200.

[20] "Report of the Technical Group on Disequilibrating Capital Flows," pp. 84–85. See also de Vries, *International Monetary Fund, 1972–1978,* vol. 1, pp. 192–193; vol. 2, pp. 930–931.

[21] De Vries, *International Monetary Fund, 1972–1978,* vol. 1, p. 77; Helleiner, *Reemergence of Global Finance,* p. 107.

In this context, the technical group recommended that the IMF develop a code of conduct for the use of capital controls. Although there was also discussion about the possibility of imposing reserve requirements on the Euromarket liabilities of banks, no consensus could be reached on the issue.[22]

The proposals of the technical group thus represented an attempt to develop new standards of behavior for the use of capital controls. Equally significant, the technical group made a modest attempt—at the insistence of U.S. officials—to advance new understandings of market behavior. Reflecting the rise of neoliberalism, U.S. officials challenged the Keynesian view that capital flows that worsened payments imbalances were necessarily "disequilibrating" or negative. On the contrary, such flows could be seen as imposing a valuable discipline on policymakers and prompting necessary policy adjustments. The technical group thus explained that "there is no simple and straightforward definition of 'disequilibrating' capital flows . . . [P]articular capital flows cannot be defined as disequilibrating simply because they increase a payments imbalance, since they may encourage a needed adjustment."[23]

The C-20 ultimately produced a final report—known as the *Outline of Reform*—that contained some concrete reform proposals. A number of these proposals reflected the U.S. position, thus potentially narrowing the scope for using controls. Although the report stopped short of developing a new code of conduct for controls, at the insistence of U.S. officials, it did suggest some limits on their use.[24] In particular, it proposes that "countries will not use controls over capital transactions for the purpose of maintaining inappropriate exchange rates or, more generally, of avoiding appropriate adjustment action. Insofar as countries use capital controls, they should avoid an excessive degree of administrative restriction which could damage trade and beneficial capital flows and should not retain controls longer than needed."[25] U.S. officials also successfully blocked efforts to strengthen cooperative capital control obligations. Instead of prescribing obligatory cooperative controls, the outline simply notes that such a strategy would be one of many options available.

After the move to generalized floating in 1974, the board turned its attention to developing guidelines for the management of floating exchange rates. U.S. officials continued to insist the IMF be given the authority to discourage governments from using controls to manipulate

---

[22] "Report of the Technical Group on Disequilibrating Capital Flows," p. 89.

[23] "Report of the Technical Group on Disequilibrating Capital Flows," pp. 78–79.

[24] Dam, *Rules of the Game*, p. 248.

[25] "Outline of Reform [14 June 1974]," in IMF, *International Monetary Reform*, pp. 7–48 at p. 12.

their balance of payments, a position that ran contrary to the preferences of European and Japanese officials.[26] A compromise was therefore struck whereby the Fund would be permitted to advocate liberalization of restrictions being used for balance-of-payments reasons, while permitting the use of controls for "economic and social reasons."[27]

The *Outline of Reform* evolved into the Jamaica accord, which institutionalized reform of the international monetary system in the second amendment to the IMF Articles. Although the substance of the amended Articles suggests that the U.S. position had largely prevailed, the resulting changes to formal rules regarding the use of capital controls turned out to be rather modest. As Pauly observes, "In the end, all that proved politically feasible was an amendment to the Articles of Agreement of the IMF which legalized floating exchange rates and gave up on trying to achieve a new consensus on the definition and management of disequilibrating capital flows."[28] The formal rule changes that did occur had little operational significance for the staff and failed to change their views about the legitimacy of controls. Thus, although the position of U.S. officials on capital controls had shifted, and they had succeeded in altering some formal IMF rules, they were ultimately unable to prevail upon other member states or the staff to alter their views as well.

One modest formal rule change was new language in the amended Article IV, Section 1, which now states that "the essential purpose of the international monetary system is to provide a framework that facilitates the exchange of goods, services, *and capital* among countries" (emphasis added). The newly amended Article IV also charges the IMF with the responsibility to exercise "firm surveillance over the exchange rate policies of members."[29] Yet the amended Articles failed to specify precisely what surveillance would entail.

A 1977 board decision clarified the concept of surveillance to some extent. Among the developments that "might indicate a need for discussion with a member of the Fund," the decision identifies "the introduction or substantial modification for balance of payments purposes of restrictions on, or incentives for, the inflow or outflow of capital," as well as "the pursuit, for balance of payments purposes, of monetary and other domestic financial policies that provide abnormal encouragement or dis-

---

[26] Helleiner, *Reemergence of Global Finance*, p. 110.

[27] "Guidelines for the Management of Floating Exchange Rates [13 June 1974]," reprinted in de Vries, *International Monetary Fund, 1972–1978*, vol. 3, p. 487. See also vol. 1, p. 215.

[28] Pauly, *Who Elected the Bankers?* p. 97.

[29] "Articles of Agreement of the International Monetary Fund [1 April 1978]," reprinted in de Vries, *International Monetary Fund, 1972–1978*, vol. 3, pp. 379–446 at pp. 381–382, emphasis added to indicate changes.

couragement to capital flows."[30] These formal rule changes clearly reflect the U.S. effort to facilitate capital freedom.

On the surface these formal rule changes appear to partially undermine the legitimacy of capital controls and to direct the IMF to encourage liberalization. But the significance of these changes should not be overstated. The newly revised Articles did not undermine the right of governments to use controls as specified in Article VI, Section 3.[31] The formal rule change also failed to lead the staff to adopt the norm of capital freedom. This was partly due to the minor operational significance of the formal rule change, as it indicated that capital freedom was the purpose of the international monetary system and not necessarily of the IMF.[32]

More significantly, most staff members continued to view controls as legitimate policy instruments and thus proved resistant to discarding their support for such measures. As I have discussed, in the context of the reform negotiations most staff members initially favored controls as means to support the Bretton Woods exchange rate system. But even after the move to generalized floating in 1974—which is commonly depicted as a crucial turning point in lessening concerns about capital mobility—most staff members continued to envision controls as one of several means that governments could use to maintain "normal zones" for their exchange rates.[33] Since the 1977 surveillance decision did not resonate with prevailing beliefs held by the staff, this formal rule change ultimately had little impact on the staff's informal approach. The staff rarely invoked the new surveillance rules, and there would be little change in their support for capital controls until the mid-1980s.[34]

U.S. officials were at the forefront of efforts to overturn what remained of Keynesian understandings and standards of behavior. This norm leadership was critical for two reasons. First, and most significantly, it removed a vital base of support for the Keynesian understandings and standards of behavior that had underpinned formal IMF rules since Bretton Woods. This does not mean that U.S. officials subsequently embarked on a global crusade for the liberalization of all controls. But, in contrast to earlier periods, U.S. officials did signal in the 1970s that the world's dominant

---

[30] Executive Board Decision No. 5392-(77/63), 29 April 1977, reprinted in de Vries, *International Monetary Fund, 1972–1978*, vol. 3, pp. 491–494 at p. 493.

[31] Joseph Gold, *The Fund Agreement in the Courts*, vol. 3 (Washington, D.C.: IMF, 1986), pp. 539–542.

[32] IEO, *IMF's Approach*, p. 18.

[33] De Vries, *International Monetary Fund, 1972–1978*, vol. 2, p. 298.

[34] Harold James, "The Historical Development of the Principle of Surveillance," *IMF Staff Papers* 42, no. 4 (1995), pp. 762–791. Interviews with a number of longtime staff members confirm that these rule changes had little influence on the staff's approach.

financial power would no longer accommodate the use of controls that impeded exchange rate adjustments. Later, especially beginning in the early 1990s, U.S. officials would also target those controls that hampered access by American financial firms. The Fund's outer structural constraint and its formal rules, because of this important shift in the preferences of its leading principal, thus became less permissive of the norm of capital control.

U.S. norm leadership was also critical because it successfully blocked initiatives for cooperative controls. By blocking cooperative control measures, U.S. officials facilitated the move to a floating exchange rate system. The collapse of the system of adjustable pegs therefore removed one of the important justifications for maintaining controls. Though many governments retained a "fear of floating," they were now free to sacrifice exchange rate stability in order to preserve policy autonomy and garner the benefits that came from permitting greater capital freedom.

But these events also further demonstrate the importance of being attentive to informal aspects of organizational behavior and internal organizational processes. Indeed, powerful U.S. norm leadership, formal rule changes, and the collapse of the Bretton Woods exchange rate system failed to induce significant changes to the informal staff approach. Prevailing staff beliefs, which continued to be shaped by a personnel configuration more or less inherited from the 1940s and 1950s, were simply not receptive to efforts that sought to narrow the scope for the use of capital controls.

To be sure, the international monetary reform negotiations of the 1970s suggest the continuing importance of preference heterogeneity and compromises among the IMF's membership. But a focus on preference heterogeneity reveals as much as it obscures. Like earlier episodes of preference heterogeneity discussed in this book, these battles among IMF principals tell us more about why the staff may be capable of acting autonomously than they do about what the staff will actually do with this autonomy. Additional insight, however, can be gained by focusing on the staff's beliefs, which during and after the reform negotiations, generally remained committed to the idea that controls still had a legitimate role to play in the international monetary system. As Polak recalls, "I don't think that ten years after the reform that [the staff's] attitude on capital controls or encouragement of capital flows was particularly different."[35]

---

[35] Author's interview with Polak.

CHAPTER SEVEN

Capital Freed

INFORMAL CHANGE FROM THE 1980s
TO THE MID-1990s

THE 1980s AND 1990s were a period of significant change to the IMF staff's informal approach. Without a legal mandate or active influence from member states or IMF management, the staff discarded their earlier attachment to Keynesianism, replacing it with beliefs that spanned the full continuum of neoliberalism. What is remarkable about the evolution of the IMF approach during this period is that it took place almost exclusively on an informal level. A new informal approach emerged that identified capital freedom as desirable, at least in the long run.

Yet beyond this broad consensus at the level of abstract principles, this chapter shows that there was considerable internal debate over how the world should proceed toward capital freedom. The staff did not fully agree on whether to proceed rapidly or slowly, and whether to proceed with various preconditions and allowances for temporary controls or not. The Fund was thus divided between gradualists and proponents of the big bang. Although these two groups agreed that controls on capital outflows were outside the boundaries of legitimate policy, this consensus did not extend to the issue of sequencing or to the introduction of temporary market-based controls on capital inflows.

This chapter shows that professionalization, administrative recruitment, organizational learning, and internal entrepreneurship were at the center of the Fund's informal adoption, interpretation, and application of the norm of capital freedom. As a result of these processes of endogenous organizational change, the Fund began to advocate capital account liberalization informally, though never indiscriminately or uniformly.

CAPITAL CONTROLS IN THE 1980s DEBT CRISIS: U.S. TREASURY
AND IMF MANAGEMENT PERSPECTIVES

U.S. officials were at the center of the response to the 1980s debt crisis. These officials initially saw the crisis as one of illiquidity in which in which market actors had reacted to an efficient reading of poor fundamentals, imposing discipline on debtor countries and forcing them to adjust. This "crisis construction" had significant implications for determining which actors bore responsibility and what policy responses were legitimated.

As Wesley Widmaier observes, "This construction placed the onus of responsibility for adjustment on debtor overborrowing rather than creditor overlending. . . . These narratives obscured the destabilising effects of private bank overlending and later capital flight, and US monetary policy shifts, such as . . . [the] decision to sharply restrict monetary growth."[1] Drawing on this construction, the initial U.S. response was built on the premise that markets, if left unfettered, would act in a manner that encouraged a return to balance-of-payments equilibrium and currency stability. The provision of large amounts of official financing was believed likely only to make matters worse by creating a moral hazard. Instead, policy adjustment and debt repayment were offered as the appropriate course of action.

Even after the Baker Plan in 1985 signaled a change of course toward providing more generous official financing and augmenting debt-servicing capacity by way of growth, U.S. officials remained wedded to their initial interpretation of the crisis. Paul Volcker, then Federal Reserve chairman, later wrote of the crisis that "for all the pain, the implications were not entirely negative . . . the agony of the debt crisis provided the jolt necessary for Latin American leaders to rethink their old approaches and set off in fresh and much more promising directions."[2] Thus, although U.S. officials belatedly recognized that market actors had perhaps reacted excessively, some nonetheless retained an underlying faith in market discipline. Debt relief would not be offered until the announcement of the Brady Plan in March 1989.

Capital flight was a major contributor to the pains of the debt crisis. For some Latin American countries the value of their residents' foreign assets was nearly equal to or even greater than the value of official foreign debt, suggesting that the pains of the debt crisis could be greatly eased if these foreign assets could be returned home. Reminiscent of Keynes's and White's arguments urging governments to cooperate to strengthen the effectiveness of capital controls, in the 1980s, some less orthodox-minded economists proposed cooperative measures that would have helped debtor governments seize and locate the foreign assets of residents and use these assets either to service debt or as collateral for further borrowing.[3]

---

[1] Wesley Widmaier, "Constructing Monetary Crises: New Keynesian Understandings and Monetary Cooperation in the 1990s," *Review of International Studies* 29, no. 1 (2003), pp. 61–77 at p. 68.

[2] Volcker and Gyohten, *Changing Fortunes*, pp. 187–188.

[3] Carlos F. Diaz-Alejandro, "Latin American Debt: I Don't Think We Are in Kansas Anymore," *Brookings Papers on Economic Activity* 1984, no. 2, pp. 335–403; David Felix, "How to Resolve Latin American's Debt Crisis," *Challenge* 28, no. 5 (1985), pp. 44–51.

But U.S. officials rejected these proposals and showed little interest in helping Latin American governments find and repatriate the assets of their residents through cooperative regulatory measures.[4] In fact, with several regulatory initiatives—such as the abolition in 1984 of the withholding tax on the interest income earned on U.S. securities by nonresidents—U.S. policy actually had the effect of encouraging the inflow of flight capital. The U.S. position partly stemmed from recognition that attracting capital flight would help underwrite U.S. fiscal and current account deficits. It also reflected the neoliberal belief that capital flight was a symptom of poor fundamentals—such as inflation and overvalued exchange rates—rather than a "cause" of Latin America's debt problem. According to Susan Strange, the failure of U.S. officials to sanction regulatory action to manage Latin American capital flight stands as one of the crucial "nondecisions" in the history of the debt crisis.[5]

Instead of taking regulatory action U.S. officials insisted that Latin American governments adjust their policies and liberalize their economies in order to stem capital flight and encourage its return. U.S. Treasury Secretary James Baker made clear in his October 1985 speech announcing the new debt plan that governments could not participate in it unless they acted to curtail capital flight in such a manner. However, U.S. officials, though viewing capital freedom as desirable in principle, devoted little, if any, effort to promoting it in most emerging markets and developing countries at this time. Instead, capital controls—particularly in Latin America—were tolerated as second-best measures that served, though only marginally, to curtail capital flight. To the extent that U.S. officials engaged in efforts to encourage liberalization, it was generally limited to specific bilateral settings in East Asia where controls prevented exchange rate adjustments.[6]

Charles Dallara, a senior Reagan and George H. W. Bush Treasury official as well as U.S. IMF director from 1984 to 1989, recalls:

[Capital account liberalization was] not a major policy priority. However, that being said, we were quite a proponent of capital account liberalization both in specific situations and in general. [We] saw it then as an integral part of globalization of the world economy and an integral

[4] Helleiner, "Handling 'Hot Money': U.S. Policy toward Latin American Capital Flight in Historical Perspective," *Alternatives* 20, no. 1 (1995), pp. 81–110; and Helleiner, "Regulating Capital Flight," *Challenge* 44, no. 1 (2001), pp. 19–34. Interestingly, reflecting the ascendance of neoliberalism in Latin America, most Latin American governments also avoided offering their support for this approach.

[5] Susan Strange, "Finance, Information and Power," *Review of International Studies* 16, no. 3 (1990), pp. 259–274 at p. 264.

[6] Jeffrey A. Frankel, "Exchange Rate Policy," in *American Economic Policy in the 1980s*, ed. Martin Feldstein (Chicago: University of Chicago Press, 1994), pp. 293–348 at p. 312.

part of countries growing up in the global financial system. In the mid to late 1980s we were engaged in an effort to allow adequate appreciation to a more market-based level of currencies in places like Japan, Korea, and Taiwan. Capital account liberalization was seen as one dimension of that overall move of exposing their economies and financial systems to global forces.[7]

Thomas Dawson, a senior Bush Treasury official and U.S. IMF director from 1989 to 1993, recollects that U.S. officials, though prioritizing policy adjustment, accommodated controls: "When I was executive director we accepted controls. We were concerned about capital flight, but did not suggest opening up markets because capital flight was a problem. Instead, we suggested they put in place better macroeconomic policies."[8] Indeed, as late as a 1993 IMF board seminar, Dawson signaled that the United States would tolerate certain types of controls.[9]

IMF management offered a similarly accommodative orientation. Under Jacques de Larosière, managing director from 1978 to 1987, the Fund was principally concerned with liberalizing controls on the current account rather than the capital account. "The focus," according to Larosière, "was on current account payments. The big test for a country was to become Article VIII status, leaving Article XIV status."[10]

Although as managing director Larosière recognized that controls "were in many senses impotent," he accommodated their use in order to partially reduce exchange rate volatility and to facilitate adjustment. Larosière believed that capital account liberalization was beneficial for developing countries in the long run and, like U.S. Treasury officials, saw capital flight as a reflection of poor fundamentals. But he insists that "it would not have been a crime for a developing country to have a bulwark of capital controls. . . . There was not a campaign for liberalization."[11] The first deputy managing director from 1984 to 1994, Richard Erb was also accommodative of controls.[12]

[7] Author's interview with Charles Dallara, Washington, D.C., 24 May 2005.

[8] Author's interview with Thomas Dawson, Washington, D.C., 17 May 2005.

[9] Minutes of the Executive Board Seminar, SEMINAR/93/3, 21 July 1993 (IMF Archives), p. 29.

[10] Author's interview with Jacques Larosière, Paris, 19 July 2006. Article VIII formally commits a member state to current account openness and thereafter permits the introduction of restrictions only upon IMF approval. Article XIV formally commits a member state to move toward current account openness, but provides a somewhat open-ended transitional period to achieve this goal during which governments can impose restrictions without the Fund's approval. However, Article XIV countries remain subject to annual IMF scrutiny of their restrictions.

[11] Author's interview with Larosière.

[12] Author's interview with Richard Erb, Washington, D.C., 8 June 2005.

Informally, Larosière and Erb therefore did little, if anything, to encourage the staff to raise or explore the issue of capital account liberalization. Nor was it a major priority for Camdessus in his early years as managing director. "The Fund," according to Camdessus, "had a full agenda in the 1980s and early 1990s in encouraging current account liberalization."[13]

The Fund's Informal Adoption of the Norm of Capital Freedom

The informal staff approach changed radically in the 1980s and 1990s. In contrast to earlier periods, beginning in the mid-1980s and continuing until the Asian crisis in the late 1990s, the informal staff approach stressed the costs of capital controls and the benefits of liberalization, while under-emphasizing the risks and vulnerabilities associated with greater openness. Staff treatment of capital controls and their liberalization was selective, with these issues becoming prominent in those cases where capital flows were a significant factor in macroeconomic developments and exchange rate management. Consequently, as capital markets became increasingly integrated in the 1980s and 1990s and capital flows became a more significant feature of the world economy, the staff became more attentive to controls and their liberalization.

Although U.S. officials and IMF management accommodated controls during the debt crisis, the staff began in the mid-1980s to challenge their legitimacy as an instrument of macroeconomic management. Initially, the staff concentrated on the efficiency gains from capital account openness and the need to attract foreign investment as the principal rationales for liberalizing controls. In accordance with this perspective, area department staff missions in the middle to late 1980s, such as those to Chile, Mexico, and Venezuela, generally advocated and welcomed measures that liberalized barriers to inward foreign direct investment.[14] Similarly, other area department staff missions, such as those to Malaysia in the mid-1980s, supported the liberalization of foreign equity ownership.[15]

[13] Author's interview with Michel Camdessus, Paris, 10 November 2006.

[14] "Chile—Staff Report for the 1988 Article IV Consultation," EBS/88/139, 15 July 1988 (IMF Archives); "Mexico—Staff Report for the 1986 Article IV Consultation," EBS/86/161 Supplement 1, 15 August 1986 (IMF Archives), pp. 28–29, 46; "Mexico—Staff Report for the 1989 Article IV Consultation," EBS/89/91 Supplement 1, 25 May 1989 (IMF Archives), p. 2; "Venezuela—Staff Report for the 1988 Midyear Article IV Consultation," SM/88/165, 3 August 1988 (IMF Archives), pp. 14–15, 22.

[15] "Malaysia—Staff Report for the 1987 Article IV Consultation," SM/87/154, 7 July 1987 (IMF Archives), pp. 10, 20, 21. Asian Department staff also welcomed initiatives from Malaysian officials to liberalize restrictions on foreign direct investment; see, for instance, "Malaysia—Staff Report for the 1985 Article IV Consultation," SM/85/180, 26 June 1985 (IMF Archives), p. 14.

Reversing decades of IMF support for controls as an essential instrument of macroeconomic management, controls were said to harm economic performance, create severe distortions, and delay policy adjustments needed to eliminate balance-of-payments disequilibria. For instance, in the 1984 *WEO* the RES staff argued that controls "have had less salutary effects on domestic economic performance . . . and do not address the underlying financial disequilibrium in the economy and often aggravate distortions in the allocation of resources."[16] Area department staff missions in the middle to late 1980s, such as those to Chile, Mexico, Nigeria, and Venezuela, also often called for or welcomed liberalization based on such arguments.[17]

With respect to the issue of capital flight, rather than seeing it, as Keynes and White had, as a principal "cause" of the problems facing some countries, the staff understood capital flight to be a "symptom" of poor fundamentals. Some staff even questioned whether assets abroad represented flight capital instead of just "'normal' portfolio diversification by domestic residents."[18] In considering policy responses to capital flight, one staff analysis representative of opinion inside the Fund concluded:

> There is evidence that capital flight in a number of countries was slowed to some extent by the degree of capital controls, but this evidence is by no means conclusive. Further, it is well known that controls are generally effective in the short run, and tend not only to be circumvented in the long run but also often create serious distortions. *By and large, capital controls are not a viable substitute for a strategy designed to correct the underlying disequilibria in the economy that give rise to capital outflows.*[19]

In cases where controls were seen to be ineffective because of extensive capital flight and use of parallel foreign exchange markets, some staff saw scope to press for liberalization on the grounds that it would increase transparency and enhance efficiency. According to a 1995 internal IMF review, arguments for liberalization based on these grounds were made in Nigeria as early as 1986, which offered "one of the first cases where convertibility for both current and capital account transactions

---

[16] IMF, *World Economic Outlook* (Washington, D.C.: IMF, 1984), p. 54.

[17] "Chile—Staff Report for the 1986 Article IV Consultation," EBS/86/135, 27 June 1986 (IMF Archives), p. 26; "Mexico—Staff Report for the 1984 Article IV Consultation," SM/84/155, 2 July 1984 (IMF Archives), p. 32; "Nigeria—Staff Report for the 1987 Article IV Consultation," SM/87/280, 25 November 1987 (IMF Archives), pp. 3, 22–23, 25; "Venezuela—Staff Report for the 1987 Article IV Consultation," SM/87/243, 19 October 1987 (IMF Archives), pp. 23–24.

[18] Mohsin S. Khan and Nadeem Ul Haque, "Capital Flight from Developing Countries," *Finance and Development* 24, no. 1 (1987), pp. 2–5 at p. 3.

[19] Khan and Ul Haque, "Capital Flight," p. 5, emphasis added.

was proposed by the Fund staff."[20] In the mid-1980s and early 1990s, the leading proponents of this view were found in ETR, which was responsible for technical assistance on capital account liberalization until the creation of the Monetary and Exchange Affairs Department (MAE) in 1992. In making these arguments in Nigeria and other countries such as Egypt (1990–1991), Guatemala (1989), Honduras (1990), and Jamaica (1990), the ETR staff would often provide country officials with estimates of the magnitude of capital flight, emphasizing that controls on outflows had been ineffective and that their liberalization would recognize the de facto situation.

These arguments contrast sharply with those espoused when the staff in the 1940s considered how to manage capital flight from Europe. Then, the Keynesian-minded staff recommended intensifying controls and urged governments to abide by the spirit of the cooperative obligations embodied in the IMF Articles. Yet the ascendance of neoliberalism within the Fund in the 1980s led the staff to prescribe a different course of action. Although the staff considered some regulatory measures developed countries could take to lessen the incentive for capital inflows, the staff stopped short of sanctioning measures that would forcibly repatriate capital flight. In the event, no regulatory action was taken and the matter became less urgent as residents of Latin America began to repatriate their assets following the success of Brady Plan restructurings in the early 1990s.

As discussed in chapter 3, for much of the postwar era the staff approach lent legitimacy to traditional arguments for using controls, such as increasing domestic investment and tax revenue, supporting financial interventionism and macroeconomic planning, permitting greater monetary policy autonomy, and managing balance-of-payments pressures. However, as the 1980s debt crisis progressed, many staff members became increasingly skeptical of these traditional arguments and began to advocate liberalization in cases where countries maintained extensive controls.

For instance, two RES staff reports in the 1980s argue that there was "considerable scope in many countries for the rationalization of existing regulations and controls" and recommend their "elimination" to strengthen savings, investment, and growth.[21] In the late 1980s and early 1990s, RES and ETR staff reports increasingly pointed to the benefits of liberalization.[22] The October 1988 *WEO*, for instance, concludes that

[20] "Capital Account Convertibility—Review of Experiences and Implications for Fund Policies—Background Paper," SM/95/164 Supplement 1, 7 July 1995 (IMF Archives), p. 27.

[21] IMF, *World Economic Outlook* (Washington, D.C.: IMF, 1985), p. 13; IMF, *World Economic Outlook* (Washington, D.C.: IMF, 1986), p. 102.

[22] IMF, *World Economic Outlook* (Washington, D.C.: IMF, 1987), p. 89; Mark Allen, Donald Mathieson, Charles Collyns, Augusto de la Torre, Mohammed El Erian, David Folkerts-Landau, Tim Lane, Liliana Rojas-Suarez, Paul Thomsen, Louis Pauly, Can Demir,

"what appears to be required in present circumstances, therefore, is a continuation of recent trends [liberalization] in those countries where most progress has been made, together with a more vigorous attitude on existing rigidities in countries where financial competition is still relatively constrained."[23] A similar perspective was shared by a number of area department staff. For example, a 1989 area department mission to South Korea argued, "The authorities have made significant progress in liberalization of domestic financial markets, but there continues to be considerable scope for action in this area. A reform of the foreign exchange market will require, besides a freer domestic financial market, a substantial liberalization of external capital transactions."[24]

The emergence within the Fund of new understandings of market behavior underpinned staff arguments for these new standards of behavior. The staff discarded their earlier Keynesian emphasis on factors intrinsic to international capital markets, and replaced it with a neoliberal focus on the role of fundamentals. One earlier mentioned indication of the emergence of these new understandings was staff arguments that some capital flight during the debt crisis could be constituted as "normal" portfolio diversification. The meaning some staff fixed to capital flight in the 1980s thus contrasts sharply with the one fixed in the 1940s and 1950s. A 1992 *International Capital Markets Report* (*ICMR*) offers another clear indication of the staff's new focus on fundamentals, noting, "International capital flows continued to reflect the current account imbalances of industrial and developing countries and the international diversification of investment portfolio."[25] Testifying to the emergence of these new understandings, the IEO concludes that the staff generally shared a "fundamentalist view of international capital flows," that is, interpreting market actors as guided largely by economic and policy trends.[26]

These new understandings led the staff to downplay the potential risks of capital flow volatility and to overlook the potential usefulness of supply-side regulatory measures that developed countries might implement to reduce it. Although the staff were aware of the potential for sudden stops

and Rosa Vera-Bunge, *International Capital Markets: Developments and Prospects* (Washington, D.C.: IMF, 1990), pp. 12, 13; IMF, *World Economic Outlook* (October) (Washington, D.C.: IMF, 1992), p. 28; Michael Mussa, Morris Goldstein, Peter B. Clark, Donald J. Mathieson, and Tamim Bayoumi, "Improving the International Monetary System," IMF Occasional Paper No. 116 (Washington, D.C.: IMF, 1994), p. 3.

[23] IMF, *World Economic Outlook* (October) (Washington, D.C.: IMF, 1988), p. 35. See also pp. 34–35.

[24] "Korea—Staff Report for the 1989 Article IV Consultation," SM/89/194, 12 September 1989 (IMF Archives), pp. 22–23.

[25] As cited in IEO, *IMF's Approach*, p. 24. The *ICMR* later became the *GFSR*.

[26] IEO, *IMF's Approach*, p. 24.

and reversals, they generally did not sufficiently highlight the risks and vulnerabilities associated with capital account openness. On the contrary, the staff often welcomed supply-side measures that offered emerging markets and developing countries greater access to international capital markets. Even though there was an explosive surge in net private capital flows to emerging markets and developing countries from less than $100 billion in 1990 to well over $200 billion in 1995, staff reports during this period devoted relatively little attention to the policy challenges that enhanced access to capital flows might pose.[27]

Although their beliefs were not monolithic, the staff's approach, and thus the informal boundaries of legitimate policy practice as defined by the IMF, had changed significantly. Whereas earlier the staff generally viewed unfettered capital mobility as undesirable and controls as essential, now most had little doubt about the long-run desirability of capital freedom. "By the time we got to the 1980s," observes Matthew Fisher, a longtime member of the staff who has worked extensively on capital issues, "the thinking that had driven the logic of Keynes's position had given way to a different paradigm."[28]

The key point of debate, which I return to below, centered on not whether capital freedom was desirable but how the world should proceed toward it. In other words, the debate dealt with how the norm of capital freedom should be interpreted and applied. As Michael Mussa, RES director from 1991 to 2001, observes, "There was a basic consensus that in the long run a liberal financial regime focused on market forces and market discipline both domestically and internationally was the objective to aim for. There was also recognition that extensive controls often were ineffective and sources of important distortion and often could be a source of corruption. . . . The debate was not on the ultimate goal but on the pace and sequencing."[29]

EXPLAINING THE FUND'S INFORMAL SHIFT

The state-centric conventional wisdom portrays IMF adoption of the norm of capital freedom as resulting from management acquiescence to pressure from U.S. officials, who in turn were shaped by private financial community demands. The evidence, however, does not support this portrayal.

[27] IEO, *IMF's Approach.*
[28] Author's interview with Matthew Fisher, Washington, D.C., 19 May 2005.
[29] Author's interview with Michael Mussa, Washington, D.C., 6 June 2005.

First, management did little, if anything, to encourage initial staff adoption of the norm of capital freedom. Larosière and Erb failed to signal to the staff that they favored capital account liberalization as a goal for the Fund to promote. They instead focused on graduating countries to current account convertibility and generally accommodated capital controls. Interestingly, as suggested above, this more accommodating orientation was somewhat at odds with the more critical stance taken by some staff.

Camdessus would emerge in the 1990s as a strong supporter of giving the Fund the mandate to promote liberalization and to have jurisdiction over the capital accounts of its members. Yet by all accounts Camdessus did not seriously consider and make these ideas public until late 1993.[30] Moreover, no specific intellectual or operational guidance appears to have been forthcoming from management until Stanley Fischer arrived as first deputy managing director in September 1994. Alongside developments in Mexico (see below) and efforts to amend the Articles (see chapter 8), the arrival of Fischer was critical in stirring active management involvement on the issue.

As first deputy managing director, Fischer likely saw the bureaucratic benefits of expanding the IMF's role in advocating liberalization. Yet his professional training at MIT, an academic department traditionally associated with the neoclassical synthesis and new Keynesianism, likely shaped how he articulated his specific position. For instance, looking ahead, in 1997, Fischer's interpretation of the Asian crisis would focus primarily on poor fundamentals, but also concede that market actors "may themselves be excessive on occasion."[31] As an academic economist Fischer had helped to elaborate the gradualist approach along with Jacob Frenkel, who served as RES director from 1987 to 1991.[32] In line with the gradualist view, Fischer, as first deputy managing director, argued that the pace of liberalization should depend on the strength of the financial sector.[33] Fischer admits, however, that he was never particularly systematic in encouraging the staff to pursue the gradualist approach.[34]

In any event, the staff had changed their normative outlook in the 1980s *prior* to any active management involvement on the issue. As Mussa recalls,

[30] Author's interview with Camdessus. See also Abdelal, *Capital Rules*, p. 140.

[31] Stanley Fischer, "Capital Account Liberalization and the Role of the IMF," IMF Seminar on Asia and the IMF, Washington, D.C., 19 September 1997, available at http://www.imf.org/external/np/speeches/1997/091997.htm (accessed 9 January 2007).

[32] Stanley Fischer and Jacob A. Frenkel, "Stabilization Policy for Israel," *Economics Quarterly* 29, no. 114 (1982), pp. 246–255.

[33] IEO, *IMF's Approach*, p. 78.

[34] Author's interview with Stanley Fischer, London, 10 November 2006. Some staff members had similar recollections. Author's interview with Mohsin Khan, Washington, D.C., 7 June 2005.

"The view that capital account liberalization was desirable was already present in the Fund prior to Camdessus's push for the amendment."[35] Other staff—who have little incentive to take responsibility for a policy orientation that has been so severely criticized—offer similar recollections.[36] Without any strong indication in the 1980s and early 1990s that management favored IMF advocacy of capital account liberalization, it is difficult to conclude that career incentives drove staff behavior. To be sure, once management signaled its support for capital freedom, career incentives likely played a role. But these incentives were limited largely to reinforcing the change that had come from within rather than initiating any significant change from above.

Significantly, as discussed subsequently, even though management did offer support from above for capital freedom in the mid-1990s, Camdessus and Fischer never spoke with one clear voice on how this norm should be interpreted and applied. Generally speaking, Fischer was more open to the use of temporary controls than Camdessus. This subtle disagreement provided the staff with additional autonomy and limited the extent to which management could informally shape the staff's norm interpretation and application.

Like management, U.S. officials were also cast in a supporting rather than a leading role in shaping the staff's approach. To be sure, in the 1980s U.S. officials saw capital freedom as desirable and sought to promote it in specific countries. But the issue was not viewed as a top priority or one on which to expend resources within the Fund.[37] U.S. officials were more focused on exchange rate management and the debt crisis, and thus little attention and effort was devoted to imposing a particular approach on the staff. IMF management and staff—who presumably would have a strong incentive to deflect responsibility for a policy orientation that has been so severely criticized—also recall no U.S. encouragement at this time.

Moreover, as noted above, U.S. policy until the early 1990s, which often accommodated controls, was occasionally at odds with IMF staff prescriptions. It was only beginning in the mid-1990s that the U.S. Treasury—under Robert Rubin and Lawrence Summers—began to make a big push for the staff to encourage liberalization.[38] Yet by this time the staff's approach had already more or less developed. U.S. officials may not have seen

[35] Author's interview with Mussa.
[36] Author's interviews with Mark Allen, 1 June 2005, Washington, D.C.; Jack Boorman, 31 May 2005, Washington, D.C.; Khan; Fisher; Claudio Loser, 26 May 2005, Washington, D.C.; and Singh.
[37] Author's interviews with Dallara; Dawson; and Erb.
[38] Author interviews with David Lipton, New York, 17 June 2005; Karin Lissakers, New York, 15 June 2005; Jeffrey R. Shafer, New York, 14 June 2005. Many staff members also recall the U.S. Treasury strongly voicing its views only under Rubin and Summers.

a need to block the staff's adoption of the norm of capital freedom, but they did not actively reflect upon or encourage it, and at times they disagreed with the staff on how it should be interpreted and applied. Thus, U.S. officials did not play a primary or direct role in the development of the staff's approach.

In the early 1990s, after countries of the EC had nearly completed their transition to capital account openness, some European officials emerged as strong supporters of capital freedom. But, like U.S. officials, European officials at best played a supporting role, actively encouraging the norm only after the staff's approach already had developed. The outer structural constraint that supported capital freedom did not begin to take shape until agreement on capital account openness within the EC had been reached in June 1988.[39] Even then some EC governments—such as Italy, Greece, Portugal, and Spain—still objected to the principle of capital freedom, though their positions changed in the early to mid-1990s. Support from European governments helped underpin the norm of capital freedom within the Fund, but it also was not the source of it. Furthermore, it should be noted that despite U.S. and European support for capital freedom in the 1990s, the IMF board, because of alternative perspectives offered by emerging market and developing country directors, could never reach a consensus on the legitimacy of controls and thus failed to issue any directives to the staff until 1995.[40]

Still, while U.S. and European officials were not the source of the staff's approach, the new ideational climate among leading Fund principals did create an outer structural constraint that was more permissive of endogenous normative change. So long as many leading principals did not support capital freedom, the staff, even if they were sympathetic to the idea, would likely have found it difficult to argue forcefully for liberalization. But once European governments began to dismantle their controls, the outer structural constraint was loosened, and the staff could encourage liberalization more actively. Although staff members likely recognized that their outer structural constraint was changing in the 1980s and 1990s, it is important to reiterate that, partly because of preference heterogeneity among board directors, they failed to receive any directives or informal

---

[39] Abdelal, *Capital Rules*, pp. 69–72.

[40] On the lack of the consensus on the board, see Executive Board Seminar SEM/93/3, 21 July 1993 (IMF Archives), pp. 29, 43, 61, 63; Executive Board Seminar SEM/93/4, 21 July 1993 (IMF Archives), pp. 5, 15; "Concluding Remarks by the Acting Chairman for the Seminar on Issues and Developments in the International Exchange and Payments System" (Executive Board Seminar 94/10), BUFF/94/106, 23 November 1994 (IMF Archives), p. 2; "The Acting Chairman's Summing Up—Capital Account Convertibility—Review of Experience and Implications for Fund Policies (Executive Board Meeting 95/73)," BUFF/95/73, 4 August 1995 (IMF Archives).

encouragement from member states that might have significantly influenced their approach.

With respect to role of the private financial community, which some see as constituting a principal of the Fund,[41] it is clear from the evidence that it exerted little influence on the staff. The Institute of International Finance (IIF), the organization that represents the interests of most of world's largest commercial banks and investment banks, did not devote serious consideration to the issue of capital account liberalization until 1993.[42] Upon such consideration, the IIF came down cautiously in its support, viewing capital freedom as desirable in principle but with its enthusiasm tempered by an awareness of the risks and vulnerabilities that can accompany premature liberalization.[43] More importantly, the IIF and financial market participants were generally not consulted by the Fund and thus had little opportunity to express their position effectively.[44]

Without firm directives or formal rules from management or member states, and in the context of preference heterogeneity among IMF principals, the staff were provided with significant autonomy to develop their approach independently. This autonomy permitted the staff members to rely on their own judgment and initiative to determine whether liberalization should be encouraged informally in a given case. A July 1995 staff paper confirms as much: "The Executive Board has not thus far considered comprehensively the specific issue of capital account liberalization with a view to developing guidelines for the membership as a whole. Rather, views of capital account issues have been expressed largely [by the staff] in the context of surveillance, the use of Fund resources, and technical assistance activities."[45] PA approaches of course expect such autonomy, but how preferences form within IOs—given such autonomy—constitutes a significant analytical blind spot.

[41] Gould, "Money Talks."

[42] Author's interview with Dallara. The IIF's semiannual policy letters to the IMF Interim Committee did not raise the issue of capital controls until September 1995; see Charles Dallara, *Letter to His Excellency Minister Philippe Maystadt, Chairman of the Interim Committee* (Washington, D.C.: Institute of International Finance, 28 September 1995).

[43] IIF, "Capital Account Convertibility as an IMF Obligation: A Briefing Note for the IIF Board of Directors," Washington, D.C., unpublished manuscript, 1997, p. 3; IIF, "Background Paper—Capital Account Convertibility as an IMF Obligation," Washington, D.C., unpublished manuscript, 1997, pp. 2–4, 11, 13; IIF, "Report of the Working Group on the Liberalization of Capital Movements," Washington, D.C., unpublished manuscript, 1999, pp. 2–4.

[44] IIF, "Capital Account Convertibility," pp. 1, 2–3; IIF, "Background Paper—Capital Account Convertibility as an IMF Obligation," p. 8. Interestingly, one of the lessons the Fund drew from the failed attempt to amend the Articles was that greater effort needed to be made to consult with the private financial community.

[45] "Capital Account Convertibility—Review of Experiences and Implications for Fund Policies," SM/95/164, 7 July 1995 (IMF Archives), p. 8.

Professionalization and Administrative Recruitment

We therefore need to turn to intraorganizational processes to better understand the evolution of the IMF approach, with particular attention to the beliefs that prevailed within the Fund. Professionalization and administrative recruitment were two critical factors shaping these beliefs. Beginning in the mid-1980s, the substantial group of individuals who had served as members of staff since the 1940s and 1950s began to retire in large numbers. These retiring staff, who because of their Keynesian training and the experiences of the 1930s were more inclined to view controls as legitimate, were subsequently replaced primarily by "neoliberal-trained" economists who had joined the staff in the 1960s and early 1970s.[46] This realignment of personnel fostered the emergence of a cadre of individuals who supported new understandings and standards of behavior.

Newly available quantitative data enables a detailed inspection of this personnel realignment. In chapter 3 I outlined a methodology to identify a specific set of academic departments where, and a time frame when, neoliberalism prevailed. Here I use this information to code the professional characteristics of a new dataset of 472 IMF staff members that was created from telephone directories found in the IMF Archives and supplemented by the IMF Communications Department. Data on professional characteristics were obtained from Digital Dissertations, Index to Theses, LexisNexis Executive, and The International Who's Who.[47]

Most researchers treat the Fund as a unitary actor, assuming, as a number of critics suggest, that it speaks with one voice and advocates a uniform set of policies for all countries on all occasions. Yet the Fund never spoke with one voice on capital account liberalization. Rather, the issue was subject to a vigorous internal debate that resulted in a fairly diverse set of policy prescriptions. I therefore use the personnel data to disaggregate the Fund as unit. Following the methodology outlined in chapter 3, I create a measure indicating the proportion of economists with "neoliberal training" in each of the IMF departments that played a key role in developing the Fund's approach.

Figure 7.1 shows the personnel realignment within the Fund from 1970 to 1998.[48] Although these data cannot differentiate between gradualist

---

[46] De Vries, in "The International Monetary Fund," p. 55, comments on this wave of retirements in the 1980s.

[47] See http://www.proquest.com/en-US/products/brands/pl_umidp.shtml; http://www.theses.com; http://www.lexis-nexis.co.uk/site/LN_Executive.asp; http://www.worldwhoswho.com/.

[48] Prior to the 1970s no staff member was coded as having neoliberal training; therefore the data are only plotted from 1970 onward; 25.4 percent of the dataset was coded as having "neoliberal training."

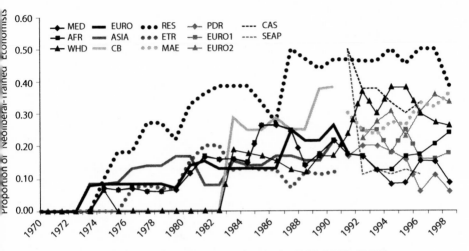

Figure 7.1. "Neoliberal-Trained" Economists at the IMF, 1970–1998

and big-bang supporters, they do offer a clear picture of the general ascendance of neoliberalism within the Fund as well as the considerable variation that existed across departments. Across the Fund as a whole the ascendance of neoliberalism seems to begin gradually in the early to mid-1970s and then accelerates in the late 1980s and early 1990s.

The personnel realignment depicted in figure 7.1 helped overturn long-standing beliefs and associated practices and facilitated adoption of the norm of capital freedom. Staff recruited in the 1940s and 1950s had shown themselves to be reluctant to adopt the norm of capital freedom, even after the formal rule changes engineered in the 1970s. Without this personnel realignment in the 1980s, the Fund's adoption of the norm of capital freedom therefore would have been, in all likelihood, delayed, more incremental, and less coherent than it was.

Indeed, several official IMF historians identify administrative recruitment patterns as a critical mechanism shaping cycles, trends, and shifts in the staff's beliefs.[49] Along these lines, Polak suggests that professionalization and recruitment were critical determinants of the staff's approach:

In the absence of general instruction from the Board it depended on individual departments and staff who judged the situation. Judgments tended to be reflective of what was learned in university. All of the [initial] staff tended to start out as Keynesians, though became less enthusi-

[49] James Boughton, *The Silent Revolution: The International Monetary Fund, 1979–1989* (Washington, D.C.: IMF, 2001), pp. 25, 27–28; de Vries, "The International Monetary Fund," p. 56.

astic about that approach. The atmosphere in the economics profession then started changing in a direction that viewed liberalization as desirable. New people and new cohorts of recruits from university were a primary source of new ideas.[50]

Others offer similar assessments. Morris Goldstein, a staff member from 1970 to 1994, observes that new ideas tend to enter the Fund "as part of the broader economics profession. There are fashions and fads and the Fund is not immune to that. Fashions and fads come about and become something that seems successful for a while. People [who came to senior staff positions in the 1980s] were representative of what was going on in the profession."[51]

Boughton also finds the evolution of the IMF to be partly driven by "trends and cycles in economic theory" and identifies new classical economics as "the theoretical development that probably had the biggest post-Keynes impact on the IMF."[52] Similarly, Mussa suggests, "Academic thought has led the way. Many of the staff were trained in Ph.D. programs in the virtues of market-oriented solutions. Academics were very critical of regulations and played an important role in motivating financial liberalization. As the climate changed intellectually it impacted how these issues were viewed within the Fund."[53]

However, as expected, figure 7.1 reveals that significant differences existed among the staff, with neoliberal economists being most prevalent in RES, MAE (and one of its principal institutional predecessors the Central Banking Department—CB), and the Western Hemisphere Department (WHD). Although RES tended to house the most neoliberal economists, there were sharp divisions within the department between gradualists—who mainly worked within the department's Capital Markets Group—and big-bang supporters.[54] Indeed, while two former RES directors, Frenkel and Mussa, were aligned more with gradualism, other influential staff members, such as Goldstein and Donald Mathieson, were reportedly initially more sympathetic to the big-bang approach. Figure 7.1 also suggests that MAE (and CB) generally was staffed with a large number of neoliberal economists. But, as I discuss below, MAE was less divided than RES and instead tended to support the big-bang approach. PDR (and its principal institutional predecessor ETR) also generally housed a modest contingent of neoliberal economists, though their relative number usually was smaller

[50] Author's interview with Polak.
[51] Author's interviews with Morris Goldstein, Washington, D.C., 19 May 2005.
[52] Boughton, "Force of History," pp. 1, 17.
[53] Author's interview with Michael Mussa, Washington, D.C., 6 June 2005.
[54] Author's interviews with Mussa; Morris Goldstein, 19 May 2005, Washington, D.C.; Liliana Rojas-Suarez, 26 May 2005, Washington, D.C., 26 May 2005; Khan.

than that found in RES or MAE. Within PDR the gradualists tended to have the upper hand, but there were also proponents of the big-bang approach as well.

Among the area departments, the WHD clearly stands out. Indeed, the evidence from country consultations, as well as that gleaned from interviews, strongly suggests that WHD was a more enthusiastic proponent of liberalization than other area departments.[55] But some WHD staff were also accommodative of, even sympathetic to, the use of selective restraints on capital inflows. For instance, when, in 1991, Chile first introduced market-based controls on inflows—a measure that fostered significant debate within the Fund and the economics profession (see below)—the WHD staff responsible for country consultations did not oppose the measure, and, in fact, later positively noted that the controls may have helped limit short-term inflows.[56]

Strong proponents of liberalization could also be found in other area departments. Figure 7.1 suggests that the Asia Department and the European Department (EURO) tended to house a fairly large contingent of neoliberal economists from the late 1970s until their reorganizations in 1991 and 1992, respectively. The Asia Department was reorganized into separate departments covering Southeast Asia and the Pacific (SEAP) and Central Asia (CAS) until 1997 when these separate departments were consolidated into the APD. The European II Department (EURO2) was created in 1992 with the task of managing relations with countries of the former Soviet Union, while the European I Department (EURO1) was created to cover countries in Eastern and Western Europe.[57] The data in figure 7.1 suggest that CAS and EURO2 were generally staffed with a larger contingent of neoliberal economists than SEAP and EURO1.

Nonetheless, archival evidence suggests each of these departments was also characterized by the division between gradualists and adherents of the big bang. In South Korea, the SEAP staff were particularly forceful in encouraging broader and more rapid liberalization despite attempts by RES's Capital Markets Group to raise concerns about the risks inherent

[55] Author's interviews with Jack Boorman, Washington, D.C., 31 May 2005; Matthew Fisher, Washington, D.C., 19 May 2005; Claudio Loser, Washington, D.C., 26 May 2005 and 8 July 2005; Michael Mussa; Washington, D.C., 6 June 2005.

[56] "Chile—Staff Report for the 1994 Article IV Consultation," SM/94/172, 6 July 1994 (IMF Archives), pp. 3, 4, 8; IEO, *IMF's Approach*, p. 28. Western Hemisphere Department staff also did not initially oppose introduction of similar market-based controls on inflows in Colombia in 1994; see IEO, *IMF's Approach*, pp. 68–69.

[57] In 2003, EURO2 was dissolved, with the Baltic countries, Belarus, Moldova, Russia, and Ukraine moving to EURO1, which was renamed the European Department. The other countries of the former Soviet Union were moved to the Middle Eastern Department, which was renamed the Middle East and Central Asia Department.

in South Korea's liberalization strategy, which had liberalized short-term foreign borrowing while maintaining restrictions on long-term flows, thus encouraging the buildup of short-term debt by weak financial institutions. Throughout the 1990s, the SEAP staff paid little attention to the problems caused by such a liberalization sequence and pressed instead for "further substantial liberalization," "a more ambitious timetable than envisaged [by the government]," and "a faster pace."[58]

But others within SEAP and CAS offered an alternative perspective. For instance, staff consultations with India routinely supported the government's gradual approach.[59] In Indonesia, which faced a high external debt burden and growing weaknesses in the state-dominated banking sector, the staff endorsed limits introduced by the government in 1991 on foreign borrowing by all public sector entities, including those with no more than indirect links to the state.[60] In contrast to consultations with South Korea, the SEAP staff responsible for Indonesia were more conscious of the vulnerabilities created by large capital inflows and associated foreign debt as well as the fragile banking system. But these staff members also underestimated the risks associated with reliance on short-term capital flows that were vulnerable to a sudden shift in market sentiment and failed to adequately recognize the extent of Indonesia's banking sector weaknesses.

In the early 1990s, the EURO1 and EURO2 staffs were extremely supportive and welcoming of liberalization in the transition economies of the former Soviet bloc. Liberalization was encouraged as a means to supplement domestic savings (Poland in 1991), to decrease domestic interest rates (Slovenia in 1993), and to foster greater price stability (Russia in early 1990s).[61] According to a 1995 internal review, the EURO1 and EURO2 staff also supported the "rapid liberalization of certain capital account transactions" in the early 1990s in several Eastern European countries under the auspices of IMF programs.[62] The EURO1 and

---

[58] "Korea—Staff Report for the 1990 Article IV Consultation," SM/90/184, 18 September 1990 (IMF Archives), p. 15 ("further substantial liberalization"); "Korea—Staff Report for the 1992 Article IV Consultation," SM/93/11, 19 January 1993 (IMF Archives), p. 16 ("a more ambitious timetable"); "Korea—Staff Report for the 1995 Article IV Consultation," SM/95/209, 18 August 1995 (IMF Archives), p. 2 ("a faster pace").

[59] IEO, *IMF's Approach*, p. 51.

[60] "Indonesia—Staff Report for the 1992 Interim Article IV Consultation," SM/92/81, 13 April 1992 (IMF Archives), pp. 15, 18; "Indonesia—Staff Report for the 1993 Article IV Consultation," SM/94/22, 25 January 1994 (IMF Archives), pp. 17, 22. The staff also pointed out that care needed to be taken to ensure the measure did not impede private sector borrowing and that the measure was not a substitute for improving bank management.

[61] IEO, *IMF's Approach*, pp. 32–33.

[62] "Capital Account Convertibility—Review of Experiences and Implications for Fund Policies—Background Paper," p. 23. See also pp. 24–25. The internal review covered IMF programs with Albania, Bulgaria, the Czech and Slovak Republics, Estonia, Hungary, Latvia, Lithuania, Poland, and Romania.

EURO2 staff also occasionally urged broader and more rapid liberalization when reforms outlined in IMF programs were not implemented. However, since liberalization could not legally be made a condition for the use of the Fund's resources, the staff, even if they wished to do so, had no direct leverage with which to impose liberalization. It should also be noted that some EURO1 staff members were cautious not to push for liberalization too rapidly. In 1992, for instance, the staff consulting with Albanian officials recommended that controls on outflows be maintained until external imbalances were resolved and the reserve position strengthened.[63]

Generally speaking, the Middle Eastern Department (MED) and the African Department (AFR) contained the fewest neoliberal economists, and this, along with the fragility of many of the economies in these regions, helped to make these staff members some of the least enthusiastic proponents of liberalization within the Fund. But despite this general lack of enthusiasm, the MED and AFR staff did not hesitate to advocate liberalization in some cases, such as Tunisia and Botswana in the mid-1990s.[64] Still, in cases where liberalization was encouraged, these staff tended to support gradualism, as exemplified by the stance taken in AFR consultations with South Africa in the mid-1990s. Here the AFR staff advised the government to move slowly toward capital account openness because of concerns about political uncertainty associated with the transition from apartheid and in light of recent speculative attacks on the currency.[65]

Organizational Learning

In the 1980s and 1990s, in addition to the role of new recruits replacing retiring staff members, learning via country experiences helped alter the normative outlook of the Fund.[66] Indeed, the IEO concludes that "the IMF has learned over time on capital account issues."[67]

[63] "Capital Account Convertibility—Review of Experiences and Implications for Fund Policies—Background Paper," p. 24.

[64] "Capital Account Convertibility—Review of Experiences and Implications for Fund Policies—Background Paper," pp. 21–22; "Tunisia—Staff Report for the 1994 Article IV Consultation," SM/94/200, 20 December 1994 (IMF Archives), pp. iv, 18, 23; "Tunisia—Staff Report for the 1997 Article IV Consultation," SM/97/107, 5 May 1997 (IMF Archives), pp. 7, 9, 14. See also IEO, *IMF's Approach*, pp. 71–74.

[65] IEO, *IMF's Approach*, p. 34; "Review of Experience with Capital Account Liberalization and Strengthened Procedures Adopted by the Fund," SM/97/32 Supplement 1, 6 February 1997 (IMF Archives), pp. 37–38.

[66] Figure 7.1 shows that not all staff in the 1980s and 1990s were neoliberal economists, suggesting some unexplained variance in norm adoption. Learning can thus help account for some of this unexplained variation.

[67] IEO, *IMF's Approach*, pp. 6, 60.

Staff reports and interviewees routinely cited the transition to capital account openness among developed countries—particularly EU countries—as critical in demonstrating the desirability of liberalization. Some staff—particularly big-bang proponents as well as those in the Asian Department—also pointed to the case of Indonesia, as it showed an emerging market could seemingly undertake rapid liberalization without much regard to sequencing and maintain a commitment to it in the face of consistent balance-of-payments imbalances.[68] Staff research also helped undermine many of the traditional arguments for controls, revealing their relative ineffectiveness in supporting monetary policy, preserving domestic savings, and managing balance-of-payments pressures.[69] Capturing the views of many IMF staff members, Michael Dooley, a senior RES staff member from 1981 to 1991, observes, "One important lesson that can be drawn from this work is that there is considerable evidence that capital control systems have not prevented successful speculative attacks on fixed exchange rate systems."[70]

This new evidence helped foster among the staff a comprehensive reappraisal of organizational goals. Underlying organizational "theories in use," in particular the desirability of controls, were fundamentally challenged. Old organizational ideologies, norms, language, and routines were largely discarded, and new ones took their place. Rather than simply adding new agendas or policy instruments to existing organizational practice, the staff experienced a deeper shift in their beliefs about desirable goals. The personnel alignment of the 1980s likely played an important part in creating an environment conducive for learning.

This personnel realignment made the organization as a whole more receptive to lessons suggesting that capital freedom was a desirable goal. The realignment of IMF personnel, in which retiring long-serving staff were replaced by new recruits with alternative beliefs, created an internal ideational environment that was permissive, if not encouraging, of particular staff research, that is, studies that furthered adoption of the norm of capital freedom. As retirements led to more long-serving staff leaving the Fund and recruitment brought in more neoliberal economists, an environment was created in which staff research that drew attention to the

---

[68] Peter Quirk, "Capital Account Convertibility: A New Model for Developing Countries," IMF Working Paper 94/81 (Washington, D.C.: IMF, 1994), p. 13; author's interview with Singh.

[69] See, for instance, Nadem U. Haque and Peter Montiel, "Capital Mobility in Developing Countries—Some Empirical Tests," IMF Working Paper WP/90/117 (Washington, D.C.: IMF, 1990); R. Barry Johnston and Chris Ryan, "The Impact of Controls on Capital Movements on the Private Capital Accounts of Countries' Balance of Payments: Empirical Estimates and Policy Implications," IMF Working Paper WP/94/78 (Washington, D.C.: IMF, 1994); and Mathieson and Rojas-Suarez, *Liberalization of the Capital Account*.

[70] Dooley, "Survey of Academic Literature," p. 3.

benefits of capital freedom and the costs of controls was likely to be given greater prominence. The new ideational environment also made it more acceptable within the Fund to analyze controls from a more critical perspective. In the absence of this realignment, the cognitive difficulties associated with learning likely would have limited the extent to which it occurred.

NORM INTERPRETATION AND APPLICATION PRIOR TO THE ASIAN CRISIS

Informal adoption of the norm of capital freedom was more or less complete by the early 1990s. However, although staff members had come to view capital freedom as desirable in the long run, they disagreed over how this norm should be interpreted and applied. The personnel realignment of the 1980s had helped foster adoption of the norm of capital freedom, but it had also resulted in the emergence of subcultures.

These subcultures developed partly as a result of new recruits bringing with them contrasting interpretations and applications that were associated with unsettled debates within the economics profession, thus providing an ideational basis for the internal bureaucratic struggle that followed. Most staff members, like most academic economists, saw liberalization as a desirable long-run goal. But these staff members, like academic economists, also disagreed over how the world should proceed toward capital freedom. The staff, like the economics profession, did not agree about whether to proceed quickly or slowly, and whether to proceed with various preconditions and allowances for temporary controls or not. The battle of ideas between the gradualists and big-bang proponents was thus very much a reflection of ongoing debates within the economics profession.

In the early 1980s, the gradualist position began to develop, with the general contours emerging from the seminal work of McKinnon and Shaw. Characterized by a neoclassical synthesist / new Keynesian understanding of market behavior, gradualists see liberalization as desirable in the long run, but also view restraints on capital mobility as often necessary to counteract distortions and correct short-run market errors. Gradualists often point to the differential speed of adjustment for goods and asset markets, for instance, as a reason for sequencing reforms.

The gradualist position also developed partly in reaction to the experiences of the Southern Cone countries of Latin America (Argentina, Chile, and Uruguay) with capital account liberalization and financial crisis in the early 1980s. Three lessons were identified from these experiences. One was that macroeconomic stability must precede capital account liberalization.[71]

---

[71] See, for instance, Michael Dooley and Donald Mathieson, "Financial Liberalization in Developing Countries," *Finance and Development* 24, no. 3 (1987), pp. 31–34; Sebastian Edwards, *The Order of Liberalization of the External Sector in Developing Countries*, Prince-

Macroeconomic policies in the Southern Cone countries had produced substantial interest-rate differentials and real exchange rate appreciations, which attracted large capital inflows and further dollar indebtedness, which in turn exacerbated the pain of the severe financial crisis when currency devaluations occurred in the early 1980s.

Another lesson focused on how current and capital account liberalization should be sequenced. Although McKinnon and Shaw had examined the "optimal" sequence for liberalization, relatively little effort had been devoted since to analyzing the issue. Renewed attention had been drawn to it, however, by the Southern Cone experiences. Argentina and Uruguay had opened the capital account first; Chile opened the current account first. The general consensus to emerge was that the "optimal" sequence placed current account liberalization prior to capital account liberalization.

Frenkel was a chief proponent of this view inside the Fund. Because of the differential speed of adjustment of goods and assets markets, Frenkel warned that capital account liberalization could produce a real exchange rate appreciation that would potentially undermine adjustments in the goods market as it moved from a protective to a freer environment. To illustrate the implications from the different speeds of adjustment, Frenkel often used the analogy of a carriage pulled by two horses, one of which was faster than the other. In such circumstances the result would be that the horses moving at different speeds would cause the cart to collapse. To avoid this disaster, the speeds of the two horses had to be equalized. This could be achieved by speeding up the slow horse or by slowing down the fast one. It stood to reason that the former course of action was not sustainable, while the latter was achieved with little effort. This analogy thus implied that the optimal policy was short-run intervention in the adjustment of asset markets to slow down capital flows while other reforms were implemented and the adjustment of goods markets occurred over the long run. As Frenkel observed, "Although it is eventually desirable to have an open capital account, prudence calls for a gradual transition to openness so as to facilitate the required change in institutions and the economic structure."[72] Others inside the Fund and the economics profession shared this conclusion.[73]

---

ton Essays in International Finance No. 156 (Princeton, N.J.: Princeton University, International Finance Section, 1984).

[72] Jacob Frenkel, "Panel Discussion on the Southern Cone," *IMF Staff Papers* 30, no. 1 (1983), pp. 164–172 at p. 166.

[73] See Edwards, *Order of Liberalization*; Mohsin Khan and Roberto Zahler, "The Macroeconomic Effects of Changes in Barriers to Trade and Capital Flows: A Simulation Analysis," *IMF Staff Papers* 30 (1983), pp. 223–282; Ronald I. McKinnon, *The Order of Economic Liberalization: Financial Control in the Transition to a Market Economy* (Baltimore: Johns Hopkins University Press, 1991), p. 160.

A small number of staff and academic economists also drew a third lesson from the Southern Cone experiences. For these individuals, the experiences demonstrated that a well-developed and regulated domestic financial sector was a vital precondition for capital account openness.[74] Drawing on the Chilean financial crisis, which some partly attributed to the decision of the government to liberalize in the absence of robust prudential financial regulations, these individuals warned of the possibility of dynamic feedback between financial sector weakness and currency crisis— an outcome that in the late 1990s became known as a "twin crisis."

Within the Fund some gradualists in RES, particularly those within the Capital Markets Group, picked up on this lesson and issued warnings about the vulnerabilities created by weak and poorly regulated financial systems in an environment where there was the potential for sharp and sudden disruptions to capital flows. These gradualists stressed the need for governments to strengthen their financial systems and prudential regulations before liberalizing controls. In their view, restraints on capital mobility were necessary while policy adjustments were implemented. Some area department missions in the early 1990s also pointed to problems posed by weak banking systems (Poland in 1991 and the Czech Republic in 1993) or raised the possibility of tightening prudential regulations as a way of dealing with capital inflow surges (Thailand in 1992 and Mexico in 1993).[75] But these were isolated incidents and such concerns usually did not translate into any staff advice on slowing down the pace or rethinking the sequence of liberalization.

Notwithstanding the Chilean experience, most of the staff and the economics profession failed to make the explicit connection between financial sector weakness, capital account openness, and the potential for crisis. As a result, this important lesson of the Chilean experience failed to register uniformly, and with the appropriate intensity, throughout the IMF. Indeed, the IEO observes that "awareness [of the need for a sound financial system] largely remained at the conceptual level and did not lead to operational advice on preconditions, pace, and sequencing until later in the 1990s."[76] The Asian Department's assessment of the offshore Bangkok International Bank Facility (BIBF) has been said to represent the "typical" staff approach to such issues until the late 1990s. The BIBF, established in

---

[74] Carlos F. Diaz-Alejandro, "Goodbye Financial Repression, Hello Financial Crash," *Journal of Development Economics* 19, nos. 1–2 (1985), pp. 1–24; Vittorio Corbo and Jaime de Melo, "Liberalization with Stabilization in the Southern Cone of Latin America: Overview and Summary," *World Development* 13, no. 8 (1985), pp. 863–866.

[75] IEO, *IMF's Approach*, pp. 33, 42.

[76] IEO, *IMF's Approach*, pp. 4–5.

1993, offered various tax incentives to attract banks to Thailand with the goal of developing a regional financial center. Rather than analyzing this policy in terms of its implications for capital inflows, the staff saw the BIBF in terms of the benefits it would provide in improving competition and technical skills in Thailand's financial system. Later, when the composition of inflows attracted by the BIBF shifted to short-term maturities, the staff paid little attention to the accumulating vulnerabilities in the financial system, instead offering support to measures to be taken to "complete the process of financial market deregulation."[77]

From the late 1980s until the mid-1990s, the big-bang approach eclipsed the gradualist position. According to the IEO, "The IMF generally supported rapid capital account liberalization in the early 1990s and offered little practical advice on pace and sequencing."[78] Internal entrepreneurs—especially in what was then called MAE—promoted this interpretation and application vigorously within the Fund. Many proponents of this view seem to have taken the desirability of liberalization as an article of faith. Several IMF staff members recall that there were a large group of "market romantics" with a "Jesuitical zeal" for and an "evangelical approach" to liberalization for whom "capital controls were an anathema."[79]

One particularly effective entrepreneur was the late Manuel Guitian, a University of Chicago–trained economist and longtime staff member described by the official IMF bulletin as an "unwavering proponent of capital account liberalization."[80] In the 1980s Guitian served as deputy director of ETR, which then had responsibility for monitoring and quality control before the creation of PDR in 1992. Guitian was thus in a position to offer input into the area department talking points for discussions with member states. Taking advantage of this capacity, Guitian strongly advocated the big-bang approach, regularly prevailing upon other staff members to back this approach in their discussions with government officials.[81]

Guitian later served as the second-highest-ranking member of the MAE staff before becoming director in 1995. From this organizational platform Guitian was among the first to make the intellectual case for amending formal IMF rules to give the Fund jurisdiction over the capital account and the mandate to advocate liberalization.[82] Guitian invoked the IMF's informal adoption of the norm of capital freedom to justify

---

[77] IEO, *IMF's Approach*, pp. 33–34.

[78] IEO, *IMF's Approach*, p. 34.

[79] Author's interviews with Allen; Fisher; and Khan.

[80] "Köhler Pays Tribute to Manuel Guitian," *IMF Survey* 30, no. 5 (5 March 2001), p. 75.

[81] Author's interview with Boorman.

[82] Manuel Guitian, *The Unique Nature of the Responsibilities of the International Monetary Fund*, IMF Pamphlet Series No. 42 (Washington, D.C.: IMF, 1992), pp. 48, 49.

changes to formal IMF rules, claiming that there was a "gap between norms and reality" and a need to bring "policy in line with reality."[83] In making their case, the MAE staff helped draft nearly every staff paper on capital account issues that went to the board for review; and Guitian made several impassioned speeches before the board to argue the case for amending the Articles.

In urging other staff to support their approach, Guitian and other big-bang proponents attacked gradualist arguments for short-run intervention and sequencing. Applying arguments about rent-seeking behavior, big-bang proponents claimed controls, temporary or otherwise, sheltered special interests that profited from such policies, often illicitly.[84] Big-bang proponents also claimed that the ineffectiveness of controls made sequencing irrelevant and that such a strategy was "the best recipe for the permanence of capital controls."[85] A big-bang approach, however, was said to prevent a prolonged transition from creating resistance from vested interests. Big-bang advocates also downplayed the importance of financial sector and regulatory development as essential preconditions for liberalization. Instead, they argued the best route to financial sector soundness and robust prudential regulations was to liberalize, as it would inject best practices and competitive pressures in the financial sector and permit market discipline to operate and ensure that governments stepped up their efforts to adjust policies.[86]

The MAE staff routinely employed technical assistance operations as a mechanism to convey these views to country officials. A 1994 technical assistance mission to Sri Lanka, for example, argued for liberalization be-

[83] Manuel Guitian, "Capital Account Liberalization: Bringing Policy in Line with Reality," in *Capital Controls, Exchange Rates, and Monetary Policy in the World Economy*, ed. Sebastian Edwards (Cambridge: Cambridge University Press, 1995), pp. 71–89; Manuel Guitian, "The Issue of Capital Account Convertibility: A Gap between Norms and Reality," in *Currency Convertibility in the Middle East and North Africa*, ed. Manuel Guitian and Saleh M. Nsouli (Washington, D.C.: IMF, 1996), pp. 169–188.

[84] See also Mathieson and Rojas-Suarez, *Liberalization of the Capital Account*, p. 18; Johnston and Ryan, "Impact of Controls," p. 3.

[85] Guitian, "Issue of Capital Account Convertibility," p. 184. See also Mathieson and Rojas-Suarez, *Liberalization of the Capital Account*, p. 1.

[86] Vincente Galbis, "Sequencing of Financial Sector Reforms: A Review," IMF Working Paper WP/94/101 (Washington, D.C.: IMF, 1994); Guitian, "Capital Account Liberalization"; Guitian, "The Issue of Capital Account Convertibility"; IEO, *IMF's Approach*, p. 43; Quirk, "Capital Account Convertibility." Other staff members sympathetic to the big-bang approach recognized financial sector soundness and robust prudential supervision as possible preconditions for openness, but concluded that "the consistency of macroeconomic, financial, and exchange rate policies is more important for sustaining an open capital account than is the sequencing of the removal of capital controls"; see Mathieson and Rojas-Suarez, *Liberalization of the Capital Account*, p. 33.

cause it would promote policy discipline.[87] In India, where the area department staff supported the government's gradualist approach, a 1995 technical assistance mission argued for the need for a broad strategy for liberalization as a precondition for developing a dynamic foreign exchange market. Controls, according to the MAE staff, were hampering financial sector development.[88]

Big-bang advocacy was aided by the overlap between its prescriptions and prevailing staff beliefs. During much of the 1980s, a number of emerging markets and developing countries had lost access to international capital markets. In the context and aftermath of the debt crisis, the staff were generally quite receptive to any market-based, as opposed to regulatory, measure that would potentially stir capital inflows and permit emerging markets and developing countries greater access to international capital markets. As a result, the staff often saw any liberalization, regardless of its sequence, as better than no liberalization at all.

Big-bang advocacy also resonated with the general enthusiasm at the end of the Cold War for "shock therapy" approaches to market reform. The big-bang approach was in many ways an extension of this approach to nontransition economies, though it seems that many in EURO1 and EURO2 may have applied it as well. Finally, the big-bang approach fit well with elements in the Fund's culture that prioritized "first-best" policy prescriptions. Arguments for sequencing based on second-best reasoning did not benefit from such fertile ground for their advocacy.

The ascendance of the big-bang approach was also facilitated by the way the IMF was organized. Prior to the creation of MAE in 1992, responsibility for monetary systems and exchange restrictions had been kept separate, with CB having control over the former and ETR having control over the latter. In the 1980s and early 1990s the CB staff had kept a close eye on developments in a number of developed economies as they moved from repressed to liberalized financial systems. The ETR staff had analyzed the same developments but had paid closer attention to the liberalization of external restrictions. Although staff members in both departments were aware of the links between domestic financial and international financial liberalization, because organizational responsibility for monetary systems and exchange restrictions was kept separate until the creation of MAE, there did not exist a strong organizational capacity to explore systematically how domestic financial and international financial liberalization might be coordinated. When organizational responsibility for monetary

[87] "Capital Account Convertibility—Review of Experiences and Implications for Fund Policies—Background Paper," p. 29.

[88] "Review of Experience with Capital Account Liberalization and Strengthened Procedures Adopted by the Fund," Supplement 1, p. 40.

systems and exchange restrictions was finally merged, it took some time for the MAE staff to develop any specific conclusions about sequencing.

It also should be pointed out that the case for capital account liberalization, though not necessarily a particular approach to it, was advanced within the Fund by the general success of the organization in fostering current account liberalization. Technical assistance missions to Sri Lanka (1994) and Trinidad and Tobago (1993), for example, argued that the liberalization of remaining capital controls was simply a logical extension of earlier reforms that eliminated current account restrictions.[89] Many staff interviewees also suggested that capital account liberalization was viewed as a natural and unproblematic extension of economic logic and IMF practice from one area to another. Others made the similar, but more heroic, assumption for capital account and trade liberalization. Guitian, for instance, portrayed the case for capital account and trade liberalization as analogous.[90]

The internal staff debate concerned not only sequencing but also the appropriateness of temporary controls. The legitimacy of such measures was perhaps the most bitterly contested issue within the Fund. Yet before proceeding, two brief observations are in order to illuminate the extent of normative change that had occurred within the Fund.

First, it is revealing that one of the principal points of internal debate focused on the legitimacy of *temporary market-based* controls rather than *permanent administrative* controls. Controls had clearly shifted from being cast as permanent and essential measures to deal with factors intrinsic to the operation of international capital markets, to being identified, even by the most sympathetic staff members, as temporary measures to deal with distortions or short-run market errors. Drawing on standard second-best arguments for intervention, much of the initial gradualist sympathy for temporary controls was that they insulated weak and poorly regulated financial systems from capital flow volatility. The presumption was that controls gave policymakers the breathing space necessary to implement, but not avoid, policy adjustments. Indeed, in some cases, some staff may have supported controls because government officials had already pledged to move ahead with a comprehensive reform program.[91]

Support for measures that prohibited or limited particular financial transactions had all but evaporated and was replaced by sympathy for measures that influenced the price of financial transactions but left them other-

---

[89] "Capital Account Convertibility—Review of Experiences and Implications for Fund Policies—Background Paper," p. 28.

[90] Guitian, "Capital Account Liberalization," p. 78; Guitian, "The Issue of Capital Account Convertibility," p. 176.

[91] IEO, *IMF's Approach*, p. 48.

wise unfettered. While sympathy and support for market-based restraints would grow in the mid-1990s (see below), it would not extend to administrative measures. Exemplifying this approach was the reaction of some Asian Department staff members to Malaysia's introduction in 1994 of a ceiling on the sale of short-term monetary instruments by residents to nonresidents. Here the staff urged the government to phase out the restriction on the grounds that it would introduce distortions and lead to an inefficient allocation of resources.[92]

A second observation to be made is that prior to the Asian crisis sympathy for temporary controls extended only to those on inflows. Despite their differences, gradualists and big-bang supporters were generally opposed to controls on outflows, especially when they were introduced in a relatively liberalized context. Recall that as early as the 1960s a view had started to emerge within the Fund that controls were an inappropriate substitute for adjusting policies that gave rise to balance-of-payments pressures. In the 1980s this view solidified. "There was," as Goldstein recalls, "a concern that controls were not a substitute for adjusting policy measures that were driving outflows."[93] The 1992–1993 European Exchange Rate Mechanism (ERM) crisis, in which the intensification of controls on outflows in Spain, Ireland, and Portugal had failed to prevent a change in the exchange rate, reinforced these views among the staff.[94]

Staff research, as suggested earlier, also challenged many of the traditional arguments for controls on outflows. R. Barry Johnston, a staff member who was at the forefront of research analyzing the effects of controls, recalls the "consensus view was that controls on capital outflows didn't work [to achieve these objectives]."[95] In contrast to the traditional arguments, staff research pointed to the (ostensible) credibility-enhancing effects of liberalization, suggesting that removing controls on outflows would strengthen rather than weaken a country's balance-of-payments position. As Liliana Rojas-Suarez, a RES staff member from 1984 to 1994, recalls, "The consensus was that outflows should be liberalized. We were of the mind that you were not going to have inflows if you controlled outflows."[96]

What a 1995 internal review calls the staff's "general distaste for such controls as a way of addressing balance of payments difficulties" is best

---

[92] "Review of Experience with Capital Account Liberalization and Strengthened Procedures Adopted by the Fund," Supplement 1, p. 36.

[93] Author's interview with Morris Goldstein, Washington, D.C., 19 May 2005. See also Guitian, "The Issue of Capital Account Convertibility," pp. 174–175; Guitian, "Reality and the Logic of Capital Flow Liberalization," p. 21.

[94] IEO, IMF's Approach, p. 27.

[95] Author's interview with R. Barry Johnston, Washington, D.C., 7 July 2005.

[96] Author's interview Liliana Rojas-Suarez, Washington, D.C., 26 May 2005.

exemplified by the views the WHD staff expressed in Venezuela, where, in 1994, extensive administrative controls on outflows were imposed in response to instability created by a domestic banking crisis.[97] Here the staff consistently argued for elimination of all controls, though it suggested such liberalization should proceed gradually. In response to concerns that liberalization would permit massive outflows, the staff explained that "complete elimination of controls need not lead to a renewal of capital outflows," if policies are adjusted appropriately.[98] Across a range of countries, such as Argentina, Brazil, Mexico, Pakistan, Romania, area department staff argued that governments should adjust policies to stem capital outflows rather than introduce or tighten controls.[99]

This general view framed the analysis that some staff brought to bear on controls on inflows. Like controls on outflows, some staff saw controls on inflows as prolonging the maintenance of unsound policies, inviting evasion, creating severe distortions, and failing to substitute for adjusting policies that were driving capital flows. A 1993 staff study best summarizes the conclusion these staff members reached: "The conventional wisdom on policies to contain the destabilizing effects of inflows is clear . . . *avoid . . . capital controls.*"[100] One staff member suggested that controls on inflows were like "killing the goose that laid the golden egg," especially for those highly indebted countries trying to attract foreign capital.[101] "Regardless of [the] cause" of the inflows, some staff members saw policy adjustment via fiscal consolidation as "the only appropriate means to prevent overheating and real exchange rate appreciation."[102] The liberalization of controls on outflows and greater exchange rate flexibility was also encouraged.

But not all the staff members shared these conclusions, with much of the debate centering on Chile's introduction of market-based controls in response to a surge in capital inflows.[103] In line with prevailing beliefs about controls on outflows, big-bang supporters saw the Chilean con-

[97] "Capital Account Convertibility—Review of Experiences and Implications for Fund Policies—Background Paper," pp. 10–11.

[98] As cited in IEO, *IMF's Approach*, p. 45.

[99] "Review of Experience with Capital Account Liberalization and Strengthened Procedures Adopted by the Fund," Supplement 1, pp. 33–34.

[100] Susan Schadler, Maria Carkovic, Adam Bennett, and Robert Kahn, "Recent Experiences with Surges in Capital Inflows," IMF Occasional Paper No. 108 (Washington, D.C.: IMF 1993), p. 1, emphasis added. See also p. 41.

[101] As cited in IEO, *IMF's Approach*, p. 27.

[102] Schadler et al., "Recent Experiences with Surges," p. 30.

[103] For an overview of the Chilean controls, see Sebastian Edwards, "Capital Flows, Real Exchange Rates, and Capital Controls: Some Latin American Experiences," in *Capital Flows and the Emerging Economies: Theory, Evidence, and Controversies*, ed. Sebastian Edwards (Chicago: University of Chicago Press, 2000), pp. 197–246.

trols—and similar measures in Colombia and Brazil—as an unsound attempt to provide greater monetary independence and prevent exchange rate adjustment. Their initial evaluations suggested the effectiveness of the Chilean controls would prove short-lived, forcing the introduction of additional restrictions to maintain the same level of control and thus introducing further distortions.[104] Although they had not initially opposed the Chilean controls, by 1994 this view had become the one the WHD staff advanced in their country consultations.[105]

What is particularly interesting about the big-bang framing of the Chilean controls is not the issues it considers, but rather the issues it fails to consider. Since big-bang supporters took the ineffectiveness of controls as an article of faith, they were inclined to give stronger consideration to evidence that supported this view. Initial big-bang evaluations therefore emphasized the fact that the Chilean controls did not appear to slow down the volume of capital flows, permit greater monetary independence, or prevent real exchange rate appreciation. There is nothing "wrong" per se with this analysis, but it suggests that big-bang supporters were somewhat blinded to information that could have disconfirmed their views and at the same time were narrowly focused on information that buttressed their views.

While accepting the broad contours of big-bang analysis, gradualists were more inclined to search for alternative information about the effectiveness of the controls. For gradualists, controls were not solely an attempt to avoid policy adjustment completely; they could also be used to counteract domestic distortions or market errors. As a result, when gradualists on the staff examined the case of Chile, they were more open to the possibility that the government was employing controls as a way of insulating the weak and poorly regulated financial system from capital flow volatility. Controls were said to give breathing space for policymakers to make adjustments and for financial sector development to proceed. Some prominent academic economists, such as Eichengreen and Wyplosz, had also raised the possibility of using taxes and taxlike instruments to curtail capital mobility when preexisting distortions, such as moral hazard in the banking system, gave rise to excessive inflows.[106]

But gradualists inside the Fund recognized that such prescriptions did not fit well with the framing offered by big-bang supporters or with the prioritization the Fund's culture places on first-best policy prescriptions. Influential RES staff members, such as Mussa and Guillermo Calvo, there-

---

[104] Mathieson and Rojas-Suarez, *Liberalization of the Capital Account*, pp. 2, 19; Schadler et al., "Recent Experiences with Surges," pp. 19, 30.

[105] IEO, *IMF's Approach*, p. 28.

[106] Eichengreen and Wyplosz, "Taxing International Financial Transactions."

fore developed a strategy of framing such measures not as restrictions designed to substitute for adjustment, but as "prudential measures" designed to safeguard the domestic financial system.[107] Members of the PDR staff also generally supported this framing.[108]

But big-bang proponents initially proved resistant; instead they continued to see the Chilean controls (and those like them) as failing to substitute for adjustment, increasing the cost of capital, generating increasing distortions, and permitting evasion over time. But the financial crisis in Mexico in 1994–1995 aided gradualist advocacy, presenting an opportunity to represent the events as a "crisis" for the big-bang approach.

The severity of the Mexican crisis, like the one in Chile in the early 1980s, was amplified by domestic financial liberalization and bank privatization in the context of weak prudential supervision and rapid capital account liberalization.[109] Poor bank supervision had resulted in excessive credit expansion and a buildup of nonperforming loans. These banking sector weaknesses in turn complicated economic management by heightening the adverse effects of using higher interest rates to defend the peso. Poor bank supervision in the context of capital account openness also exposed the banking sector to currency-mismatch problems. The devaluation of the peso in December 1994 and January 1995 placed additional strains on the banking sector and induced a "twin crisis."

Although the possibility of "twin crises" would seem obvious after the Asian crisis, at the time most of the Fund's staff and the economics profession had failed to make the explicit connection between banking sector soundness and capital account openness.[110] The theoretical literature on currency crises had seen some advances in the early 1990s with the development of second-generation models after the ERM crisis.[111] These second-generation models (re)introduced the possibility of self-fulfilling market expectations triggering financial crises. Yet awareness of the possi-

---

[107] Author's interview with Mussa. See also Guillermo A. Calvo, Leonardo Leiderman, and Carmen Reinhart, "Capital Inflows and Real Exchange Rate Appreciation in Latin America: The Role of External Factors," *IMF Staff Papers* 40, no. 1 (1993), pp. 108–151.

[108] Executive Board Seminar 93/3, 21 July 1993 (IMF Archives), pp. 49, 51; Executive Board Seminar 93/4, 21 July 1993 (IMF Archives), p. 12.

[109] See Shalendra Sharma, "The Missed Lessons of the Mexican Peso Crisis," *Challenge* 44, no. 1 (2001), pp. 56–89.

[110] A notable exception is Guillermo Calvo, "Varieties of Capital-Market Crises," Inter-American Development Bank Research Department Working Paper No. 306 (Washington, D.C.: IAD, 1994).

[111] Seminal contributions to second-generation models include Barry Eichengreen, Andrew Rose, and Charles Wyplosz, "Contagious Currency Crises," NBER Working Paper 5681 (Cambridge, Mass.: NBER, 1996); and Maurice Obstfeld, "The Logic of Currency Crises," *Cahiers Economiques et Monetaires* (Bank of France), 43 (1994), pp. 189–213.

bility of self-fulfilling market expectations did not translate into Keynesian concerns about uncertainty and conventions.

In second-generation models, a crisis need not be motivated by policy failures and misaligned fundamentals observed before the crisis. Instead, the crisis itself induces policy change that makes the crisis self-validating. "Thus," observes a 1997 IMF paper, "whereas first-generation models use excessively expansionary precrisis fundamentals to push the economy into crisis, second-generation models use the expectation of fundamentals expansion ex post to pull the economy into a crisis that might have been avoided."[112] These self-fulfilling expectations generate the possibility of multiple equilibria, that is, that a given set of fundamentals may be consistent with more than one value of the exchange rate. The value of the exchange rate therefore can conceivably experience dramatic swings as the market switches from equilibrium to another. Eichengreen, Tobin, and Wyplosz argued that the possibility of multiple equilibria justified market-based controls as "a temporary measure to be applied exclusively by countries en route to EMU [Economic and Monetary Union], since monetary union offers them a permanent solution posed by exchange rate fluctuations."[113]

Although allowing for self-fulfilling elements, second-generation models consider only the effect of forward-looking market actors responding to transparent economic information. Second-generation models thus resemble first-generation models in one important respect: crises are said to result from market actors rationally reacting to an efficient use of information regarding fundamentals. Not surprisingly, because of prevailing beliefs, when the Mexican crisis erupted, most IMF staff members pointed their finger at poor fundamentals and paid insufficient attention to the interaction of financial sector weakness and capital account openness. Most of the staff, according to the IEO, believed that "the crisis had largely resulted from inconsistency between a pegged exchange rate and the pursuit of discretionary monetary policy, and not necessarily from wrong sequencing in capital account liberalization."[114]

Management also turned its attention to poor fundamentals in Mexico. Instead of inferring that the Mexican crisis suggested reining in capital mobility, Camdessus claimed it underscored the urgency of sound government policies. Volatile capital flows were cast as a symptom of fundamentals rather than as a contributing problem per se. Market actors

[112] Robert P. Flood and Nancy P. Marion, "Policy Implications of 'Second-Generation' Crisis Models," International Monetary Fund Working Paper WP/97/16 (Washington, D.C.: IMF, 1997), p. 4.

[113] Eichengreen, Tobin, and Wyplosz, "Two Cases for Sand," p. 167.

[114] IEO, IMF's Approach, p. 26.

were simply imposing discipline on Mexico and other countries through contagion by forcing them to adjust their unsound policies. "Let me make clear here," Camdessus declared, "that it is not a lesson of the Mexican crisis that countries should retreat from globalization, or that countries should regress toward less open markets . . . [T]o fall back on restrictions because of financial market reactions to policy inadequacies would be akin to shooting the messenger. It is policy inadequacies that have to be addressed."[115]

But gradualists appear to have been successful in convincing some staff members that Mexico's rapid liberalization represented a "policy failure" for the big-bang approach and that Chile's relative stability through its capital controls represented a "policy success" for the gradualist approach. Discursive attempts to paint the turmoil as a "crisis" for the big-bang approach prompted greater awareness of the risks of rapid liberalization, enhanced receptivity to arguments stressing a need for "prudential measures," and heightened support for sequencing and temporary controls.[116] Adaptation also likely played a part, though gradualist advocacy probably helped ensure that a broader range of information was considered and that it was filtered in such a manner as to match the gradualist approach. For instance, in the aftermath of the Mexican crisis, Goldstein, who earlier was sympathetic to the big-bang view, moderated his opinion and expressed support for gradualism and for temporary controls.[117]

As Goldstein recalls, "With more evidence of capital account crises, it sounded a warning bell. The interaction of liberalization with weak financial systems began to make some people more cautious."[118] The notion of preconditions became more prominent in some of the area department consultations with country officials, with an increasing number of staff members questioning the wisdom of rapidly liberalizing controls on outflows and short-term inflows. The 1996 EURO2 staff mission to the Slo-

---

[115] Camdessus, "Prospects and Challenges in Our Globalizing World Economy," Wharton School, University of Pennsylvania, 4 April 1995, available at http://www.imf.org/external/np/sec/mds/1995/MDS9506.HTM (accessed 24 March 2009)

[116] David Folkerts-Landau and Takatoshi Ito, *International Capital Markets: Developments, Prospects, and Key Policy Issues* (Washington, D.C.: IMF, 1995), pp. 27, 108; IMF, *World Economic Outlook* (October) (Washington, D.C.: IMF, 1996), pp. 57, 151; IMF, *World Economic Outlook* (October) (Washington, D.C.: IMF, 1997), pp. 88, 116; Mohsin S. Khan and Carmen Reinhart, "Capital Flows in the APEC Region," IMF Occasional Paper No. 122 (Washington, D.C.: IMF, 1995), pp. 28, 29; Peter J. Quirk and Owen Evans, "Capital Account Convertibility: Review of Experience and Implications for IMF Policies," IMF Occasional Paper No. 131 (Washington, D.C.: IMF, 1995), pp. 4, 6, 22–23.

[117] Morris Goldstein, "Coping with Too Much of a Good Thing: Policy Responses for Large Capital Inflows in Developing Countries," World Bank Policy Research Working Paper No. 1507 (Washington, D.C.: World Bank, 1995), p. 39.

[118] Author's interview with Goldstein.

vak Republic, for instance, cautioned against further liberalization until external imbalances were resolved. Similarly, area department staff working in India advised against liberalizing restrictions on nonresident purchases of government bonds until fiscal consolidation had been achieved. Concerns about banking and financial sector weaknesses in Slovenia and China also led area department staff to suggest greater caution in liberalizing. Some area department staff, such as those assessing Thailand, also began to give greater attention to the potential vulnerabilities associated with a buildup of short-term external liabilities in the context of financial sector weakness.[119]

The Mexican crisis also helped the gradualists to undermine the big-bang framing of the Chilean controls. As a result, other staff members turned their attention away from information about the controls' relative ineffectiveness in providing monetary policy independence and preventing real exchange rate appreciation and toward alternative information that suggested their effectiveness in lengthening the maturity structure of inflows, which in turn was seen as helping to minimize vulnerabilities to the financial sector.[120] Although the general consensus within the Fund remained that controls on inflows were distortionary, that their effectiveness waned over time, and that they were not a long-run substitute for policy adjustments, there was now increased support for the claim that "such measures may be justified on prudential grounds and on a temporary basis."[121]

Indeed, in the immediate aftermath of the Mexican crisis, some area department staff seem to have become willing to accommodate temporary controls on inflows as a second-best policy response. For example, in 1995, the introduction of a tax to discourage short-term inflows into the Czech Republic was supported by the EURO2 staff partly because of political constraints on other macroeconomic policy instruments and partly because of growing weakness in the banking system. The 1996 EURO2 staff consultation later positively noted that the Czech controls had "helped lengthen the maturity of banks' foreign liabilities," though the measures, like the Chilean controls, had been "less successful in limiting the total volume of capital inflows."[122] In 1995 and 1996, the EURO2 staff also

---

[119] IEO, *IMF's Approach*, p. 34.

[120] See Vicente Galbis, "Currency Convertibility and the Fund: Review and Prognosis," IMF Working Paper WP/96/39 (Washington, D.C.: IMF, 1996); Bernard Laurens and Jaime Cardoso, "Managing Capital Flows: Lessons from the Experience of Chile," IMF Working Paper WP/98/168 (Washington, D.C.: IMF, 1998).

[121] Quirk and Evans, "Capital Account Convertibility," p. 4.

[122] IEO, *IMF's Approach*, p. 65. See also p. 44 and "Review of Experience with Capital Account Liberalization and Strengthened Procedures Adopted by the Fund," Supplement 1, p. 35, 37.

endorsed the decision of officials in Slovenia and Hungary to introduce market-based controls to manage inflow surges.[123] Market-based restraints on inflows were also accommodated in Thailand (1995, 1996) and Brazil (1995) as a way of creating breathing space for policy adjustments.[124]

Although some staff members now placed more emphasis on sequencing and attached greater legitimacy to selective restraints on capital inflows, the shift in their interpretation and application of the norm of capital freedom should not be overstated. The staff's approach would continue to evolve, and support for temporary controls remained extremely controversial. In spite of the evidence from Mexico and Chile, Fisher recalls that "a big division had opened within the staff."[125] Indeed, staff in some area departments, such as those responsible for Chile, Romania, Russia, and South Korea, continued to advocate liberalization enthusiastically.

The case of South Korea offers an interesting example of how this battle of ideas played out within the Fund. Here, and in other cases, contrasting norm interpretations offered by area department staff and those in the Capital Markets Group led to uneven attention being given to vulnerabilities created by the buildup of short-term debt in a weak and poorly regulated financial system. Issues of sequencing and financial sector weakness had attracted increasing attention from the Capital Markets Group since the Mexican crisis. Warnings about the risks of financial sector weakness and the implications of reversals in market sentiment became increasingly prominent in the *WEO* and the *ICMR* in the period leading up to beginning of the Asian crisis in July 1997.[126] Some RES staff members also started to circulate to area departments their doubts about the sequencing of liberalization undertaken in some countries, such as South Korea.[127]

But SEAP staff responsible for South Korea had a different view. "The focus on capital account liberalization in Korea," the IEO reports, "reflected the [big bang] . . . belief that liberalization of its external accounts would encourage the authorities to pursue genuine reforms of the domestic financial sector, including improvements in supervision."[128] Consequently, the SEAP staff gave little attention to the issue of sequencing. Prevailing beliefs that located the "cause" of financial instability primarily

[123] IEO, *IMF's Approach*, p. 44, 66.

[124] IEO, *IMF's Approach*, p. 44; "Review of Experience with Capital Account Liberalization and Strengthened Procedures Adopted by the Fund," SM/97/32, pp. 35, 36.

[125] Author's interview with Fisher.

[126] IMF, *External Evaluation of IMF Surveillance*, pp. 107–111.

[127] David Folkerts-Landau and Carl-Johan Lindgren, "Toward a Framework for Financial Stability," *World Economic and Financial Surveys* (Washington, D.C.: IMF, 1998). A draft of this manuscript had begun to circulate internally in 1997; see IEO, *IMF and Recent Capital Account Crises: Indonesia, Korea, Brazil* (Washington, D.C.: IMF, 2003), p. 95.

[128] IEO, *Recent Capital Account Crises*, p. 95.

in poor macroeconomic trends also led the SEAP staff to remain fixated largely on traditional fundamentals, which were sound in South Korea in the months leading up to the crisis, and to fail to appreciate sufficiently microeconomic weaknesses in the financial sector. As a result, as late as September 1997, even after Thailand, the Philippines, Indonesia, and Malaysia had already been hit by pressures from the emerging Asian financial crisis, and even though Mussa, in August 1997, had warned of a need for a downward adjustment, the SEAP staff continued to offer optimistic growth forecasts for South Korea.[129]

This optimism remained in October 1997 when a SEAP staff mission, along with a member of the MAE staff, visited South Korea and concluded that the economy was "relatively well equipped" to handle further external pressures even though the mission acknowledged the possibility of a spillover from the financial sector to the capital account and even though an earlier Capital Markets Group mission had alerted the SEAP staff of several important sources of risk in the financial system.[130] With little resonance between the warnings of the Capital Markets Group and the beliefs of the SEAP staff, and because of the "silo mentality" of and bureaucratic competition among the Fund's departments, there was little opportunity for gradualists to shape how things played out on the ground in South Korea.

The big-bang approach favored by many of the SEAP staff members responsible for South Korea appears to have solidified into an article of faith. The staff consistently screened out or failed to forcefully seek out alternative information or warnings that could have potentially led to a different conclusion about the health of the South Korea economy. For instance, as early as August 1997 the yield spread on Korean Development Bank dollar-denominated bonds had begun to widen, and this, along with other signals of increasing market unease, should have been picked up in surveillance conducted by the SEAP staff. But it was not. Moreover, although the South Koreans sought to conceal information from the Fund about its reserve position and short-term debt obligations, the SEAP did not forcefully request more complete data nor did it seek out relevant alternative data sources, such as the BIS, which were readily available.[131]

Beliefs and the way they channel data gathering and interpretation help us to understand how the SEAP staff responded to their poor information environment. If the beliefs of the SEAP staff had been more in line with those advocated by gradualists, they would have, in all likelihood, been

---

[129] IMF, *External Evaluation of IMF Surveillance*, pp. 45, 109; IEO, *Recent Capital Account Crises*, p. 97.

[130] IEO, *Recent Capital Account Crises*, pp. 96, 98–99.

[131] IEO, *Recent Capital Account Crises*, pp. 25–26, 96–97, 99.

more forceful in seeking to gain access to better information on the financial system. Yet because the SEAP staff's beliefs were more focused on macroeconomic fundamentals than microeconomic weaknesses, they failed to do so. This proved to be particularly significant because had the staff attained such data in a timely manner the IMF would have been better prepared to respond to and possibly to prevent or ease the eventual crisis.[132]

In addition to these types of internal battles of ideas, there were also some interesting cases where the staff from various departments clashed in the advice they offered directly to country officials. For instance, whereas area department staff endorsed the use of controls on inflows in the Czech Republic, a MAE technical assistance report argued that the restrictions had proven ineffective except in the very short run. PDR also opposed the cautious approach of the EURO2 staff.[133] This was by no means an isolated incident. When Hungary introduced market-based controls in 1996 to manage a surge in short-term inflows, the staff were once again divided. In this case, the area department staff, along with PDR and RES, accommodated the restrictions, while the MAE was adamantly opposed.[134] The MAE also opposed the cautious approach taken by AFR staff in South Africa.[135] In addition, the RES staff occasionally sought to counter WHD advocacy for liberalization, for instance, by privately dispatching Calvo to advise country officials on the use of market-based restraints on inflows, often soon after they had heard opposition to such measures from WHD staff missions.[136]

A 1995 staff report provides another clear indication of the extent of the division within the Fund. The report was written by a team led by Peter Quirk, then a member of the MAE staff and a proponent of the big-bang approach, and Owen Evans, a gradualist supporter then serving in

[132] Another important idea at the time that transcended the divide between gradualists and adherents of the big bang and that contributed to the surveillance failures in South Korea concerns the belief that the capital account consisted solely of transactions between residents and nonresidents. Consequently, large short-term borrowing by overseas branches and subsidiaries of South Korean banks—a vulnerability that placed great strain on South Korea's reserve position—was not recognized as an important issue. A 1997 MAE study of capital account liberalization in South Korea, for instance, catalogued such borrowing as outward foreign direct investment rather than as potentially equivalent to borrowing by their parent financial institutions. The result was that the staff underestimated vulnerabilities in the South Korean economy. See R. Barry Johnston, Salim M. Darbar, and Claudia Echeverria, "Sequencing Capital Account Liberalization: Lessons from the Experiences in Chile, Indonesia, Korea, and Thailand," IMF Working Paper 97/157 (Washington, D.C.: IMF, 1997) and IEO, *Recent Capital Account Crises*, p. 97.

[133] IEO, *IMF's Approach*, p. 65.

[134] IEO, *IMF's Approach*, p. 65.

[135] Author's interview with Leslie Lipschitz, Washington, D.C., 20 May 2005.

[136] Author's interview with Mussa.

PDR. This report offers statements that lend support to controls on inflows as prudential measures, while at the same time making strong caveats that reflect the position that controls are distortionary, ineffective in the long run, and a poor substitute for adjusting policies.[137]

Yet not all the team shared these conclusions. As discussed in chapter 2, the Fund's team-oriented work practices generally lead the staff to present a united view in papers. Internal debate therefore often is stifled because the staff strives to ensure that a common position is obtained. Traditionally, to indicate that a staff team was united behind the conclusions of a particular report, the Fund would have identified the aforementioned 1995 report as "Prepared by a staff *team* headed by Peter Quirk and Owen Evans." But this report contains a hidden reference to signal the report had been written by a divided camp, indicating that it was "Prepared by staff *teams* headed by Peter Quirk and Owen Evans." It was a subtle, yet significant, indication of the extent of the divide within the Fund.[138] Even the strong conforming elements in the Fund's culture could not paper over the deep divide between gradualists and big-bang supporters.

Significantly, the strengthening of staff support and accommodation for temporary controls diverged somewhat from the preferences of management, which often at times appeared divided. Following the Mexican crisis, Camdessus suggested a willingness to accommodate temporary market-based controls on inflows "until domestic financial markets and institutions become well established and resilient." But even in this statement Camdessus made it clear that he saw such controls as generally "undesirable because they have highly distorting effects and erode fairly quickly."[139] In later statements this mildly accommodating attitude was replaced by one that was much more hostile to the use of controls. "It would be a mistake," Camdessus claimed, "to try to avoid such crises by reverting to closed economic systems with exchange controls and less open markets: to do this would be to run the clock back and forgo the benefits of globalization."[140] Fischer, however, saw merit in the use of temporary controls on inflows, and reportedly "shocked" the board with his expressions of support.[141]

[137] See, for instance, Quirk and Evans, "Capital Account Convertibility," p. 4. Similar conflicting statements are offered in Folkerts-Landau and Ito, *International Capital Markets*, p. 27; and Khan and Reinhart, "Capital Flows in the APEC Region," p. 28.

[138] Author's interview with Fisher.

[139] Michel Camdessus, "The IMF Way to Open Capital Accounts," *Wall Street Journal*, 27 September 1995, p. A14.

[140] Michel Camdessus, "Luncheon Remarks," Conference on Banking Crises in Latin America, Washington, D.C., 6 October 1995, available at www.imf.org/external/np/sec/mds/1995/mds9513.htm (accessed 9 January 2007).

[141] Author's interview with Fischer. See also Tobin, "Prologue," pp. xi–xii; and "International Issues Prominent at AEA Meeting," *IMF Survey*, 22 January 1996, p. 32.

The normative outlook of the Fund changed radically in the 1980s and early 1990s. The argument advanced in this chapter is that this process of normative change had six bases of support, four that facilitated the initial normative change and two that reinforced it.

Professionalization and administrative recruitment served as two critical bases of support. The ascendance of the neoliberal continuum of thought within the economics profession meant that generations of economists had been instilled with a set of beliefs that contrast sharply with those espoused by Keynesians. Following a wave of retirements by long-serving members of staff, the IMF's recruitments offered a pathway through which these beliefs could be transmitted to the Fund.

However, unsettled debates within the economics profession provided an ideational basis for an internal bureaucratic struggle. As Eichengreen observes, economists "make very different assumptions about market efficiency depending on their predisposition and training."[142] Although similarities in professional training had led most staff members to view liberalization as desirable in the long run, subtle differences in the content of this training were a crucial determinant of the formation of subcultures and the battle between gradualists and big-bang proponents.

Along with professionalization and administrative recruitment, organizational learning also fostered normative change "from within." Country experiences and staff research led some staff to become convinced of the desirability of liberalization and to advocate it within the Fund. This comprehensive reappraisal of the staff's approach was in turn facilitated by the personnel realignment of the 1980s that made it easier to bring alternative perspectives to bear on experiences. But, along with subtle differences in professional training, the application of gradualist and big-bang frames to the same experiences contributed to divisions among the staff. As Dooley notes, those who define the effectiveness of controls as their "ability to maintain an inconsistent macroeconomic policy regime forever . . . argue that controls are not effective . . . [Conversely,] those who see controls as a short-term device to allow the government time to react and adjust other policy tools generally argue that controls can be effective."[143]

Internal entrepreneurship was a fourth crucial base of support, particularly in terms of how the norm of capital freedom was interpreted and applied. Gradualists and big-bang supporters engaged in a process of strategic social construction whereby they sought to prevail upon others to accept their interpretations and applications of the norm. Their efforts often were aided by the extent to which their arguments overlapped with

---

[142] Eichengreen, "The Tobin Tax: What Have We Learned?" in Haq, Kaul, and Grunberg, *The Tobin Tax*, pp. 273–288 at p. 274.

[143] Dooley, "Survey of Academic Literature," p. 29.

existing organizational beliefs, principles, and practices. Although it remains difficult to predict ex ante when it might occur, success in peddling one's paradigm was also facilitated when staff members were able to present particular events as representing a "crisis" for opposing views.

These endogenous sources of normative change were reinforced by exogenous developments among member states, such as the completion of Western Europe's transition to capital account openness. Although neither U.S. nor European officials were the source of the staff's approach, their support for capital freedom loosened the Fund's outer structural constraint, providing the staff with greater autonomy in their approach to liberalization. The absence of any formal or informal encouragement from IMF principals, along with preference heterogeneity among principals over the legitimacy of controls, furthered this autonomy.

Management also reinforced endogenous sources of normative change. Some scholars place Camdessus at the center of the IMF's encouragement of liberalization.[144] Although Camdessus was a key figure in pushing to amend the Articles, he was largely not responsible for the staff's approach. The staff had already developed their approach *prior* to any guidance from Camdessus. Although management's support for capital freedom reinforced the staff's views, differences between Camdessus and Fischer limited the extent to which they could shape interpretation and application of norms by the staff.

Finally, the evidence in this chapter again underscores the importance of being attentive to informal aspects of IOs' behavior. For instance, Abdelal's focus on formal IMF rules leads him to conclude that "within the Fund, the 1980s were relatively uneventful with regard to the capital account."[145] While this may have been the case in terms of the evolution of formal IMF rules, it does not accurately describe the evolution of the staff's informal approach. Although there were no significant changes to formal IMF rules during the period examined in this chapter, it is abundantly clear from the evidence that this period was in fact one of profound normative change at the level of the informal staff approach. And significantly, it was this change, not the development of formal rules, that ultimately shaped the IMF's behavior, leading the staff to advocate informally, though not uniformly or indiscriminately, the liberalization of capital controls.

[144] Abdelal, *Capital Rules*.
[145] Abdelal, *Capital Rules*, p. 135.

CHAPTER EIGHT

Capital in Crisis

FINANCIAL TURMOIL IN THE LATE 1990s

THE LATTER HALF OF THE 1990s witnessed within the Fund both the high-water mark and demise of enthusiasm for capital freedom. It was a period of gradual, albeit incomplete, ideational and institutional convergence in which an attempt was made to align formal IMF rules with the informal staff approach. By the mid-1990s many members of the staff had been informally advocating liberalization for nearly a decade. This was in an environment in which leading IMF principals had completed their transition to capital account openness and sought to institutionalize capital freedom as a formal requirement for all IMF member states. IMF management initiated this proposal and supported it enthusiastically and unwaveringly.

The proposal failed, however. Although some governments had privately voiced misgivings about the amendment prior to the Asian crisis, the severity of the crisis and criticism of the Fund's response to it undermined support. Inside the Fund, the staff attributed the crisis to policy and institutional failures, legitimating policy adjustment and structural reform, rather than controls on outflows, as the appropriate response. The U.S. Treasury and IMF management offered a similar view.

Yet as the crisis unfolded, it spawned within the Fund an important reassessment of prevailing beliefs about capital freedom. But, significantly, these prevailing beliefs, which identified capital freedom as a desirable long-run goal, served to channel how this reassessment played out. Rather than implicating capital account openness per se as responsible for the crisis, prevailing beliefs led the staff to identify "disorderly liberalization" as a principal culprit. This interpretation in turn presented a "crisis" for the big-bang approach and led to an almost complete unraveling of support for it within the Fund. However, the reassessment of this particular norm interpretation and application did not induce reconsideration for the norm of capital freedom itself.

Nevertheless, this reassessment did lead some staff and academic economists to reappraise prevailing standards of behavior for capital controls. Here Malaysia's experience with controls on outflows also was of great significance. Prevailing beliefs had led many to expect the controls to prove ineffective, harmful to growth, and damaging to Malaysia's credibility with the private financial community. But when these expectations were not fully met, a number of staff members and academic economists interpreted this outcome as evidence of a "crisis" for prevailing standards of behavior that ruled out the use controls on outflows. Following the Malaysian experience, such controls, while controversial, have received much greater accommodation from the Fund.

A few influential staff members and academic economists also advocated an alternative Keynesian-inspired interpretation of the crisis. This advocacy in turn fostered renewed appreciation for factors intrinsic to international capital markets that can give rise to financial instability, which in turn led some staff members and academic economists to suggest the possibility of permanent controls on inflows, albeit controls of a market-based nature. Although the staff generally do not dispute the long-run desirability of capital account liberalization, in the aftermath of the Asian crisis there has been much greater legitimacy attached to selective limitations on capital mobility.

Support for the Amendment?

In the mid-1990s informal standards of behavior, as defined and advocated by the staff, and formal IMF rules specifying the obligations of membership began to converge. Prior to 1995 the board and management had failed to issue any operational guidance. In the late 1980s, the board had given greater attention to international capital flows, but, as the IEO indicates, their focus "tended to be a *positive* analysis of what motivated capital flows, and what the consequences would be, rather than an attempt to make a *normative* case for a particular capital account policy."[1]

In the early 1990s, in an environment where virtually all developed countries had removed nearly all their controls, many board directors offered broad endorsement to staff papers that advocated liberalization. The 1993 IMF *Annual Report,* for instance, stated, "Directors were unanimous in their support for open capital markets and in their rejection of the use of temporary capital controls [on outflows] during an exchange crisis."[2] But this public display of enthusiasm for capital freedom understated the degree of private support and accommodation for capital controls. Some directors at the time—including the U.S. director—failed to rule out the use of controls to manage inflows, while other directors, particularly those representing emerging markets and developing coun-

---

[1] IEO, *IMF's Approach,* p. 20.
[2] IMF, *Annual Report, 1993* (Washington, D.C.: IMF, 1993), p. 53.

tries, continued to make the case for using controls on outflows to manage crisis pressures.

Camdessus appears to have started seriously considering the idea of making capital account liberalization an objective for the Fund in 1993. He recalls that "a long discussion about capital account liberalization" began late that year and "accelerated after the Mexican crisis."[3] In late 1993, Camdessus reportedly first privately approached the chairman of the Interim Committee with the idea of amending the Articles by giving the Fund the mandate to advocate liberalization and to have jurisdiction over the capital account.[4] Camdessus maintains that his experience dismantling French capital controls in the 1980s informed his belief in the desirability of liberalization.

Yet the norm of capital freedom also resonated with the bureaucratic interests of Camdessus and other actors and enabled them to articulate these interests. Historically, the IMF has shown itself to be quite adaptable; transforming itself from an overseer of exchange rates to a coordinator of petrodollar recycling in 1970s, then to a sovereign debt manager in the 1980s. Yet the success of the Brady Plan restructurings and subsequent capital inflow surges to emerging markets in the early 1990s threatened the IMF with increasing irrelevance. However, the norm of capital freedom—both its advocacy and its jurisdiction—stood to reposition the Fund at the center of financial governance.

In addition to helping to expand the bureaucratic mandate of the Fund, the proposed amendment also would have helped the Fund outmaneuver the encroaching authority of "rival" IOs. In the mid-1990s, several initiatives were progressing that had expanded the number of IOs with some potential authority over capital flows. The World Trade Organization (WTO) had started to tackle financial service liberalization, and the OECD had moved forward with its abortive attempt to craft a Multilateral Agreement on Investment. Asserting IMF jurisdiction over capital flows would ensure that global discussions would be lodged within the Fund and not rival IOs.

In addition to the IMF's management, the norm of capital freedom resonated with and served to articulate the bureaucratic interests of some staff members, helping to build an ideational and bureaucratic coalition of like-minded actors. For instance, Boorman, then PDR director, was not only convinced of the benefits of greater capital freedom but also believed that there was a hole in the international architecture and that the Fund was the IO best positioned to fill it. He contended that the array of IOs, which lodged clear authority over the current account and trade with the

---

[3] Author's interview with Camdessus.

[4] Abdelal, *Capital Rules*, p. 140.

IMF and WTO, respectively, had left a hole in the architecture with respect to the capital account. Boorman argued that capital flows, which were becoming increasingly discussed within the WTO and OECD as well as part of bilateral trade and investment treaties, required "international organization supervision."[5] But, according to Boorman, permitting the WTO or OECD to have authority would have resulted in "a second-best architecture." Although the near universal membership of the WTO ensured country coverage would have been sufficiently broad, the consensual decision-making procedures of the institution would have, in all likelihood, produced an insufficiently high enough standard. The reverse would have applied to the OECD.

The proposed amendment involved a fundamental transformation of formal IMF rules. It would, to paraphrase Guitian's call to arms, help bring formal IMF policy in line with the informal reality that some staff members were advocating liberalization. Although some within the Fund had been informally encouraging liberalization for a decade, they had lacked a legal mandate to do so. There was an "asymmetry" in the Articles that had by design given the staff the mandate to encourage current but not capital account liberalization. But, as suggested in chapter 7, this asymmetry had failed to deter the staff. The staff was forthright in conceding as much in a 1997 internal review: "Notwithstanding this asymmetry the Fund has in recent years sought to promote capital account liberalization in view of the benefits that can accrue from capital movements and their importance in the international monetary system."[6] Without any formal mandate, some staff members, largely because of processes endogenous to the Fund, had come to define liberalization as an "appropriate" policy and one that the Fund should promote.

The proposed amendment would formally institutionalize the standard of behavior that controls were outside the boundaries of legitimate policy practice. The logic of the amendment would reverse a critical aspect of the norms established at Bretton Woods. Keynes and White had envisioned a system where capital controls would be the norm, and where the presumption would be that they were permitted for any reason. Although proponents of the amendment envisioned a transition period for countries moving to capital account openness, the amendment would have committed governments to justifying existing restrictions and prohibited them from introducing new ones without the Fund's approval. "The burden of

---

[5] Author's interview with Boorman.

[6] "Capital Account Convertibility and the Role of the Fund—Review of Experience and Consideration of a Possible Amendment of the Articles," SM/97/32, 5 February 1997 (IMF Archives), p. 1.

proof," as Abdelal observes, "was to be shifted; restrictions would have to be justified as deviations from openness."[7]

In 1994, Camdessus first offered a series of public statements supporting liberalization.[8] Although Camdessus signaled his support, in principle, for liberalization, he failed to offer any specific guidance to the staff. Management reportedly did not offer any specific guidance until Fischer replaced Erb as first deputy managing director in September 1994.[9] Fischer subsequently offered considerable intellectual support for the amendment.

Interestingly, as noted in chapter 7, Camdessus and Fischer did not always see eye to eye on the issue of temporary market-based controls on inflows. Fischer tended to side with the arguments of Mussa and Calvo, who claimed that such controls could serve as "prudential measures" for countries with weak and poorly regulated financial systems. Camdessus, however, seems to have been more reluctant to sanction such measures. But despite Fischer's support for gradualism and temporary market-based controls on inflows, some staff members viewed him as more open than Erb to a campaign to make advocating liberalization a formal goal of the Fund.[10]

Guitian had made the intellectual case for amending the Articles as early as 1992. After noting the "growing freedom of capital movements and their increasing importance in international transactions" Guitian observed:

As this century closes, the time has come for updating the code of conduct so as to bring it into conformity with economic logic, which argues against restrictions regardless of the nature of the transaction, and with the current prospective world economic environment, where capital movements have established a permanent and prominent presence. Now that there is a prospect for the world economic order to become fully global in geographical scope, extending the code of conduct to cover all international transactions would be most appropriate for the establishment of true universality.[11]

In July 1994, the MAE staff, headed by Guitian, further elaborated the case for amending the Articles: "Under the Bretton Woods system controls were seen to make it more difficult for market participants to test the

[7] Abdelal, *Capital Rules*, p. 140.
[8] Michel Camdessus, "The IMF at Fifty—an Evolving Role but a Constant Mission, Address at the Institute for International Economics," MD/Sp/94/6, 7 June 1994 (IMF Archives); IEO, *IMF's Approach*, p. 78.
[9] Author's interview with Khan.
[10] Author's interview with Allen.
[11] Guitian, *Unique Nature of Responsibilities*, p. 49.

authorities' resolve to defend an exchange rate parity. However, the advent of floating exchange rates and the rapid integration of capital markets has shifted the balance of costs and benefits away from controls."[12] MAE and Guitian in particular were enthusiastic about the amendment throughout the board's deliberations.[13]

PDR was also at the center of the board's deliberations. Although supportive of the amendment, Boorman and Fisher were concerned about sequencing and ensuring that appropriate safeguards and transition mechanisms were in place.[14] Indeed, recall from chapter 7 that PDR usually sided with the arguments of Mussa and Calvo. In the context of the board's deliberations, Boorman and Fisher were concerned that support for the amendment from Guitian, who was perhaps the most vocal advocate and did most of the writing about the topic, had inadvertently and wrongly colored the IMF as in favor of rapid liberalization. Moreover, Boorman and Fisher feared that this portrait of the IMF would be used to validate the proposition that it was imposing liberalization on its member states.

The initiative to amend the Articles came from inside the Fund not, as some critics suggest, from the U.S. Treasury or private financial community.[15] U.S. Treasury officials did not develop, nor did they uniformly embrace, the proposal. The strength of the U.S. position on the board meant that the proposal needed at least a certain degree of support from the U.S. director for deliberations to proceed. However, though capital freedom was in principle the U.S. position, some U.S. officials offered only lukewarm and tacit support.

As with their general failure to actively shape the informal staff approach, some Treasury officials simply did not see the amendment as a top priority. They were more interested in getting Congress to approve the pending contribution for the IMF quota increase than in pushing through an amendment that faced stiff opposition. But despite their reservations, these Treasury officials were also reluctant to take a stance that seemed to contradict the principle of capital freedom. Thus, some senior Treasury officials—such as Jeffrey Shafer and Timothy Geithner—publicly accepted the proposal but not passionately.[16] Others, such as David Lipton and U.S.

---

[12] "Issues and Developments in the International Exchange and Payments System," SM/94/202, 29 July 1994 (IMF Archives), p. 25.

[13] Nearly every member of the IMF board and staff whom I interviewed suggested that Guitian was a tireless advocate and played an essential role in the board's deliberations. See also an interview with Guitian in "IMF's Role Evolves in Financial and Exchange Rate Arenas," *IMF Survey* 26, no. 11 (9 June 1997), pp. 169–171.

[14] Author's interviews with Boorman and Fisher.

[15] See also Abdelal, *Capital Rules*.

[16] Author's interview with Shafer.

IMF director Karin Lissakers, offered stronger support, arguing that the amendment was an architectural step in the right direction. Lipton and Lissakers were especially troubled by the asymmetry in the Articles and by the 1961 board reinterpretation, which they saw as not expansive enough to cover the capital account crises the Fund faced in the 1990s. Both concerns led these officials to believe that the Fund needed the explicit authority to advocate liberalization and to use its resources to manage capital account crises.[17] At the top of the Treasury leadership, Summers was reportedly more supportive of the amendment than Rubin.[18]

Another reason some senior Treasury officials were reluctant to support the amendment enthusiastically was that they were never fully interested in promoting liberalization per se on a global scale, though priorities at lower levels of leadership may not always have been so clear. In the 1980s the Treasury primarily sought to encourage liberalization of controls that interfered with exchange rate adjustments in particular countries, such as Japan, South Korea, and Taiwan. In 1990s, the focus shifted to improving market access and establishing national treatment in foreign markets for American financial firms.

But Treasury officials sought to draw a sharp distinction between capital account liberalization and extending the right of establishment and national treatment. Summers insisted at the time that capital account liberalization "is logically separable from the degree of market access enjoyed by foreign financial institutions" but also acknowledged that in practice the two tended to be linked.[19] Shafer claims, "The most important U.S. interest at stake was not to get rid of capital controls, but was to improve the terms of access of U.S. financial institutions and business in foreign markets on a national treatment basis. [Capital account liberalization] was left in the background."[20]

Although the Fund generally failed to consult it on either the initial proposal or its subsequent development, the IIF nonetheless stood in opposition. The IIF was never overly enthusiastic about capital account liberalization, and therefore offered only tentative support to the idea of giving the Fund the mandate to encourage it. Following the currency crisis in Thailand in July 1997, Charles Dallara, IIF managing director, emphasized the "need for caution" at a time when the IMF was pro-

[17] Author's interviews with Lipton; Lissakers.

[18] Author's interviews with Lipton; Lissakers; Shafer. See also Abdelal, *Capital Rules*, p. 139.

[19] Lawrence Summers, "Building a Global Financial System for the 21st Century, Address to the Congressional Economic Leadership Council," U.S. Treasury Release RR-1879, Washington, D.C., 12 August 1997.

[20] Author's interview with Shafer.

ceeding with its deliberations on the proposed amendment.[21] Dallara and the private financial community were particularly concerned about the possibility of crises in countries where "banking regimes . . . are not adequately strong."[22]

In addition to concerns about financial stability, the IIF was also staunchly opposed to giving the IMF jurisdiction. The jurisdictional element of the amendment heightened concerns within the private financial community about a potential expansion of IMF powers to resolve sovereign debt crises. Opposition was directed principally at potential "standstills" and financing that could be authorized for debtors under Article VIII, Section 2b of the Articles of Agreement and under the IMF lending into arrears policy. Under the proposed amendment governments could potentially gain IMF approval to suspend debt repayments in the midst of restructuring negotiations and still gain access to IMF resources, thus strengthening their position against creditors.

These concerns were augmented when, in 1996, in the aftermath of the Mexican crisis, the G-10 issued a report that recommended extending the existing IMF lending into arrears policy so that it applied to bondholders as well as commercial banks.[23] The Asian crisis would prompt further consideration of this recommendation, and, in September 1998, the IMF board formally modified its policy to apply to bondholders "and other marketable debt instruments." According to the analysis of the IIF, these developments provided "sufficient reason for the private financial community to oppose at this time any amendment that would formally extend the jurisdiction of the IMF over capital movements."[24]

THE STAFF APPROACH AND GUIDANCE FROM THE BOARD AND MANAGEMENT

By October 1994 there was sufficient consensus among leading Fund principals for the Interim Committee to issue what became known as the Madrid Declaration. This statement "welcomed the growing trend toward

[21] "Fuse Lit under IMF Powers: Proposed New Powers for the IMF, Intended to Help Avert or Lessen the Impact of a Financial Crisis, Have Caused Alarm in Sections of the Financial Community," *The Banker*, 1 September 1997.

[22] "IMF/World Bank: Can Banking Systems Cope? The Historic Hong Kong Meetings Will Discuss Controversial New Powers for the IMF in Response to Recent Financial Crises," *The Banker*, 1 September 1997.

[23] G-10, *The Resolution of Sovereign Liquidity Crises* (Basle: Bank for International Settlements, 1996).

[24] IIF, "Report of the Working Group on the Liberalization of Capital Movements," p. 23.

currency convertibility and encouraged member countries to remove impediments to the flow of capital."[25] Although this statement confirmed the existence of a new ideational climate among leading IMF principals, it was not a directive to the board or the staff, and, more importantly, it masked private misgivings about the benefits of capital freedom among some of the Fund's membership.

Several board directors, particularly those representing emerging markets and developing countries, privately continued to offer concerns about capital flow volatility unrelated to fundamentals and to view controls as legitimate policy instruments.[26] In fact, throughout its deliberations preference heterogeneity prevented the board from reaching a consensus on the legitimacy of controls. The outer structural constraint of the IMF had clearly shifted, but public displays of enthusiasm for capital freedom often understated the degree of preference heterogeneity among IMF principals.

Nonetheless, the enthusiasm for liberalization, particularly among developed countries, continued largely unabated. In a June 1995 statement, the G-7 urged other IMF members to "consider extending existing obligations regarding the convertibility of current account transactions to the staged liberalization of capital account transactions." Yet in the aftermath of the Mexican peso crisis, most G-7 officials began to shy away from the big-bang approach and to lend support to gradualism. The June 1995 statement went on to note that the IMF "should encourage an integrated approach to ensure that adequate supervisory, regulatory and policy structures are in place to support the sound development of financial markets in countries which are removing these restrictions."[27] Still, some U.S. officials remained supportive of the big-bang approach; "there was hope," according to Bradford DeLong and Barry Eichengreen, "that by forcing the pace of financial liberalization, countries might be compelled to more quickly upgrade their domestic regulations and institutions. Conversely, encouraging them to open only after the requisite domestic reforms were well advanced applied no pressure for reform; it was a road map to a destination that might never be reached."[28]

[25] Quirk and Evans, "Capital Account Convertibility," p. 1.

[26] See "Concluding Remarks by the Acting Chairman for the Seminar on Issues and Developments in the International Exchange and Payments System," p. 2; "Summing Up by the Chairman, International Capital Markets—Developments, Prospects, and Key Policy Issues," 30 May 1995, BUFF/95/44 (IMF Archives), pp. 2–3; "The Acting Chairman's Summing Up—Capital Account Convertibility—Review of Experience and Implications for Fund Policies," p. 1.

[27] G-7, The Halifax Review of the International Financial Institutions, 16 June 1995, available from www.g8.utoronto.ca/summit/1995halifax/financial/6.html (accessed 22 October 2004).

[28] Bradford DeLong and Barry Eichengreen, "Between Meltdown and Moral Hazard: The International Monetary and Financial Policies of the Clinton Administration," in *Amer-*

Significantly, though the preferences of some Fund principals for capital freedom and a gradualism had become clearer, the board and management still had not issued any operational guidance to the staff. In other words, actors operating from above had yet to instruct the staff on how to adopt, interpret, and apply the norm of capital freedom. The formal rules governing IMF surveillance still reflected a world where current account transactions were of paramount importance. Therefore, as part of efforts to strengthen surveillance and respond to the new world of increasingly integrated capital markets, the board, in April 1995, had amended the 1977 surveillance decision, directing the staff to pay greater attention to "unsustainable flows of private capital" and capital account developments. But, as the IEO indicates, "While unambiguously noting the importance of the capital account for the purposes of IMF surveillance, the decision neither implied the encouragement nor discouragement of capital account convertibility."[29] Moreover, the directive had little effect on actual behavior since most of the staff, particularly after the Mexican crisis, already recognized the importance of considering private capital flows when conducting surveillance.[30]

By July 1995 many staff members, largely through their own initiative, had been encouraging liberalization informally for nearly a decade. In developed countries, the staff recognized that their advocacy had little, if any, impact on their general move toward openness: "The Fund has been supportive of liberalization of capital flows in industrial countries, although the impetus for such liberalization was provided by the frameworks of the OECD Code and the EU Directives."[31] With emerging markets and developing countries, the staff took a "case-by-case approach to capital account liberalization in its consultations." But the staff's general orientation was clear:

> The Fund has tended in the context of its multilateral surveillance discussions and bilateral policy advice to welcome members' actions taken to liberalize capital account transactions, and to urge such liberalization in cases where this was deemed to be a crucial element of broader structural reforms. . . . While generally eschewing an activist policy of urging rapid liberalization, the institution in some cases encouraged developing countries to open their economies to foreign capital inflows and to liberalize restrictions on capital account transactions . . . [Moreover,]

---

ican Economic Policy in the 1990s, ed. Jeffrey A. Frankel and Peter R. Orszag (Cambridge: MIT Press, 2002), pp. 191–254 at p. 251.

[29] IEO, *IMF's Approach*, p. 18.

[30] Author's interviews with Fisher; and Willy Kiekens, Washington, D.C., 27 June 2005.

[31] "Capital Account Convertibility—Review of Experience and Implications for Fund Policies," p. 9.

the tightening of controls over capital movements . . . was generally discouraged. Although the Fund has generally supported a gradual approach to capital account liberalization, it has encouraged an acceleration of the process in some cases . . . [A]n effort to facilitate capital liberalization [also] has been made more generally through the medium of technical assistance to develop foreign exchange markets. Traditionally, the Fund's technical assistance in the area of foreign exchange systems focused on efforts to facilitate current account convertibility in its member countries; however, from the mid-1980s the focus shifted toward encouraging the adoption of full current and capital account convertibility.[32]

In a context where the absence of board or management directives created ambiguity about formal policy, the "battle of ideas" between the gradualists and big-bang supporters led the Fund to advance diverse views to the outside world. The staff generally welcomed liberalization and viewed controls skeptically. But whereas some staff members urged an acceleration of liberalization, others suggested gradualism and accommodated or recommended the use of controls. The result, as one staff member suggests, was that "one side of the house was stepping on the accelerator, while the other side was applying the brake."[33]

In July 1995, in its first operational guidance to the staff, the board "encouraged the staff to enhance the Fund's role in the liberalization of the capital account through surveillance and technical assistance."[34] The staff were directed to pay closer attention to capital account issues, to assess the scope for liberalization in technical assistance operations and consultations with government officials, and to examine possible changes to the Articles. As part of their follow-up work, the MAE staff began to improve the IMF's knowledge base by gathering more detailed information on member state regimes governing capital account transactions; first for a pilot group of thirty-one countries, then later for the entire membership.[35]

The staff also prepared a series of internal notes that were designed to give detailed operational guidance to area department missions. The intention of these notes was to encourage advocacy of liberalization. Yet a

[32] "Capital Account Convertibility—Review of Experience and Implications for Fund Policies," pp. 8, 10, 11.
[33] Author's interview with Fisher.
[34] "Capital Account Convertibility and the Role of the Fund—Review of Experience and Consideration of a Possible Amendment of the Articles," p. 7.
[35] "Capital Account Convertibility and the Role of the Fund—Review of Experience and Consideration of a Possible Amendment of the Articles," SM/97/32 Supplement 1, 6 February 1997 (IMF Archives), pp. 41–49.

clear policy direction from management and senior staff was not entirely forthcoming. As I have discussed, Camdessus and Fischer, though both generally supporters of gradualism, apparently disagreed over the degree of legitimacy to attach to temporary controls on inflows. Senior staff also offered conflicting guidance to the area departments. For instance, Mussa, in October 1995, circulated a note to area department staff that suggested they might accommodate the use of temporary controls to manage inflow surges when the use of conventional macroeconomic tools was limited because of political constraints or general ineffectiveness. Mussa, in spring 1997, later clarified his views, insisting that accommodation for temporary controls on inflows should not be confused with an endorsement for their use in all cases: "[The] staff was not endorsing the use of capital controls; and some of the countries had resorted to controls that were undesirable."[36]

Then, in December 1995, a "staff operational note" authored by the directors of MAE and PDR, Guitian and Boorman, respectively, was circulated to area departments. The purpose of the note was to outline the "next steps to be followed by the staff in adapting Fund practices to elicit greater emphasis on capital account issues, and to promote more actively capital account liberalization."[37] This note, like the paper written by the staff teams led by Quirk and Evans, suggests a significant divide among the staff in terms of how to approach liberalization from an operational perspective. The note, reflecting internal advocacy and the lessons some staff members gleaned from the Mexican crisis, places greater emphasis on sequencing; but the issue of temporary controls seems to have generated greater controversy.

Drawing on the second-best logic that underpinned the legitimacy gradualists attached to temporary controls, the note directs the staff to recognize "the possibility that some capital account restrictions could in principle be useful, including by neutralizing the effect of pre-existing distortions" and that "in certain circumstances, the use of capital controls to deter or slow down inflows may provide some temporary breathing space for the authorities, while more fundamental policy adjustments are being prepared." But the note then goes on to offer strong caveats that reflect the big-bang position and the first-best culture of the Fund, suggesting that "empirical research . . . generally points to the ineffectiveness of . . . controls in sustaining inconsistent macroeconomic policies . . . and [suggests that] their effectiveness will diminish over time." The note then directs the staff to highlight the "potential distortionary effects" of controls on capital inflows and to recognize "their ineffectiveness over

---

[36] IEO, *IMF's Approach*, p. 21, 28.
[37] "Capital Account Convertibility and the Role of the Fund," Supplement 1, p. 50.

time."[38] The conflicting nature of these directions provided area department staff with additional autonomy, especially since the PDR director had coauthored one of the notes.

The year 1995 was thus pivotal, in that it saw the Fund move toward greater ideational and institutional convergence. Although significant disagreements remained, the gradualists were slowly gaining the upper hand, with staff reports and country consultations placing greater emphasis on sequencing and the risks of premature liberalization in the context of poor prudential supervision, but with the use of temporary controls remaining more controversial.[39] All that remained was amending the Articles, though here consensus remained elusive as well.

In September 1996, the Interim Committee asked the board to heighten its focus on capital account issues and to examine possible changes to the IMF Articles.[40] The vast majority of developed countries—albeit not all—supported the amendment. In addition to the U.S. director, the Belgian, British, Dutch, Japanese, and Russian directors indicated their support. Capturing the views of many supporters of the amendment, Willy Kiekens, the Belgian director, argued that the amendment would be for the benefit of emerging markets and developing countries. By accepting the obligation to refrain from controls without IMF approval, Kiekens argued, these countries would send a clear signal to international capital markets of their commitment to openness, making capital flows more stable, deeper, and less costly.[41] Fischer and Guitian elaborated a similar logic in support of the amendment.[42]

But the board remained divided. Directors from emerging markets and developing countries continued to oppose the amendment. Some directors, such as Iran's Abbas Mirakhor, expressed concerns about whether capital account openness per se was desirable, arguing that there was no definitive evidence that it improved growth prospects. Mirakhor and others, such as Egypt's Abdel Shakour Shaalan, also opposed the jurisdictional aspect of the proposed amendment.[43] Their concerns over jurisdiction

[38] "Capital Account Convertibility and the Role of the Fund," Supplement 1, p. 54.

[39] David Folkerts-Landau, Donald J. Mathieson, and Garry J. Schinasi, *International Capital Markets: Developments, Prospects, and Key Policy Issues* (Washington, D.C.: IMF, 1997), p. 51; IMF, *World Economic Outlook* (October) (Washington, D.C.: IMF, 1996), pp. 57, 62, 151; IMF, *World Economic Outlook* (October) (Washington, D.C.: IMF, 1997), pp. 88, 93, 116.

[40] "Communique of the Interim Committee of the Board of Governors of the International Monetary Fund," IMF Press Release No. 96/49, 29 September 1996.

[41] Author's interview with Kiekens.

[42] Fischer, "Capital Account Liberalization and the Role of the IMF" (seminar); see a summary of Guitian's remarks in Sara Kane, "Seminar Discusses the Orderly Path to Capital Account Liberalization," *IMF Survey* 27, no. 6 (23 March 1998), pp. 81–84 at pp. 83–84.

[43] Author's interviews with Abbas Mirakhor, 28 June 2005, Washington, D.C.; A. Shakour Shaalan, 20 May 2005, Washington, D.C.

were partly based on the desire to retain the capacity to impose controls in crisis situations without the Fund's approval. These countries were also especially fearful that the staff would become overly enthusiastic in their advocacy of liberalization. Interestingly, Polak, then a consultant to the managing director, later made similar remarks in opposing the amendment.[44] Emerging markets and developing countries were particularly concerned that since the Articles forbade the use of conditionality to promote liberalization, the primary purpose of the amendment was to enable the Fund to do so.

These countries, however, were forced to tread carefully because of their dependence on management's support for Fund programs. Stiffer opposition was forthcoming from a somewhat unlikely source: Canadian director Thomas Bernes. The Canadian position had been partly outlined in the context of negotiations with Chile over a 1996 free trade agreement. This agreement recognized that controls on short-term inflows—such as those employed at the time by Chile—often proved useful. Breaking with the convention of presenting a unified position within the IMF, Canada parted ways with other G-7 countries, questioning the need for the amendment. Bernes, while not contesting the desirability of capital freedom, stressed the need for a greater understanding about preconditions and sequencing as well as the legal aspects before giving the Fund jurisdiction.[45]

Financial Turmoil in Asia and Beyond: Undermining Norm Institutionalization

Between April and October 1997, efforts to amend the Articles reached their peak. In April 1997, the Interim Committee announced its intention to embark on a fundamental revision of the Articles "to make the promotion of capital account liberalization a specific purpose of the IMF and give it jurisdiction over capital movements."[46] As Benjamin J. Cohen observes,

---

[44] Polak, "The Articles of Agreement of the IMF and the Liberalization of Capital Movements," in *Should the IMF Pursue Capital-Account Convertibility?* Princeton Essays in International Finance No. 207 (Princeton, N.J.: International Finance Section, Department of Economics, Princeton University, 1998), pp. 50, 52.

[45] Abdelal, *Capital Rules*, pp. 148–149; author's interview with Thomas Bernes, 23 June 2005, Washington, D.C.; John J. Kirton, "Canada as a Principal Financial Power: G-7 and IMF Diplomacy in the Crises of 1997–99," *International Journal* 54, no. 4 (1999), pp. 603–624 at pp. 607–608.

[46] "Communique of the Interim Committee of the Board of Governors of the International Monetary Fund," IMF Press Release No. 97/22, 28 April 1997.

"The tide was clearly moving toward the consecration of free capital mobility as a universal norm."[47]

Consensus, however, continued to prove elusive.[48] Momentum for securing agreement was further slowed when, following the defeat of the Conservative government in May 1997, the new British director demonstrated less enthusiastic support for the amendment.[49] Yet Camdessus continued to offer public statements that masked the degree of private opposition to the amendment: "As far as the IMF is concerned, there is unanimity in the membership to give us the mandate to promote capital account liberalization, thereby adding a chapter to the uncompleted work of Bretton Woods."[50]

Proposed provisions for transitional arrangements, "carve outs," greater flexibility in approving controls, and language emphasizing the role of the IMF in ensuring "orderly" (as opposed to rapid) liberalization failed to assuage concerns about the amendment. By the time the Interim Committee met in Hong Kong in September 1997 the financial crisis that would envelop much of Asia and spread to other emerging markets already had begun in Thailand. But at the time the crisis had yet to spread fully, and there was hope that the crisis would be limited to Thailand.

The Interim Committee signaled its resolve to push ahead with the amendment by producing a statement that came to be known as the Hong Kong Communiqué. "It is time," the statement argues, "to add a new chapter to the Bretton Woods agreement."[51] The Hong Kong Communiqué went on to direct the board to complete its work on the proposed amendment. Interestingly, emerging markets and developing countries did not evidence much opposition to the amendment within the Interim Committee. In the event, the capital account amendment was not the only issue on the agenda; a proposed Special Drawing Right (SDR) allocation to countries that joined the Fund after 1981 (more than one-fifth of the

[47] Benjamin J. Cohen, "Capital Controls: Why Do Governments Hesitate?" in *Debating the Global Financial Architecture*, ed. Leslie Elliott Armijo (Albany: State University of New York Press, 2002), pp. 93–117 at p. 104.

[48] "Concluding Remarks by the Chairman, Capital Account Convertibility and the Role of the Fund: Review of Experience and Consideration of a Possible Amendment of the Articles," Executive Board Seminar 97/2, BUFF/97/21, 3 March 1997 (IMF Archives); "Summing Up by the Chairman, Capital Account Convertibility and a Possible Amendment to the Articles," Executive Board Meeting 97/38, BUFF/97/39, 18 April 1997 (IMF Archives).

[49] Author's interview with Fisher.

[50] "Camdessus on Globalization, Capital Account, IMF Support for Social Spending," *IMF Survey*, 26, no. 9 (12 May 1997), p. 134.

[51] "Communique of the Interim Committee of the Board of Governors of the International Monetary Fund," IMF Press Release 97/44, 21 September 1997. For the IMF's coverage of the Hong Kong annual meeting, see *IMF Survey* 26, no. 18 (6 October 1997), pp. 289–320.

current IMF membership) and a 45 percent quota increase were also under consideration. Emerging markets and developing countries were perhaps modest in their opposition to ensure that the SDR allocation and quota increase would be approved.[52]

Still, in its communiqué the Group of Twenty-Four (G-24), the organization responsible for coordinating the position of emerging markets and developing countries on international financial issues, did suggest some lingering concerns, noting that "the capital account liberalization process could put additional stress on the economies that are already straining to adjust to globalization." The statement also reveals continued support for controls, noting that "in particular circumstances, precautionary and price-based measures could help protect economic stability and sound macroeconomic management." The statement also indicates a lingering fear among these countries that the Fund would use conditionality to impose liberalization, as it stresses that "liberalization of the capital account should not be made a condition for the use of IMF resources."[53]

The cause of the Asian crisis, like earlier episodes of financial instability, did not contain a necessitarian logic. Actors had to interpret the events and use these interpretations to arrive at an "appropriate" course of action. Rival interpretations were advanced that legitimated different courses of action with respect to the proposed amendment and crisis management. These interpretations would evolve over time and shape the development of the formal IMF rules and the informal staff approach.

Fischer sought to counter concerns that the crisis undermined the case for liberalization, arguing that developments in Asia "[did] not suggest that the capital account is more often the source of economic difficulties and risk rather than benefit, and therefore that capital account liberalization should be put off as long as possible."[54] Camdessus also sought to placate fears about the crisis by representing it as rational market discipline. "The lesson to be drawn from recent developments," Camdessus argued, "is not about the risks of globalization—and still less about demonizing the markets—but rather about the importance of exercising good citizenship when tapping them. Indeed, countries cannot compete for the blessings of the global capital markets and refuse their disciplines." Camdessus made an impassioned plea for governments not to interpret the turmoil as evidence for greater hesitancy in supporting the amend-

---

[52] Author's interview with J. Onno de Beaufort Wijnholds, 8 June 2005, Washington D.C.

[53] "Communique of the Intergovernmental Group of Twenty-Four on International Monetary Affairs," 20 September 1997 reprinted in "Ministers Call for Progressive, Flexible Approach to Capital Account Liberalization," *IMF Survey* 26, no. 18 (6 October 1997), pp. 306–308.

[54] Fischer, "Capital Account Liberalization and the Role of the IMF" (seminar).

ment: "Far from being discouraged by recent events in southeast Asia, the IMF is all the more motivated to continue work on an amendment to the Articles of Agreement that will allow the Fund to promote freedom of capital movements."[55]

But the subsequent spread of the crisis in November to South Korea, a country with relatively sound macroeconomic fundamentals, greatly dampened enthusiasm for the amendment. It now appeared to some directors that market discipline had been replaced by market panic. Although IMF management and some directors claimed the crisis strengthened the case for the amendment, the tone on the board had shifted, and members were increasingly reluctant to discuss it.[56] Opponents used the crisis in South Korea, which the Fund and the U.S. Treasury had used as a window of opportunity to work closely with domestic reformers to press for greater liberalization, to suggest that the IMF was imposing liberalization on countries and therefore should not be given jurisdiction. The events in Asia also added strength to Keynesian-inspired views among some board directors, many of whom claimed that herding behavior evident from the crisis undermined the theoretical arguments for liberalization and thus the proposal to give the Fund the authority to promote it. But for proponents of the amendment, the crisis suggested more than ever that the amendment was vital for enabling the Fund to deepen its understanding of capital account crises and "to help bring order to the international economy."[57] Progress on the amendment thus proceeded, but enthusiasm was clearly waning.

In March 1998 a seminar was held at the Fund to discuss the amendment, with participants including board directors, IMF management and staff, senior government officials, members of the private financial community, and prominent academic economists. The seminar revealed significant disagreements among the participants. Although some participants argued that "it was not liberalization per se, but its form and sequence that rendered countries vulnerable to changes in market sentiment," others expressed "severe doubts" about "whether capital account liberalization per se was a good idea." Differing views were also expressed on the desirability of temporary market-based controls on inflows, with a "fairly wide cross-section of participants—from developed and developing countries and representing both the public and private sector" supporting their use,

[55] Camdessus, "Address to the Board of Governors of the Fund," Hong Kong, , 23 September 1997, available at http://www.imf.org/external/np/speeches/1997/mds9711 .htm (accessed 9 January 2007).

[56] Author's interview with Wijnholds.

[57] Fischer, "Capital Account Liberalization and the Role of the IMF" (seminar). In interviews with the author, Camdessus and Fischer maintained that the amendment remains vital to improving the international financial architecture.

while "a number of speakers" claimed they were "generally undesirable" and "a way of avoiding necessary policy adjustment."[58] Most participants interpreted the Asian crisis as necessitating greater attention to sequencing. Still, there remained a modicum of support for the big-bang approach, with some participants expressing the fear that too much emphasis on preconditions would lead to unnecessary delays in implementing reforms. These participants claimed that not all governments should wait for other reforms to be completed; instead, they should take "advantage of windows of political opportunity" to liberalize.[59]

From within the IMF, Fischer and Boorman restated their arguments for the amendment.[60] Other seminar participants argued that the IMF should be given the mandate to advocate liberalization but not given jurisdiction.[61] Summers, offering the U.S. perspective, backed the amendment and criticized the use of controls as a means "to avoid necessary policy adjustments . . . [and] a sure-fire route to . . . introducing new economic distortions and creating scope for official rent-seeking and corruption."[62] The fact that Summers still publicly supported the amendment in March 1998 suggests that he was still pushing it hard in private before that point.

In April 1998, the Interim Committee reaffirmed its commitment to the amendment.[63] But opposition had spread among the Fund's membership, with an increasing number of directors now speaking more forcefully about the need for caution.[64] Opponents on the board had a critical opportunity to discursively represent financial events in Asia as a "crisis" for proponents of the amendment.[65] For these actors, the haphazard rush to liberalize in countries such as Thailand and South Korea had resulted in policy failure, while the maintenance of extensive controls and the cautious approach taken in countries such as China and India had produced greater success by enabling these economies to escape the worst effects of the crisis. Opponents therefore increasingly implicated capital account

---

[58] IMF, *Annual Report, 1998* (Washington, D.C.: IMF, 1998), pp. 74, 76, 77.

[59] IMF, *Annual Report, 1998*, p. 76. See also p. 77.

[60] "Press Conference on International Monetary Fund Seminar on Capital Account Liberalization," 10 March 1998, available at http://www.imf.org/external/np/tr/1998/tr980310.htm (accessed 9 January 2007).

[61] IMF, *Annual Report, 1998*, p. 76.

[62] "Deputy Treasury Secretary Summers' Remarks before the International Monetary Fund," U.S. Treasury Press Release RR-2286, 9 March 1998.

[63] "Communique of the Interim Committee of the Board of Governors of the International Monetary Fund," IMF Press Release 98/14, 16 April 1998.

[64] Minutes of the Executive Board Meeting, EBM/98/38, 2 April 1998 (IMF Archives).

[65] Ralf J. Leiteritz, "Explaining Organizational Outcomes: The International Monetary Fund and Capital Account Liberalization," *Journal of International Relations and Development* 8, no. 1 (2005), pp. 1–25.

openness as the "cause" of the crisis, warranting extreme caution in pushing ahead with the amendment.

Equally significant was growing opposition to the amendment from within the leading IMF principal. In the context of the congressional debate over the U.S. quota increase to the Fund, legislators, in part because of increasing NGO advocacy, subjected the IMF to severe criticism over a range of concerns about the environment, labor standards, and moral hazard. In May 1998, several leading Democratic legislators, having learned of the proposed amendment, sent a letter to Rubin threatening to withhold support for the quota increase if the Treasury continued to support the amendment. Their threat was clear: "Our support for the additional IMF funding will be in jeopardy if the U.S. government continues to press for the addition of capital account liberalization to the IMF charter."[66] The course of action for senior Treasury officials was equally clear; priority was to be given to securing approval of the quota increase, and support for the amendment was to be quietly withdrawn.[67]

Without U.S. or British support on the board, those in favor of the amendment clearly faced a losing battle. The spread of the crisis to Russia in August 1998 seems to have sounded the death knell for the amendment. Opposition to the amendment, already fueled by growing concerns about herding behavior, was further amplified by critical perceptions of the Fund's role in Russia. The IMF had strongly encouraged the Russian government to liberalize restrictions on foreign investment in high-yield government securities.[68] The subsequent Russian devaluation and default were directly linked to this decision. Critics saw these events as evidence that the IMF's advice, which in this case had recommended liberalization prematurely, was questionable at best, and as an indication that the staff could not be entrusted to advocate liberalization cautiously.

FINANCIAL TURMOIL IN ASIA AND BEYOND: INFORMAL RECONSIDERATIONS

The crisis also led many economists within the Fund and the academic community to reconsider their views on capital freedom. In addition to views about the crisis itself, Malaysia's experience with the introduction of controls on outflows also was of great significance. Perceiving this expe-

---

[66] Letter to the Honorable Robert E. Rubin, Secretary, Department of the Treasury, from Reps. Richard Gephardt, David Bonior, Nancy Pelosi, Barney Frank, Maxine Waters, and Esteban Edward Torres, 1 May 1998, available from www.house.gov/frank/imf-letter.html (accessed 1 June 2006). See also Abdelal, *Capital Rules*, pp. 158–159.

[67] Author's interview with Lissakers.

[68] Stone, *Lending Credibility*, pp. 147–148; Woods, *The Globalizers*, pp. 125–127.

rience to have been a qualified success, some inside the Fund and the academic community represented it as a "crisis" for beliefs that ruled out the use of controls on outflows in crisis situation.

In the months leading up to the crisis, fundamentals in most Asian countries had been fairly strong and the Fund had continued to praise key practices of the development model that had led to the "East Asian miracle." Indeed, what is particularly striking is the fact that most observers generally failed to predict the extent, depth, and breadth of the coming crisis. Yet later in diagnosing the reasons for the crisis after its onset, the "causes" were clear, with IMF and U.S. officials identifying key practices associated with the Asian development model—such as bank-firm-state collaboration—as synonymous with "crony capitalism."[69]

Neoliberal arguments were consistently drawn upon to represent these practices as "policy errors" and as structural institutional sources of instability that "caused" the turmoil. Rubin, for instance, argued the turmoil was the "consequence of structural deficiencies and bad policies" and urged crisis-afflicted governments to "re-commit to the sound policies that create confidence and encourage a steady flow of capital." In a series of speeches, Summers focused on "maintenance of mutually inconsistent monetary policy and exchange rate regimes" and "excess inflows of private capital channeled into unproductive investments . . . [as well as] . . . significant failures of debt management that led to unsustainable quantities of short-term debt." Institutional structures were also blamed for triggering the crisis. Rubin and Summers referred to "close links between governments, banks and corporations [that] led to fundamentally unsound investments by corporations funded by unsound banks" and "inadequate financial regulation and supervision" as well as "lax lending standards."[70]

Failing to see the crisis as related to capital account openness and factors intrinsic to the operation of international capital markets, this interpretation placed the onus firmly on countries that had been recipients of capital inflow surges that were now suddenly being reversed. In accordance with this interpretation, macroeconomic policy adjustment and structural reform, such as the closure or merger of insolvent financial institutions and

[69] Rodney Bruce Hall, "The Discursive Demolition of the Asian Development Model," *International Studies Quarterly* 47, no. 1 (2003), pp. 71–99.

[70] Robert Rubin, "Address on the Asian Financial Situation to Georgetown University," U.S. Treasury Press Release RR-2168, 21 January 1998; and Rubin, "Remarks to the National Center for APEC," U.S. Treasury Press Release RR-1937, 18 September 1997; Lawrence H. Summers, "Testimony before the House Committee on Banking and Financial Services," U.S. Treasury Press Release RR-2062, 13 November 1997; Summers, "Emerging from Crisis: The Beginnings of a New Asia, Economic Strategy Institute," U.S. Treasury Press Release RR-2217, 11 February 1998.

the strengthening of prudential regulations, was defined as the "appropriate" response. This interpretation also ruled out the introduction of restraints on outflows. Summers stated that crisis-affected countries were to absorb the costs by "making the macroeconomic policy adjustments needed." "The primary burden of responsibility," Summers insisted, "must continue to fall on the countries concerned."[71]

Capital flow volatility, according to U.S. officials, was a symptom of underlying policy and institutional failures, not a cause of the turmoil per se. Market actors in general and speculators in particular were cast as rationally reacting to policy and institutional failures, imposing discipline, perhaps excessively, on crisis-affected countries. Indicative of the views of U.S. officials at the time were the December 1997 remarks by then Federal Reserve chairman Alan Greenspan:

> Belatedly perhaps, they [Asian governments] have perceived the problems to which their systems are prone and recognized the unforgiving nature of the new global market forces. . . . A well-functioning international financial system will seek out anomalies in policy alignments and exchange rates and set them right . . . [S]peculation forces currencies through arbitrage into a closer alignment with underlying market values to the benefit of the international economic and financial system as a whole. We used to describe capital flight as "hot money." But we soon recognized that it was not the money that was "hot," but the place it was running from.[72]

The IMF's interpretations also located the cause of the crisis in policy and institutional failures and represented the market's reaction as imposing discipline. Camdessus located the initial trigger for the crisis in the buildup of "large macroeconomic imbalances" in Thailand. "Substantial real exchange rate appreciation; a marked slowdown in export growth; a persistently large current account deficit financed by portfolio inflows, including a substantial amount of short-term capital; and rising external debt," according to Camdessus, "exposed other weaknesses in the economy, including substantial, unhedged borrowing by the private sector, an inflated property market, and a weak and over-exposed banking system." The crisis then spread elsewhere as "problems in the Thai economy promoted markets to take a closer look at the risks in other countries."[73] Simi-

---

[71] Summers, "Testimony before the House Committee on Banking and Financial Services."

[72] Alan Greenspan, "Growth and Flexibility: Lessons from Asia," Economic Club of New York, New York, 2 December 1997, available from www.federalreserve.gov/boarddocs/Speeches/1997/19971202.htm

[73] Camdessus, "Rebuilding Confidence in Asia," remarks at the ASEAN Business Forum, Kuala Lampur, Malaysia, 2 December 1997, available at http:///www.imf.org/external/np/speeches/1997/120297a.htm; Camdessus, "Lessons from Southeast Asia," Remarks at

larly, Fischer noted that "weak financial institutions, inadequate bank regulation and supervision, and the complicated and non-transparent relations among governments, banks and corporations were central to the economic crisis."[74] The staff offered a similar construction that focused on policy and institutional failures.[75]

What is particularly noteworthy about this construction of the crisis is not the "causes" it identifies, but rather the "causes" it fails to identify. In focusing exclusively on domestic economic, policy, and institutional sources of the turmoil, this particular crisis construction obscures the impact of self-fulfilling market expectations and the possibility the crisis was triggered by more pervasive market failures of the type Keynesians highlight.

To be sure, Rubin, Summers, and Greenspan recognized that "financial markets tend to go to extremes . . . perhaps overshooting the long-term equilibrium," thus making it seem "difficult to avoid the judgment that . . . the [market's] punishment was in a sense disproportionate to the crime."[76] But the statements from U.S. officials surveyed earlier make it clear that they regarded the pain of excessive market discipline as having been brought on by trends in affected countries, and not factors intrinsic to the operation of international capital markets. As Summers concluded, "It seems difficult to point to any emerging-market economy that experienced a financial crisis but did not have significant fundamental weaknesses that called into question the sustainability of its policies. . . . The point is that preventing crises is heavily dependent on avoiding a situation where the bank-run psychology takes hold, and that will depend heavily on strengthening core institutions and fundamentals."[77]

Press Briefing, Singapore, 13 November 1997, available at http://www.imf.org/external/np/speeches/1997/mds9716.htm.

[74] Stanley Fischer, "In Defense of the IMF: Specialized Tools for a Specialized Task," *Foreign Affairs* 77, no. 4 (1998), pp. 103–106 at p. 105.

[75] IMF, *World Economic Outlook* (October) (Washington, D.C.: IMF, 1997), pp. 14, 96; IMF, *World Economic Outlook* (April) (Washington, D.C.: IMF, 1998), pp. 3, 16–18, 101–102; Charles Adams, Donald J. Mathieson, Garry Schinasi, and Bankim Chada, *International Capital Markets: Developments, Prospects, and Key Policy Issues* (Washington, D.C.: IMF, 1999), pp. 6, 11, 57, 63, 73, 148–150.

[76] Rubin, "Remarks to the National Center for APEC" ("Financial markets tend to go to extremes"); Summers, "International Financial Crises: Causes, Prevention, and Cures," *American Economic Review* 90, no. 2 (2000), pp. 1–16 at p. 7 ("difficult to avoid the judgment . . . "); Greenspan, Testimony before the Committee on Banking and Financial Services, U.S. House of Representatives, 13 November 1997, available at http://federalreserve.gov/boarddocs/testimony/19971113.htm ("perhaps overshooting . . .").

[77] Summers, "International Financial Crises," p. 7.

Camdessus expressed similar views, claiming "it would be a mistake to blame hedge funds or other market participants for the turmoil in Asia." Instead, Camdessus argued that "turbulence in the market is only a symptom of more serious underlying problems."[78] While conceding that "markets have overreacted," Camdessus maintained the behavior of market participants was based on a "rational" reading of fundamentals, and that "contagion does not strike out of the clear blue sky."[79] Speaking of the requirements for "solidarity" in a world of financial globalization, Camdessus suggested it was up to governments, not financial market participants, to maintain harmony, remarking that the "first tenet of a charter for world solidarity is to 'keep your house in order.'"[80] Fischer, while conceding there were "examples of market overreactions and unjustified contagion effects," argued that "capital movements are mostly appropriate: currency crises do not blow out of a clear blue sky, but rather start as reactions or external shocks."[81] Thus, few actors within the Fund and its leading principal were yet willing to consider the crisis as partly the result of autonomous self-fulfilling market expectations where market actors fail to use "all available information."[82]

By September 1998 the crisis had already swept through much of Asia and on to Russia, with most governments approaching the Fund for programs. Malaysia had not been immune to the effects of the crisis, suffering significant exchange rate depreciation and a collapse in asset prices.[83] Initially, the Malaysian government responded with orthodox policy adjustments—such as interest rate hikes—that won praise from Camdessus.[84] But as the effects of the crisis became more severe and serious questions were raised about whether the IMF response had spooked rather than reassured investors, and whether it had exacerbated the material downturn

[78] Camdessus, "Rebuilding Confidence in Asia."

[79] Camdessus, "Reflections on the Crisis in Asia," address to the Extraordinary Ministerial Meeting of the Group of 24, Caracas, Venezuela, 7 February 1998, available at www.imf.org/external/np/speeches/1998/020798.htm

[80] Camdessus, "Address to the Board of Governors of the Fund."

[81] Fischer, "Capital Account Liberalization and the Role of the IMF" (seminar).

[82] By "autonomous self-fulfilling market expectations" I mean the type of expectations that Keynes had in mind, that is, those that develop independently from any reading of fundamentals. Instead, expectations are shaped by the social context in which investment decisions are made. For prominent analyses of the crisis stressing policy and institutional errors, see Morris Goldstein, *The Asian Financial Crisis: Causes, Cures, and Systemic Implications* (Washington, D.C.: Institute for International Economics, 1998); Giancarlo Corsetti, Paolo Pesenti, and Nouriel Roubini, "Paper Tigers? A Model of the Asian Crisis," *European Economic Review* 43, no. 7 (1999), pp. 1211–1236.

[83] For an overview see Laura Alfaro and Rawi Abdelal, "Capital and Control: Lessons from Malaysia," *Challenge* 46, no. 4 (2003), pp. 36–53.

[84] Camdessus, "Address to the Board of Governors of the Fund."

rather than lessened it, Malaysia's leader, Prime Minister Mahathir Mohammad, rather than approach the Fund for assistance, decided on a new course of action.[85] Mahathir proceeded to sack and jail his finance minister (and then heir apparent), discontinue his orthodox policies, and introduce controls on outflows. Mahathir also unleashed a barrage of neocolonialist and anticapitalist rhetoric, blaming the crisis on speculators, hedge funds, and a Western conspiracy. The capital controls were designed to curtail the offshore market in the Malaysian currency, which had been a source of significant pressure of the exchange rate, and to restore a degree of monetary independence so that interest rates could be reduced to increase output and employment.[86]

Although some prominent economists had urged expansionary monetary policy as a route to recovery, few, with the exception of Paul Krugman, had raised the possibility of controls on outflows.[87] The IMF's management, staff, and leading principals, as well as much of the economics profession, saw the introduction of such measures, especially in a relatively liberalized financial setting such as Malaysia, as outside the boundaries of legitimate policy. Later, Krugman noted the "radical" nature of the Malaysian controls and suggested that "Malaysia got away with economic heresy." Indeed, prior to the outbreak of a full-blown crisis, Thailand's imposition of controls on outflows in May and June 1997 had been severely criticized.[88]

Two weeks after imposing its controls, Malaysia faced similar criticism.[89] Rubin and Summers opposed the decision, arguing that controls are inef-

---

[85] For criticisms of the IMF response, see, for instance, Feldstein, "Refocusing the IMF"; and Steven Radelet and Jeffrey D. Sachs, "The East Asian Financial Crisis: Diagnosis, Remedies, Prospects," *Brookings Papers on Economic Activity* 1998, no. 1, pp. 1–90.

[86] The government also was anxious to avoid IMF structural conditionality, which likely would have mandated the elimination of subsidies and other schemes that give economic preference to descendants of the indigenous Malay population as opposed to those descended from Chinese immigrants. These policy measures are a key source of political support for the government, and their elimination would have threatened the political survival of the government.

[87] Paul Krugman, "Saving Asia: It's Time to Get Radical," *Fortune* 138, no. 5 (1998), pp. 74–80. See also Krugman, "Capital Control Freaks: How Malaysia Got Away with Economic Heresy," *Slate*, 27 September 1999, available from www.slate.com/id/35534. For recommendations for expansionary monetary policies, see Radelet and Sachs, "East Asian Financial Crisis"; and the proposals of Joseph Stiglitz covered in "World Bank Questions IMF Plan: Austerity in Asia May Worsen Crisis," *Wall Street Journal*, 8 January 1998.

[88] IEO, *IMF's Approach*, pp. 45–46.

[89] Malaysia introduced controls on outflows twice in connection with the Asian crisis, first in August 1997 and then in September 1998. The first set of measures was aimed specifically at regulating swap-transactions by banks with nonresidents, while leaving other flows unfettered. The second set of measures tightened restrictions by introducing a one-year holding limit on the repatriation of portfolio investment. In February 1999, the one-year holding

fective over time, cannot substitute for policy adjustment, introduce distortions, and deter inflows and damage credibility, particularly when introduced in a relatively liberalized setting. Rubin, for instance, claimed the Malaysian controls were "misguided" and "would effectively prevent the return of capital [and] . . . postpone recovery and the restoration of economic growth."[90] Summers similarly remarked, "We should all be able to agree on the danger of . . . denying a country's own citizens the capacity to convert their own currency and invest abroad. Such measures represent substantial intrusions on freedom. They make unsustainable policy errors more tempting. They repel new capital inflows. And in an age of the internet they are more unlikely to be successful in the long run."[91] Some U.S. officials reportedly "quietly expressed the hope" that the controls "would fail so spectacularly that the smouldering ruins of the Malaysian economy would act as a caution to other countries."[92]

The IMF management and staff initially offered a similar assessment of the Malaysian controls. Camdessus praised governments for "relying increasingly on measures to strengthen economic fundamentals, rather than on controls," while going so far as to identify the Malaysian controls as "dangerous and indeed harmful."[93] Controls on outflows, Camdessus argued, were counterproductive and "a sure-fire way to send the herd scrambling for safer pastures and set back efforts to restore confidence."[94] Fischer urged the gradual removal of the controls.[95]

The initial views of the Asian Department and MAE staff in their consultations with the Malaysian government, as well as the appraisal offered by RES staff, were equally negative. In line with neoliberal standards of

---

period was replaced by a graduated system of exit levy. In September 1999, the exit levy was abolished, except for profits from portfolio investment brought in after February 1999. The system was entirely abolished in February 2001.

[90] Robert Rubin, "Statement at the 58th Development Committee of the World Bank and the International Monetary Fund," U.S. Treasury Press Release RR-2738, 5 October 1998.

[91] Summers, "Building an International Financial Architecture for the 21st Century, Remarks to the Cato Institute, Washington, D.C.," U.S. Treasury Press Release RR-2770, 22 October 1998.

[92] As quoted in Jonathan Kirshner, "The Study of Money," World Politics 52, no. 3 (2000), pp. 407–436 at p. 435.

[93] Camdessus, "Address to the Board of Governors of the Fund" ("relying increasingly on measures . . ."); and as quoted in Robert Wade, "The Asian Crisis and the Global Economy: Causes, Consequences, and Cure," Current History 98 (November 1998), pp. 361–373 at p. 368 ("dangerous and indeed harmful").

[94] Camdessus, "Lessons from Southeast Asia," remarks at Press Briefing, Singapore, 13 November 1997, available at www.imf.org/external/np/speeches/1997/mds9716.htm

[95] Fischer, "Reforming the International Monetary System," revised and preliminary draft of David Finch Lecture, Melbourne, 9 November 1998, available at www.imf.org/external/np/speeches/1998/110998.htm

behavior, the controls were said likely to prove ineffective and offer a poor substitute for policy adjustments and structural reforms. The staff also believed the controls would damage Malaysia's credibility, making it an international financial pariah and creating difficulties in accessing capital markets in the future. Interestingly, the staff did not oppose maintaining controls on inflows that had been in place prior to September 1998 while policies were adjusted. The staff even suggested the government consider introducing a market-based "prudential" restraint on inflows of the type implemented in Chile.[96]

However, as the crisis unfolded it sparked a reconsideration among a small, but prominent, group of academic economists and IMF and World Bank staff of prevailing understandings of market behavior and standards of behavior for controls. An alternative crisis construction, very much in the Keynesian tradition, began to emerge, arguing that factors intrinsic to the operation of international capital markets had also played a role in the crisis and the herding behavior accompanying it. In this alternative construction, the crisis was identified as more a market panic than the result of policy errors and institutional deficiencies. For instance, a 1998 World Bank report, which was drafted when Joseph Stiglitz was chief economist of the organization, indicated, "It is important to note that domestic policy failure explains only part of the . . . crisis. Herd instincts in financial markets have not served East Asia well."[97] Stiglitz was fiercely critical of the IMF's response to the crisis and strongly opposed to unfettered capital mobility.[98]

Some prominent academic economists also increasingly argued that crises could occur even when fundamentals were sound, because of factors intrinsic to the operation of international capital markets, such as information asymmetries, that can give rise to autonomous self-fulfilling expectations. Like Stiglitz, when these economists examined some of the crisis-affected countries they discovered capital flow volatility driven not by fundamentals, but rather by such autonomous self-fulfilling expectations. Jeffrey Sachs, for instance, pointedly argued, "There is no 'fundamental' reason for Asia's financial calamity except financial panic itself. Asia's need for significant financial reform is real, but not a sufficient cause for the

[96] IMF, *World Economic Outlook* (October) (Washington, D.C.: IMF, 1998), pp. 6, 18; IEO, *IMF's Approach*, p. 46.

[97] World Bank, *East Asia: The Road to Recovery* (Washington, D.C.: World Bank, 1999), p. 16. See also World Bank, *Global Economic Prospects and the Developing Countries, 1998/ 99: Beyond Financial Crisis* (Washington, D.C.: World Bank, 1999), p. xi.

[98] See, for instance, Joseph Stiglitz, "How to Fix the Asian Economies," *New York Times*, 31 October 1997; Stiglitz, "What Caused Asia's Crash? Bad Private Sector Decisions," *Wall Street Journal*, 4 February 1998; Stiglitz, "What I Learned." See also "World Bank Questions IMF Plan: Austerity in Asia May Worsen Crisis," *Wall Street Journal*, 8 January 1998.

panic. . . . Asia is reeling not from a crisis of fundamentals, but from a self-fulfilling withdrawal of short-term loans, one that is fuelled by each investor's recognition that all other investors are withdrawing their claims."[99] The perceived inadequacy of understandings that stressed policy and institutional errors alone led some economists, such as Krugman, to criticize existing academic models of currency crises.[100] Some economists have subsequently endeavored to incorporate the role of market panic into a new generation of currency crisis models, but the extent to which self-fulfilling expectations and herding behavior develop autonomously remains, as Krugman acknowledges, one of several "disputed issues."[101]

Perhaps most influential in shifting the beliefs of many economists was a widely cited 1998 article by Bhagwati. Bhagwati's status as a prominent supporter of free trade brought renewed attention to question of whether unfettered capital mobility was inherently stable or desirable. Bhagwati argued that the crisis provided "striking evidence of the inherently crisis-prone nature of freer capital movements" and revealed claims that unfettered capital mobility was desirable as a "myth."[102]

By the autumn of 1998 the climate of opinion among economists had clearly shifted toward a genuine reappraisal of neoliberalism. Greater attention to the role of market panic and herding behavior translated into what Wade and Veneroso describe as "the gathering support for capital controls."[103] Many economists saw the financial instability afflicting emerging markets as a "crisis" for certain beliefs that prevailed in the profession. As Bhagwati concluded: "Despite the . . . assumption that the ideal world is indeed one of free capital flows, the weight of evidence and the force of logic point in the opposite direction, toward restraints on capital flows. It is time to shift the burden of proof from those who oppose to those who favor liberated capital."[104] In applying this perspective, many economists, like some board directors, pointed to China and India as examples of countries that had maintained controls and therefore managed

---

[99] Jeffrey Sachs, "Power unto Itself," *Financial Times*, 11 December 1997. See also Radelet and Sachs, "East Asian Financial Crisis."

[100] Krugman, "Bahtulism: Who Poisoned Asia's Currency Markets," *Slate*, 14 August 1997; and Krugman, "Currency Crises," October 1997, available at http://web.mit.edu/krugman/www

[101] Krugman, "Currency Crises." On this new generation of currency crisis models, see B. N. Ghosh, "Financial Crisis in the MIT Countries: Myths and Realities," in *Global Financial Crises and Reforms: Cases and Caveats* (London: Routledge, 2001), pp. 77–101.

[102] Bhagwati, "The Capital Myth," p. 7. See also Bhagwati's contribution to IMF Economic Forum: "Capital Account Liberalization: What's the Best Stance?" (2 October 1998), available at http://www.imf.org/external/np/tr/1998/tr981002a.htm

[103] Wade and Veneroso, "The Gathering Support for Capital Controls," *Challenge* 41, no. 6 (1998), pp. 14–26.

[104] Bhagwati, "The Capital Myth," p. 12.

to escape the worst effects of the turmoil. In addition to Bhagwati and Krugman, a number of other prominent economists later offered their support for selective restraints on capital mobility.[105]

To be sure, many prominent economists, such as Sebastian Edwards, continued to oppose the use of controls based on conventional arguments.[106] Differences also remained even among those economists who supported controls. Krugman, for instance, lent support to controls on outflows, while Eichengreen limited his support to controls on inflows. Others—such as Bhagwati, Cohen, and Richard Cooper, failed to make a distinction between controls on inflows and outflows in offering their sympathy or support for controls. In spite of these differences, as Bhagwati suggested, the "burden of proof" shifted, and since the Asian crisis the economics profession has devoted significantly greater attention to examining the consequences of controls, and whether and under what conditions they might be effective.[107] Although the beliefs expressed by most economists remain far from those elaborated by Keynes and his supporters, since the Asian crisis the economics profession has lent greater support than in years past to selective restraints on capital mobility. As Cohen concludes, "A policy approach once dismissed as obsolete, left over from a more interventionist era, was back on the agenda."[108]

Arguments for gradualism had been gathering steam within the IMF since the Mexican peso crisis and with it a renewed legitimacy for temporary controls on inflows. Although the informal staff approach continued to evolve until the Asian financial crisis, "the idea of sequencing," according to the IEO, "became more prominent in staff analysis" following the Mexican crisis.[109] Support for gradualism and sequencing came not

[105] See, for instance, Benjamin J. Cohen, "Taming the Phoenix? Monetary Governance after the Crisis," in *The Asian Financial Crisis and the Architecture of Global Finance*, ed. Gregory W. Noble and John Ravenhill (Cambridge: Cambridge University Press, 2000), pp. 192–212; Richard N. Cooper, "Should Capital Controls Be Banished?" *Brookings Papers on Economic Activity* 1999, no. 1, ed. William C. Brainard and George L. Perry, pp. 89–125; Eichengreen, *Toward a New International Financial Architecture: A Practical Post-Asia Agenda* (Washington, D.C.: Institute for International Economics, 1999); James Tobin, "The Money Changers: Why We Need Sand in the Market's Gears," *Washington Post*, 21 December 1997; John Williamson, *Exchange Rate Regimes for Emerging Markets: Reviving the Intermediate Option* (Washington, D.C.: Institute for International Economics, 2000).

[106] Sebastian Edwards, "How Effective Are Capital Controls?" *Journal of Economic Perspectives* 13, no. 4 (1999), pp. 65–84.

[107] For an overview of this research, see Nicholas Magud and Carmen M. Reinhart, "Capital Controls: An Evaluation," in *Capital Controls and Capital Flows to Emerging Markets*, ed. Sebastian Edwards (Chicago: University of Chicago Press, 2007), pp. 645–674.

[108] Cohen, "Taming the Phoenix?" p. 199.

[109] IEO, *IMF's Approach*, p. 26. See also pp. 75–77 and chapter 7 of this book.

just from RES and PDR staff but also from some staff inside MAE. For instance, following the Mexican crisis, and before the Asian crisis, an MAE staff paper examined the sequence of liberalization followed in several emerging markets, and concluded that the pace should depend on macroeconomic and exchange rate policies.[110]

Along with the Mexican crisis, the emphasis that many academic economists began to place on institutions as a critical determinant of economic performance reinforced staff receptivity to gradualism.[111] By the mid-1990s many academic economists had reached the conclusion that a well-functioning market economy depends not solely on "getting policies right" but also on "getting institutions right." It became clear to many, particularly after the uneven performance of many Latin American economies in the 1990s, that even if countries liberalized restrictions on trade and capital flows, reduced fiscal deficits, and eliminated currency overvaluation, they often failed to achieve sustainable strong economic performance because of weak institutions. What became clear to many academic economists, as well as many staff members inside the Fund, was that policy reforms would not have any lasting effect if institutional conditions were poor.[112] Sound policies needed to be embedded in solid institutions. This line of argument lent support for gradualist arguments to slow down the pace of capital account liberalization until the necessary institutional reforms and development took place.

But it was interpretations of the Asian financial crisis that seem to have led most staff members to adapt their views and abandon support for the big-bang approach. Erstwhile big-bang supporters, because of the experiences of some emerging markets as well as gradualist advocacy, came to see financial instability in some countries, such as South Korea, where "disorderly liberalization" was undertaken without regard to sequencing, as a policy failure. Moreover, they also came to view the relative stability of other countries, such as India, which maintained controls and sought to coordinate liberalization with other reforms, as offering a policy success. This posed a "crisis" for the big-bang approach. Indicative of this process of adaptation are the conclusions reached by a July 1998 MAE staff paper:

---

[110] Johnston, Darbar, and Echeverria, "Sequencing Capital Account Liberalization."

[111] Douglass C. North, *Institutions, Institutional Change, and Economic Performance* (Cambridge: Cambridge University Press, 1990).

[112] See, for instance, Anoop Singh, Agnes Belaisch, Charles Collyns, Paula De Masi, Reva Krieger, Guy Meredith, and Robert Rennhack, "Stabilization and Reform in Latin America: A Macroeconomic Perspective of the Experience since the 1990s," IMF Occasional Paper No. 238 (Washington, D.C.: IMF, 2005).

The Asian country experiences confirm that it is necessary to approach capital account liberalization as an integral part of a more comprehensive program of economic reform, coordinated with appropriate macroeconomic and exchange rate policies, and including policies to strengthen financial markets and institutions. The question is not so much one of capital liberalization having been too fast, since some of the countries in Asia have followed a very gradualist approach. Rather, it is more to do with the appropriate sequencing of the reforms and, more specifically, what supporting measures need to be taken.

Following the outbreak of the Asian crisis, the notion of sequencing became increasingly prominent in MAE technical assistance operations. For instance, in a December 1997 seminar held in China, the MAE staff emphasized the need to coordinate liberalization with measures aimed at strengthening the financial system. In the aftermath of the "crisis" for the big-bang approach, even Guitian adapted his beliefs, conceding that "the actual speed with which countries move toward liberalization would depend on individual cases."[113] Since the Asian crisis there has been a proliferation of staff research on sequencing, enabling the staff to develop an increasingly sophisticated understanding of the optimal preconditions and modalities for "successful" liberalization.[114] Greater recognition of financial sector soundness as a precondition for liberalization led, in 1999, to the creation of the Financial Sector Assessment Program (FSAP), which has been administered jointly by the IMF and the World Bank. The intention of the FSAP has been to strengthen the focus of IMF surveillance, which until the late 1990s was insufficiently attentive to financial sector vulnerabilities.

After the Asian crisis the informal staff approach thus became one of relative caution, retaining capital freedom as a long-run goal but placing greater emphasis on sequencing and attention to preconditions. Expressions of caution were no longer isolated incidents within the Fund; in fact, they tended to be the norm. The staff became increasingly attentive to potential sources of vulnerability, such as weak financial systems, that need to be addressed before liberalizing. This approach was evident in area department consultations with Bulgaria (1999), Croatia (2001), and Russia (2002). Building on this approach, a July 2001 staff paper to the board proposed that the IMF adopt an "integrated" (gradualist) approach as its

[113] Kane, "Seminar Discusses Orderly Path," p. 84.

[114] See, for instance, R. Barry Johnston, "Sequencing Capital Account Liberalizations and Financial Sector Reform," IMF Paper on Policy Analysis and Assessment No. 98/8 (Washington, D.C.: IMF, 1998); R. Barry Johnston and V. Sundararajan, eds., *Sequencing Financial Sector Reforms: Country Experiences and Issues* (Washington, D.C.: IMF, 1999).

formal policy toward capital account liberalization.[115] Still, some staff did not shy away for advocating liberalization when conditions appeared to warrant it. Following the Asian crisis, for those countries, such as Chile, Hungary, Israel, Poland, and South Africa, which broadly met certain preconditions, some staff endorsed the move toward greater openness.[116]

Although officials from the United States and other leading developed countries gave greater priority to institutional reform in the aftermath of the Asian crisis, little of the staff shift toward gradualism seems directly attributable to the influence of these member states. In fact, some officials from these countries remained committed to the principles of the big-bang approach.

Recall from the earlier discussion that after the Mexican crisis some U.S. officials continued to seek to force the pace of liberalization. In April 1998, in the midst of the Asian crisis, this view received support from the Scandinavian board director, who argued that "appropriate sequencing should not mean that the liberalization of capital movements should wait for all reforms to be completed. . . . In economics, as in life, there is no reward without risk."[117] More recently, in its ongoing dialogue with China, the U.S. Treasury has sought to force the pace of liberalization even though some IMF staff members have suggested that, without prior institutional reforms, this would be "putting the cart before the horse." Some IMF staff members also opposed recent efforts by officials in Brissels to force the pace of liberalization in some EU accession countries.[118] It is therefore not surprising that, though gradualism has come to define the informal staff approach, the Fund's principals have refused to sanction gradualism and the "integrated approach" as formal policy. Although some directors believe gradualism to be appropriate, others still cling to the big-bang approach and argue that policy measures can be implemented simultaneously and that governments might want to "use windows of opportunity" to move ahead rapidly with liberalization.[119]

Inside the Fund the reappraisal of beliefs about sequencing translated into stronger and broader support for the use of temporary market-based controls on inflows as a "prudential measure."[120] Even MAE technical as-

---

[115] This board paper was later published as Shogo Ishii, Karl Habermeier, Jorge Ivan Canales-Kriljenko; Bernard Laurens, John Leimone, and Judit Vadasz, "Capital Account Liberalization and Financial Sector Stability," IMF Occasional Paper No. 211 (Washington, D.C.: IMF, 2002).

[116] IEO, *IMF's Approach*, p. 35.

[117] As quoted in Leiteritz, "Explaining Organizational Outcomes," p. 15.

[118] Abdelal, *Capital Rules.*

[119] IEO, *IMF's Approach*, p. 23.

[120] Kenneth Rogoff, "Rethinking Capital Controls: When Should We Keep an Open Mind?" *Finance and Development* 39, no. 3 (2002), available at http://www.imf.org/external/pubs/ft/fandd/2002/12/rogoff.htm (accessed 24 March 2009).

sistance operations became more accommodative of restraints on capital inflows, especially those implemented for prudential reasons. In January 1999, for example, the MAE staff advised the Russian government to implement restrictions for such reasons.[121] "Limitations on capital mobility," as Cohen observes, "thus seemed to gain new legitimacy as an instrument of monetary governance."[122] It is worth noting that this strengthening and broadening of staff accommodation and support for the use of controls on inflows also appears to have occurred without strong influence from member states or management.

In fact, growing staff accommodation and support for controls on inflows initially ran contrary to what Camdessus and the U.S. Treasury were advocating. Although Fischer had earlier raised the possibility that controls on inflows could play a useful role in some circumstances, Camdessus appears to have remained more reluctant to sanction their use, even in the immediate aftermath of the Asian crisis. In the early months of the crisis, Rubin and Summers, often referring specifically to Chilean experience, routinely opposed the use of market-based controls on inflows. In April 1998, Rubin did concede that it "may be worth exploring narrower, prudential limits on banks to prevent an excessive buildup of short-term foreign currency liabilities"; but some Fund staff members, the most prominent being Eichengreen, who had joined the Fund on secondment in 1997, criticized this approach because it failed to deal with non-bank borrowing, thus leaving the risks to the financial system essentially unchanged.[123] For Eichengreen and others the appropriate approach was "taxes or non-remunerated deposit requirements on all capital inflows, not just on inflows into the banking system. These are the kind of policy recommendations to which the IMF has and should continue to gravitate."[124]

By late spring 1999 the position of Camdessus and the U.S. Treasury officials became more accommodative. Despite strong caveats that controls "do not deal effectively with fundamental imbalances," that "they

[121] IEO, *IMF's Approach*, p. 32.

[122] Cohen, "Taming the Phoenix?" p. 204.

[123] Robert Rubin, "Strengthening the Architecture of the International Financial System, Address to the Brookings Institution, Washington, D.C.," U.S. Treasury Press Release RR-2236, 14 April 1998.

[124] Eichengreen, "The International Monetary Fund in the Wake of the Asian Crisis," in Noble and Ravenhill, *Asian Financial Crisis*, pp. 170–191 at p. 189. See also Barry Eichengreen and Michael Mussa, "Capital Account Liberalization: Theoretical and Practical Aspects," IMF Occasional Paper No. 172 (Washington, D.C.: IMF, 1998), p. 26, and Eichengreen's contribution to IMF Economic Forum: "Capital Account Liberalization: What's the Best Stance?" (2 October 1998), available at http://www.imf.org/external/np/tr/1998/tr981002a.htm

work best when they are price-based and temporary," and that they "may only be useful in certain circumstances," Camdessus suggested that they "may have a place when there is a risk of a crisis."[125] According to DeLong and Eichengreen, the U.S. Treasury also eventually became "at least acquiescent" to Chilean-style measures where they were already in place, but failed to actively urge their widespread use.[126] Indicative of this new approach was a June 1999 G-7 finance ministers report, which concluded that "the use of controls on capital inflows may be justified for a transitional period as countries strengthen the institutional and regulatory environment in their domestic financial systems. Where financial sectors and supervisory regimes are weak, safeguards may be appropriate to limit foreign currency exposure of the banking system."[127] Still, despite this statement, in recent free trade agreements with Chile, Singapore, and South Korea, U.S. officials insisted on clauses that limit the scope for using capital controls, while EU officials did the same in accession negotiations with recent new members.

Controls on outflows remain quite controversial; but the Malaysian experience, along with advocacy for the alternative Keynesian-inspired crisis construction, engendered a subtle, but important, change of views within the Fund. Despite dire predictions, the Malaysian economy did not collapse after the imposition of the controls. The Malaysian economy declined in 1998 but then rebounded to experience two years of robust growth, with the controls being removed in February 2001. Although it had initially opposed their use, by 1999 the APD staff became more accommodating, recognizing that the controls had been effective in creating temporary "breathing room" that government officials used to adjust policies.[128] Some later studies suggested that the controls had slowed outflows, and some IMF officials even conceded the Malaysian approach may have been the appropriate one.[129] But even today the jury remains out

[125] Camdessus, "Governments and Economic Development in a Globalized World," remarks to the 32nd International General Meeting of the Pacific Basin Economic Council, Hong Kong, 17 May 1999, available at www.imf.org/external/np/speeches/1999/051799.htm

[126] DeLong and Eichengreen, "Between Meltdown and Moral Hazard," p. 237 n. 99.

[127] G-7 Finance Ministers, "Strengthening the International Financial Architecture," report of G-7 Finance Ministers to the Cologne Economic Summit, 18–20 June 1999, available at http://www.ustreas.gov/press/releases/pr3210b.htm

[128] "Malaysia—Staff Report for the 1999 Article IV Consultation," SM/99/141, 16 June 1999 (IMF Archives), p. 22. See also pp. 1, 5, 15 and IMF, *World Economic Outlook* (October) (Washington, D.C.: IMF, 1999), pp. 54–56.

[129] See, for instance, Akira Ariyoshi, Karl Habermeier, Bernard Laurens, Inci Ötker-Robe, Jorge Iván Canales-Kriljenko, and Andrei Kirilenko, "Capital Controls: Country Experiences with Their Use and Liberalization," IMF Occasional Paper No. 190 (Washington, D.C.: IMF, 2000), pp. 53–55; Wayne Arnold, "Debt Rating of Malaysia Is Upgraded," *New York Times*, 21 August 2002.

on whether the controls "worked" as intended, or if their effectiveness depended on supporting policies, Malaysia's institutional capacity, or favorable external conditions. As Krugman has written, "The truth is that while Malaysia's recovery has proved the hysterical opponents of capital controls wrong, it has not exactly proved the proponents right."[130]

Despite the ongoing debate, the significance of the Malaysian experience, particularly within the Fund and the economics profession, was to challenge conventional views on monetary management, which assumed the inviolable primacy of capital mobility. For members of the IMF staff and the economics profession the Malaysian experience undermined the prevailing belief that controls on outflows could not "work," demonstrating that such measures could be used effectively, if only under a limited set of conditions. As Krugman observes, "Malaysia at least proved a point—namely, that controlling capital in a crisis is at least feasible.[131] To be sure, most IMF staff members remain in principle opposed to the use of controls on outflows and much more sympathetic, even supportive, of controls on inflows. Yet it is clear that the staff have become much more accommodating of the selective use of controls on outflows in the wake of the Malaysian experience.

The position of IMF management also has become more accommodative of controls on outflows, though not necessarily to the same extent as the staff. In May 1999, Camdessus indicated that such measures could potentially be useful in a limited number of circumstances "to allow breathing space;" however, he then quickly went on to point out that controls on inflows were more effective than on outflows.[132] Camdessus also indicated that policy adjustments and structural reforms—not controls per se—were the key factors behind the success of countries that imposed controls after the Asian crisis. In 2002, Horst Kohler, who succeeded Camdessus and served as managing director from 2000 to 2004, offered similar remarks.[133] In 2001, Anne Krueger, who succeeded Fischer and served as first deputy managing director from 2001 to 2006, gave her support to the use of controls on outflows in crisis situations as part of her proposed new approach to sovereign debt restructuring, the Sovereign Debt Restructuring Mechanism (SDRM).[134]

---

[130] Krugman, "Capital Control Freaks."

[131] Krugman, "Capital Control Freaks."

[132] Camdessus, "Governments and Economic Development."

[133] IEO, *IMF's Approach*, pp. 78–79.

[134] Anne O. Krueger, "International Financial Architecture for 2002: A New Approach to Sovereign Debt Restructuring," address to the National Economists' Club Annual Members' Dinner, American Enterprise Institute, Washington, D.C., 26 November 2001, available at http://www.imf.org/external/np/speeches/2001/112601.htm

But following the Asian crisis the U.S. Treasury has remained opposed to the use of controls on outflows, blocking a 1998 French proposal for a "financial safeguard clause" as well as Krueger's SDRM proposal, both of which would have given added legitimacy to the use of controls on outflows during a crisis. Treasury officials in the George W. Bush administration also made clear their opposition to any significant reversal of the norm of capital freedom.[135] Rather than focusing on supply-side developments and factors intrinsic to the operation of international capital markets, U.S. officials have instead prioritized policy adjustment and institutional reform in emerging markets and developing countries.

However, Keynesian-inspired understandings that stress factors intrinsic to the operation of international capital markets have featured much more prominently in IMF staff analyses since the Asian crisis. Internal entrepreneurs appear to have been critical in triggering this shift of views. The arrival of Eichengreen at the Fund on secondment in 1997 added strength to arguments that drew on Keynesian-inspired understandings and that sought to legitimate controls. As indicated in chapter 7, Eichengreen's earlier work had advocated the possibility of using controls in circumstances where preexisting domestic distortions or multiple equilibria were present. Eichengreen had also been an early prominent supporter of the view, reflected in the later staff assessment of the Malaysian experience, that controls could prove effective in providing a breathing space for policymakers to adjust policies.[136]

At the Fund, Eichengreen teamed up with Mussa and other members of the staff to craft an influential report on capital account liberalization. The 1998 report drew renewed attention to problems of domestic distortions and factors intrinsic to international capital markets that could create the possibility of "sharp investor reactions [that] can give rise to unpredictable market movements and, in the extreme, financial crises."[137] The October 1998 WEO followed up on this argument, suggesting that it would be wrong "to attribute financial crises exclusively to policy shortcomings in crisis countries," and called on others to "recognize the inherently fragile and volatile nature of capital flows."[138] The conclusion of the

---

[135] See, for instance, U.S. Government, *Economic Report of the President* (Washington, D.C.: Government Printing Office, 2004), chap. 13; John B. Taylor, "Testimony before the Subcommittee on Domestic and International Monetary Policy, Trade and Technology, Committee on Financial Services, U.S. House of Representatives," U.S. Treasury Press Release JS-149, 1 April 2003.

[136] Eichengreen and Wyplosz, "Taxing International Financial Transactions," pp. 22–23, 28–29.

[137] Eichengreen and Mussa, "Capital Account Liberalization," p. 2.

[138] As cited in IEO, *IMF's Approach*, p. 25.

report by Eichengreen and Mussa, which is worth quoting at some length, testifies to the strengthening of Keynesian-inspired understandings and standards of behavior within the Fund:

> To the extent that the problem is information asymmetries that are intrinsic to the operation of financial markets, that cannot realistically be removed, and that give rise to significant systemic risks, *this creates an argument for the permanent application of policies designed to influence the volume of certain types of financial transactions.* If these policies are operationalized through the use of taxes and taxlike instruments that make their effect felt by altering relative prices, rather than through the use of administrative controls, there is no reason why they should be viewed as incompatible with the still-desirable goal of capital account liberalization.[139]

This conclusion suggests a remarkable emergence (revival) within the Fund of arguments that reflect Keynesian-inspired beliefs; factors intrinsic to international capital markets, not fundamentals alone, are identified as possibly responsible for financial instability, and permanent, as opposed to temporary, controls are seen as potentially essential. Of course the similarities should not be exaggerated. The report's proposed new standard of behavior is limited to market-based controls on inflows, and strictly rules out the use of administrative measures. More significant is the fact that the staff team clearly retains a fundamental belief in the long-run desirability of capital freedom. Enthusiasm for rapid liberalization may have been abandoned, but not for the goal of liberalization itself.

Nevertheless, following the Asian crisis the Fund has devoted greater attention to problems intrinsic to the operation of international capital markets and to the role of herding behavior.[140] Yet, as I explore in more detail in chapter 9, until the subprime crisis, staff attention to these issues failed to translate into policy prescriptions that developed countries could take to promote financial stability. Instead, the staff remained largely focused on measures that emerging markets and developing countries could implement.

Consideration of the proposed amendment to the Articles has been suspended indefinitely. In a May 2005 board meeting, "Most directors did not wish to explore further at present the possibility of giving the Fund jurisdiction over capital movements."[141] Disagreements among member

---

[139] Eichengreen and Mussa, "Capital Account Liberalization," p. 30, emphasis added.

[140] For an overview, see Marco Cipriani, "Herding in Financial Markets," *IMF Research Bulletin*, 9, no. 4 (2008), pp. 1–2.

[141] As cited in IEO, *IMF's Approach*, p. 101. See also "Summing Up by the Acting Chairman of Countries' Experiences with the Use of Controls on Capital Movements and Issues in Their Orderly Liberalization," BUFF/99/45, 6 April 1999 (IMF Archives).

states persisted over the relative emphasis that should be placed on preconditions and sequencing. While offering their broad endorsement for an "integrated" approach, the board was divided over whether certain preconditions are necessary before liberalization or whether some governments can implement measures simultaneously or even use "windows of opportunity" to move ahead with rapid liberalization.[142] IMF formal policy on liberalization thus remains to this day clouded in ambiguity.

The events in this chapter reveal several key themes developed in this book. First, formal rules alone often tell us little about how IOs behave; to better understand their behavior we must turn to the decisive influence of the staff operating on an informal level. Despite all the rule changes and directives surveyed in this chapter and others, the IMF Articles still specify the right of any member state to use controls. Yet this formal rule did little to constrain the staff from adopting, interpreting, and applying the norm of capital freedom. Even today, without a formal IMF policy on capital account liberalization, the staff has been left to develop autonomously its own informal "integrated" approach.

Second, exogenous developments, especially the presence of significant preference heterogeneity among and within IMF principals, help us to understand the evolution of the IMF approach. Divisions over the amendment, particularly after the Asian crisis, ensured that the legitimacy of controls remained contested. Underscoring how collective action problems within IMF principals and NGO "fire alarms" can affect organizational behavior, the proximate cause of the failed formal institutionalization of the norm of capital freedom appears to have been the threat of the U.S. Congress to withhold support for the IMF quota increase, which in turn was partly prompted by NGO advocacy.

A third and related theme is that preference heterogeneity among IMF principals loosened the outer structural constraint in which the staff operated. The absence of board guidance until 1995, which was partly due to EU countries not completing their transition to capital account openness until the early 1990s, and partly due to misgivings among emerging markets and developing countries about capital freedom, provided the staff with a considerable autonomy in how they approached liberalization. The lack of clear guidance from IMF management and PDR, as well as the subtle differences between Camdessus and Fischer, generated additional staff autonomy.

Yet a more significant determinant of staff autonomy was the fact that U.S. officials did little to shape the staff's approach and were divided over

---

[142] IEO, *IMF's Approach*, p. 101.

their enthusiasm for a bitterly opposed amendment to the Articles. This gave the staff space to develop their approach largely autonomously from U.S. influence. While this approach was consistent with U.S. interests, it was not imposed upon them, and it was ultimately the staff that largely determined how, among the range of alternatives, these interests were best advanced.

To understand how the staff determined their approach we must turn to processes internal to the IMF. Professionalization was an important determinant, helping to foster among the staff a shared belief in the long-run desirability of liberalization, but also contrasting beliefs on how to proceed toward it. These beliefs in turn helped to channel the lessons gleaned from particular experiences, such as the Mexican and Asian crises.

Yet these experiences also reveal that belief systems are not static, particularly during moments of "crisis" when they can be challenged and overturned. The Mexican crisis opened the door for gradualist advocacy, but most staff members failed to see it as a "crisis" for the big-bang approach, Guitian's relatively successful entrepreneurship continued until the Asian crisis. It took this experience, which many staff attributed to "disorderly liberalization," to help undermine staff support for the big-bang approach. Growing support for gradualism was also aided by the new emphasis placed on "getting institutions right."

Also of crucial importance to the evolution of the staff's approach was the reconsideration by a small, but prominent, group of key actors of prevailing understandings of market behavior and standards of behavior for capital controls. The Asian crisis, in conjunction with this important reconsideration, opened up discursive space for advocacy of alternative Keynesian-inspired views. Internal advocates of these Keynesian-inspired views, who could point to countries, such as China, India, and Malaysia, as evidence that controls could help minimize crisis pressures, enhanced the receptivity of many staff members to lending greater legitimacy to controls.

But in the absence of a personnel realignment within the Fund that could enable these alternative beliefs to flourish, learning proved to be cognitively difficult and beliefs channeled how the staff interpreted experiences. After the Asian crisis, most staff members adapted their position, placing greater emphasis on sequencing, recognizing that controls could work, and devoting more attention to factors intrinsic to the operation of international capital markets that can trigger financial instability. Yet while the Asian crisis largely undermined support for the big-bang approach (but, interestingly, not among some member states), it failed to displace the belief that capital freedom was desirable in the long run. Prevailing belief in the long-run desirability of liberalization led staff members to attribute the means that were used to proceed toward this goal ("disorderly liberalization") rather than the goal itself as responsible for financial instability. Instead, exceptions were carved out for market-based controls on inflows and for the use of controls on outflows in crisis situations, which in turn were embedded in a principled normative framework that constitutes capital freedom as desirable in the long run. Today staff members generally do not question the desirability of capital freedom, but their preferred methods for achieving this goal, and their willingness to accommodate exceptions to it, have changed significantly since the financial turmoil of the late 1990s.

CHAPTER NINE

Norm Continuity and Organizational Legitimacy from the Asian Crisis to the Subprime Crisis

IN THE DECADE after the Asian crisis, the IMF and its member states implemented a number of reforms to the international financial architecture. Yet the norms that underpinned this architecture changed little. The Fund's staff and principals generally remained cautious in supporting gradualism, though some continued to be optimistic that "windows of opportunity" could be exploited to move ahead rapidly with liberalization. The use of selective restraints on capital mobility also failed to elicit the cries of outrage that it once did in the 1990s. Still, some leading principals, especially U.S. and EU officials, remained adamant that the norm of capital freedom should not be reversed.

There was thus a high degree of norm continuity in the decade after the Asian crisis. In fact, most of the reforms to the international financial architecture can be seen as a direct reflection of a particular interpretation advanced to explain financial instability in the late 1990s, namely that it resulted primarily from poor fundamentals and institutions in crisis-afflicted countries, which in turn legitimated policy adjustment and structural adjustment in these countries. Consequently, developing, monitoring, and encouraging the implementation of standards and codes for macroeconomic policy and domestic financial systems in emerging markets and developing countries became a principal focus of the IMF and the G-7. This focus left little space for consideration of other policies, such as regulatory measures aimed at financial market participants in developed countries, that would be consistent with an alternative interpretation that stresses factors intrinsic to the operation of international capital markets as partly responsible for financial instability.

While standards and codes serve a useful purpose, such measures alone cannot guarantee financial stability. Yet prior to the subprime crisis, despite having developed an increasingly sophisticated understanding and appreciation of factors intrinsic to the operation of international capital markets that can trigger financial instability, the IMF showed little willingness to entertain additional measures, such as regulations aimed at financial market participants in developed countries. This chapter begins by explaining norm continuity within the Fund between the Asian and subprime crises. The preferences of leading principals are, of course, important since these actors generally opposed taking regulatory action to limit the actions of financial market participants that are largely based in them. The outer structural constraint imposed by these preferences thus helped rule out policy prescriptions for greater regulation. But this is not the entire story. Intraorganizational factors, such as the absence of institutional tools to influence developed country policies and the presence of beliefs that directed staff attention toward fundamentals and institutions in emerging markets and developing countries, also helped to keep calls for greater regulation off the policy agenda.

The failure of the IMF to give much consideration to greater regulation of financial market participants in developed countries also has had important implications for its legitimacy. The content of the standards and codes it promotes tend to reflect developed country interests and experiences in general and American and British ones in particular. Moreover, these standards and codes effectively serve to transfer the blame and responsibility for financial instability to emerging markets and developing countries, which until recently were underrepresented in the institutional forums where these standards and codes were developed. This generated much resentment. But in making the case for developed countries to take regulatory action, the Fund could enhance its legitimacy by demonstrating that it is responsive to the interests and experiences of emerging markets and developing countries who seek to shift some of the blame and responsibility for financial instability to developed countries.

To prevent emerging markets and developing countries from permanently turning their back on the Fund and the standards and codes it helps promote, some suggest reforms to formal governance of the IMF (and other institutional forums) as a way of increasing the weight of emerging markets and developing countries within the Fund, which, according to the argument would help enhance the legitimacy of the IMF by making the organization more responsive to their interests and experiences. While potentially useful, such reforms overlook many of the key arguments and themes developed in this book, namely that the staff and their internal debates can have a decisive influence on organizational behavior. Indeed, such formal governance reform proposals presume that much of what the Fund does is exogenously rather than endogenously driven. However, as this book has demonstrated, a great deal of what the Fund does is rooted in beliefs collectively shared by the staff and in intraorganizational processes rather than in the preferences of, and directives from, leading principals. Reform of formal IMF governance structures could therefore end up being an empty victory for emerging markets and developing countries if it has little impact on staff beliefs and intraorganizational processes.

A more promising approach to enhancing the legitimacy of the IMF would be to also turn our attention toward the staff and the internal processes that shape "how things should be done." In this spirit, this chapter concludes by offering some potentially useful reforms that target processes that shape behavior from within. The overriding logic of all of these proposals is to encourage greater intellectual diversity and debate within the Fund so that the beliefs collectively shared by the staff better reflect the diverse interests and experiences of the IMF membership, thereby enhancing the sense of "ownership" felt by emerging markets and developing countries.

NORM CONTINUITY BETWEEN THE ASIAN AND SUBPRIME CRISES

Norm continuity within the Fund manifested itself in several ways. First, the staff generally remained committed to gradualism, an approach area department staff pursued in China, India, Iran, Kazakhstan, Libya, Morocco, Tunisia, and Russia.[1] Some RES staff members also supported this approach in their empirical analysis, finding that countries that meet certain "thresholds" before liberalizing, such as sound macroeconomic policy and financial systems, are likely to enjoy enhanced growth prospects and lower macroeconomic volatility and crisis frequency.[2] But this commitment to gradualism did not mean the staff entirely shied away from encouraging governments to liberalize more quickly when conditions appeared optimal. A 2004 area department mission to South Africa, for example, argued that, given the relative soundness of the banking system, the strength of the South African currency presented "an opportune time to move ahead" to relax controls.[3]

In addition to the continued emphasis on gradualism, there was also much continuity in the standards of behavior the staff defined for controls. The Fund's response to policy challenges faced by emerging markets experiencing capital inflow surges from early 2002 to late 2007 illustrates this continuity quite well. From a post-Asian crisis nadir of less than $50 billion in 1998, net private capital inflows to emerging markets reached nearly $650 billion in 2007.[4] These inflows resembled the surge to emerging markets in the early to middle 1990s in that they raised the challenge of how to harness their benefits, while avoiding overheating, a loss of competitiveness, and increased vulnerability to crisis.

In evaluating this challenge the Fund showed little change from the norms it advocated in the 1990s, prioritizing policy adjustment, namely

---

[1] IEO, *IMF's Approach*, pp. 49–53.
[2] IMF, "Reaping the Benefits of Financial Globalization." See also IMF, *Global Financial Stability Report* (October) (Washington, D.C.: IMF, 2007), chap 3.
[3] IEO, *IMF's Approach*, p. 53.
[4] IMF, *World Economic Outlook* (October) (Washington, D.C.: IMF, 2008).

fiscal consolidation, rather than the use of controls. Controls were cast as legitimate only in select circumstances, and even then the staff tended to offer strong reservations. The October 2007 *WEO*, for instance, observes: "While capital controls might have a role in certain cases, they should not be seen as a substitute for sound macroeconomic policies that include a prudent fiscal stance and a supporting exchange rate and monetary policy framework, as well as appropriate prudential measures."[5] "Capital controls," according to the October 2007 *GFSR*, "should be used only as a last resort and as part of a package of macroeconomic and prudential measures. They may be able to throw sand in the gears of a surge of short-term speculative inflows under certain circumstances, especially if the infrastructure is already in place. [But,] in addition to the challenge of effectiveness, there are reputational costs to be considered."[6] Controls, the October 2007 *WEO* suggests, can "temporarily tilt the composition [of capital flows] toward longer maturities in a few cases," but there is little evidence that this actually reduces a country's vulnerability to crisis. In a similar vein, a 2007 RES staff study uncovers little evidence that the output costs of financial instability are lower in countries that seek to restrict capital mobility.[7]

Still, this did not prevent the staff from accommodating or even encouraging the use of controls in certain circumstances, especially in contexts where liberalization threatened to expose countries with weak and poorly regulated financial systems to greater risk. For instance, in 2004, in Bulgaria and Romania, although it went against encouragement for capital freedom coming from EU officials, the EURO staff advised officials to consider, if necessary, market-based controls on inflows to contain credit growth. The EURO staff offered similar advice to Croatia that year. The following year the EURO staff even recommended that Romania tighten its controls to restrict credit growth. In a wide range of cases since the Asian crisis the staff saw virtue in controls as a means of protecting countries from contagion (as in Slovenia, Romania, and India in 1998, and China and Tunisia in 1999) or as a way of permitting breathing space for reforms to proceed (Russia in 2002). On occasion, the staff even accommodated administrative controls on inflows, such as those imposed by Colombia in 2004 when it was faced with sharp currency appreciation.[8]

---

[5] IMF, *World Economic Outlook* (October) (Washington, D.C.: IMF, 2007), chap. 3, p. 12.

[6] IMF, *Global Financial Stability Report* (October) (Washington, D.C.: IMF, 2007), p. 92. See also Atish Ghosh, Manuela Goretti, Bikas Joshi, Uma Ramakrishnan, Alun Thomas, and Juan Zalduendo, "Capital Inflows and Balance of Payments Pressures—Tailoring Policy Responses in Emerging Market Economies," IMF Policy Discussion Paper PDP/08/02 (Washington, D.C.: IMF, 2008), pp. 11, 17.

[7] IMF, "Reaping the Benefits of Financial Globalization."

[8] IEO, *IMF's Approach*, pp. 35, 51, 53, 54, 73. For additional insight on Brussels's position in Romania and Croatia, see Abdelal, *Capital Rules*, pp. 210–211.

Accommodation was also extended to administrative restrictions on outflows, such as those Venezuela erected in 2003. The Venezuelan case is particularly interesting because it illuminates quite well the shift in the staff's approach that occurred after the Asian crisis. This case marked the second time Venezuela had imposed controls on outflows in less than a decade, the previous occasion being in 1994. Recall that in 1994 the WHD staff argued for eliminating controls. When policymakers at the time raised concerns that liberalization might lead to capital flight, the staff responded that policy adjustment would prevent significant outflows. By contrast in 2004 the staff accommodated the use of controls to reduce capital flight and manage crisis pressures.[9]

Norm continuity was also apparent in the Fund's continued emphasis on poor fundamentals and institutions as the primary cause of financial instability, and in its insistence on policy adjustment and structural reform. This particular interpretation led to the development and promotion of new international standards and codes for macroeconomic policy and financial regulation. The interpretation underpinning these standards and codes is both simple and appealing: by strengthening macroeconomic policy and the financial systems of emerging markets, the standards and codes should facilitate better-informed lending and investment decisions, improve market integrity, and thus reduce the risk of financial instability. These standards and codes, which are largely Anglo-American in content, have been drafted under the umbrella of the Financial Stability Forum (FSF) and backed by the G-7. Created in 1999, for much of its history the FSF comprised representatives of monetary authorities and financial regulators from developed countries, key international financial institutions (including the IMF), and international regulatory and supervisory groupings. Emerging markets were excluded from membership until March 2009.[10]

[9] IEO, *IMF's Approach*, pp. 54–55, 70–71.

[10] Until March 2009, the FSF consisted of Australia, Canada, France, Germany, Hong Kong, Italy, Japan, the Netherlands, Singapore, Switzerland, the United Kingdom, the United States, the IMF, the World Bank, the BIS, the OECD, the Basel Committee on Banking Supervision, the International Accounting Standards Board, the International Association of Insurance Supervisors, the International Organization of Securities Commissions, the Committee on Payment and Settlement Systems, the Committee on the Global Financial Systems, and the European Central Bank. But, as discussed in the epilogue, the FSF decided in March 2009 to broaden its membership and to invite as new members the G-20 emerging market countries that were not in the FSF. These countries are Argentina, Brazil, China, India, Indonesia, South Korea, Mexico, Russia, Saudi Arabia, South Africa, and Turkey. In addition, Spain and the European Commission also became new members of the FSF.

Much of the focus of the IMF, the FSF, and the G-7 has been on improving transparency; that is, the availability and quality of information. Many key officials, including those inside the Fund, pointed to a lack of transparency as a leading cause of financial instability in the 1990s. The emphasis on transparency, like the broad focus on standards and codes, reflects a particular interpretation that places blame for financial instability on crisis-afflicted countries. In this interpretation, unfettered international capital markets are not to blame for financial instability; after all, financial market participants cannot be expected to make efficient decisions when they do not have enough information, especially when governments seek to conceal it.

In such a context, financial market participants have little way of differentiating "good" borrowers from "bad" borrowers. Thus once market confidence begins to erode, many claim, there is no way to stabilize expectations. As Alassane Ouattara, former AFR director and deputy managing director, noted: "In the absence of adequate information, markets tended to fear the worst and to doubt the capacity of governments to take timely corrective action."[11] As a result, as Camdessus observed in 1999, "There is a strong consensus for making transparency the 'golden rule' of the international financial system."[12]

The Fund adroitly maneuvered itself to be at the center of efforts to develop and monitor standards and codes for macroeconomic policy and data transparency. The first formal proposals to improve transparency came in the aftermath of the Mexican peso crisis in 1994–1995.[13] The IMF subsequently developed data dissemination standards in 1996–1997 to guide countries in their provision of economic and financial data. To improve the capacity of financial market participants to assess the soundness and conduct of fiscal and monetary policy, the Fund developed in 1998–1999 standards and codes for transparency in fiscal policy and monetary and financial policy.

The Fund also developed new forms of surveillance to monitor implementation of the standards and codes. At the request of a member state the Fund prepares Reports on Observance of Standards and Codes

---

[11] Alassane D. Ouattara, "The Asian Crisis: Origins and Lessons," Address to the Royal Academy of Morocco Seminar "Why Have the Asian Dragons Caught Fire?" Fez, Morocco, 4 May 1998, available at http://www.imf.org/external/np/speeches/1998/050498a.htm

[12] Camdessus, "Stable and Efficient Financial Systems for the 21st Century: A Quest for Transparency and Standards," address to the XXIVth Annual Conference of the International Organization of Securities Commissions, Lisbon, Portugal, 25 May 1999, available at http://www.imf.org/external/np/speeches/1999/052599.htm

[13] G-7, Communique of the Halifax Summit; G-10, *The Resolution of Sovereign Liquidity Crises*.

(ROSCs). The ROSCs are meant to provide a certification of sorts that helps countries access international capital markets. Since the Asian crisis, the Fund has also sought to sharpen its surveillance of domestic financial systems and international capital markets as it moves away from its traditional narrow focus on exchange rate policy and attendant fiscal and monetary policy. Indeed, a recent IMF reform strategy paper seeks "to put financial and capital market issues at the heart of its macroeconomic analysis in emerging markets."[14]

One aspect of strengthening surveillance, discussed in chapter 8, has been the creation of the FSAP. An important institutional innovation in 2001 has been the elevation of the Capital Markets Group from being a subdepartmental unit largely within RES (and earlier within ETR) to being the separate ICM within the Fund. The ICM (now called MCM after its 2006 merger with the Monetary and Financial Systems Department, which was created in 2003 following the reorganization of MAE) has been a central part of the Fund's effort to better understand global financial markets.

Eschewing Supply-Side Regulation

The standards and codes project and the strengthening of IMF surveillance have been important initiatives. But in the period between the Asian and subprime crises the focus tended to be asymmetric, prioritizing what emerging markets and developing countries should do to minimize financial instability with little corresponding attention given to developed countries. Why was this the case?

Prior to the Asian crisis, the Fund staff, though aware of the potential for abrupt and sudden capital flow reversals, generally devoted little attention to analyzing how developments in developed countries shaped capital flow volatility and risk implications for emerging markets and developing countries. But, as discussed in chapter 8, in the aftermath of the Asian crisis the IMF staff developed a much greater appreciation for factors intrinsic to the operation of international capital markets that can give rise to financial instability. As a result, since the Asian crisis the staff have highlighted more forcefully the risks inherent in international financial integration, as well as the linkage between developments in developed countries and their capital flow volatility and risk implications for emerging markets and developing countries. Recent staff reports have explored herding behavior in international capital markets,[15] the "feast and famine" dynamics

---

[14] IMF, *Report on Medium-Term Strategy,* p. 6.
[15] Cipriani, "Herding in Financial Markets."

and the "boom-and-bust pattern and volatility" of capital flows to emerging markets,[16] the relationship between financial market returns in developed countries and capital flows to emerging markets,[17] the investor base of emerging market financing,[18] and "spillovers" from developed countries to emerging markets.[19]

Yet this increasingly sophisticated understanding of international capital markets failed to translate into much attention being given to regulatory actions developed countries might take to foster greater financial stability. To be sure, the staff were clearly aware of how such actions might be beneficial. For instance, as part of its effort to minimize moral hazard on the "supply side," the Fund has sought to limit access to financing during crises, proposed the SDRM, and encouraged the use of collective action clauses in debt contracts.

The Fund staff also raised supply-side concerns about the New Basel Capital Accord ("Basel II") to the Basel Committee on Banking Supervision (BCBS), a committee of supervisors from developed countries that meets at the BIS to consider issues related to the regulation of international banks and global financial stability. Basel II, which is currently being implemented, replaces the Basel (I) Accord, an agreement that emerged during the 1980s debt crisis in response to lax banking standards in many developed countries. The principal innovation of Basel I was the development of a standardized risk-weighting scheme that requires banks to set aside varying levels of capital depending on asset risk. Initially proposed in 2004, Basel II provides for greater flexibility by permitting larger banks with sophisticated risk-assessment capabilities to develop and rely upon their own internal models to assign risk-weightings, subject to the supervision of national regulators, rather than to use the standardized model required of smaller banks. Until these internal models were developed, larger banks, along with smaller banks, were to use risk-weights based on ratings issued by external credit rating agencies (CRAs), such as Moody's and Standard and Poor's. Because CRA upgrades and downgrades tend to follow, not lead, economic cycles, the IMF staff warned the BCBS that tying lending to rating agency assessments would increase market volatility and procyclicality.[20] However, the warning was not heeded.

[16] IMF, *Global Financial Stability Report* (March) (Washington, D.C.: IMF, 2003), especially pp. 63–68; IMF, *Global Financial Stability Report* (September) (Washington, D.C.: IMF, 2003).

[17] IMF, *International Capital Markets Report* (Washington, D.C.: IMF, 2001).

[18] IMF, *Global Financial Stability Report* (March) (Washington, D.C.: IMF, 2004), especially pp. 111–151; IMF, *Global Financial Stability Report* (April) (Washington, D.C.: IMF, 2006), especially pp. 85–126.

[19] IMF, *Global Financial Stability Report* (October) (Washington, D.C.: IMF, 2008), especially pp. 131–152.

[20] IEO, *IMF's Approach*, p. 25 n. 34.

The Fund staff also addressed some supply-side issues raised by hedge funds, which are largely based in major financial centers in developed countries, particularly the United States and Britain. Until the subprime crisis, hedge funds were a rapidly growing part of the financial industry, with their assets, estimated to total $1.6 trillion, having grown more than fivefold between 1999 and 2007.[21] Their legal status places few restrictions on their operations, although, as I discuss in the epilogue, regulatory reforms are currently being considered. Hedge funds raise their capital from high net worth individuals and institutional investors, rather than on organized exchanges, and are therefore subject to only limited public disclosure requirements. They are also subject to little direct regulatory or supervisory oversight and therefore do not find themselves constrained by capital requirements, limits on credit concentration, and standards for risk and liquidity management that apply to most regulated financial firms.

Because hedge funds often are alleged to precipitate major asset price movements, either through the sheer volume of their own transactions or via their tendency to act as the "lead steer" when the financial herd begins to move, previous episodes of financial instability, such as the 1992 ERM crisis and 1994 Mexican crisis, had brought attention to these actors. But hedge funds did not become a prominent policy issue until several episodes in the late 1990s.

The first episode, the Asian crisis, focused attention on market dynamics; that is, the concern that hedge funds can dominate or manipulate markets. Led by Malaysia's Mahathir, officials from several crisis-afflicted countries charged hedge funds with destabilizing the Asian economies. These charges led an IMF staff team, headed by Eichengreen and Mathieson, to conduct a study in the winter of 1997–1998.

Drawing on currency crisis models with multiple equilibria, Eichengreen and Mathieson claimed the principal concern of crisis-afflicted countries was "the fear that large traders can precipitate a crisis that arbitrarily shifts an economy from a 'good' to a 'bad' equilibrium."[22] But while problems of incomplete information and herding feature prominently in the report, Eichengreen and Mathieson found that hedge funds did not play a major role in precipitating the crises in Asia. Therefore, overall, the report concluded that "the case for supervisory and regulatory initiatives directed specifically at hedge funds is not strong."[23]

---

[21] FSF, *Update of the FSF Report on Highly Leveraged Financial Institutions* (Basel: FSF 2007), p. 8.

[22] Barry Eichengreen, Donald Mathieson, Bankim Chadha, Anne Jansen, Laura Kodres, and Sanil Sharma, "Hedge Funds and Financial Market Dynamics," IMF Occasional Paper No. 166 (Washington, D.C.: IMF, 1998), p. 3.

[23] Eichengreen et al., "Hedge Funds and Financial Market Dynamics," p. 20.

Still, it did offer some recommendations should policymakers wish to proceed. Although the report pointed to factors intrinsic to the operation of international capital markets as giving rise to significant risks, it offered little support for actions that could be taken by developed countries. In order to limit herding that might occur when the news or rumor of a particular hedge fund investment spreads, the report raised the idea of improving information disclosure from financial market participants by having G-10 countries install large trade and position reporting systems. But without a comprehensive and internationally coordinated system, which Eichengreen and Mathieson doubted would be feasible, the report suggested that many transactions would escape monitoring, leading its authors to question the utility of such a system.

The report's main recommendation centered on improving information disclosure and strengthening macroeconomic policies in countries on the receiving end of hedge fund investment. Improving information, the report argues, would "encourage investors to trade on fundamentals rather than to run with the herd." In addition, strengthening macroeconomic policies would remove from the eye of speculators "the irresistible combination of inconsistent policies and unsustainable currency pegs.[24]

The report also claimed that measures to limit position-taking, such as Chilean-style taxes on capital inflows, could be useful in increasing the cost of putting on and taking off positions and in limiting a country's vulnerability to capital flow reversals. But the report cautioned that controls could also prevent hedge funds and other investors from acting as valuable "contrarians," that is, purchasing assets that have recently depreciated and are trading for prices lower than warranted by fundamentals.

In autumn 1998, the near-collapse of Long-Term Capital Management (LTCM) raised new concerns about the potential systemic risks, should a hedge fund collapse, to those counterparties who supply it with credit, as well as to market liquidity and prices. The spread of financial turmoil from Asia to a number of other countries during the course of 1998 also renewed concerns about the impact of hedge funds on market dynamics. The FSF therefore convened a Working Group on Highly Leveraged Institutions. The Working Group issued a report that was accompanied by an analysis from the Market Dynamics Study Group, which reviewed the activities of hedge funds in Australia, Hong Kong, Malaysia, New Zealand, Singapore, and South Africa.[25] Charles Adams, then director of the IMF's Capital Markets Group, served as convener of the study group and played an important in part in crafting its report.[26]

[24] Eichengreen et al., "Hedge Funds and Financial Market Dynamics," p. 23.

[25] FSF, *Report of the Working Group on Highly Leveraged Institutions* (Basel: FSF, 2000).

[26] Charles Adams, "Hedge Funds and Financial Market Dynamics: Some Perspectives from the Asian Experience," paper presented at Nanyang Technological University, Singa-

The FSF rejected the proposal that, to manage systemic and market dynamics risks, regulatory action should be taken against hedge funds, and instead proposed and subsequently developed a regime of indirect supervision. Emphasis has been placed on improving the quality and flow of information that is aggregate in nature between hedge funds and the public, on strengthening the risk management systems of hedge fund counterparties, and on enhancing the ability of regulators to scrutinize hedge fund counterparties. In the view of the FSF, market discipline could substitute for direct regulation. Better information would strengthen the market discipline felt by hedge fund managers from their clients; it, along with stronger risk management systems, would enable banks to better monitor their exposure to highly leveraged clients; and it would permit the public to impose market discipline on the banks. Initially, some envisioned a system of mandatory disclosure, but this vision was abandoned when a set of voluntary guidelines, designed with the participation of five major hedge funds, was released in 2000. Presumably under the threat of legislation mandating disclosure, a number of hedge funds moved to implement them.[27]

This regulatory approach rested in part on the belief that financial market participants were not to be blamed for the emerging market crises of the late 1990s. This faith in markets pushed G-7 governments, led by the United States and Britain, to delegate an increasing range of regulatory functions to private market actors.[28] Regulators encouraged innovation through a belief in "light-touch" regulation and "self-regulation" based on the assumption that market discipline would provide an effective check on risk-taking by lightly regulated and unregulated institutions. As Britain's financial service regulator recently observed, "The predominant assumption behind financial market regulation—in the US, the UK, and increasingly across the world—has been that financial markets are capable of being both efficient and rational and that a key goal of financial regulation is to remove the impediments which might produce inefficient and illiquid markets."[29] Applying regulation to hedge funds and a wider range

---

pore (September 2005), available at http://www.hss.ntu.edu.sg/egc/seminar_papers/Paper%20by%20Dr%20Charles%20Adams.pdf

[27] Eichengreen, "Governing Global Financial Markets: International Responses to the Hedge-Fund Problem," in *Governance in a Global Economy: Political Authority in Transition*, ed. Miles Kahler and David A. Lake (Princeton, N.J.: Princeton University Press 2003), pp. 168–198 at pp. 188–189.

[28] Eric Helleiner and Stefano Pagliari, "Between the Two Storms: Patterns in Global Financial Governance, 2001–2007," in *Global Financial Integration: Thirty Years On*, ed. Geoffrey Underhill, Jasper Blom, and David Mügge (Cambridge: Cambridge University Press, forthcoming).

[29] Financial Services Authority, *The Turner Review: A Regulatory Response to the Global Banking Crisis* (London: Financial Services Authority, 2009), p. 39.

of institutions was seen as being too costly and hampering innovation. Hence, a regime based on light-touch regulation, self-regulation, and market discipline could substitute for direct regulatory scrutiny. In contrast to the Eichengreen and Mathieson report, the Report of the Market Dynamics Study Group expressed stronger concerns about the large positions of hedge funds in some markets and their implications for market integrity. But the group could not reach a consensus on their role or importance. The group also supported self-regulation rather than direct regulation as the appropriate means to manage the potential risks to market dynamics. By limiting the leverage to which hedge funds have access, a regime of self-regulation and market discipline, it was argued, would not only minimize systemic risks but also, by limiting the position-taking ability of hedge funds, minimize their risks to market dynamics.

Yet this approach had asymmetric distributional implications, namely that information that was aggregate in nature would be of more use to developed country investors, counterparties, and regulators concerned about systemic risk than it would be to emerging market governments concerned about market dynamics. In addition, rather than advocating imposition of the outcome through regulation, the study group encouraged leading foreign exchange market participants to self-regulate by developing a code of good conduct. The group also considered installation of large trade and position reporting systems, but it echoed the skepticism of the earlier IMF report.

These responses to the challenges posed by hedge funds reveals how little willingness the Fund's staff showed for entertaining proposals to take regulatory action against financial market participants based in developed countries. The staff certainly did not suffer from a lack of available regulatory options. For instance, the staff could have supported direct regulation of hedge funds. The staff also could have drawn on arguments from analysts who argued that regulators could mandate that creditors include contract provisions that entitle debtors to extend the maturity of any obligation for a specified period at a penalty, thereby relieving liquidity pressures that can trigger or worsen the crisis.[30] Recalcitrant creditors could face suspension of amortization payments subject to approval by an international body, such as the IMF.[31] Other analysts proposed charging banks that have lent to any country that requires an official bailout an ex post insurance premium related to the magnitude of their withdrawals in the

---

[30] Willem H. Buiter and Anne C. Sibert, "UDROP: A Contribution to the New International Financial Architecture," *International Finance* 2, no. 2 (1999), pp. 227–248.

[31] John Williamson, *Curbing the Boom-Bust Cycle: Stabilizing Capital Flows to Emerging Markets* (Washington, D.C.: Institute for International Economics, 2005), especially chap. 6.

preceding period, thus deterring banks from cutting and running when a crisis materializes.[32] Bank regulators and supervisors could also enforce higher risk weights for loans to particularly risky borrowers, such as highly leveraged hedge funds or emerging markets with weak financial systems. They could subject banks that rely on their internal models to stiff fines should they be found to have underrated the risks to particular borrowers. Regulators also could limit herding behavior among banks through internationally coordinated tightening of capital requirements.[33]

Some analysts considered even more radical reform, such as regulating the remuneration structure of financial market participants.[34] Standard industry practice is to pay asset managers a base salary that is augmented by the possibility of earning a substantial bonus for superior performance. The bonus is normally based on the extent to which a given asset manager achieves a higher return than the norm for a given asset class. Bonuses are usually paid on a quarterly or annual basis. This problem with this remuneration structure is that it creates incentives for herding and favoring short-term returns irrespective of long-term consequences. Such herding and short-termism, some claim, often contributes to financial instability. As a result, some argued that regulators could insist that bonus payments be deferred until the long-term consequences of short-term investments are realized, or that paid bonuses be "clawed back" should short-term gains turn out to be overstated in light of long-term performance.

Other radical reformers argued that developed country regulators, following the lead of Spain, could mandate that their banks set aside more capital in good times and adopt dynamic provisioning so as to mitigate procyclicality through countercyclical prudential regulation.[35] Standard practice creates procyclical tendencies; banks set aside less capital and expand lending during economic upturns and then contract lending and raise capital to cover recognized loan losses during downturns. Dynamic provisioning would require banks to set aside capital not just for recognized loan losses but also for the statistically expected level of future loan losses over the full business cycle. Therefore, when an economy experienced a downturn, banks that had been required to set aside more capital

---

[32] Henri Bernard and Joseph Bisagnano, "Information, Liquidity and Risk in the International Interbank Market: Implicit Guarantees and Private Credit Market Failure," BIS Working Paper No. 86 (Basel: Bank for International Settlements, 2000).

[33] Wendy Dobson and Gary Hufbauer, *World Capital Markets: Challenge to the G-10* (Washington, D.C.: Institute for International Economics, 2001).

[34] Williamson, *Curbing the Boom-Bust Cycle*, especially chap. 5.

[35] Jose A. Ocampo and Maria Luisa Chiappe, *Counter-cyclical Prudential and Capital Account Regulations in Developing Countries* (Stockholm: Almqvist and Wiksell International, 2003).

during good times and to use dynamic provisioning would have significant reserves on hand for the loan losses that materialized and thus would not need to cut back on lending at the time when it would be needed to avert a deepening of the downturn.

Why did the IMF eschew these and other supply-side regulatory measures prior to the subprime crisis? First, the preferences of the Fund's principals are important. Because of these preferences, it was much easier for the staff to focus on poor fundamentals and institutions in crisis-afflicted countries.

There is nothing wrong per se with this approach, but historically it has led the staff to generally overlook policy prescriptions aimed at external factors that can heighten vulnerability. As Tony Killick observes, this approach led the IMF to see balance-of-payments adjustment "primarily as something to be undertaken by deficit countries, with no equivalent pressure for action on surplus countries."[36] The staff's unwillingness to entertain supply-side regulatory measures can be read in a similar light. One problem for the staff, even if they were sympathetic to strengthening supply-side regulation, is that such measures ran contrary to the preferences of many of the Fund's most powerful principals, particularly the United States and Britain, as well as members of the private financial community based in them.

Representative of the view of many G-7 country officials about where the burden of policy responsibility lay are the remarks offered by Frederic Mishkin, a former member of the Federal Reserve Board of Governors:

> I have argued strongly that the financial-sector problems of emerging market countries arise primarily from within the countries themselves and not from outside agents. . . . Thus, while shocks from outside emerging market countries can trigger financial crises in some countries, their vulnerability to financial crises from these shocks results from the flawed policies of the countries themselves. The only way to make financial crises less likely in emerging market economies and for those countries to enjoy the full benefits of financial globalization is for them to adopt fundamental reforms. The reform of the international financial architecture, no matter how worthwhile, is not the answer for helping these countries harness the power of globalization to help them grow.[37]

While G-7 officials did seek to improve transparency on the supply side, few showed much willingness to entertain greater regulation until the subprime crisis.

---

[36] As quoted in Woods, *The Globalizers*, p. 146.

[37] Frederic Mishkin, *The Next Great Globalization: How Disadvantaged Nations Can Harness Their Financial Systems to Get Rich* (Princeton, N.J.: Princeton University Press, 2006), p. 201.

Consider again the challenges that hedge funds pose. In calling for the IMF to study their impact on market dynamics, many Asian emerging market officials, who saw hedge funds as playing a major role in destabilizing their economies, advocated direct regulation. But most developed country officials saw hedge fund activity as merely a symptom of poor fundamentals and institutions. Interestingly, at the time many Latin American governments, which had not shared the Asian experience and which sought to attract hedge fund capital, also saw the threat of hedge funds as less pressing. The Eichengreen and Mathieson report subsequently failed to support direct regulation, in part because of the preference heterogeneity among the Fund's principals on the severity of the problem.[38]

The subsequent near-collapse of LTCM and the spillover effects of the Asian crisis altered this state of affairs somewhat. The near-collapse of LTCM focused the attention of developed country officials on systemic risks, though they, along with some Latin American governments, continued to view market dynamics risks as less pressing. Meanwhile, the spillover effects from the 1997–1998 crises in Asia and Russia led an increasing number of countries outside of Asia, such as Australia and South Africa, to raise concerns about market integrity and to support some form of direct regulation. Against this background, the FSF Working Group on Highly Leveraged Institutions was created to assess and develop responses to systemic risks, and, in response largely to concerns of Asian countries and others, the Study Group on Financial Market Dynamics was formed to examine market dynamics concerns.

But the lack of a common diagnosis of the nature of the problem led officials from developed countries and emerging markets to prescribe different policy responses. While U.S. and British officials favored indirect measures aimed at strengthening market discipline, emerging market officials tended to argue that direct regulation of the leverage, trades, and positions of hedge funds was necessary. The strength of the Anglo-American position, as well as the absence of emerging market representation in the FSF, ensured that direct regulation was not supported, despite the fact that representatives from Australia and Hong Kong were members of the FSF Working Group and had raised concerns about market dynamics.

To be sure, Australia and Hong Kong were not the only members of the FSF less committed to relying on market discipline. Many European and Japanese officials were sympathetic to considering some form of direct

---

[38] In addition, opponents of direct regulation pointed to other obstacles, such as ensuring comprehensive and timely information disclosure and problems of evasion. See Eichengreen, "Governing Global Financial Markets," pp. 180–181.

regulation. In fact, in 1999–2000 and 2006–2007, Germany pressed other G-7 countries to devise a modest form of direct regulation through development of a government-sponsored code of conduct and an international registry of hedge fund holdings. In principle, a regime of indirect supervision could have been combined with such modest direct regulations to tackle both systemic and market dynamics risks. But, as Eichengreen explains, a primary reason both policy options were not adopted "is that the first set of measures is compatible with the mind-set and terms of reference of the international community of financial supervisors while the second set of recommendations is not."[39]

Indeed, the preferences of the United States and Britain, where most hedge funds and their counterparties are headquartered, and which adopted "light" indirect regulatory approaches, left little room for serious consideration of direct regulation. Moreover, because any system of direct regulation would require extensive international coordination, U.S. and British preferences ruled out an international response in favor of various national responses. In response to the threat posed by Germany's regulatory proposal, hedge funds did eventually move forward more quickly in developing an industry-sponsored voluntary code of conduct, but U.S. and British preferences ensured that "self-regulation" rather than "direct regulation" was pursued.[40]

As the example of hedge funds reveals, the Fund's outer structural constraint prior to the subprime crisis severely limited the viability of policy prescriptions for greater regulation. If the Fund staff pushed for supply-side regulatory measures, they would have eventually run up against the preferences of their most powerful principals. Hence, this outer structural constraint discouraged the staff from arguing for developed countries to take regulatory action.

But the preferences of leading principals are not the full story. The institutional tools available to the Fund, which partly reflect prior delegation from IMF principals, make it easier for the staff to insist on reforms in emerging markets and developing countries than to press for regulatory measures in developed countries. While most developed countries can

---

[39] Eichengreen, "Governing Global Financial Markets," p. 194.

[40] For elaboration of the American and British positions prior to the subprime crisis, see Ben Bernanke, "Speech to the Federal Reserve Bank of Atlanta's 2007 Financial Market Conference," Sea Island, Georgia, 15 May 2007, available at http://www.federalreserve .gov/newsevents/speech/Bernanke20070515.htm; President's Working Group on Financial Markets, *Principles and Guidelines Regarding Private Pools of Capital* (22 Feb-ruary 2007), available at http://www.treasury.gov/press/releases/reports/hp272_principles.pdf; and Callum McCarthy, "Hedge Funds: What Should Be the Regulatory Response?" speech to European Money and Finance Forum, 7 December 2006, available at http://fsa.gov.uk/ pages/Library/Communication/Speeches/2006/1207cm.shtml

borrow extensively in their own currencies, and thus do not need to draw on IMF resources, emerging markets and developing countries do not enjoy this luxury. Conditional lending, surveillance, and the coordinating role these instruments play for official creditors and financial market participants provide the Fund with a range of tools it can use to promote policy adjustment and structural reforms in emerging markets and developing countries.

The Fund does not enjoy equivalent leverage or influence over developed countries. No developed country has approached the IMF for a loan since 1977, and it is difficult to imagine a situation where a G-7 country would draw on IMF resources. Surveillance over developed countries has also not proven to be a particularly effective means to influence policy. As Boughton notes, "Nowhere is the difficulty of conducting surveillance more apparent than in the relations between the IMF and the major industrial countries."[41] Indeed, as discussed in the epilogue, for several years prior to the onset of the subprime crisis the Fund was not sufficiently critical and even-handed in applying its surveillance to its leading principals.

The IMF still plays an important part in shaping market confidence in developing countries, and a critical, though declining, role in shaping perceptions about emerging markets, but it has little such capacity with respect to most developed countries or countries with large reserve holdings. For instance, until 2008 the United States refused to agree to an FSAP review of its financial system, even though over the previous decade it had pushed the IMF to look more closely at financial sector vulnerabilities in emerging markets. Along similar lines, in its recent attempt to help address global macroeconomic imbalances found in large and consistent deficits in the United States and corresponding surpluses in the Eurozone, Japan, China, and Saudi Arabia, the Fund found it could do little to mandate a specific time frame for implementing agreed policy actions or to develop a specific mechanism for enforcing them.[42]

The preferences of leading principals and the institutional tools available to the Fund thus play an important part in shaping its willingness to entertain supply-side regulatory measures, creating an environment where it becomes difficult for the staff to support such measures. But these factors alone do not provide us with an adequate understanding of why the Fund shied away from supply-side regulatory measures. We must also turn our attention to staff beliefs.

[41] Boughton, *The Silent Revolution*, p. 135.

[42] Scheherazade Daneshkhu, "Biggest Economies Promise to Cut Imbalances," *Financial Times*, 15 April 2007; Krishna Guha, "IMF Cools on Talks on Global Imbalances," *Financial Times*, 30 November 2006.

Here recruitment patterns played an important role, generating a personnel configuration that generally shared a similar, albeit narrow, understanding of the economic problems countries face and the appropriate solutions to them. The vast majority of Fund economists has been trained to view poor fundamentals and institutions in crisis-afflicted countries as the primary cause of financial instability, and therefore has been inclined to prescribe policy adjustment and structural reforms as necessary to prevent it. Reflecting on the unassailable nature of this claim across much of the economics profession, John Williamson associates these beliefs with "motherhood-and-apple-pie."[43]

These beliefs were closely linked to a tacit presumption that prevailed within the Fund, until the subprime crisis, that the main risks to systemic stability lay with emerging markets. Certainly, the wave of emerging market crises in the late 1990s had demonstrated that significant risks could emanate from emerging markets, but a case could also have been made that supply-side developments had important implications for these risks and capital account management. But the Fund's staff generally failed to examine wider sources of risk and a broader range of tools aimed at managing capital flows. Tellingly, although since the Asian crisis the Fund spent significant resources on surveillance in developed economies, as of February 2009, the Fund's formal vulnerability exercise involved only emerging markets.[44]

This made it difficult for proposals outside this prevailing view, even if staff were sympathetic to them, to be taken seriously or to percolate into the collectively shared beliefs that shape organizational behavior. Ideationally, despite an increasingly sophisticated understanding of the causes of financial instability, the staff's expertise biased their prescriptions toward recommending reforms in crisis-afflicted countries rather than on the supply side.

Recruitment patterns also played a role in creating blind spots in the way some staff members understood supply-side risks. Since the late 1990s, the Fund, as part of its effort to strengthen surveillance, has sought to recruit more midcareer staff with work experience in the public financial sector, such as central banks, financial regulatory agencies, or the BIS. Many of these staff members were steeped in the "micro-prudential" ethos that prevailed among regulators and supervisors since the creation of Basel I in the 1980s. This ethos directs the limited resources of regulators and supervisors to focusing on firm-level supervision in the formal banking sector, the presumption being that if each bank is safe, then the system as

---

[43] Williamson, *Curbing the Boom-Bust Cycle*, p. 9.
[44] IMF, *Initial Lessons of the Crisis for the Global Architecture and the IMF* (Washington, D.C.: IMF, 2009), p. 6.

a whole will be too. Yet this ethos fails to recognize that severe problems can arise through the correlation of risks across banks, which are presumed to be independent.

An alternative "macro-prudential" ethos would stress systemic risks and would be less concerned with the risks to and failure of individual banks per se and more with the correlation of risks across banks and the macroeconomic costs of financial instability as the basis to formulate policy. A macro-prudential orientation would fully recognize how financial instability can result from common exposures to similar assets across the system and therefore pay greater attention to procyclical tendencies. A core element of a macro-prudential orientation would be to ensure that financial institutions build up buffers during booms in order to run them down during downturns. "Leaning against the wind" in this fashion, as well as through the use of monetary policy, could therefore end up reducing the amplitude of the economic cycle.

But prior to the subprime crisis, regulators, supervisors, and academic economists did little to develop this macro-prudential orientation.[45] To be sure, regulators and supervisors possessed some "macro-prudential" tools geared toward systemic risks, but these often remained underdeveloped and inattentive to the buildup of risk over the full economic cycle. Because of the increasingly popularity of inflation targeting, few, if any, central banks took sufficient account of systemic risks stemming from asset price bubbles or leverage. This "benign neglect," prominently espoused by Alan Greenspan, suggested that central bankers should not seek to lean against the wind because it was difficult to distinguish speculative bubbles from "rational exuberance." This view was also associated with the perception that monetary policy was too blunt an instrument to counteract asset price booms and that financial stability was a task best left to prudential regulation. If and when asset bubbles burst, the effects on activity could be largely counteracted, as they seemingly had been after the dot-com bubble had burst in 2001, through lower interest rates. As two BIS economists noted in 2004, developing and employing macro-prudential tools would require "a cultural change among regulatory and supervisory authorities. . . . Countercyclical adjustments to prudential instruments, be these discretionary or rule-based, may be thought to be too intrusive and inconsistent with the current trend toward relying increasingly on firms' internal risk management systems . . . [C]ulturally,

---

[45] For notable exceptions, see Claudio Borio, "Towards a Macroprudential Framework for Financial Supervision and Regulation," Bank for International Settlements Working Paper No. 128 (Basel: Bank for International Settlements, 2003); Andrew Crockett, "Marrying the Micro- and Macro-Prudential Dimensions of Financial Stability" (Basel: Bank for International Settlements, 21 September 2000).

prudential authorities still remain rather reluctant to address financial instability through the instruments at their disposal if the origin is somehow seen to lie with broader macroeconomic developments, regardless of what the contribution of financial factors might be."[46] For some IMF staff members, this micro-prudential ethos thus created blind spots in their analysis of systemic risk and biased their prescriptions against countercyclical regulatory measures.

This is not to say that there were no staff members within the Fund sympathetic toward supply-side regulation. Indeed, the fact that the IEO, which is staffed primarily by Fund economists who have been rotated there as part of the regular interdepartmental staff transfers, advocated greater consideration of supply-side regulations suggests that there was some sympathy among the staff for such measures. However, the hierarchical, bureaucratic, and conforming elements of the IMF's culture likely made it difficult for these staff members to advocate such measures. The emphasis that IMF management places on maintaining intellectual discipline left little room for considering alternative policy prescriptions, particularly when the IMF had established a "line" on a given issue. Extensive bureaucratization and standardization, the monitoring and quality control responsibilities of PDR, and team-oriented work practices also combined to inhibit debate, creating pressures to conform to a standard way of doing things. Although the Fund has not established a formal approach toward capital account issues, it is clear from its emphasis on codes and standards, as well as the micro-prudential ethos that prevailed among regulators and supervisors, that the Fund "line" prior to the subprime crisis prioritized policy adjustments and structural reforms in emerging markets and developing countries. Staff with dissenting views were thus likely to either forgo advocacy of such views or to find their views drowned out or silenced by internal processes. Intraorganizational processes thus ensured a high degree of conformity centered on prescriptions for policy adjustment and structural reform.

NORM CONTINUITY AND ORGANIZATIONAL LEGITIMACY

The formal governance structures of the IMF clearly play an important part in shaping its willingness to entertain particular policy prescriptions. With respect to supply-side regulatory measures, the preferences of leading principals and the institutional tools available to the Fund combined

[46] Claudio Borio and William White, "Whither Monetary and Financial Stability? The Implications of Evolving Policy Regimes," Bank for International Settlements Working Paper No. 147 (Basel: Bank for International Settlements, 2004), pp. 26–27.

to create an environment where it became difficult for the staff to support such measures. Yet this created an asymmetric burden of responsibility: emerging markets and developing countries were expected to adjust their policies in line with developed country norms, largely Anglo-American in content, with no corresponding mechanism for encouraging developed countries to adjust their policies in a way consistent with the interests of emerging markets and developing countries. The Fund's failure to entertain supply-side regulatory measures thus fed the resentment felt by many emerging markets and developing countries toward the organization after the Asian crisis, thereby contributing to its legitimacy crisis.

Many of the Fund's legitimacy problems are linked to the criticisms by officials from emerging markets and developing countries that IMF conditionality is excessively intrusive. Although IMF conditionality has historically aroused controversy, it was not until the 1980s and 1990s that the Fund began to deepen its involvement in the local institutions of its borrowers. In the 1980s the Fund became increasingly convinced of the need for "structural adjustment," while in the 1990s, particularly after the Asian crisis, it turned its attention to "governance failures." Governance-related conditionality, which led the Fund to expand the scope of its leverage over borrowers from its traditional narrow focus on macroeconomic parameters to a broader concern with local institutions, has triggered much resentment among emerging markets and developing countries. Although it did seek to "streamline" its conditionality, as the standards and codes project suggests, the Fund nonetheless continued to place the burden of responsibility and adjustment on emerging markets and developing countries.

To some extent the prioritization of institutional reforms is unavoidable, as too many aspects of a country's domestic economy and its governance are critical to the Fund's goal of macroeconomic stability. Thus, one cannot expect the Fund to pursue the goal of macroeconomic stability without exercising at least some surveillance over domestic institutional arrangements that can affect it. Still, the deepening of the IMF's involvement in local institutions and the resulting resentment has caused a number of emerging markets and developing countries to lose faith in the Fund. As a result, many of them have pursued a policy of "mock compliance"[47] with standards and codes, moved toward greater regulatory decentralization, and embarked on a path of self-insurance as means of avoiding future IMF borrowing.

The result of this loss of faith was a "twin crisis" of legitimacy and budgetary finance for the Fund, with the organization subsequently mov-

---

[47] Andrew Walter, *Governing Finance: East Asia's Adoption of International Standards* (Ithaca, N.Y.: Cornell University Press, 2008).

ing to implement governance reforms and a new income model. Advocates of IMF governance reform claim the ongoing reallocation of Executive Board chairs and quota shares will go a long way in strengthening the legitimacy of the Fund. Although any agreed final reallocation will potentially leave U.S. veto power intact and do little to eliminate informal G-7 influence, it should, the argument goes, give disgruntled emerging markets and developing countries a greater opportunity to influence policy and programs. Greater voice should then translate into greater legitimacy.

The emphasis on IMF governance reforms may be justified. Such reforms could play a vital role in restoring the faith of many emerging markets and developing countries in the organization. By giving these countries the opportunity for more participation in IMF decision-making, these governance reforms could translate into greater commitment on the part of these countries to the norms of financial governance that the Fund helps create and diffuse. These reforms could also help broaden the range of policies that the Fund entertains by potentially creating a new outer structural constraint where the experience and interests of emerging markets and developing countries are given greater weight, thereby enhancing the IMF's legitimacy.

But focusing solely on the IMF's relationship with its principals as a way of understanding its reluctance to consider supply-side regulatory measures, and as a way of strengthening organizational legitimacy, overlooks many of the key arguments and themes developed in this book. In particular, it neglects the decisive influence that the staff and their internal debates have on organizational behavior. As I have shown in this book, much of what the Fund does is rooted less in directives from IMF principals than it is in the staff, their beliefs, and their internal debates. A large part of what the Fund does is thus derived from the informal approach of the staff as opposed to the formal rules constructed by IMF member states. Factors highlighted by both PA theorists and constructivists—such as ambiguous mandates, preference heterogeneity and collective action problems among and within IMF principals, expertise, information asymmetries, and specialization—have combined to provide the staff with considerable autonomy. Consequently, understanding the legitimacy problems facing the IMF and its reluctance prior to the subprime crisis to consider supply-side regulatory measures, as well as ultimately addressing these issues, requires attention to intraorganizational processes and informal aspects of IMF behavior.

Any realignment of chairs and shares on the IMF board may therefore end up being a hollow victory for emerging markets and developing countries if it ends up having little impact on "how things are done" inside the Fund. This is not to deny the power of votes on the board; but since much of what the Fund does is rooted in the staff, their beliefs, and their internal debates, reform proposals that overlook these internal factors could end up having little substantive effect on actual organizational behavior. Indeed, such proposals would risk making cosmetic changes to formal IMF rules without any corresponding change in the staff's informal approach. Reforming formal governance structures, while essential, is, in all likelihood, not sufficient to revive the Fund's legitimacy.

What is also required to enhance the IMF's legitimacy is that the staff entertain proposals, such as supply-side regulatory measures, that demonstrate that it is responsive to the interests and experiences of emerging markets and developing countries. The link between such measures and strengthening the IMF's legitimacy is clear. In a context where many of the IMF's traditional borrowers are pursuing self-insurance policies, the financial leverage of the Fund over emerging markets has declined significantly.[48] Much of the IMF's influence and authority now depends on its ability to define, disseminate, and legitimate ideas about appropriate policy. As Best aptly puts it, "As the Fund's own financial resources have declined relative to the role of private capital, it has come to rely increasingly on discursive strategies to achieve its goals."[49]

But unless the Fund entertains prescriptions, such as supply-side regulatory measures, that draw substantial input from alternative viewpoints that reflect the experiences and interests of emerging markets and developing countries, its policies and programs will be increasingly handicapped by a weak sense of "ownership." The risk, then, is not only the likelihood of policy reversals and perhaps greater financial instability but also that those emerging markets and developing countries that can, will in fact permanently turn their backs on the Fund and the norms it promotes. To help avert this outcome, genuine ownership requires that government officials play a lead role in determining policy goals; it requires political negotiations and debate over alternatives and priorities to provide the "policy space" to enable government officials to have a real choice about the trajectory of policy. But the mind-set of the IMF tends to be one that assumes that there is one best solution that can be defined through the application of expertise. Moreover, this expertise, because of the priority placed by the Fund's culture on first-best policy prescriptions, tends to blind the staff to the second-best reality of policymaking in many member states.

There is thus a strong need to broaden the collectively shared beliefs that prevail within the Fund. There are often many credible alternatives to its policy prescriptions, and intellectual diversity should be encouraged

---

[48] However, as noted in the epilogue, a few emerging markets have been forced to borrow from the Fund as a result of "sudden stops" in capital flows associated with the subprime crisis.

[49] Best, *The Limits of Transparency*, p. 143.

to foster meaningful debate among these theories. After all, the point of diversity is—or should be—precisely to acknowledge that no one knows for sure what set of ideas is "best." Intellectual diversity also should enhance genuine ownership of the Fund by emerging markets and developing countries, and thus its legitimacy, by giving emerging markets and developing countries a greater sense that their experiences and interests are being taken into account. Such ownership in turn requires that the Fund embrace intellectual diversity as a goal, thus becoming more representative of the heterogeneity of views that exist among its membership and the economics profession.

How could such intellectual diversity be encouraged? Any reforms that seek to increase intellectual diversity must begin with IMF recruitment practices. Recruitment procedures are of crucial importance because of the IMF's reliance on claims of expertise to legitimate its authority. Indeed, claims to expert-based legitimacy necessarily raise prior questions about how these experts are selected.[50] The Fund often claims that it selects individuals based on their technical skills, recruiting those who have a command of the "best" available theory and techniques for analyzing the world economy. Although it is difficult to call into question the credentials that most of the Fund's economists possess, this argument tends to be overstated.

To begin with, it overlooks the fact that there are often many credible alternatives to the policy prescriptions that the Fund claims are derived from the "best" available theory and techniques. Economic theory rarely produces a unique singularly true solution to matters of policy, and this should lead us to question arguments that seek legitimate authority based on such claims. Perhaps more importantly, arguments that suggest the Fund recruits only those that have a command of the "best" available theory and techniques neglect the fact that such experts bring not only technical skills with them but also value judgments about how to assess various trade-offs. These value judgments speak to important questions: Should efficiency be valued over equity? Should price stability take precedence over growth? And there are many other such questions. We therefore should be wary of claims to expert-based authority when such expertise tends to prioritize one set of value judgments over another.

An accommodation of a wider range of alternative judgments about these trade-offs would encourage greater ownership. But the scope for such accommodation is currently severely constrained by the Fund's tendency to engage in "intellectual monocropping." Most worrying is the fact that such monocropping appears to most prevalent in RES (see figure

[50] Best, "Legitimacy Dilemmas: The IMF's Pursuit of Country Ownership," *Third World Quarterly* 28, no. 3 (2007), pp. 469–488.

7.1), the department within the Fund that is expected to contribute greatly to policy innovation. A number of changes to recruitment procedures could help the Fund respond to these shortcomings.

Expanding the number of IMF economists with alternative professional characteristics is one way of fostering intellectual diversity. This could be accomplished in a number of different ways. The Fund could make a special effort to attract recruits from academic institutions—such as "HKCE" departments or those in emerging markets and developing countries— that traditionally bring less orthodox perspectives to bear on economic problems. The Fund could also seek to expand the number of economists with experience in emerging market and developing country institutions so as to increase the extent to which the experiences and interests of these members are reflected in policy formulation.[51]

One possible way to achieve this goal would be to enhance opportunities for lateral entry inside the Fund by making more midcareer appointments from emerging markets and developing countries and by recruiting fewer staff via the EP. Currently, an overwhelming majority of midcareer appointees come from developed countries, and many of the appointees from emerging markets and developing countries receive their professional training in the same academic institutions from which the Fund traditionally recruits.[52] The Fund therefore could make a special effort to increase the proportion of midcareer appointees from emerging markets and developing countries who received their training from academic institutions from which the Fund does not conventionally recruit. Because of their training and policy-related experience, such midcareer appointees are likely to bring alternative perspectives from their previous experience, be more attuned to the second-best reality of policymaking, and be unlikely to shy away from challenging prevailing beliefs inside the Fund.

Finally, the Fund could also seek to inject alternative perspectives by making greater use of individuals based in academic institutions and think-tanks in emerging markets and developing countries to serve as subcontractors and consultants for IMF programs.[53] However, special care would have to be taken to ensure that such individuals were not exclusively drawn from institutions whose perspective more or less aligns with that of the IMF. The increasing "internationalization" of the economics profession in recent years, however, could make this, and the earlier sugges-

---

[51] Evans and Finnemore, "Organizational Reform," pp. 12, 16–18; Momani, "IMF Staff," p. 52.

[52] In 2005, over 60 percent of midcareer appointees came from the developed world; see IMF, *Annual Report, 2006*, p. 118. Data on the professional characteristics of such appointees are not available.

[53] Evans and Finnemore, "Organizational Reform," p. 12.

tion to recruit more from departments in emerging markets and developing countries, a challenging task.[54] But there still remains a sufficient degree of intellectual diversity to justify the effort.

However, in making greater use of midcareer appointees, subcontractors, and consultants, the Fund would need to manage resistance from existing staff members who opposed actions inconsistent with the conventional way of doing things. In fact, changes to recruitment procedures alone will likely not be sufficient to ensure that alternative perspectives affect the informal approach of the staff. The IMF's culture and intraorganizational processes would likely continue to favor conformity and homogeneity. Thus, reform also must be targeted at these internal factors and dynamics, particularly those that inhibit debate and innovation. One important reform would be to loosen the grip of PDR's monitoring and quality control responsibilities so as to better facilitate internal debate and consideration of alternative ideas. While PDR's role helps ensure coherence and uniformity of treatment among members, it also leads the staff often to self-censor references to particular country problems or alternative ideas, as they recognize that PDR will remove such statements from reports before they reach the board or the public. The monitoring and review process conducted by PDR also encourages carbon-copy documentation of member country information.

To encourage greater internal debate, the staff requires greater "space" to consider alternative ideas. Currently, much of the work that PDR conducts is segmented; an individual staff member responsible for a particular issue (for instance, capital account policy) reviews and comments on reports in an effort to bring greater coherence and uniformity to them regarding that issue. But this practice provides little opportunity for alternative viewpoints and perspectives to be considered. Some suggest one way to do so would be to better unify the work of PDR by developing a team-based approach to monitoring and quality control.[55] Non-PDR staff could also be brought in to ensure alternative institutional perspectives are considered.

But a team-based approach to monitoring and quality control could also end up simply replicating similar problems that arise from team-based work practices across the Fund as a whole. Team-based PDR work could produce reports where the staff focus more on reaching internal agreement than on considering alternative perspectives. Dissenting views would still be inhibited. To address this potential shortcoming, it would be worth considering opening up staff reports to internal and external debate before submitting any report to the board. Along these lines, Camdessus has

[54] Coats, *Post-1945 Internationalization of Economics.*
[55] See also Momani, "IMF Staff," p. 54.

suggested "submitting the staff's preliminary conclusions to a broader debate before transmission to the Executive board. With due precautions, this consultation could be open to academic observers and regional partners."[56] Subjecting staff reports to greater internal and external debate would help break down pressures to conform, and it might also help the Fund become more representative of the heterogeneity of views that exist among its membership and the economics profession. In addition, greater space for alternative ideas could be carved out by having the staff present its internal disagreements and views before the board, rather than a homogenized staff report.[57]

Attention also needs to be paid to certain organizational routines within the Fund that inhibit learning and adaptation, and thus the uptake of new and alternative ideas. For more than fifty years the IMF had no independent evaluation office that could enable the Fund to better absorb the lessons from past experience, although internal and external evaluations were occasionally undertaken on an ad hoc basis. It was not until 2000 that the IEO was created to improve the "learning culture" of the Fund. Although a recent external evaluation of the IEO finds that "staff attest that the IEO has created greater space for debate and criticism," it also uncovers "little evidence that findings and recommendations of specific IEO reports are being systematically taken up and followed up by senior management and the Board."[58] There is thus clearly room for more systematic monitoring of follow-up to IEO reports.[59]

Greater effort also needs to be devoted to breaking down the "silo mentality" that prevails within the Fund. The IMF needs to encourage greater lateral movement across departments. This would facilitate greater cross-fertilization of the various perspectives that the departmental staff members bring to their tasks and help discovery of new ideas and of shortcomings with existing policy. Some of the other measures discussed earlier could also enhance the learning culture of the Fund. With new recruitment procedures and organizational routines in place, the Fund would be more likely to bring a wider range of perspectives to bear on experiences, thus helping to minimize the likelihood that learning is channeled by a particular set of prevailing beliefs.

---

[56] Quoted in L. Wallace, "How Should the IMF Be Reshaped?" *Finance and Development* 41, no. 3 (2004), pp. 27–29 at p. 27.

[57] IMF, *External Evaluation of IMF Surveillance*, p. 34.

[58] Lissakers, Husain, and Woods, *Report of External Evaluation*, p. 4.

[59] In 2008, in an attempt to follow up more systematically on IEO reports, the IMF began to monitor progress of board-endorsed recommendations of the IEO; see "First Periodic Monitoring Report on the Status of Board-Endorsed Recommendations of the Independent Evaluation Office," Public Information Notice No. 08/125 (Washington, D.C.: IMF, 2008).

A final set of reforms worth considering would be those directed at the intraorganizational processes that often bias the staff toward unrealistic first-best policies and away from feasible second-best policies. Staff biases for first-best policies undermine genuine ownership, giving government officials little space to debate alternative policies and priorities. Earlier, it was suggested that recruiting more midcareer staff with experience inside emerging market and developing country institutions could increase consideration of second-best policy prescriptions. In addition, the Fund also might consider broadening its recruitment net, casting it in such a manner as to bring in fewer macroeconomists and more individuals with policy and political economy training.

The internal staff promotion and appointment system could also be redesigned so as to encourage the staff to strike a better balance between academically convincing and politically feasible policies. Momani, for instance, suggests the staff could be required to pass "diplomatic service" equivalency examinations and to attend political economy seminars and conferences. The staff promotion system could also be reengineered so as to strike a better balance in evaluations between successful policy implementation in member states, on the one hand, and tenure of service and technical skills, on the other.[60]

Some also recommend that area department staff be rotated less frequently so as to better harness local knowledge of member state institutions and policymaking as a means of bringing in new ideas and alternative perspectives. Although there is some merit in this proposal, it also suffers from some important shortcomings that warrant caution. First, it would undermine efforts to encourage greater lateral movement across departments, thus potentially constraining the learning culture of the Fund. Second, and perhaps far more worrisome, is the possibility that longer assignments could encourage clientism. Recent external evaluations of IMF interactions with country officials have highlighted this tendency, and the departure of the long-serving WHD director in 2002 was attributed by many to the failure of the staff in the 1990s to insist on the need for fiscal restraint in Argentina—a failure directly implicated in the subsequent crisis. It therefore would seem advisable to continue staff rotation practices, while pushing forward with other reforms, such as changes to recruitment procedures, which could enhance the uptake of local knowledge.

All of these reform proposals should not only strengthen debate of policy alternatives and priorities, and thus enhance genuine ownership and IMF legitimacy; they should also improve policy implementation in mem-

[60] Momani, "IMF Staff."

ber states. The Fund would have a broader array of knowledge—both abstract theoretical principles from an array of disciplines and local contextual understandings of the way institutions work and of policy implemented in various member states—that could be employed to better design programs and policies so that they stand a better change of being implemented. The logic behind these proposals is not to supplant the current beliefs that prevail within the Fund, but rather to complement these beliefs with a broader array of knowledge that can provide a fuller understanding of the complexities of policymaking and implementation.

The Fund experienced a strong continuity of norms in the period between the Asian and subprime crises. This continuity was evident through persistent support for gradualism, accommodation for selective restraints on capital mobility, the development of the standards and codes project, and the eschewal of supply-side regulatory prescriptions. The preferences of leading principals, the availability of institutional tools, and intraorganizational processes were shown to be crucial determinants of this continuity. Yet the distributional implications of this continuity, which place the burden of responsibility and adjustment on emerging markets and developing countries, aroused significant resentment among the IMF's membership.

The Fund's near universal membership and mandate for financial stability makes it the optimal IO for developing norms of financial governance. But resentment among the IMF membership has increasingly called into the question the legitimacy of the organization, the norms it promotes, and the project of developing universalist standards and codes. Without meaningful reform of the IMF—at the level of formal governance and intraorganizational processes—and consideration of measures that reflect the interests and experiences of emerging markets and developing countries, it risks becoming increasingly illegitimate.

A Subprime "Crisis" for Capital Freedom?

THE SUBPRIME CRISIS has generated signs that the norms of financial governance are changing, with governments having implemented dramatic measures that fly in the face of long-held policy taboos and norms. Many developed country governments have partially nationalized their financial systems and embarked on Keynesian-style fiscal expansion. Even the IMF, traditionally a preacher of fiscal discipline, has pushed governments to loosen their purse strings to combat the global downturn. Amid growing calls for reregulation of the financial system, advocates of liberalization and self-regulation find themselves on the defensive. But it is not yet clear how radical or extensive reform will be or whether the turmoil will ultimately turn out to be a "crisis" for capital freedom.

Indeed, despite the growing calls for reregulation and the role that capital inflows played in fueling housing bubbles in the United States and other developed countries, unlike the Asian crisis, the subprime crisis has yet to stir many politically prominent calls for restricting capital mobility and overturning the norm of capital freedom. However, the Fund has accommodated in some countries the use of controls on outflows to manage pressures from the crisis, and has pointed once again to the potential role that controls on inflows can play in minimizing vulnerabilities associated with inflow bonanzas. More significantly, the subprime crisis has led the Fund to shift toward supporting regulatory measures aimed at financial market participants based in developed countries, signaling a change in the organization's interpretation and application of the norm of capital freedom. This shift constitutes an important step toward demonstrating that the Fund is able and willing to entertain measures that reflect the interests and experiences of emerging markets and developing countries. Such a step could prove useful in contributing to ongoing efforts to enhance the Fund's legitimacy.

Because events and policies are evolving quickly at the time of writing, any assessment of the scope of this policy shift and the reasons behind it are necessarily preliminary. With this important caveat in mind, it appears that this shift has been driven by preference changes and heterogeneity among the Fund's principals as well as adaptation and the efforts of norm entrepreneurs within the Fund. Although the agenda for reforming the international financial architecture has been wide-ranging in scope, the focus here is largely on a narrower set of issues related to capital account management; in particular, supply-side regulatory proposals related to procyclicality and the use of capital controls.

Significantly, the subprime crisis has also triggered a breakthrough in the form of international financial governance, as revealed by the decision to convene the leaders of the G-20, rather than the G-7, to develop the reform agenda. This change in form could subsequently translate into a change in substance where the interests and experiences of emerging markets are more adequately represented in international regulatory outcomes. But if this breakthrough turns out to be more symbolic than substantive, the risk is that emerging markets will turn their backs on these forums and the norms they promote through strategies of self-insurance and regulatory decentralization.

REWRITING FINANCIAL ORTHODOXY ONE STEP AT A TIME

The subprime crisis was the culmination of an exceptional boom in credit and debt. A number of factors fueled the boom. Since the early 2000s, many central banks in developed countries pursued exceptionally loose monetary policy, which encouraged the development of housing bubbles. Although central bankers were aware of these bubbles, the widely shared "benign neglect" view led many to see their task as one of reacting to asset price bubbles after they had burst so as to minimize damage to the economy, rather than "leaning against the wind" by seeking to identify the bubbles and determining the proper way to deflate them. The capital inflow bonanzas associated with the recycling of savings and trade surpluses from China and other emerging market countries and oil-producing countries to the United States and other deficit countries also fueled housing bubbles. Taken together, central bank policies and global macroeconomic imbalances generated historically low real interest rates and abundant liquidity, which increased the amount of debt and risk that borrowers, investors, and intermediaries were willing to take on.

Financial institutions responded to these benign conditions by developing innovative models of securitization for mortgages and other assets. Traditionally, lenders bore the risk on the mortgages they issued. But the new originate-to-distribute model of securitization enabled financial institutions to transform their assets, such as loans for subprime and prime mortgages, automobiles, credit cards, and students, into asset-backed securities (ABS), of which mortgage-backed securities (MBS) were an important subset, and collateralized debt obligations (CDOs) that could be sold off to investors. Other financial innovations, such as credit default swaps (CDSs), which insured holders against defaults of various securities and structured credit products, also emerged. The result was an extraordinary expansion of the market for credit risk transfer instruments. Banks and other financial institutions fueled this expansion by creating MBS-backed off-balance-sheet funding and investment vehicles (structured investment vehicles—SIVs), which tended to invest heavily in structured credit products. Many central bankers and regulators praised this new model of securitization, believing it to have strengthened systemic stability by diffusing risk and deepening the liquidity of the market for risk. Yet the model became increasingly dependent on originators' underwriting standards, the risk and liquidity management practices of financial institutions, and the performance of CRAs in evaluating risks.

Starting in the summer of 2007, a steady rise in U.S. subprime mortgage delinquencies triggered a sharp fall in the price for subprime MBS, which in turn produced losses and margin calls for leveraged investors. The problems in the subprime market quickly spread to other markets. Multiple CRA downgrades of formerly highly rated structured products caused a loss of confidence and broad reassessment of risk across the wider market, and, in August 2007, money market investors in asset-backed commercial paper refused to roll over investments made in bank-sponsored conduits and SIVs backed by structured credit products.

Banks became unwilling to provide liquidity to one another as they sold assets and cut lending to repair their balance sheets and increased their demand for liquid assets to fund commitments to their conduits and SIVs. This caused the interbank and other credit markets to freeze. Many banks subsequently found they lacked the liquidity to finance their lending commitments.

As the credit crunch materialized, a vicious cycle developed. Financial institutions were forced to sell assets at fire sale prices, thereby depressing asset prices and generating valuation losses for assets that remained on balance sheets, which in turn forced additional asset sales and led to lower asset prices and further valuation losses. The use of fair value accounting, which requires assets to be marked according to their current market value, reinforced this feedback loop by forcing banks to take immediate losses on their balance sheets after each price drop. As market liquidity for structured credit products evaporated, banks faced difficult challenges valuing their holdings and became less confident in their assessments about the exposure and capital strength of other institutions. Without any buyers for their distressed ABS, major financial institutions absorbed them onto their balance sheets, sustaining large losses to their capital cushions. Major uncertainties developed about the soundness of financial institutions, the value of structured credit products, and the general macroeconomic outlook. These uncertainties, along with heightened risk aversion and reduced liquidity, caused financial intermediation in much of the developed world to grind to a halt.

The response of policymakers has reflected an assumption that problems are largely due to illiquidity rather than insolvency, and that the financial system has been experiencing a correction. These officials see their task as one of ensuring that this correction is orderly by providing liquidity to financial institutions so as to prevent further fire sales and help banks finance their holdings of hard-to-value securities. As the crisis has unfolded, the Bank of England (BoE), the European Central Bank (ECB), the Federal Reserve, and other central banks have responded by aggressively cutting interest rates, pumping larger amounts of liquidity into financial institutions on increasingly generous terms and across a wider range of collateral and counterparties, and introducing U.S. dollar swap lines. In an effort to unfreeze credit markets, some central banks have also introduced credit guarantees and direct purchases of private and public sector securities.

In the period prior to the crisis, the Fund had failed to send a strong wakeup call to policymakers about risks building up in the financial system. The Fund, like other observers such as the BIS, FSF, and BoE, managed to issue only scattered and unspecific warnings, few of which provided operational policy guidance. Over time the Fund did become increasingly concerned that securitization might not have dispersed risk as widely as was being assumed. But, like other observers, it did not see that these risk concentrations remained with the core banking system. As a 2009 IMF review of lessons of the crisis for the international financial architecture concedes, "The failure to diagnose the risk to the core system also led to a failure to propose a concrete policy solution—the need to raise capital charges on off-balance sheet exposures and nonbanks."[1]

The Fund also missed the connection between financial market developments and risks to the real economy. For instance, despite the experience with the failure of LTCM in 1998, the Fund devoted little attention to how a loss of market liquidity could affect the growing, complex web of financial relationships. Finally, the Fund also tended to offer an optimistic view on developed countries and financial innovation, particularly on the performance and prospects for the United States and Britain, whose liberal market economies were widely perceived to have out performed other varieties of capitalism. In line with the tacit presumption that systemic risks lay mainly in emerging markets, the Fund devoted insufficient attention to vulnerabilities in developed economies. As suggested in chapter 9, this optimistic view also reflected the political difficulties the Fund staff faced in offering sufficiently critical assessments of their leading principals. As a result, the risk that a financial crisis might emanate from the developed world was never seriously considered.

[1] IMF, *Initial Lessons*, p. 5.

During the first year of the financial turmoil, the IMF was relegated largely to the sidelines. The crisis was initially confined to developed countries, which could mobilize sufficient resources by borrowing in their own currencies, thus freeing them from the need to borrow from the Fund or heed its advice. This, of course, did not prevent the IMF from offering its views. For instance, in April 2008 the *GFSR* estimated that losses on U.S.-originated assets and securities could total $945 billion.[2] Also that month IMF managing director Dominique Strauss-Kahn was among the first to break with orthodoxy by suggesting solvency was becoming a concern and that government recapitalization of the banking system could be necessary: "With respect to the banks, if capital buffers cannot be repaired quickly enough by the private sector, use of public money can be examined."[3] But the G-7 dismissed this analysis and advice, with one senior U.S. Treasury official calling the IMF forecast "unduly pessimistic" and suggesting there was "no consensus" on the need for government intervention.[4] Later the IMF would be entitled to some righteous vindication when its forecasts and policy proposals proved rather accurate.[5]

Emerging markets, the Fund's traditional client base, initially appeared well positioned to weather the crisis, as many of them were less exposed to MBS and enjoyed trade surpluses and a commodity price boom that continued through summer 2008. Some observers even speculated that emerging markets could "decouple" from the downturn occurring in developed economies. But by autumn 2008 "decoupling" proved to be wishful thinking.

Indeed, the crisis worsened significantly in 2008, as losses on MBS piled up, credit markets remained frozen, and share prices, especially for financial institutions, plummeted. Yet, as suggested by the G-7's dismissal of the IMF's April 2008 estimate of losses, policymakers were slow to recognize the magnitude of the crisis, leading to an institution-by-institution approach that tended to address the symptoms of financial stress while the balance sheets of financial institutions and the real economy deteriorated. As some banks came under severe funding pressures, governments intervened on an ad hoc, institution-specific basis that reflected the belief that the financial system remained solvent. In January, Britain nationalized Northern Rock, following almost six months of providing liquidity

---

[2] IMF, *Global Financial Stability Report* (April) (Washington, D.C.: IMF, 2008).

[3] As quoted in Krishna Guha, "IMF Heads Calls for Global Action on Turmoil," *Financial Times*, 6 April 2008.

[4] Chris Bryant and Krishna Guha, "IMF Rejects Criticism over Global Turmoil," *Financial Times*, 10 April 2008.

[5] Interestingly, the April 2008 estimate actually proved to be unduly optimistic, with the October 2008 *GFSR* forecasting that losses on U.S.-originated assets will ultimately total $1.45 trillion, and the April 2009 *GFSR* forecasting that losses could reach $2.7 trillion.

and seeking to avoid such an outcome through private sector involvement. Later that year, U.S. officials intervened in Bear Stearns, Countrywide, and IndyMac, with the former two being acquired by healthier financial institutions and the latter converted to a bridge bank.

In the final months of 2008, amid heightened uncertainty about the soundness of financial institutions, the pace of government intervention accelerated sharply. In early September, U.S. officials effectively nationalized the nation's two largest government-sponsored enterprises (GSEs)—the Federal National Mortgage Association and the Federal Home Loan Mortgage Corporation, which exist to provide liquidity to the residential mortgage market by purchasing mortgages, securitizing them, and then selling them off to investors. With panic gripping the market, credit markets frozen, losses piling up, and share prices of financial institutions plunging, the financial landscape of the United States and other developed countries was radically reshaped over the next few months.

Unlike the treatment of earlier failures, the decision of the U.S. government to permit the closure of Lehman Brothers in mid-September imposed significant losses on creditors. The result was a marked deterioration in market sentiment, as creditors shifted their concerns from the soundness of individual financial institutions arising from narrow issues in the subprime market to the broader stability of the entire financial system. The subprime crisis thus became a wider financial crisis. Many governments first moved to minimize creditors' panic by providing assurances that they would not permit a collapse of the financial system. These assurances included strengthening creditor protection programs through the introduction of measures such as enhanced deposit insurance schemes and bank debt instrument guarantees.

Governments also moved to shore up confidence in the system through a series of interventions and recapitalizations, though these resolution strategies, reflecting a belief that the system was solvent, remained institution-specific rather than systemic in scope. In late September, British officials provided liquidity and waived competition rules to arrange for the merger of HBOS with its rival Lloyds, and then nationalized Bradford and Bingley. Following the closure of Lehman, U.S. officials also closed Washington Mutual, arranged the private sector sale of Merrill Lynch and Wachovia, and took a significant ownership stake in the insurance firm American International Group (AIG). Belgium and the Netherlands moved to break up and recapitalize the regional bank Fortis.

Following the AIG intervention, concerns about heightened congressional scrutiny and the Federal Reserve's overstretched balance sheet mounted within the Bush Treasury. In late September, U.S. Treasury Secretary Henry Paulson unveiled to Congress the Troubled Assets Relief Program (TARP), a plan for using public money to purchase distressed assets from financial institutions and then sell them in auctions. The plan essentially assumed that the financial system was solvent but illiquid and that public money could substitute for market liquidity, thus jump-starting the market for these distressed assets and enabling banks to value them on their balance sheets. Once cleansed, banks could then tap capital and begin lending again.

The initial proposal to Congress did not permit the use of TARP funds to recapitalize banks, nor did it contain restrictions on executive compensation or bonuses, as pushed by Democratic legislators. Yet at the time the idea of using public money to effectively nationalize parts of the financial system was unthinkable within the Bush administration. This was partly due to a deep principled opposition within the U.S. Treasury to the degree of government intervention that such an action would entail. "Some said we should just stick capital in the banks, take preferred stock in the banks. That's what you do when you have failure," Paulson told congressional legislators in late September. "This is about success."[6] The Treasury also opposed capital injections and limits on executive compensation on the grounds that both measures would deter financial institutions from participating in the scheme. Paulson thus informed legislators that it made more sense to jump-start credit markets with "market measures" to purchase and sell distressed assets. But the Bush administration was forced to give in to congressional opposition. Although the Treasury insisted that public money would be used to purchase distressed assets, the approved version of TARP also gave the government the authority to inject capital and subject financial institutions receiving public assistance to modest limits on executive compensation.

The IMF, for its part, called for an aggressive response to the crisis. Strauss-Kahn argued that "a systemic crisis demands systemic solutions" and pressed for a three-pronged response to the crisis based on liquidity provision, government purchase of distressed assets, and government recapitalization of financial institutions.[7] The October 2008 *GFSR* offered a similar line of argument.[8]

With creditor protection schemes failing to shore up confidence and a global equity sell-off wiping out bank capital, policymakers in developed countries abandoned long-standing policy taboos and norms. The British government acted first, announcing what few contemporary developed country politicians or observers could ever have imagined implementing: the partial nationalization of the financial system through a government

[6] As quoted in Edmund Andrews, "White House Overhauling Rescue Plan," *New York Times*, 12 October 2008.

[7] Dominique Strauss-Kahn, "A Systemic Crisis Demands Systemic Solutions," *Financial Times*, 22 September 2008.

[8] IMF, *Global Financial Stability Report* (October) (Washington, D.C.: IMF, 2008).

recapitalization scheme. EU officials soon reached agreement on a similar coordinated recapitalization plan tailored to national circumstances.[9]

Although the Bush Treasury was opposed in principle to using public money to recapitalize banks, the collapse of share prices and the prospect of American financial institutions being at a competitive disadvantage vis-à-vis their British and European rivals forced their hand. Paulson announced that the government would deploy some TARP funds to recapitalize weakened financial institutions. "Government owning a stake in any private U.S. company," Paulson explained, "is objectionable to most Americans—me included. Yet the alternative of leaving businesses and consumers without access to financing is totally unacceptable."[10] (Later, in November, the U.S. Treasury, abandoning its initial strategy of purchasing distressed bank assets, announced that all available TARP funds would be allocated to recapitalize the banking system.)

With orthodoxy effectively rewritten, many governments moved to intervene in financial institutions, while delicately avoiding outright nationalization. In the six weeks following the collapse of Lehman, twenty-five large financial institutions based in G-20 countries required public intervention. As of February 2009, nine of the G-20 countries had directly injected approximately $400 billion of public money into financial institutions, with the largest share—almost two-thirds of the total—coming from the United States, followed by Britain.[11]

By October, after weeks of difficulty coordinating their policies, governments from leading developed countries finally managed to develop a consensus of sorts, though one that still emphasized national rather than international action. This consensus, as spelled out in an October 2008 G-7 statement, centered on preventing the failure of systemically important financial institutions, recapitalizing banks, strengthening deposit guarantees, and unfreezing credit markets.[12]

Government asset management policies for the purchase of distressed assets have evolved slowly. Largely reflecting the difficulties in valuing these assets, at the time of writing only two countries have authorized distressed asset purchase schemes, although many have developed schemes to purchase a wide range of higher-quality assets. In October, Germany became the first country to commit to using public funds to purchase

[9] "Full Statement from Eurozone Summit," *Financial Times*, 12 October 2008.

[10] As quoted in Andrews, "White House Overhauling Rescue Plan." See also Krishna Guha, "US Shift as UK Sets Out to Recapitalize," *Financial Times*, 8 October 2008; James Politi, "US Unveils $250 Billion Rescue Plan," *Financial Times*, 14 October 2008.

[11] IMF, *Stocktaking of the G-20 Responses to the Global Banking Crisis* (Washington, D.C.: IMF, 2009), pp. 8–9.

[12] G-7, "G-7 Finance Ministers and Central Bank Governors Plan of Action," U.S. Treasury Press Release HP-1195, 10 October 2008.

distressed assets. Following the decision to use TARP funds for recapitalization, the U.S. Treasury spent months debating schemes to remove distressed assets from the balance sheets of financial institutions. At the time of writing, Treasury officials from the new administration of Barack Obama were seeking to create a new public-private investment fund to manage assets purchased from banks. Some countries, including the United States and Britain, have also announced selective insurance schemes for losses on distressed assets.

The IMF has been critical of the slow pace and lack of specificity surrounding government asset management schemes. At the time of writing, most governments have failed to unveil precise mechanisms for dealing with distressed assets on bank balance sheets. The IMF has warned that governments, by ducking the critical issue of cleaning up distressed assets, risk prolonging the economic downturn. In April 2009, based on the staff's analysis of 124 banking crises, Strauss-Kahn argued that "you will never recover before cleaning up of the banking sector has been done. . . . They are not yet moving quickly enough in doing the cleaning up of the financial system."[13]

Initially, many European officials watched the financial storm brew in the United States and identified its self-regulatory framework as the principal culprit. For these officials, the events of mid-September strengthened their conviction that the concerns about self-regulation they had expressed in the past were warranted. Peter Steinbrück, the German finance minister, claimed that the U.S. belief in "laisser-faire capitalism; the notion that markets should be as free as possible from regulation; these arguments were wrong and dangerous. This largely under-regulated system is collapsing today." Reregulation, not self-regulation, Steinbrück insisted, would become the new norm, and governments must act to "civilize financial markets."[14] German chancellor Angela Merkel cited the crisis as proof that she was right at earlier international meetings to press for tougher regulation of hedge funds and financial markets—and that the United States and Britain were wrong to resist it.[15]

For many in Europe the crisis seemed to validate earlier remarks from German president Horst Kohler, who had served as IMF managing director in the early 2000s, that global financial markets had become a "mon-

[13] Chris Giles, George Parker, and Gillian Tett, "G20 Leaders Accused over Toxic Assets," *Financial Times*, 1 April 2009; Luc Laeven and Fabian Valencia, "Systemic Banking Crises: A New Database," IMF Working Paper WP/08/224 (Washington, D.C.: IMF, 2008).

[14] As quoted in Bertrand Benoit, "US 'Will Lose Financial Superpower Status,'" *Financial Times*, 25 September 2008.

[15] Ralph Atkins, "Merkel Vents Annoyance over US and UK," *Financial Times*, 21 September 2008.

ster" that "must be put back in its place."[16] French president Nicolas Sarkozy, for instance, declared, "The idea of an all-powerful market without any rules and any political intervention is mad. Self-regulation is finished. Laisser faire is finished. The all-powerful market that is always right is finished."[17] Sarkozy called for a summit of world leaders to be convened aimed at building a "regulated capitalism . . . in a way to allow European ideas to flourish."[18] Strauss-Kahn, who remains a leading figure in the French Socialist Party after becoming IMF managing director in 2007, more diplomatically observed: "It is because there were no regulations or controls, or not enough regulations or controls, that this situation was born. We must . . . regulate, with greater precision, financial institutions and markets."[19]

British prime minister Gordon Brown has also sought to position himself as the scourge of unfettered capitalism, noting that 2008 would be remembered as the year in which the "old era of unbridled free market dogma was finally ushered out."[20] In its March 2009 report on the causes of the crisis, the Financial Services Authority (FSA), Britain's financial services regulator, similarly observed that the crisis "raises important questions about the intellectual assumptions on which previous regulatory approaches have been built . . . [and in particular] the theory of efficient and rational markets."[21] Lord Turner, chair of the FSA, has gone so far as to label Britain's reliance on light-touch regulation and self-regulation as a "fundamental intellectual failure."[22] In publicly advocating greater regulation, Brown, who has long been an advocate of strengthening the IMF's early warning system, has insisted that he raised earlier alarms about the need for greater regulation but that they were ignored.[23] Yet France and Germany, having over the last decade observed Britain often side with the United States in opposing direct regulation, and watched as it resisted their efforts to extend European financial regulation to the City of London, remain skeptical of Brown's intentions. In fact, though British offi-

---

[16] As quoted in Bertrand Benoit and James Wilson, "Köhler Attacks Markets 'Monster,'" *Financial Times*, 14 May 2008.

[17] As quoted in John Thornhill, "Sarkozy Sets Out Bigger State Role," *Financial Times*, 25 September 2008.

[18] As quoted in Harvey Morris, "Sarkozy Presses for Capitalism Summit," *Financial Times*, 24 September 2008 ("regulated capitalism"); Ben Hall, "Eurozone Set to Pledge Billions in Rescue Bid," *Financial Times*, 12 October 2008 ("European ideas").

[19] As quoted in Daneshkhu Scheherazade, "IMF Welcomes Step to Reform," *Financial Times*, 28 September 2008.

[20] As quoted in Jim Pickard, "Brown Promises Stability in Difficult Year," *Financial Times*, 1 January 2009.

[21] Financial Services Authority, *The Turner Review*, p. 39.

[22] As quoted in Jennifer Hughes, "UK Banks to Face Tougher Rules," *Financial Times*, 25 February 2009.

[23] George Parker, "Brown Says His Warnings Were Ignored," *Financial Times*, 21 September 2008.

cials have displayed an interest in promoting greater regulation, the degree of support from Britain for new Franco-German initiatives at this point remains unclear. However, Britain has recently moved closer to the Franco-German position, with the Chancellor of the Exchequer and Lord Turner both backing a new body to coordinate regulation across the EU. Many emerging market officials have been sympathetic to European calls for reregulation. These officials, who over the past decade had faced routine lectures from the G-7 on the need to strengthen their financial systems and prudential regulations, were quick to point to similar problems in developed countries. "Allow me to point out the irony of this situation," stated Brazil's finance minister: "countries that were references of good governance, of standards and codes for the financial systems," were now the same countries where financial problems were raging.[24] Or, as China's vice-premier reportedly told his U.S. counterparts at an October 2008 meeting, "The teachers now have some problems."[25] One Chinese financial regulator also added that "the western consensus on the relation between the market and the government should be reviewed. In practice, they tend to overestimate the power of the market and overlook the regulatory role of the government and this warped conception is at the root of the sub-prime crisis."[26]

But the global schadenfreude over the financial storm in the United States did not last long. After the storm swept across the Atlantic to Europe in late September, it moved on to affect emerging markets and developing countries. Although liquidity support, credit protection schemes, and bank recapitalization had prevented a collapse of financial systems in the developed world, emerging markets now began to feel the fallout from the turmoil. Many emerging market stock exchanges and currencies plunged in value, as the risk appetite of investors declined, credit lines were cut, capital was repatriated to cover losses, and commodity prices fell because of plunging global demand. Emerging market officials also raised concerns that some of the rescue measures, such as pressure on financial institutions receiving public money to increase domestic lending, were a form of "financial protectionism" that deprived them of much needed credit. This sudden stop and reversal in capital flows left a number of Eastern and Central European countries as well as Brazil, Turkey, South Africa, Pakistan, Indonesia, and South Korea looking increasingly vulnerable to the shift in market sentiment.

[24] As quoted in Steven R. Weisman, "Tables Turned: Poor Countries Wage Fingers at Rich Ones," *New York Times*, 22 October 2007.
[25] As quoted in "When Fortune Frowned," *The Economist*, 9 October 2008.
[26] As quoted in Jamil Anderlini, "China Says West's Lack of Market Oversight Led to Subprime Crisis," *Financial Times*, 28 May 2008.

Concerns about intrusive IMF conditionality led some of these governments to seek out bilateral or regional alternatives, but most were forced to turn reluctantly to the IMF. Thus, after initially appearing irrelevant to resolving the subprime crisis, the IMF was thrust back into the lending business. Iceland was the first country to receive a loan, in late October. This program was soon followed by new programs with the Ukraine, Hungary, Pakistan, Latvia, Belarus, Romania, and Serbia. At the time of this writing, it appears that a handful of other emerging markets also might turn to the IMF for assistance.

The Fund, mindful of the criticisms of its response to the Asian crisis, has overhauled how it lends money by offering higher amounts and tailoring loan terms to circumstances in the borrowing country. Unlike traditional IMF programs, the Fund has also developed new lending instruments that provide resources unconditionally to select borrowers. Reminiscent of the now defunct Contingent Credit Line (CCL), a facility the Fund developed in the aftermath of the Asian crisis, these new instruments are precautionary lending programs for countries with sound policies, not at risk of a crisis of their own making, but vulnerable to contagion effects from crises in other countries. Unlike the CCL, which was unsuccessful in attracting any borrowers because of a perceived stigma attached to it, the new IMF lending instruments have found greater success in getting countries to take out insurance in good times, with Mexico announcing in April 2009 that it had taken out a $47 billion credit line—the largest funding arrangement in IMF history. The Fund has designated as a high priority the overhaul of all its lending facilities.

The increased demand for Fund resources led it to disburse nearly $50 billion in loans between October 2008 and April 2009. Such heightened demand fostered new concerns over whether IMF resources, which stood at around $250 billion in October, were sufficient should additional borrowers emerge. Some observers also questioned whether these resources could have much impact when the assets at the disposal of financial market participants and many emerging market central banks are significantly larger.

To shore up the liquidity needs of Brazil, Mexico, Singapore, and South Korea, the Federal Reserve established a new $30 billion swap line with each country's central bank. Each of these emerging markets was judged to be systemically important and well managed, and where the additional liquidity would make a difference. To meet potential future demands on its resources, the IMF managing director asked member states to double the Fund's financial resources.

Under a February 2009 bilateral loan agreement, Japan agreed to lend the Fund up to $100 billion of its reserves. In April 2009, the G-20 committed to a $750 billion increase in IMF resources—triple what IMF management had initially requested. The new resources will come in several forms, with $500 billion likely to come from additional bilateral loan agreements and an enlargement of existing borrowing arrangements—the GAB as well as the New Arrangements to Borrow (a set of credit arrangements with member states, like the GAB, that was established in 1998).[27] An additional $250 billion will come in the form of a SDR allocation. These measures have received strong support from the United States and Britain.

The G-20 and the IMF also have been in discussions about floating the IMF's first bond—a mechanism through which China and others prefer to make their contributions. Although pleased by the commitment to increase IMF resources, officials in emerging markets, particularly large reserve-holding countries, such as Brazil, Russia, India, and China—the so-called BRICs—fear that there will be pressure to contribute ad hoc increases now against promises of governance reform in the future. They therefore are seeking alternative mechanisms through which to make their contributions and are also pushing strongly for a general quota increase.

Convening the G-20: Agendas for Reform

In October, Brown and Sarkozy, feeling some relief from the urgency of the crisis, turned to pressuring Bush, the outgoing U.S. president, to convene the leaders of the G-20 for a summit on international financial reform. Although less convinced of the need for what Sarkozy and others were billing as "Bretton Woods II," Bush agreed to hold the summit in mid-November. A second summit was convened in London in April 2009. (All the time of writing, a third is scheduled to be held in September 2009.) The decision to convene for the first time a summit of the leaders of the G-20 rather than the G-7 was a significant development for a number of reasons.

First, it marked recognition of the growing power of emerging markets in the world economy. Although emerging market leaders generally have kept a low profile at these summits, their mere presence has offered a symbolic breakthrough in form and has opened up the possibility for future substantive breakthroughs by which the interests and experiences of emerging markets will be more adequately reflected in international regulatory outcomes. Second, the summits have marked the beginning of reform negotiations that have the potential to fundamentally reshape the norms of financial governance. There is little doubt left from the rhetoric of some European and emerging market officials that they see the financial

---

[27] G-20 London Summit Communique, 2 April 2009.

turmoil as a "crisis" for beliefs that prioritized liberalization and self-regulation, and as an opportunity to reregulate the financial system. Indeed, in invoking the phrase "Bretton Woods II" these officials have cast this crisis as a foundational moment in the world economy. The financial turmoil has put advocates of liberalization and self-regulation on the defensive. That the United States and Britain, leading advocates of these norms, implemented a partial nationalization of their financial systems, and that this response was widely considered appropriate, is a striking indicator of how the financial turmoil has overturned long-held policy beliefs. Indeed, it is remarkable the extent to which government responses to the subprime crisis have turned orthodoxy on its head. Over the past decade the G-7 had lectured crisis-afflicted countries on the need to restore confidence by closing insolvent financial institutions, strengthening fiscal discipline, and raising interest rates. Then, when faced with their own financial crises, G-7 countries pursued precisely the opposite policies. Reflecting on the shift in long-held policy norms, one informed observer suggested that now "intervention is [a] capital idea."[28]

But it is not yet clear whether greater regulation and intervention has become the new orthodoxy. Advocates of liberalization and self-regulation, though weakened, still resist efforts to reregulate. As the subprime crisis unfolded, the private financial community once again sought to preempt—or at least weaken—government regulatory efforts by developing voluntary codes of conduct. Over the past decade this had proven to be an effective strategy because of the Anglo-American belief in self-regulation. The IIF released two reports on the crisis that, while admitting mistakes bankers had made, claimed that the industry should develop new codes of conduct to regulate itself.[29] Addressing "skepticism about whether voluntary industry best practice is a credible alternative to sound supervisory arrangements," Charles Dallara insisted that "recent painful experience combined with market pressures are likely to be the strongest drivers of higher standards of conduct."[30]

But in the midst of what the IMF has called "the most dangerous shock in mature financial markets since the 1930s," governments have proven to be less sympathetic to self-regulatory initiatives.[31] Indeed, many G-7

[28] Peter Thal Larsen, "Amid Tumult, Intervention Is Capital Idea," *Financial Times*, 7 October 2008.

[29] IIF, *Interim Report of the IIF Committee on Market Best Practices* (Washington, D.C.: IIF, 2008); IIF, *Final Report of the IIF Committee on Market Best Practices: Principles of Conduct and Best Practice Recommendations* (Washington, D.C.: IIF, 2008).

[30] Charles Dallara, "How Banks Can Put Their Houses in Order," *Financial Times*, 12 May 2008.

[31] As quoted in Alan Beattie, "IMF Sees Greatest Shock since 1930s," *Financial Times*, 8 October 2008.

officials have made it clear that banks will have to accept greater regulation.[32] Prominent observers, such as Martin Wolf, have responded similarly, noting that the Bear Sterns rescue had revealed "liberalisation's limit" and that the implication of the rescue was that "there will have to be far greater regulation of such institutions."[33] "The end of lightly regulated finance," writes Wolf, "has come far closer."[34] Even Christopher Cox, SEC chairman during the Bush administration and a prominent advocate of self-regulation, conceded in September 2008 that "the last six months have made it abundantly clear that voluntary regulation does not work."[35]

Initially, in April 2008, former Federal Reserve Chairman Greenspan sought to defend self-regulation based on conventional arguments that regulation could not keep pace with marketplace innovation and would only harm economic performance. But following the intensification of the crisis in September, Greenspan was forced to concede, "I made a mistake in presuming that the self-interest of organizations, specifically banks and others, was such that they were best capable of protecting their own shareholders."[36] With one of the most prominent prophets of self-regulation admitting problems with the approach, remaining advocates of self-regulation clearly face an uphill battle.

The position of the United States as the leading advocate of liberalization and self-regulation has been weakened at the G-20 summits. Following the largest government intervention in the economy since the New Deal, it has become increasingly difficult for the United States to sell market-oriented policy norms. Until the subprime crisis, it was possible to hold up the U.S. system as a model for other countries to emulate. But the subprime crisis has made it hard for the United States to persuade other countries that its failures were not due to the principles of liberalization and self-regulation.

But this weakened normative authority has not prevented the United States from pressing its views at the summits, often, as discussed below, with some success. U.S. officials have come to the summits determined to resist what they perceive as European efforts to impose heavy-handed

[32] Chris Giles and Krishna Guha, "Banks' Self-Regulation Plan Shunned," *Financial Times*, 13 April 2008.

[33] Martin Wolf, "The Rescue of Bear Sterns Marks Liberalisation's Limit," *Financial Times*, 25 March 2008. See also Wolf, "Why Financial Regulation Is Both Difficult and Essential," *Financial Times*, 16 April 2008.

[34] Martin Wolf, "The End of Lightly Regulated Finance Has Come Far Closer," *Financial Times*, 16 September 2008.

[35] As quoted in Stephen Labaton, "S.E.C. Concedes Oversight Flaws Fueled Collapse," *New York Times*, 26 September 2008.

[36] As quoted in Alan Beattie and James Politi, "'I Made a Mistake' Admits Greenspan," *Financial Times*, 23 October 2008.

regulation. In their view, Europe had suffered similar problems despite its tougher regulations. U.S. officials also sought to shift some of the blame for the crisis from regulatory failures to the global macroeconomic imbalances, and in particular reserve accumulation and low consumption in Asia and oil-exporting countries as well as structural issues in Europe.

On the other hand, the Europeans, with France and Germany leading the charge, have pushed for greater regulation and to place blame for the crisis on deregulation. China has also sided with this position, with one central bank official recently referring to the view that Asian policy practices helped trigger the subprime crisis as "extremely ridiculous and irresponsible and it's 'gangster logic.' The 'China-responsible theory' is an attempt by major western economies to find an excuse for their own policy and regulatory failures."[37] Britain has joined France and Germany in focusing on the broad outlines of reform, but it has also sought to protect the City of London from European regulatory initiatives.

In keeping with their preference for reregulation, France and Germany also have sought to remake the IMF into a global supervisor of financial regulators. In the past the United States had been rather successful in sidelining Franco-German efforts to strengthen the IMF. Stanley Fischer, who was IMF first deputy managing director at the time, claims that the FSF was set up in a way that ensured the IMF could not be closely involved in financial regulation. Fischer insists that the creation of the FSF was a move by some developed countries to keep the IMF in its place, that is, an institution that the G-7 would not have to listen to.[38] Although the subprime crisis has weakened the U.S. hand, the United States has been joined by some European countries in opposing a global financial regulator. Interestingly, indicative of how an organization's professional norms can trump bureaucratic motives for task expansion, Strauss-Kahn also has argued against the idea because of concerns that it is not supported by the organization's professional expertise and skill set.[39] A recent IMF staff report on lessons from the crisis for the international financial architecture also stops short of supporting the transformation of the IMF into a global financial regulator, saying that mechanism for information sharing and risk assessment generally worked well in normal times.[40]

[37] As quoted in "China Central Bank Attacks Paulson's 'Gangster Logic,'" Bloomberg News, 16 January 2009.

[38] Camilla Andersen, "Future Role of IMF Is Debated as Financial Crisis Takes Toll," *IMF Survey* 37, no. 11 (2008), pp. 176–177.

[39] Beattie and Guha, "IMF Chief Curbs Summit Expectations," *Financial Times*, 7 November 2008.

[40] IMF, *Initial Lessons*.

Unlike the 1944 Bretton Woods Conference, the G-20 summits, as Eric Helleiner and Stefano Pagliari observe, did "not begin with a tabula rasa."[41] In addition to the IIF reports discussed earlier, the IMF, the FSF, the BIS, and other organizations had been developing regulatory responses to the crisis since early 2008. The most politically prominent diagnosis has focused on outdated and inadequate prudential regulations. In this "crisis construction," securitization, which transferred credit risk to parties far from the original source, obscured the ability and weakened the diligence of market participants, regulators, and CRAs to monitor and evaluate risk. Many aspects of the securities market had been left with little or no regulation because of support for self-regulation as well as a belief that the originate-to-distribute model had enhanced systemic risk and deepened market liquidity.

But once the crisis broke, the opaqueness and dispersion of risk associated with that model intensified the loss of confidence and uncertainties about the exposure of financial institutions to particular assets. "Over-the-counter" (OTC) derivatives, and CDS in particular, proved to be particularly opaque and to pose enormous challenges. These derivatives, which are negotiated privately without a centralized exchange that can minimize counterparty risk and force margin requirements for all contracts, were left unregulated over the last decade. During the crisis these derivatives were at the heart of AIG's near collapse, and exacerbated investors' concerns after the collapse of Lehman, as market participants struggled with uncertainty about the amount of CDS issued on Lehman debt.

In addition to securitization, another important development was the creation of off-balance-sheet SIVs, which banks used to evade capital regulatory requirements. Alongside the growth of this "shadow banking system," other financial institutions, such as investment banks and hedge funds, became increasingly entangled in the financial system even though they were not covered by the same regulations as commercial banks. When one of these institutions, Bear Sterns, became "too entangled to fail" and public money was used to rescue it, the event focused the attention of U.S. officials (and others) on whether investment banks should be covered by the same regulations as commercial banks.

Many officials and observers have concluded that securitization and the development of SIVs revealed the failure of capital adequacy rules developed by the BCBS. Some argue that the entire Basel II framework should be scrapped, as the crisis has discredited its chief innovations of relying on CRAs and the internal risk management systems of large banks.

[41] Eric Helleiner and Stefano Pagliari, "The G20 Leaders' Agenda for International Financial Regulation," *New Political Economy* (2009), forthcoming.

But amid these calls to scrap Basel II, many believe it can be salvaged. The answer, they suggest, is to close the regulatory loopholes, focus more on systemic risks, and strengthen transparency and risk management. Overall, this diagnosis and response offers a modest reform agenda, one that seeks to update the existing regulatory framework but that has thus far stopped short of more radical regulatory measures. Nonetheless, this is the agenda the FSF, backed by the G-7, has supported in most of its analysis and recommendations.

During the course of the crisis, the FSF outlined over sixty recommendations to modernize the existing regulatory framework.[42] The British Treasury's white paper on finanacial reform, the FSA's Turner review, as well as a February 2009 regulatory review completed for the European Commission by a group of experts chaired by former IMF managing director Larosière, have backed most of these recommendations.[43] Many of the FSF's recommendations are also consistent with potential changes being considered for the EU's Capital Requirements Directive, a supervisory framework that provides rules on capital measurement and adequacy for financial institutions. The views of the Obama administration, which in March 2009 proposed a sweeping overhaul of the U.S. regulatory framework, are also broadly in line with many of the FSF's recommendations.[44] In addition to the changes outlined in the proposed regulatory overhaul, a January 2009 report from a group of experts chaired by Paul Volcker, the former Federal Reserve chairman and a key advisor in the Obama administration, was also in broad agreement with the FSF's recommendations.[45]

Banks will be forced to set aside more capital against complex structured products and off-balance-sheet vehicles. Banks will also be required to follow new BCBS guidelines on liquidity management to respond to future abrupt changes in market liquidity.[46] The FSF endorsed ongoing measures to enhance disclosure and transparency, as well as the creation of a "college of supervisors" from different countries to strengthen monitoring of large cross-border financial institutions. It also urged strengthening of the oversight of CRSs and their methodologies. The FSF also encouraged market participants to develop a more robust infrastructure and

[42] FSF, *Report of the Financial Stability Forum on Enhancing Market and Institutional Resilience* (Basel: FSF, 2008).
[43] HM Treasury, *Reforming Financial Markets* (London, July 2009); Financial Services Authority, *The Turner Review*; High-Level Group on Financial Supervision in the EU, *Report* (Brussels, 25 February 2009).
[44] "Treasury Outlines Framework for Regulatory Reform," U.S. Treasury Press Release TG-72, 26 March 2009.
[45] Working Group on Financial Reform, *Financial Reform: A Framework for Financial Stability* (New York: Group of Thirty, 2009).
[46] BCBS, *Principles for Sound Liquidity Management and Supervision* (Basel: BIS, 2008).

clearing system for OTC derivatives. The organization representing this sector, the International Swaps and Derivatives Association (ISDA), has since moved forward in working with U.S. and European regulators to develop such an infrastructure.

The FSF also asked leading international accounting-standard-setting bodies to explore revision of their practices, which were found to suffer weaknesses in valuing assets in illiquid markets and in shining light on the opaque relationship between financial institutions and their off-balance-sheet vehicles. The International Accounting Standards Body (IASB), whose standards are employed in over one hundred countries, is currently revising its standards to address these weaknesses. Some actors, critical of the procyclicality of fair value accounting, have called for a fundamental rethinking of these standards. In May 2008, the IIF, though it had supported this principle when asset prices were rising, pressed for a relaxation of it when the financial turmoil worsened. In September 2008, it sent a confidential memo to the IASB and its U.S. counterpart, the Financial Accounting Standards Board (FASB), asking for a suspension of fair value accounting for "sound" assets suffering "undervaluation."

But some members of the IIF opposed this request. Goldman Sachs, for instance, resigned from the organization in protest at what it called "Alice in Wonderland accounting."[47] While recognizing the procyclicality of fair value accounting, the IMF staff have also opposed abandoning the principle. The October 2008 *GFSR* proposed some minor modifications to the principle, but accepted it as "the preferred accounting framework for financial institutions."[48]

Nonetheless, critics of the principle have moved ahead with measures to relax fair value accounting. In late September, Sarkozy pressed for suspension of the principle to give European financial institutions breathing space in the midst of the panic.[49] In mid-October, the IASB responded to this pressure by suspending the principle for some holdings and later published guidelines on the application of fair value accounting in distressed market conditions. In April 2009, the FASB, also in response to political pressure, introduced its own changes that will make it easier for firms to value their assets using their own internal models rather than market prices. Despite pressure for the IASB to follow suit, it announced it would forgo further relaxation of its standards until it could complete a thorough review.

[47] Francesco Gerrera, "Goldman Set to Sever IIF Links," *Financial Times*, 23 May 2008.

[48] IMF, *Global Financial Stability Report* (October) (Washington, D.C.: IMF, 2008), p. 105. See also Alicia Novoa, Jodi Scarlata, and Juan Solé, "Procyclicality and Fair Value Accounting," IMF Working Paper WP/09/39 (Washington, D.C.: IMF, 2009).

[49] Ben Hall and Nikki Tait, "Sarkozy Seeks EU Accounting Change," *Financial Times*, 30 September 2008.

Yet some European officials seem keen to do more, with the Larosière review calling for "a wider reflection on the mark-to-market principle and in particular recommends that . . . accounting standards should not. . . promote pro-cyclical behavior."[50] A prominent member of the European Commission has also warned the IASB that it did "not live in a political vacuum" but "in the real world" and that the EU could yet move ahead with different rules.[51] However, the FSA has been more supportive of fair value accounting, and has suggested that some of the procyclical tendencies it induces can be counteracted through dynamic provisioning and capital adequacy requirements.[52]

Although some leading Democratic legislators were successful in pressuring the FASB to relax fair value accounting, U.S. Treasury Secretary Timothy Geithner and Federal Reserve Chairman Ben Bernanke have expressed some reservations about suspending the practice.[53] In fact, the FASB's decision complicates the Obama administration's asset management plan. If banks can select between keeping assets on their balance sheets, at value of their choosing, and selling them to the government, written down to a fair price, the risk is that they will select the former option rather than the latter. Banks could thus potentially continue on for an indefinite period saddled with distressed assets valued at unrealistic prices. In addition, the pressure on standard setters to relax accounting rules and give bank managers greater discretion oddly contrasts with the current thrust toward reregulation, which seeks to bring private market actors under greater public control. Not surprisingly, since the FASB's decision the Obama administration has rolled out a significantly scaled back version of its original plan.

Despite the broad consensus on the need for reregulation, agreement on how to manage the challenges posed by hedge funds has proven elusive. As in the past, hedge funds have been accused in the subprime crisis as having amplified downward pressure of asset prices through short selling. As a result, some officials have renewed the push to regulate the industry. Sarkozy, for instance, has called for creating a "regulated capitalism in which whole swathes of the financial activity won't be left to the sole judgment of market dealers." "No financial institution," Sarkozy insisted,

---

[50] High-Level Group on Financial Supervision in the EU, *Report*, p. 22.

[51] As quoted in "Messenger, Shot," *The Economist*, 11 April 2009. In July 2009, the ISAB proposed new rules that would give institutions more freedom in how they report their assets but that also underline the principle of using market prices where possible.

[52] Financial Services Authority, *The Turner Review*, pp. 62–67.

[53] Ben S. Bernanke, "Financial Reform to Address Systemic Risk," Speech at the Council on Foreign Relations, Washington, D.C., 10 March 2009; Tom Braithwaite and Sarah O'Connor, "Congress Warns on Mark-to-Market Rule," *Financial Times*, 12 March 2009.

"should escape regulation and supervision."[54] Support for comprehensive financial regulation has come from Germany as well as the European Parliament, which, in September 2008, passed a resolution calling on the European Commission to propose measures that would cover "all relevant actors and financial market participants, including hedge funds and private equity" and make them subject to mandatory capital requirements.[55] The Commission has since proposed a new directive that seeks to create a comprehensive framework for the direct regulation of hedge funds and private equity, with its president signaling his intention that "no financial player should be exempt from regulation and oversight. This is a clear commitment on our part. It means that hedge funds and private equity must be covered."[56]

Pressure to regulate the hedge fund industry thus is likely to continue to grow. The subprime crisis has taken its toll on the industry, weakening the viability of its business model, which depends on high levels of leverage, and undermining the persuasiveness of its arguments that hedge funds help the process of price discovery and stabilize markets by acting as "contrarian" investors. In addition, hedge funds have also been weakened by recent poor performance and a wave of redemptions that saw assets under their management fall in 2008 for the first time in their recorded history, ending eighteen years of asset growth.[57]

Nonetheless, hedge funds continue to find some allies among U.S. and British officials. For instance, while conceding that "in principle" comprehensive regulation "would appear well justified," Bernanke recently cautioned that "this more comprehensive approach would be technically demanding and possibly very costly both for the regulators and the firms they supervise."[58] In June 2008, Timothy Geithner, then president of the FRBNY, argued against extending capital regulatory requirements to hedge funds and instead supported strengthening counterparty risk management.[59] As Treasury secretary in the Obama administration, Geithner has moved closer to the Franco-German position, indicating his support,

[54] As quoted in Helleiner and Pagliari, "G20 Leaders' Agenda."
[55] Nikki Tait, "McCreevy Firm on Financial Regulation," *Financial Times*, 10 September 2008.
[56] As quoted in Nikki Tait, "Private Equity Funds Must Be Regulated," Says EU, *Financial Times*, 14 January 2009. "Financial Services: Commission Proposes EU Framework for Managers of Alternative Investment Funds," Europa Press Release IP/09/669 (29 April 2009).
[57] Deborah Brewster, "Money Flows Out of Hedge Funds at Record Rate," *Financial Times*, 30 December 2008.
[58] Bernanke, "Reducing Systemic Risk," speech at the Federal Reserve Bank of Kansas City's Annual Economic Symposium, Jackson Hole, Wyoming, 22 August 2008.
[59] Geithner, "Reducing Risk in the Financial System," *Financial Times*, 8 June 2008.

as part of the proposed regulatory overhaul, for requiring for the first time that all hedge funds register with the government and disclose information on a confidential basis on their trades and debt levels. Such information would then been passed to a "systemic risk regulator" that could judge whether risks were building in the financial system. Diverging from the view he expressed in June 2008, Geithner also has proposed as part of the regulatory overhaul that hedge funds of systemic importance would be subject to bank-like prudential regulation. The FSA's Turner review has outlined a similar approach, suggesting that hedge funds that are sufficiently bank-like in scale would have bank-style rules on capital and liquidity applied to them.

With the Obama administration moving closer to the European position, space has opened for a compromise position of sorts to be potentially staked out whereby all hedge funds would be subject to greater disclosure requirements, while only those that are of systemic importance would have additional bank-like prudential requirements imposed on them. In the run-up to the April 2009 G-20 summit, some European officials seemed open to considering such a compromise. However, while the Larosière report called for such a regulatory framework, the European Commission's proposed directive is tougher and more comprehensive than preferred by the U.S. and Britain.

The IMF staff, for their part, have supported many of the FSF recommendations, including strengthening risk and liquidity management, enhancing disclosure and transparency across all actors of the securitization chain, improving valuation standards in illiquid markets, and extending capital adequacy standards against structured credit products and off-balance-sheet vehicles.[60] But, significantly, the Fund has not hesitated from advocating more radical measures that at the time were not supported by some of its leading principals. Recall that in April 2008 the IMF managing director was one of the first prominent voices to break from orthodoxy and call for using public money to recapitalize the banking system. The FSF considered these measures at the time, but rejected them. Also recall that the Fund's staff have spoken out against the efforts of some governments to depart from fair value accounting.

Staff reports now argue for a more radical reform of existing regulation than those released prior to the subprime crisis. In the months prior to the first G-20 summit, the IMF staff began to highlight more forcefully the procyclical nature of existing regulations and industry practices and to call for creating a macro-prudential regulatory framework. Although

---

[60] IMF, "The Recent Financial Turmoil—Initial Assessment, Policy Lessons, and Implications for Fund Surveillance" (Washington, D.C.: IMF, 9 April 2008).

there is now a consensus among its leading principals in favor of mitigating procyclicality and strengthening macro-prudential regulation, the IMF staff began pressing for such reforms before widespread agreement had been reached. The April 2008 *WEO*, for instance, addressed directly the need for countercyclical regulatory policy, suggesting that "prudential and regulatory financial policies are also essential tools for constraining the procyclical mechanism in financial markets that tend to amplify the business cycle."[61] Similarly, in autumn 2008, Olivier Blanchard, the current RES director, argued, "Counter-cyclical macro-prudential rules appear to be a promising way to reduce the buildup of systemic risks, particularly if some regulators have responsibility for overall financial stability."[62] Blanchard also suggested measures to regulate the remuneration structure of financial market participants, arguing that "better incentive and executive compensation schemes can be introduced to limit excessive risk taking and too much focus on short term returns."[63]

With respect to regulating remuneration, the IMF has seemingly found many allies among its members. Amid a growing outcry against excesses in the financial system and the use of public money to rescue financial institutions, many of the Fund's leading principals, including the United States, Britain, France, and Germany, have made commitments to address compensation issues as part of their interventions. In Britain, in an October 2008 letter to chief executive officers of leading financial institutions, the FSA criticized the remuneration structure of many institutions for being "inconsistent with sound risk management."[64] In February 2009, it issued a draft code of conduct for remuneration policies and indicated that it would raise capital requirements on institutions that failed to comply.[65] Such restrictions would apply not only to senior management but also those below the management suite who absorb the bulk of the bonuses. The draft code contained prescriptive regulations that sought to delink bonuses from annual results and short-term indicators by providing deferred disbursements and permitting clawbacks as risks are realized over the long term. In October 2008, Australia's prime minister promised similar action, and, in May 2009, the Australian financial regulator issued a set

---

[61] IMF, *World Economic Outlook* (April) (Washington, D.C.: IMF, 2008), p. 123 n. 25. See also IMF, *Global Financial Stability Report* (October) (Washington, D.C.: IMF, 2008), pp. xiv, 109, 116, 129; IMF, *World Economic Outlook* (October) (Washington, D.C.: IMF, 2008), pp. xviii, 39.

[62] Olivier Blanchard, "The Tasks Ahead," IMF Working Paper WP/08/262 (Washington, D.C.: IMF, 2008), p. 6.

[63] Blanchard, "The Tasks Ahead," p. 6.

[64] Financial Services Authority, "Dear CEO" letter (13 October 2008)

[65] Financial Services Authority, "FSA Draft Code on Remuneration Policies" (26 February 2009; updated 18 March 2009).

of draft standards on remuneration.[66] Similar codes of conduct also have been unveiled or are being developed in France, Germany, the Netherlands, and Switzerland.[67]

But is unclear how serious governments are about drawing up regulations that delve into the detail of compensation. In the run-up to the April G-20 summit, Gordon Brown called for an international code on remuneration practices, but indicated that it should take the form of a set of guiding principles rather than binding perscriptive rules. Later, out of concern that its initial proposal could put Britain at a competitive disadvantage, the FSA's final code backed away from the draft code's prescriptive regulations on deferred bonus disbursements and clawbacks in favor of voluntary guidelines.[68] In addition, even though some financial market participants[69] have indicated that prescriptive regulation could be useful in some areas such as specifying the percentage of remuneration that should be deferred, the codes unveiled or being developed in Australia, France, Germany, the Netherlands, and Switzerland each explicitly highlight their continued reliance on a principles-based approach and voluntary compliance.

Before leaving office, Bush Treasury officials had imposed relatively modest restrictions on compensation that did not extend below the board level, leading one informed observer to suggest that they "look remarkably easy to meet."[70] Upon taking office, the Obama administration announced tighter restrictions on pay for executives at financial institutions that received public were money. But even these restrictions were not particularly radical; pay curbs were to be applied only to those institutions receiving future "exceptional assistance," with those receiving "general assistance" under TARP permitted to waive them if they fully disclosed their pay and

---

[66] Peter Smith, "Rudd Calls for Crackdown on Executive Pay," *Financial Times*, 15 October 2008; Australian Prudential Regulation Authority, "Discussion Paper: Remuneration" (28 May 2009); Australian Prudential Regulation Authority, "Prudential Practice Guide: PPG 511-Remuneration" (28 May 2009).

[67] French Banking Federation, "FBF Adopts Common Guidelines on the Compensation of Financial Market Professionals" (7 February 2009); Federal Financial Supervisory Authority, "New Minimum Requirements for Risk Management (MaRisk): BaFin Implements International Risk Management Standards" (14 August 2009); De Nederlandsche Bank and the Netherlands Authority for the Financial Markets, "Principles for Sound Compensation Policies" (May 2009); Swiss Financial Market Supervisory Authority, "Circular 2009/Remuneration Systems: Minimum Standards for Remuneration Systems of Financial Institutions" (June 2009).

[68] Financial Services Authority, "Reforming Remuneration Practices in Financial Services," Policy Statement 09/15 (August 2009).

[69] IIF, *Compensation in Financial Services: Industry Progress an the Agenda for Change* (Washington, DC: IIF, 2009).

[70] Andrew Hill, "It Will Be Bloody If Regulators Take Axe to Bonuses," *Financial Times*, 14 October 2008.

held nonbinding shareholder votes. The pay curbs also were aimed mainly at top executives, suggesting that other employees could escape the restrictions. Later, Congress introduced tougher restrictions by capping bonuses for institutions that had already received public money, not just those receiving funds in the future. However, as in Britain, concerns about competitiveness have since led the Obama administration to scrap its earlier pay curbs and emphasis on prescriptive regulations in favor of voluntary guidelines and stronger shareholder oversight. Although the Obama administration has indicated its approac is intended to mark the start of a long-term effort to reform remuneration in the financial sector, at the time of writing it is not clear how radical such reforms will be.

Even in France, where the economy minister once attacked "perverse" pay structures that lead to "greedy and blind behavior," the government left it to the private sector to design a code of conduct for pay based largely on IIF recommendations.[71] However, France was the first developed country to impose restrictions on future bonuses in an effort to prevent excessive risk-taking, and the country's financial regulator has indicated it will monitor compliance with the code of conduct. Among pan-European regulators, the Larosière review recommends delinking bonuses from short-term results and calls on regulators to monitor the suitability of remuneration practices and, where necessary, to raise capital requirements on institutions that fail to comply. Although the Larosière review envisions implementing such reforms in a gradual fashion over several years, the European Commission, after unveiling two non-binding recommendations on remuneration in April 2009, has fast-tracked such reforms as part of potential changes being considered for the EU's Capital Requirements Directive, which, if implemented, would give regulators the power to raise capital requirements on institutions with compensation policies that fail to comply.[72]

The FSF, for its part, has developed a set of principles for compensation.[73] Yet while identifying compensation schemes as one issue that merits scrutiny, the FSF has stopped short of making a firm commitment on regulating them. Instead, one FSF report suggested that regulators should

[71] As quoted in Michael Peel and George Parker, "Brown Attacks 'Irresponsible' City Bonuses," *Financial Times*, 21 September 2008. Hall, "Paris Warns on Executive Pay," *Financial Times*, 7 October 2008.

[72] Europa, "Directors' Pay: Commission Sets Out Further Guidance on Structure and Determination of Director's Remuneration," IP/09/673 (29 April 2009); Europa, "Financial Services Sector Pay: Commission Sets Out Principles on Remuneration of Risk-Taking Staff in Financial Institutions," IP/09/674 (29 April 2009); Europa, "Commission Proposes Further Revision of Banking Regulation to Strengthen Rules on Bank Capital and on Remuneration in the Banking Sector," IP/09/1120 (13 July 2009).

[73] FSF, "Principles for Sound Compensation Practices," 2 April 2009.

work with the private sector to help mitigate risks.[74] Ultimately, despite public outrage over perceived excesses in the financial system, especially the payment of bonuses at some institutions after they had received public money, politicians and regulators have gradually backed away from radical measures to restrict remuneration practices.

After the initial onset of the crisis, there was some reluctance to reform the content of the existing regulatory framework by supporting dynamic provisioning as well as dynamic capital adequacy requirements that would force banks to build up capital in good times that they can draw upon in weaker times. The IIF opposes such requirements on the grounds that they will add more conservatism to banking and act as a drag on growth. Yet the Fund's leading principals opened the door to considering such regulations in June 2008, and since then a head of steam has been building behind such reforms.

Following their June 2008 meeting, for example, the G-8 finance ministers indicated that they "look forward to work on mitigating pro-cyclicality in the financial system."[75] In describing "an increased focus on system-wide risks by regulators and supervisors" as "inevitable and desirable," Bernanke argued in August 2008 that "we should critically examine capital regulations, provisioning policies, and other rules applied to financial institutions to determine whether, collectively, they increase procyclicality of credit extension beyond the point that is best for the system as a whole."[76] Bernanke has since spoken out more strongly in favor of strengthening macro-prudential supervision and reducing procyclical tendencies through dynamic provisioning and dynamic capital adequacy requirements.[77] Geithner, as part of the Obama administration's proposed regulatory overhaul, has also indicated that capital requirements and provisions against loan losses will also likely be made countercyclical for systemically important entities. The British Treasury, the FSA, the European Commission, the Larosière review, the FSF, and the BCBS have also moved forward in exploring measures to mitigate procyclicality.[78] In December 2008, fore-

[74] FSF, *Report of the Financial Stability Forum on Enhancing Market and Institutional Resilience: Follow-Up on Implementation* (Basel: FSF, 2008), p. 14.

[75] G-8 Finance Ministers, Statement of the G-8 Finance Ministers Meeting, Osaka, Japan, 14 June 2008, available at www.g7.utoronto.ca/finance/fm080614-statement.pdf

[76] Bernanke, "Reducing Systemic Risk."

[77] See, for instance, Ben S. Bernanke, "The Crisis and the Policy Response," Stamp Lecture, London School of Economics, 13 January 2009.

[78] HM Treasury, *Reforming Financial Markets*; Financial Services Authority, *The Turner Review*; High-Level Group on Financial Supervision in the EU, *Report*; FSF, in "Report of the Financial Stability Forum on Addressing Procyclicality in the Financial System," 2 April 2009; Nout Wellink, Basel Committee Initiatives in Response to the Financial Crisis, Remarks before the Committee on Economic and Monetary Affairs of the European Parliament, Brussels (30 March 2009).

shadowing the move toward a new macro-prudential regulatory ethos, Swiss regulators introduced new measures that aim to restrain asset growth when times are good. The country's largest banks now face higher risk-weighted capital requirements and a new cap (or leverage ratio) on the amount of total assets that they can hold regardless of their risks.

Although there is now widespread consensus about the importance of addressing procyclicality, at the time of writing there were still lingering differences on what should be done to mitigate it. Accountants, for instance, have taken a determined stand to resist efforts to implement dynamic provisioning. After years of promoting greater transparency in accounting, many in the accounting industry are concerned that dynamic provisioning could give rise to accounting gimmicks designed to smooth and flatten earnings. Provisioning, many accountants argue, could permit the use of one of the best-known gimmicks—"cookie jar accounting"—where executives pad out provisions in good times, then quietly let the excess flow out in tough times to hide poor performance. Dynamic provisioning, accountants fear, could therefore make banks' balance sheets less transparent. The IASB is currently in discussions with regulators about having regulatory provisions reported separately from normal loan loss reserves to avoid the risk of cookie jars reappearing.

Others suggest that the success of Spain's system of dynamic provisioning has been oversold. Heading into the crisis, its two largest banks had an extra buffer equivalent to about 1.5 percent of risk-weighted assets, but banks like UBS or Citigroup had write-offs that went far beyond the extra buffer that would have been provided had dynamic provisioning been used.[79] There are also challenges for implementing dynamic capital adequacy requirements, such as the choice of index of systemic risk and the degree of procyclicality that regulators wish to mitigate. Divisions over these issues were revealed in a recent IMF board discussion of staff recommendations to consider countercyclical regulatory measures. The board "generally saw merit in giving consideration to introducing a macroeconomic element in the financial prudential framework to weigh against the inherent procyclicality of credit creation." But "a number" of directors "pointed to the complexities that this involves and questioned the potential benefits."[80]

Some economists have suggested that more radical measures are needed. Like the emerging markets crises before it, the subprime crisis has led some economists to renew calls for restricting capital mobility. These economists diagnose excessive capital mobility as having amplified, if not caused, the

---

[79] "Regulating Banks: Inadequate," *The Economist*, 12 March 2009.

[80] IMF Executive Board Discussion of the Outlook, September 2008, printed in IMF, *World Economic Outlook* (October) (Washington, D.C.: IMF, 2008), pp. 241–245 at p. 245.

subprime crisis. As Rodrik and Subramanian observe, "Even though the roots of the subprime crisis lie in domestic finance, international capital flows magnified its scale." This alternative crisis construction points to the capital flow bonanza the United States (and other developed countries) experienced in the years prior to outbreak of the financial turmoil and the manner in which it created housing bubbles that soon burst.

Renewing earlier arguments that capital controls could be used to protect poorly regulated financial systems, advocates of this view suggest restricting capital mobility as a more effective means of minimizing financial instability than updating regulations. "If the risk-taking behavior of financial intermediaries cannot be regulated perfectly," Rodrik and Subramanian argue, "we need to find ways of reducing the volume of transactions."[81] To achieve this reduction, the two economists argue that emerging markets and developing countries should raise Chilean-style taxes on capital inflows.

The fragmented nature of European financial regulation has led other economists to make similar arguments for EU countries. "In cases where there is not a single regulator/supervisor for the markets/instruments or for the entities and their foreign parents, subsidiaries and branches in all countries where they are active," Willem Buiter argues, the EU should "permit capital controls and barriers to entry by foreign entities."[82] A recent report from a United Nations advisory panel on international monetary and financial reform, chaired by Stiglitz, has also called for the use of capital controls, particularly by developing countries. "In the absence of better systems of risk mitigation," the report argues, "it is especially important for developing countries to be wary of measures that expose them to greater risk and volatility, such as capital market liberalization. Developing countries should use all the tools at their disposal, price interventions, quantitative restrictions, and prudential regulations, in order to manage international capital flows."[83] The report also calls for the Fund to return to its "first principles" and support governments that impose controls in support of domestic countercyclical policy. Others, such as Calvo, point to controls as "useful tools" for offsetting sudden-stop disruptions in capital flows, such as those faced by emerging markets and developing countries when contagion from the subprime crisis spread.[84]

The subprime crisis has also heightened the skepticism some developed country governments have of capital mobility, particularly speculative prac-

---

[81] Rodrik and Subramanian, "We Must Curb Global Flows."

[82] Willem H. Buiter, "Some Suggestions for the G20 on November 15th," in Eichengreen and Baldwin, *What G20 Leaders Must Do*, pp. 17–20 at p. 19.

[83] The Commission of Experts on Reforms of the International Monetary and Financial System, *Recommendations* (New York: United Nations, 2009).

[84] Calvo, "New Bretton Woods Agreement."

tices. Sarkozy, for instance, has called for "a capitalism in which banks do their job, and the job of the banks is to finance economic development, it isn't speculation."[85] Along these lines, German officials suggested a permanent ban on "purely speculative" short-selling at the October 2008 meeting of the G-7.[86] Emerging market officials have tended to support capital controls, along with "self-insurance" policies, as being an effective way to minimize pressures from contagion. India, for instance, which suffered massive capital outflows from its stock market after the spread of the crisis, has pushed for a global monitoring system for stock markets to prevent capital flight.[87]

A number of emerging markets, such as Argentina, Indonesia, Russia, and Ukraine, also have recently imposed controls on outflows as a way of managing pressures from the crisis. Although controls on outflows are often used as a way of managing crisis pressures, their use has raised concern among some financial market participants that they could become a legitimate part of policymakers' toolkits well beyond emergency measures. As one recent Citigroup report notes, "A policy consensus dominated by a focus on reregulation might be expected to place less emphasis on the wisdom of globally unrestricted capital movements."[88]

But the call for restraining capital mobility has not been very prominent. While the IMF accommodated temporary controls on outflows as part of its programs with Iceland and Ukraine, it has not encouraged others to follow suit.[89] Indeed, while noting the role that capital flow bonanzas played in contributing to the crisis, a 2009 IMF staff report noted, "Surely, the lesson is not that capital flows should be sharply curtailed."[90] However, this has not prevented some financial market participants from expressing concerns that the IMF has accommodated controls on outflows in these countries as a way of "bailing in" private sector creditors by ensuring IMF loans did not finance capital flight.[91] Yet arguments about burden sharing have thus far not featured in the IMF's discussions of crisis management. Nonetheless, the staff have observed that the crisis, as well as many crises before it, showed the potential dangers of capital inflow

[85] As quoted in Helleiner and Pagliari, "G20 Leaders' Agenda."

[86] FT Reporters, "UK Plan to Support Lending Rebuffed," *Financial Times*, 9 October 2008.

[87] Michiyo Nakamoto, "Japan to Lend $100bn for Emerging Nations," *Financial Times*, 13 November 2008.

[88] David P. Lubin, "Emerging Markets: The Return of Capital Controls?" unpublished manuscript, Citigroup, 5 January 2009.

[89] Camilla Andersen, "Iceland Gets Help to Recover from Crisis," *IMF Survey* 37, no. 12 (2008), pp. 185–187.

[90] IMF, *Initial Lessons*, p. 6.

[91] Lubin, "Emerging Markets."

bonanzas and pointed to the "potential role of prudential measures to reduce systemic risk associated with large capital inflows—e.g. through constraints on the foreign exchange exposure of domestic institutions and
other borrowers."[92]

Despite the severity of the crisis, leading IMF principals have not yet
wavered in their commitment to capital freedom. Britain's Chancellor of
the Exchequer, for example, wrote to his G-20 colleagues that "the key to
retaining faith in financial markets is to establish and maintain a consensus
within the G20 and elsewhere as to the importance of open capital markets."[93] The United States has also remained steadfast in its commitment
to capital freedom. Helleiner suggests this is likely due to the fact that the
United States has yet to experience the type of capital outflow surge and
exchange rate crisis that many emerging market countries suffered in
1997–1998.[94] Yet Helleiner speculates that controls could command
greater political support from the United States and other developed countries if the subprime crisis were to spill over into a dollar crisis, a possibility
that he and others, such as George Soros, have not ruled out.[95]

RESULTS OF THE G-20 SUMMITS

The leaders of the G-20 countries came together at their November 2008
and April 2009 summits to discuss these diagnoses and prescriptions. The
result of the November summit was a declaration that included a statement
of principles and an action plan for reform.[96] The April summit communiqué followed with a more specific statement of principles, largely focused
on strengthening financial regulation and key international financial institutions.[97] In identifying the "root causes" of the crisis, the November
declaration concluded that "policymakers, regulators and supervisors, in
some advanced countries, did not adequately appreciate the risks building
up in financial markets, keep pace with financial innovation, or take

[92] IMF, *Initial Lessons*, p. 8. See also IMF, *Lessons of the Global Crisis for Macroeconomic Policy* (Washington, D.C.: IMF, 2009), p. 4.

[93] Alistair Darling, Chancellor's Letter to G20 Members, 7 January 2009.

[94] Helleiner, "Crisis and Response, The Story So Far: Five Regulatory Agendas in Search of an Outcome," *International Politics and Society* (2009), forthcoming.

[95] Helleiner, "Political Determinants of International Currencies: What Future for the US Dollar?" *Review of International Political Economy* 15, no. 2 (2008), pp. 352–376; George Soros, *The New Paradigm for Financial Markets: The Credit Crisis of 2008 and What It Means* (New York: Public Affairs, 2008).

[96] G-20, Declaration, Summit on Financial Markets and the World Economy (15 November 2008).

[97] G-20 London Summit communiqué, 2 April 2009.

into account the systemic ramifications of domestic regulatory actions." The April communiqué offered similar language, indicating that "major failures in the financial sector and financial regulation and supervision were fundamental causes of the crisis." Yet the November declaration, reflecting the efforts of U.S. officials to shift some of the blame away from regulatory failures, also identified global macroeconomic imbalances as a "major underlying" factor. Interestingly, the April communiqué contained no such language.

The tone of the two statements, which seek to strengthen regulation, represents a partial victory for the Europeans who initially brought the Americans to the negotiating table and got them to sign on to a regulatory agenda. But the United States has also been successful in resisting the inclination of some to blame free market capitalism for the crisis, securing agreement in the November declaration that "reforms will only be successful if grounded in a commitment to free market principles." Similarly, the United States gained a victory in the April communiqué by securing agreement "that the only sure foundation for sustainable globalization and prosperity for all is an open economy based on market principles."

The November declaration opened up the possibility that new regulatory action will be comprehensive in scope, pledging to "ensure that all financial markets, products and participants are regulated or subject to oversight as appropriate to their circumstances." But Bush Treasury officials insisted at the time that this language, pushed by the Europeans, did not imply that all hedge funds and other private pools of capital would be subject to direct regulation. Emphasis, U.S. officials claimed, would be placed on the phrase "as appropriate to their circumstances." Indeed, in a clear defeat for Germany, the November declaration simply notes the development of industry-led codes of conduct for hedge funds and other private pools of capital and asks "private sector bodies" to "bring forward" additional proposals that the G-20 will monitor.

But, as suggested above, in the period between the November and April summits, U.S. and British officials moved closer to the European position, indicating they were prepared to impose bank-like prudential regulation on hedge funds of systemic importance as well as tougher disclosure requirements on all hedge funds. This permitted agreement to be reached on extending the regulatory net to some hedge funds. As the April communiqué notes, "We agree . . . to extend regulation and oversight to all systemically important financial institutions, instruments, and markets. This will include, for the first time, systemically important hedge funds."[98] Still, the G-20 remains split, primarily between the United States and

[98] In addition to the April G-20 communiqué, see also G-20 Declaration on Strengthening the Financial System, 2 April 2009.

Britain, on the one hand, and France and Germany, on the other, over how aggressively to regulate hedge funds. France and Germany favor a tougher regulatory regime for all hedge funds, while U.S. and British officials continue to place the emphasis primarily on enhancing disclosure. It also remains to been seen how regulators will define hedge funds of "systemic importance"—often which funds meet this designation is only known after they fail. Moreover, designating certain funds as "systemically important" could encourage them to take on excessive risk if they are "too big to fail." Funds not designated "systemically important" could also face an incentive to increase the size and scope of their operations so as to gain implicit government protection. The development of new regulations for institutions deemed "too big to fail" is thus a top priority.

The November declaration, drawing on many of the FSF's recommendations, also outlined principles for financial regulation that included enhancing sound regulation and strengthening transparency, reinforcing international cooperation and promoting integrity in financial markets, reforming the IMF, and reforming the World Bank and multilateral development banks. It opened the door to extensive reform by directing finance ministers to convene G-20 working groups, cochaired by one developed country official and one emerging market official, to formulate additional recommendations in these areas. These working group reports fed into the April summit discussions.[99]

The November declaration also gave high priority to directions to accounting standard-setting bodies to addresses weaknesses in disclosure and accounting for complex financial instruments and off-balance-sheet vehicles. Accounting standard-setting bodies were also directed to enhance their valuation guidance for illiquid products during times of stress, though, as suggested, some countries are keener than others to weaken fair value accounting principles. The G-20 also set in a motion a review of the governance structure of the IASB, a private sector body that serves a public sector role, which has raised important questions about accountability. In response, a new external monitoring board composed of public authorities, including some emerging markets, has been established to oversee the IASB.

Turning to regulation and oversight, the G-20 tasked the IMF, the FSF, and other regulators and bodies with developing regulatory recommenda-

---

[99] See G-20 Working Group 1: "Enhancing Sound Regulation and Strengthening Transparency: Final Report," 25 March 2009; G-20 Working Group 2: "Reinforcing International Cooperation and Promoting Integrity in Financial Markets (WG2): Final Report," 27 March 2009; G-20 Working Group 3: "Reform of the IMF: Final Report," 4 March 2009) G-20 Working Group 4: "The World Bank and Other Multilateral Development Banks: Final Report," March 2009, all available at http://www.g20.org/366.aspx

tions to mitigate procyclicality. The G-20 declaration framed this task in a general way, charging the IMF and others with a "review of how valuation and leverage, bank capital, executive compensation, and provisioning may exacerbate cyclical trends." Considerable acceptance among G-20 officials that procyclicality issues need addressing has thus led to a decision to delegate to the Fund, as well as some other bodies, the autonomy to propose how, among the range of available alternatives, greater countercyclical tendencies can be induced. Although a head of steam is building behind reforms to mitigate procyclicality, the lack of institutional tools at the Fund's disposal to compel developed country regulators to adopt its recommendations raises questions about how influential its recommendations will be.

Moreover, it is unclear how much political support such initiatives will command from leading IMF principals. European officials, for instance, seem much keener to develop alternatives to fair value accounting than some officials within the United States, who have sought to hold the line more firmly on fair value accounting. Questions over the issue of compensation also linger. While U.S. officials made a concession to the Europeans to open up discussions on compensation, Bush Treasury officials all but ruled out taking regulatory action, instead talking of "universal encouragement for firms to address this issue."[100] Moreover, despite using populist rhetoric to assuage public outrage, the Obama administration has also yet to pursue radical action. Indeed, as suggested earlier, it is still unclear how serious governments are about drawing up binding international rules to regulate the detail of compensation. In fact, the November G-20 declaration left open the possibility of "voluntary effort or regulatory action to avoid compensation schemes which reward excessive short-term returns or risk-taking."

Still, the April communiqué did contain stronger language, endorsing the "FSF's tough new principles on pay and compensation." Such principles are meant to root out short-termism by adjusting payouts for long-term performance. The FSF principles mark the first attempt by regulators to agree to an international framework on compensation. Such an attempt underscores how much conventional thinking has changed since before the crisis, when few regulators monitored or controlled compensation because of a belief that they should not interfere with a free and highly mobile labor market. Nevertheless, the principles are not particularly radical. Even if they could be implemented globally, financial institutions could

[100] Press Briefing by Senior Administration Officials on Summit on Financial Markets and the World Economy, 15 November 2008, Washington, D.C., available at http://georgewbush-whitehouse.archives.gov/news/releases/2008/11/20081115-7.html (accessed 24 March 2009).

still set their own remuneration structures and there would be no limit on the amount of compensation. It is also not clear what steps regulators could take to deal with noncompliance. Although the G-20 has signaled that "where necessary they will intervene with responses that can include increased capital requirements," it remains to be seen how this will work in practice or whether it will be enforced globally.[101]

However, there appears to be greater consensus among governments on mitigating procyclicality associated with leverage, capital requirements, and provisioning. For example, in March 2009, the G-20 finance ministers committed to ensuring "financial regulators dampen rather amplify economic cycles, including by building buffers of resources during good times and measures to constrain leverage."[102] At the April summit, the G-20 leaders agreed that "regulation must prevent excessive leverage and require buffers of resources to be built up in good times." They also agreed "to reshape our regulatory systems so that our authorities are able to identify and take account of macro-prudential risks." The G-20 has also directed regulators and accounting standard setters to push forward with implementation of their recommendations to mitigate procyclicality, including a requirement for a supplementary leverage ratio and building buffers of resources in good times that can be drawn down when conditions deteriorate. At the time of writing, for the purposes of building up buffers in good times it seems that dynamic capital adequacy requirements command somewhat greater support than dynamic provisioning.[103]

Actions to be taken in other areas have also commanded consensus. The G-20 declarations have made it a high priority for regulators to enhance supervision of risk and liquidity management, to strengthen their oversight of CRAs, to extend capital requirements to structured credit products, and to speed efforts to improve the resiliency and infrastructure of the OTC derivative market in general and the CDS market in particular. The declarations also enhance cooperation by endorsing creation of regulatory colleges for all systemically important financial institutions. This represents a modest concession for the United States, which opposes the creation of any regulatory agency with cross-border authority, but it falls well short of the international regulatory agency favored by the French.

Significantly, the November declaration gave high priority to a pledge to broaden the membership of the FSF and other key forums to include

---

[101] G-20 Declaration on Strengthening the Financial System.

[102] G-20 Finance Ministers' and Central Bank Governors Communiqué, 14 March 2009.

[103] The FSF, in "Report of the Financial Stability Forum," p. 4, supports implementation of dynamic capital adequacy requirements but simply notes that standards setters should "reconsider their current loan loss provisioning requirements and related disclosure including by analyzing . . . dynamic provisioning."

emerging market economies. This pledge marks a symbolic recognition of the shift in the balance of economic power. Since the November declaration the FSF has broadened its membership to include the emerging market members of the G-20. The FSF has also invited Spain to join, suggesting that regulators hold its regulatory model in high regard. The BCBS has expanded its membership to include Brazil, China, India, South Korea, and Russia, and the International Organization of Securities Commissions (IOSCO) has broadened its membership to include Brazil, China, and India. Similarly, in an effort to ensure geographical diversity, the IASB has committed to expanding its membership by 2012. In its April communiqué, the G-20 announced that the FSF would be reestablished as the Financial Stability Board (FSB), with a strengthened mandate to promote financial stability.

In February 2009, the G-20 finance ministers also pledged to accelerate reforms to increase the voice of emerging markets at the IMF. In a sign that a global bargain on IMF reform may be close to agreement, the G-20 agreed to move the next quota review to 2011 from 2013. The G-20 finance ministers also promised to end the convention whereby the United States and Europe appoint the heads of the IMF and World Bank. The April G-20 leaders' communiqué reiterated these commitments.

This collection of governance reforms offers an important first step in giving emerging markets greater "voice" within the key international bodies that set financial standards. These reforms, along with greater emphasis on supply-side regulatory reforms, could potentially give emerging markets a greater sense of "ownership" over the norms of financial governance, as standards and codes come to reflect better their interests and experiences. But there is still reason for skepticism.

These expanded forums could, as Helleiner suggests, come to resemble the G-20, which, though offering emerging markets the opportunity to be at the negotiating table, has to date largely followed the G-7 line, with distinctive ideas emanating from non-G-7 countries having little influence on the agenda, especially when these ideas impose costs on G-7 countries.[104] Indeed, while the BRICs have signaled their growing political resolve to shape economic affairs by issuing their first joint communiqué in February 2009, for the November summit and for much of the buildup to the April summit, emerging markets generally kept a low profile.

However, there are signs that some emerging markets are keen to contribute more to the reform debate. For instance, in the days prior to the April summit, China signaled its desire to play a much more decisive role by proposing a set of monetary reforms that would replace the current

---

[104] Helleiner, "International Payments Imbalances and Global Governance," CIGI Policy Brief #8 (Waterloo: CIGI, 2008).

dollar standard with an SDR standard.[105] Some observers have even taken to describing the G-20 as the "G-2," reflecting the reality that on a growing range of issues, little can happen without agreement between the United States and China.

There is one important additional reason to be skeptical about current efforts to better incorporate the interests and experience of emerging markets. Reforming the Fund's intraorganizational processes, which this book finds to be so central to better incorporating the interests and experiences of emerging markets, has not featured in the G-20 declarations or in statements from prominent politicians. This is not because of a lack of awareness on the part of key officials that such intraorganizational processes are a key determinant of the IMF's behavior. For instance, Trevor Manuel, South Africa's long-serving finance minister, recently observed, "[There is] a sense of sameness about the people [the IMF staff]. . . . They go to the same Ivy League universities and get their PhDs. It is not innovative. It is not meant to be."[106] Yet a March 2009 report on governance reform, produced by a committee chaired by Manuel, and forming a key input into ongoing reform efforts, fails to propose any measures to encourage intellectual diversity.[107]

If emerging markets are not offered meaningful participation in shaping the norms of financial governance, the risk is that they will turn their back on the forums developing and promoting these norms. In addition to strategies of "self-insurance," one increasingly prominent approach has been the pursuit of regulatory decentralization.[108] The development of standards and codes in the aftermath of the Asian crisis was essentially an effort to construct universalist norms of financial governance, albeit norms with a largely Anglo-American content. The push to update and strengthen regulation in the context of the subprime crisis reflects a continuing commitment to such universalist norms.

Yet emerging markets, particularly those in Asia, have been skeptical of this agenda. In the aftermath of the Asian crisis, this skepticism stemmed partly from resentment of the dominant interpretation put forth by the IMF and the G-7 that the crisis resulted primarily from poor fundamentals and institutions rather than factors intrinsic to the operation of international capital markets. Equally important has been resentment that the

[105] Zhou Xiaochuan, "Reform the International Monetary System," available at http://www.pbc.gov.cn/english//detail.asp?col=6500&ID=178

[106] As quoted in Quentin Peel, "Political Will for Meaningful Reform of IMF Is Still Lacking," *Financial Times*, 17 March 2009.

[107] Committee on IMF Governance Reform, *Final Report* (Washington, D.C.: IMF, 2009).

[108] Helleiner, "Reregulation and Fragmentation."

standards and codes have been developed and promoted by forums dominated by developed countries.

The subprime crisis has revealed considerable weaknesses in the supposed superiority of Anglo-American norms of financial governance and has raised questions about the legitimacy of these norms and the universalist standards and codes informed by them. The legitimacy and survival of these standards and codes thus depends on ensuring that they, and the forums that develop and promote them, better reflect the interests and experiences of emerging markets and developing countries. Along with greater support for supply-side regulation, the decision to convene the G-20 rather than the G-7 is a promising first step, as is the broadening of the membership of key forums to include emerging markets. But it is too soon to assess whether the G-7 countries will be willing to make significant concessions to non-G-7 countries.

If the interests and experiences of emerging markets are genuinely incorporated into the key international forums, these governments are more likely to embrace these forums, and the standards and codes they promote, as legitimate. As Helleiner warns, without such meaningful change, resistance to the universalist project is likely to grow and lead to a interest in a decentralized regulatory system where norms of financial governance come to be defined by various fragmented groupings.

If reforms to key international forums and financial governance fail to meet the expectations of emerging markets (as well as European officials), then, Helleiner suggests, we are likely to see "centrifugal tendencies" in international financial regulation grow in intensity. Asian and European countries are likely to chart an increasingly independent course of action that diverges from Anglo-American norms and threatens to undermine the universalist project. As Helleiner notes, if this route is taken, "We will be moving towards a more decentralized regulatory order, one which is more compatible with diverse forms of capitalism but which might also sit less comfortably with entirely liberal regime for the movement of capital and financial services."[109]

Norm Reinterpretation and Application

Ultimately, a key question stemming from all of this discussion is whether the subprime crisis constitutes a "crisis" for capital freedom and associated neoliberal norms of financial governance. Is this crisis a "critical juncture" in which the world now moves away from the norms that have underpinned the financial system for over two decades? Some prominent

[109] Helleiner, "Crisis and Response."

observers believe this to be the case. Harold James, for instance, notes, "The response to the Asian crisis of 1997–98 was the reinforcement of the American model of financial capitalism, the so-called Washington Consensus. The response to the contagion caused by the U.S. subprime crisis of 2007–8 will be the elaboration of a Chinese model."[110]

While the subprime crisis has put advocates of liberalization and self-regulation on the defensive, it is still far from clear that they have been permanently banished, and much will depend on the approach taken by the Obama administration. The Asian crisis initially sparked much interest in radically reforming the international financial architecture. Yet once the severity of the crisis passed, and the resolve of advocates of liberalization and self-regulation stiffened, support for radical reform faded. Instead, we witnessed a drive, as James suggests, that reinforced neoliberal norms through the development of standards and codes.

We may yet witness a similar evolution in the current reform debate. At present, the predominant efforts to strengthen and update regulations, as Helleiner notes, "represent more continuity than dramatic change in the sense that they build upon the international regulatory project that the G-7 promoted in the wake of the 1997–98 crisis."[111] Moreover, calls to restrict capital mobility have thus far been much less prominent today than in the aftermath of the Asian crisis, and the IMF has not significantly increased its support for capital controls.

Nonetheless, it is clear the prominent diagnosis underpinning the current reform debate is strikingly different from the one offered following the emerging market crises of the late 1990s. In the late 1990s, the G-7 and the IMF attributed financial instability to problems in crisis-afflicted countries. In response, the IMF offered large financing packages, but with stringent conditionality. Financial market participants were relieved of most of the blame and were not subject to tighter regulation. On the contrary, faith in markets led governments to delegate greater regulatory authority to private actors.

However, in the current reform debate there is a strong consensus that the same market participants who over the past decade had been permitted to "self-regulate" were responsible for triggering the crisis. Financial markets are now being "reregulated" because policymakers either blame markets or because they recognize that large bailouts of financial institutions would not be politically acceptable to taxpayers without some reassurance that such institutions will be subject to tighter regulation. The IMF, for

[110] James, "The Making of a Mess: Who Broke Global Finance, and Who Should Pay for It?" *Foreign Affairs* 88, no. 1 (2009), pp. 162–168 available at http://www.foreignaffairs.com/articles/63590/harold-james/fixing-global-finance."
[111] Helleiner, "Crisis and Response."

its part, has developed new unconditional lending facilities that are meant to ensure against crisis. Taken together, these developments represent a shift in the way financial crises are understood. The current consensus has shifted from a view that sees crises largely as homegrown, to a view that allows for the existence of externally induced crises that can spread to otherwise sound economies.

Perhaps the most significant change to the Fund's approach since the subprime crisis has been new support for regulatory measures aimed at financial market participants based in developed countries. In a series of reports outlining initial lessons from the crisis,[112] the Fund's staff have called for expanding the regulatory perimeter to encompass all financial institutions that pose a systemic risk. In line with the emerging consensus among policymakers, the staff also suggest that institutions should be regulated by the activities they conduct rather than the legal form they take. In terms of mitigating procyclicality, the staff have called for regulators to implement dynamic provisioning and dynamic capital adequacy requirements and to impose a supplementary leverage ratio. The staff have also urged regulators to assess compensation structures to ensure they do not create incentives for excessive risk-taking. Overall, the staff have urged a shift toward greater macro-prudential regulation. As I have discussed, many of these recommendations, which fed into the G-20 process, have featured prominently in reform negotiations.

Addressing more forcefully supply-side issues, such as the procyclicality of regulatory policies and the remuneration structure of financial market participants, should enable the Fund to draw stronger links between regulatory measures in developed countries and the capital flow volatility and risk implications for emerging markets and developing countries. As a result, in line with the current emphasis on reregulation, we are likely to see even greater onus being placed on developed countries to take action to foster financial stability. By placing greater pressure on developed countries, the Fund could go a long way in demonstrating that it is responsive to the interests and experiences of emerging markets and developing countries, thus enhancing its legitimacy. However, we are also likely to see greater pressure put on Asian and oil-exporting countries to tackle their own "supply side" issues that have given rise to "uphill" capital flows to the United States and other developed countries that contributed to asset price bubbles and the subsequent crisis.

Although it is too soon to draw any definitive conclusions, many of the factors highlighted in this book suggest themselves as likely candidates for

---

[112] IMF, *Initial Lessons*; IMF, *Lessons of the Financial Crisis for Future Regulation of Financial Institutions and Markets for Liquidity Management* (Washington, D.C.: IMF, 2009); IMF, *Lessons of the Global Crisis for Macroeconomic Policy* (Washington, D.C.: IMF, 2009).

stirring this change to the Fund's approach. First, changes to the power and preferences of some of the Fund's leading principals likely have been important. There is now a widespread consensus among developed country finance ministers, central bankers, and regulators in favor of moving toward a more macro-prudential regulatory orientation. The subprime crisis has also weakened the position of the United States and Britain, which in the past have successfully resisted regulatory initiatives, while emboldening the Europeans (as well as officials from emerging markets), who in the past have sought to extend and strengthen regulation. As a result, the former have been forced to concede to the latter the need to open up discussions on issues such the scope of regulation, procyclical regulations, and compensation structures. But there is still some disagreement among the Fund's principals over what should be done. For the Fund the result of this preference shift and heterogeneity has been a loosening of the outer structural constraint imposed on its ability to entertain regulatory measures aimed at financial market participants based in developed countries.

Although the Fund's principals have signaled an interest in mitigating procyclicality, they have delegated to the staff the task of proposing how, among the various policy alternatives, this interest can be best advanced. As detailed earlier, the staff have used this space for autonomous action by suggesting dynamic capital adequacy regulations, dynamic provisioning, and reforms to compensation practices. The staff, as part of their efforts to support the move toward a greater macro-prudential regulatory orientation, have also proposed various metrics to help identify systemic risks.[113] These recommendations, as well as those produced by the FSF, have provided key inputs for the G-20 summits.

In chapter 9 it was suggested that, in addition to preferences of its leading principals, the availability of institutional tools, which made it easier for the staff to insist on reforms in emerging markets, also shaped the Fund's earlier failure to entertain supply-side regulation. The subprime crisis has done little to change the institutional tools available to the Fund. To be sure, in lending to some emerging markets in autumn 2008, the Fund has imposed fewer conditions on its conventional programs and developed new flexible lending facilities without conditionality for countries affected by contagion from the crisis. But the ability of developed countries thus far to borrow extensively in their own currencies and to deflect the influence of IMF surveillance has provided the Fund with little new leverage or influence over their policies. For instance, in spring 2008, the IMF urged the United States to spell out a distressed asset purchase plan

---

[113] IMF, *Global Financial Stability Report* (April) (Washington, D.C.: IMF, 2009), chaps. 2 and 3.

and handed Treasury officials a detailed plan for doing so. But Treasury officials ignored it.[114]

In addition, contrary to the preferences of some European governments, the Fund is unlikely to be transformed into a global supervisor of regulators with greater influence over developed countries. Thus, institutionally, it has not become easier for the Fund to insist on reforms by developed countries. Although the April G-20 declaration commits to strengthening IMF surveillance over its members, it remains to seen whether the Fund will have the muscle, or the will, to make its assessments heard.

Ideationally, however, it would appear to have become easier for the Fund to support supply-side regulation. There is now widespread recognition that the crisis resulted from regulatory failures in developed countries. The weakened normative position of the Anglo-American financial model has put traditional opponents of supply-side regulation on the defensive. As the financial turmoil unfolded, it triggered an important reassessment of beliefs about financial regulation. Policymakers were initially slow to open the door to a more macro-prudential orientation and exploring countercyclical regulatory measures. As a result, some economists and BIS officials pushed hard to cast the subprime turmoil as a "crisis" for prevailing beliefs about financial regulation.

Charles Goodhart, Avinash Persaud, Radhuram Rajan, and some BIS officials have been influential in shifting the beliefs of many economists, observers, and policymakers. "The main problem," Goodhart and Persaud argue, "is not the structure of regulatory oversight, either national or international, but the lack of counter-cyclical control mechanism and instruments. . . . The crash of 2007–08 has laid bare the poverty of the current regulatory philosophy." To mitigate procyclicality, Goodhart, Persaud, and others have called for new regulations that will work against market trends, forcing financial institutions to build up reserves during asset price booms so that they are available for release when asset prices fall.[115] Taking

[114] Stephen Fidler, Bob Davis, and Carrick Mollenkamp, "World Leaders Agree on Global Response," *Wall Street Journal*, 3 April 2009.

[115] Charles Goodhart and Avinash Persaud, "A Proposal for How to Avoid the Next Crash," *Financial Times*, 31 January 2008. See also Borio, "Towards a Macroprudential Framework"; Borio and White, "Whither Monetary and Financial Stability?"; Markus Brunnermeier, Andrew Crockett, Charles Goodhart, Avinash D. Persaud, and Hyun Shin, *The Fundamental Principles of Financial Regulation*, Geneva Reports on the World Economy No. 11 (Geneva: International Center for Monetary and Banking Studies, 2009); Crockett, "Marrying the Micro- and Macro-Prudential Dimensions"; John Eatwell and Avinash Persaud, "A Practical Approach to the Regulation of Risk," *Financial Times*, 26 August 2008; Persaud, "The Inappropriateness of Financial Regulation," in *The First Global Financial Crash of the 21st Century*, ed. Andrew Felton and Carmen Reinhart (London: Vox EU, CEPR Publication, 2008), pp. 155–157; Ashley Taylor and Charles Goodhart, "Procyclicality and Volatility in the Financial System: The Implementation of Basel II and IAS 39," in *Procycli-*

issue with compensation practices, Rajan, who served as RES director from 2003 to 2007, has suggested regulating such practices as a way to mitigate procyclicality and short-termism.[116]

Others have gone further, seeking to implicate the operation of markets, rather than regulatory failure alone, and, more generally, beliefs of the economics profession as key reasons for the crisis. "Part of the reason for inadequate regulation," observes the U.N. advisory report, "was an inadequate appreciation of the limits of markets—what economists call 'market failures.' . . . More generally, the current crisis has exposed deficiencies in the policies of national authorities and international institutions based on previously fashionable economic doctrines, which held that unfettered markets are, on their own, quickly self-correcting and efficient."[117] In a similar fashion, prominent behavioral economist Robert Shiller, who in the late 1990s presciently warned about "irrational exuberance" in stock markets, and later in housing markets, has sought to renew appreciation for Keynes's argument that "animal spirits" play a critical role in triggering asset bubbles and busts.[118] Both the UN advisory report—which in addition to Stiglitz also included input from Goodhart and Persaud—and Shiller argue that such "market failures" can be minimized, in part, by moving toward a more macro-prudential regulatory orientation and by drawing more on insights from behavioral finance.

Taken together, these arguments have helped prompt the Fund to adapt its approach to supply-side regulation. In 2006, the Fund convened a conference on macro-prudential supervision where staff members were exposed to the views of experts on the subject.[119] In drawing conclusions about the need to develop countercyclical tendencies, the Fund's staff often cited the work of BIS officials.[120] The subprime crisis also seems to have revealed to many staff members the shortcomings of micro-pruden-

---

cality of Financial Systems in Asia, ed. Stefán Gerlach and Paul Gruenwald (Basingstoke: Palgrave Macmillan, 2006), pp. 9–37.

[116] Radhuram Rajan, "Bankers' Pay Is Deeply Flawed," *Financial Times*, 8 January 2008. See also Martin Wolf, "Regulators Should Intervene in Bankers' Pay," *Financial Times*, 15 January 2008.

[117] Commission of Experts on Reforms of the International Monetary and Financial System, *Recommendations*, pp. 3, 4.

[118] Robert J. Shiller, *Irrational Exuberance*, 2nd ed. (Princeton: Princeton University Press, 2005); George A. Akerlof and Robert J. Shiller, *Animal Spirits: How Human Psychology Drives the Economy, and Why It Matters for Global Capitalism* (Princeton: Princeton University Press, 2009).

[119] Macroprudential Supervision Conference: Challenges for Financial Supervisors, Seoul, South Korea (7—8 November 2006), available at http://imf.org/external/np/seminars/eng/2006/macropr/.

[120] See, for instance, IMF, *World Economic Outlook* (April) (Washington, D.C.: IMF, 2008), p. 123.

tial supervision. For instance, the October 2008 *GFSR* observes, "This period of change provides an opportunity to rethink the financial architecture with fewer constraints about the need to preserve existing market practices than in the past. . . . There is an opportunity and a need to move toward a macroprudential and regulatory framework that is more integrated in its approach and uniform in its standards."[121]

Adaptation, rather than learning, appears to be an important mechanism at work. As I have suggested, the subprime crisis has not prompted the Fund to change its belief in the desirability of capital freedom per se. Instead it has led to a reassessment of how the norm of capital freedom should be interpreted and applied. Rather than focusing primarily on measures that emerging markets can take to minimize financial instability, the Fund is now much more forceful in stressing the need for developed countries to take regulatory action.

In addition to these processes, internal norm entrepreneurship also has likely shaped the IMF's recent receptivity to supply-side regulatory mechanisms. Jaime Caruana, who served as MCM director from August 2006 to April 2009, was, in all likelihood, a key figure in this regard.[122] Before joining the Fund, Caruana served a six-year term as governor of the Bank of Spain, where held up his country's now well-regarded system of countercyclical and macro-prudential regulation as a possible template for other countries to emulate.[123] Prior to the G-7 signaling a strong interest in mitigating procyclicality, Caruana, as MCM director, encouraged "supervisors to recognize this inherent bias towards procyclicality in the financial system, ensure that banks prepare themselves in good times to meet the rigors of the bad times and do not take measures in bad times that unduly amplify the cycle."[124] Since the FSF recommendations and the G-20 declaration in November, the Fund's managing director and first deputy managing director have also offered statements on the need to develop countercyclical macro-prudential rules to reduce the buildup of systemic risks.[125]

[121] IMF, *Global Financial Stability Report* (October) (Washington, D.C.: IMF, 2008), pp. 53–54. See also Blanchard, "The Tasks Ahead," p. 6.

[122] In April 2009, Caruana left the Fund to become general manager of the BIS.

[123] Jaime Caruana, "Monetary Policy, Financial Stability and Asset Prices," Documentos Ocasionales No. 0507 (Madrid: Banco de España, 2005). Caruana also served as chairman of the BCBS during negotiations over Basel II.

[124] Caruana, "Remarks at the Institute of International Bankers' Seminar on Basel II," New York (11 December 2007), available at http://www.imf.org/external/np/speeches/2007/121107a.htm. See also Caruana, "Dealing with the Downturn—Lessons and Opportunities," keynote remarks at the Eighth Annual International Seminar on Policy Challenges for the Financial Sector: Financial Market Turbulence and Response, Washington, D.C. (5 June 2008), available at http://www.imf.org/external/np/speeches/2008/060508.htm.

[125] John Lipsky, "Toward a Post-crisis World Economy," speech at the Paul H. Nitze School of Advanced International Studies, Johns Hopkins University, Washington, D.C. (17 November 2008), available at http://www.imf.org/external/np/speeches/2008/

Support from these individuals for engaging procyclicality issues more forcefully likely helped to open up space within the Fund to consider policy recommendations that previously may have been seen as out of keeping with the standard way of doing things.

While the IMF has shifted its interpretation and application of the norm of capital freedom through greater support for supply-side regulatory measures, it is not clear how much support such measures will draw from its leading principals and those governments that participate in the FSB and the BCBS. Nonetheless, the Fund, while not at the initial forefront of efforts to develop supply-side regulatory measures, appears well positioned to play a leading role in crafting them in the future and in distilling lessons from the crisis. Indeed, as part of its work since the onset of the crisis, the G-20 has tasked the Fund, along with the FSB, with taking a lead role in distilling lessons from the crisis and with enhancing efforts to better integrate regulatory responses into a macro-prudential framework and conduct early warning exercises. Moreover, at the time of writing it appears that the IMF has emerged as an early winner from the G-20 summit process, having received a substantial increase in its resources and a stronger mandate for monitoring and assessing its member states' policies.

Time will tell whether the subprime crisis marks a fundamental turning point in the norms of financial governance. For the time being, although we are likely to witness greater regulation of the financial system, a fundamental overturning of the norm of capital freedom appears unlikely. As Helleiner suggests, support for restricting capital could grow among leading governments if the turmoil were to spill over into a dollar crisis. However, a more likely outcome is further regulatory decentralization, which might sit less comfortably with capital freedom. The weakened economic and normative position of Anglo-American financial models could thus usher in a new era of diverse, regionally based norms of financial governance. Much depends on whether decentralization can command political support among European, Japanese, and emerging market officials.

A more serious threat to future financial stability could be the continued pursuit of self-insurance by emerging markets. After the emerging market crises of the late 1990s, many G-7 countries sought to scale back IMF lending for fear it generated moral hazard. Emerging markets were determined never to be forced to borrow from the Fund again. Along with an export-led growth strategy, self-insurance helped fuel global imbalances and asset bubbles in the developed world, helping to generate the underlying conditions for today's crisis. This cycle could repeat itself.

111708.htm; and "World Leaders Launch Action Plan to Combat Financial Crisis," *IMF Survey* 37, no. 11 (November 2008), pp. 169, 171 at p. 171.

In many emerging markets, the subprime crisis has strengthened the case for pursuing self-insurance. Large reserve-holding countries, such as China, appear well positioned to escape the worst effects of the crisis, with sufficient room to boost government spending. Other countries may therefore conclude that self-insurance is their best option.

But recent actions taken by the G-20 and the IMF could work against this conclusion. With more resources at its disposal, the IMF offers a potentially more viable alternative than reserve accumulation. Moreover, if countries with sound fundamentals and policies believe they will have unconditional access to IMF resources when conditions worsen, they may choose collective insurance over self-insurance. Of course, many countries will still require traditional conditional lending facilities, which governments will continue to use reluctantly.

But significantly, Mexico's decision to tap the IMF's new credit line suggests that if it genuinely incorporates the interests and experiences of emerging markets, the Fund can still attract borrowers. Indeed, Mexico's deputy finance minister indicated that his country was attracted not just by the size and flexibility of the new lending instrument, but also by the fact that the IMF consulted emerging markets when it designed the instrument to ensure it met their needs.[126] Moreover, if the Fund can muster the resolve to criticize with sufficient rigor the policies of its leading principals, then it could go some way in demonstrating that it is responsive to the interests and experiences of emerging markets, which have pressed for some time their preference for greater evenhandedness in the exercise of surveillance. Indeed, such a preference was reflected in the G-20's April communiqué.

Ultimately, whether decentralization and self-insurance intensify and pose a profound challenge depends largely on whether the IMF (and other key international forums) open themselves up to genuine participation from emerging markets as well as non-Anglo-American norms of financial governance that draw on alternative experiences and interests. Genuine participation in turn depends not only on governance reform, but also on changes to intraorganizational processes that are often decisive in shaping IOs' behavior.

Indeed, the core theoretical implication of this book is that scholars and policymakers who ignore intraorganizational processes do so at their own peril. Without attending to such factors, we cannot adequately understand how IOs work and evolve or how to reform them to make them more accountable. Formal rules and member states' influence are often important; in fact, scholars who focus on such features of an IO's environ-

---

[126] "Mission: Possible," *The Economist*, 11 April 2009.

ment are likely to find plenty of evidence in this book to support their interpretations. But we also need to understand better how the staff operate within the autonomous space they have carved out or been delegated. As a step toward that understanding, I have sought to demonstrate the importance of evolving IOs' personnel configurations, beliefs, debates, and the strategic agency of their staffs in fostering the adoption, interpretation, and application of norms. Ultimately, this book has sought to reveal that normative and behavioral change, as well as meaningful organizational reform, comes not just "from above" or "from below" but also "from within" IOs.

Index